Temple University

125 Years of Service to Philadelphia, the Nation, and the World

Temple University

125 Years of Service to Philadelphia, the Nation, and the World

James W. Hilty

Foreword by Ann Weaver Hart

Additional Research and Illustrations Editing by Matthew M. Hanson

Temple University Press
Philadelphia

To the Temple Family—and to my own

Temple University Press
Philadelphia, Pennsylvania 19122
www.temple.edu/tempress

Copyright © 2010 by Temple University
All rights reserved
Published 2010

Design by Phillip Unetic, UneticDesign.com

Library of Congress Cataloging-in-Publication Data

Hilty, James W.
    Temple University: 125 years of service to Philadelphia, the nation, and the world /
James W. Hilty; with additional research and illustrations editing by Matthew M. Hanson;
foreword by Ann Weaver Hart.
        p. cm.
    Includes bibliographical references and index.
    ISBN 978-1-4399-0019-2 (cloth : alk. paper)
1. Temple University—History. I. Hanson, Matthew M. II. Title.
    LD5275.T52H55 2010
    378.748'11—dc22

                                2009022168

This book is printed on acid-free paper for greater strength and durability.

Printed in Italy

2 4 6 8 9 7 5 3 1

Contents

Key to School and College Abbreviations   vi

Temple University Board of Trustees   vii

Foreword by President Ann Weaver Hart   viii

Chapter 1   The Man, the Speech, the "Temple Idea"   1

Chapter 2   Growing Pains, 1907–1928   22

Chapter 3   Depression and War, 1929–1945   46

Chapter 4   Middle Passage, 1945–1965   72

Chapter 5   Vehicle for Social Change, 1965–1982   98

Chapter 6   Temple's Ambassadors   140

Chapter 7   Multiversity and Globalversity, 1982–2009   184

Chapter 8   From Sidewalk Campus to Urban Village   220

Chapter 9   Access to Excellence   280

Chronology   291

Acknowledgments and Notes on Resources   294

Illustration Sources   298

Index   299

Key to School and College Abbreviations

CHP	College of Health Professions and Social Work
CLA	College of Liberal Arts
CST	College of Science and Technology
DEN	Maurice H. Kornberg School of Dentistry
EDU	College of Education
ENG	College of Engineering
LAW	Beasley School of Law
MED	School of Medicine
MUS	Boyer College of Music and Dance
PHR	School of Pharmacy
POD	School of Podiatric Medicine
SBM	Fox School of Business and Management
SCT	School of Communications and Theater
SED	School of Environmental Design
SSA	School of Social Administration
THM	School of Tourism and Hospitality Management
TYL	Tyler School of Art

Note The names and programs of Temple's schools and colleges have changed over the years. The list above is current as of this writing. Alumni references in the text give the abbreviation of the current names of the graduating school or college.

Foreword

Temple University is a quintessential American success story: a tutorial exercise that has grown into the twenty-seventh-largest university in the nation and the fifth-largest provider of professional education in the United States. Beginning with seven students who gathered for evening instruction in a private office in 1884, Temple today enrolls 37,000 students engaged in full- and part-time studies at nine campuses in Pennsylvania, Europe, and Asia. Its faculty employ a full array of traditional and cutting-edge pedagogies to prepare Temple students for lives of professional and civic leadership, and the faculty conduct research that broadens the range of human understanding of the most pressing issues of our age.

Temple's history is also a classic Philadelphia story. The university continues to fulfill a mission that arose from the democratic ideals of opportunity and equality that rang forth from our home city a century before the arrival of our first students. When these ideals struggled for new expression in the post–Industrial Revolution period, Temple University opened its doors to a burgeoning working-class population that yearned for a greater role in the future and prosperity of their city, ushering in a new era of educational access previously reserved for a privileged few. Temple today continues to embody the timeless value of its mission throughout its educational programs and its research enterprise and through the contributions of Temple graduates to social, economic, and cultural advancement in the global society.

Temple University is a great American institution, rooted deeply in one of America's oldest and greatest cities. It serves as one of the most important providers of education for Pennsylvania, as more than 70 percent of our students come from the commonwealth. More than half of Temple's alumni live and work in the Greater Philadelphia area, and nearly 60 percent live in Pennsylvania. One in every eight college-educated residents in the Philadelphia metropolitan area holds a Temple degree, providing invaluable intellectual capital and responsible citizenship to the city and the region. In 1965, the Pennsylvania General Assembly and the governor named Temple a state-related university within the Commonwealth System of Higher Education. The university deeply values its relationship with the Commonwealth of Pennsylvania and works closely with the state on many critical projects.

At the same time, Temple continues to expand its reach and influence throughout the world. Temple students come from every state and more than 120 nations. The university led the way among American institutions in establishing international programs at overseas sites. The first was a French-language study program in Paris in 1950, and today the university supports international campuses in Rome (established in 1966) and in Tokyo (established in 1982). Since 1999, a unique collaboration with Tsinghua University in Beijing has enabled Temple to train Chinese lawyers in U.S. and Chinese law. Additional international partnerships support student exchange and study abroad opportunities designed to prepare Temple students to be truly global citizens with deep international perspectives. Global research collaborations are multiplying the impact of Temple faculty as they work with scholars around the world.

James Hilty's wonderful narrative of Temple University's history that follows in these pages enables us to look back on the remarkable set of circumstances and the dedicated individuals that have brought this institution into the twenty-first century. Anniversaries also invite us to look forward, and Temple has taken advantage of that opportunity during its 125th anniversary year, a year that has turned out to be one of the most challenging in our history. This story, too, will be instructive to future generations.

Temple University marks its historic 125th anniversary in the midst of a global economic crisis and the worst economic conditions in the United States since the Great Depression. Like all colleges and universities, Temple finds its resources strained as traditional income sources are diminished and credit is more difficult to obtain. Yet these constraints pale by comparison with those faced by our students and their families. At this writing, we are in danger of returning to a stratification of our society resembling that which existed when Temple was founded, where only a privileged few can afford a college education.

In March 2009, *The Princeton Review* released the results of its annual "College Hopes & Worries Survey." More than 70 percent of those surveyed said their greatest worries were (1) getting into the school of their choice but not being able to afford to attend and (2) having to take on unmanageable debt to attend any college at all. That same month Eduventures, Inc., a national education consulting firm, released results of its study of adult students, an important segment of Temple's student body. The study revealed that 36 percent of adult students were "slow[ing] down or delay[ing]" their plans to pursue higher education and 61 percent were more likely to require scholarships to attend school than in the year before.

Temple has taken dramatic steps to manage its finances in this unprecedented economic climate. What the studies and statistics I cite above make clear is that our actions are directed at more than just our balance sheets; they are intrinsically linked to the lives of our current and prospective students. When so many aspiring students believe their goal of a college education—and their ability to contribute to a sustainable economic recovery when they graduate—is beyond their reach, our responsibility to assist them in achieving their educational ambitions takes on greater urgency.

I am extremely proud that the entire Temple community has risen to these challenges with the same determination as our early leaders. With remarkable commitment and willingness to sacrifice for the benefit of our students, today's university leaders, faculty, and staff have taken measures that have allowed us to keep tuition increases at their lowest level in more than a decade. We have also redirected resources into the largest infusion of financial aid funding in our history to assist students and families who face the greatest hardships in financing a college education in the current economy.

Temple University remains true to its original mission of welcoming capable students regardless of their status in life and providing them with the support they need to succeed. Our mission once again finds new expression and increasing relevance today as it has throughout our history. With this strong foundation as our guide, we can all look forward to Temple University's future with the assurance that this institution will always serve its students, its city, the commonwealth, and the world in the manner in which it was intended by those who gave so much to make its first 125 years possible.

Ann Weaver Hart
President, Temple University   Fall 2009

Chapter 1
The Man, the Speech, the "Temple Idea"

Temple University did not spring from the generosity of a captain of industry or the munificence of a financial wizard. Unlike other multi-purpose universities of today, Temple was not the creation of the state or the beneficiary of federal land grants. Neither did it have roots extending back scores of decades with connections to America's aristocracy; nor was it the vehicle of a religious order or an offshoot of a training institute, as were so many colleges founded in the latter part of the nineteenth century during America's Gilded Age.

Conwell begins
program of
evening study.
1884

The Temple
(aka the Baptist
Temple) opens.
1891

The Law School
of Temple College
is introduced.
1895

TEMPLE UNIVERSITY TIMELINE

1888
Temple College
receives its Charter
of Incorporation.

1894
College Hall, Temple's first
building, opens at 1834
North Broad Street.
The football and basketball
programs start.

1901
Conwell opens the
School of Medicine.

Indeed, Temple's founding was principally the work of one man—not a captain of industry, but a captain of erudition, an educational entrepreneur—who sought to democratize, diversify, and widen the reach of higher education. He challenged prevailing values and norms regarding the purposes of higher education and who should benefit. Rather than serve America's affluent classes, he provided deserving working men and women right of entry to an education otherwise denied them by circumstances of birth or life's station. Rather than provide only the esoteric classic curriculum, he prepared students for life's vicissitudes and for success in the modern world.

Universities are among the Western world's oldest and most stable institutions with continuous histories. Only the Roman Catholic Church, the law courts of certain European countries, some army regiments, and a few town and craft corporations can claim similar longevity. But, once Temple was begun, its survival and growth were far from certainties. Over the 125 years of its existence Temple has faced many precarious moments, considerable adversity, and more than its share of financial difficulties.

In those 125 years, as it has grown physically and intellectually, Temple has evolved the ideals and purposes of its founder into a simple, compelling mantra: "Access to Excellence." By *access* we mean maintaining allegiance to the founder's pledge to serve deserving students from all stations in life, keeping an open mind on academic issues, and maintaining diversity in the student body, faculty, and staff. By *excellence* we mean providing the highest-quality education possible, advancing and disseminating knowledge and new discoveries through research and scholarly inquiry, developing and applying new approaches to learning, and sustaining an unshakable commitment to serve the community, the city, and the world.

Before there was Temple: This sketch from 1839 is looking north on Broad Street from just above Girard Avenue, which was the city limit at the time. The location of the covered wagon is approximately Cecil B. Moore Avenue (formerly Columbia Avenue). The fourth carriage is about where Mitten Hall is today. Approximately three blocks north of that was Lamb's Tavern, where winter sleigh parties would go to dance at night. It was demolished in 1894.

The Man and the Vision

Russell Herman Conwell's life story and his aspirations for Temple University resonate with the personal life narratives of Temple University's students, faculty, staff, and alumni. He is connected to us all. Conwell played many roles—as an actor, showman, brilliant orator, journalist and editor, lawyer, minister, educator, real estate speculator, promoter, entrepreneur, and founder of Temple University. Most compellingly, Conwell grasped the meaning of his time, understood the moving forces of his generation, and demonstrated the courage to capture and control those forces and, in effect, bend history. His greatest contribution was the "Temple Idea"—the conviction that a great university must do more than discipline the mind and conscience, expand knowledge, and prepare students for the workplace. It must also serve its community, uplift its people, and be a vehicle for social justice.

Conwell was a complex man, a mingling of myth and reality, and details of his early life remain unclear despite several biographies and despite Conwell's many autobiographical insertions in his lectures and writings. For whatever reasons, Conwell embellished significant episodes in his young adult life. Perhaps Professor J. Douglas Perry explained it best: Conwell understood intuitively that "to gain support for a cause or an institution, one must give to people an image on which they would look with wonderment, yet one with which they also could identify."

Born February 15, 1843, Russell Conwell was reared on a 350-acre hardscrabble subsistence farm in the Berkshires in western Massachusetts, near South Worthington, about fifteen miles from Westfield, Massachusetts. He attended Wilbraham Academy for two years and then taught school in South Worthington. Alas, most of Conwell's descriptions of his early adult life cannot be independently corroborated or verified through written records, although several historians have put considerable effort into the task.

Piecing together major elements of Conwell's early life, we learn that at a young age he developed exemplary elocutionary skills and a wondrous capacity for extemporaneous speaking, combined with an exceptional ability to attract attention. Conwell left home in 1861 to enroll at Yale University, where he planned to study law. To earn money for tuition he held several jobs near campus but apparently spent only a few months actually enrolled in classes. In later years Conwell freely admitted that he felt humiliated by the Yale students, many of whom mocked his shabby clothing, rural manners, and ungentlemanly resort to menial labor in a New Haven hotel.

When Civil War broke out, Conwell returned to Massachusetts, where he proved a persuasive recruiter for the Union cause, giving rousing patriotic speeches that made young men enlist on the spot. Credited with recruiting an entire company of volunteers, though only nineteen, he was elected captain, Company F, Forty-sixth Massachusetts Volunteer Militia. His men presented him with a fancy dress sword inscribed *Vera Amicitia Est Sempiterna* ("True friendship is eternal"). Company F was mustered out in July 1863, after seeing light action. Conwell reenlisted in August and was commissioned captain of Company D, Second Regiment, Massachusetts Heavy Artillery.

Conwell's personal orderly was a slight young man and a neighbor of the Conwell family named Johnny Ring. Johnny greatly admired Russell Conwell, served as his personal servant, and shared his tent. A staunch Christian, Ring read the Bible daily and nightly, to the great annoyance of Conwell, who, even though raised in a devout Methodist home, boasted of being an atheist.

The Conwell birthplace in the Berkshires, South Worthington, Massachusetts. His modest background would make Conwell feel ill at ease socially when he enrolled at Yale College in 1861, but it did not restrain his ambition throughout his adult life.

FACT

One in every eight Greater Philadelphia college graduates holds a Temple University degree.

According to Conwell, Ring sacrificed his life for him during a Confederate attack when the unit was overrun and Ring ran across a burning bridge and through enemy fire to retrieve Conwell's ceremonial sword from his tent. In Conwell's various versions of the story, Ring's last full measure of devotion evoked an epiphany, bringing Conwell to kneel in prayer at the side of Johnny's cot when the young man died a few days later. Conwell pledged to work sixteen hours a day from then on—"eight hours for myself and eight hours for Johnny Ring who died for me." He repeated the story in sermons, books, and a motion picture script.

Unfortunately, war records indicate the place and circumstances of Ring's death were not as Conwell later described them. Nor was Conwell even present. Records reveal instead that Conwell was absent from his post during the attack, subsequently court-martialed (later expunged by President Ulysses S. Grant), and separated from the service on May 20, 1864. Conwell claimed to have served beyond that date, telling biographers that a private, unrecorded high-level arrangement allowed the twenty-one-year-old to remain in the service to serve on General James McPherson's staff as a lieutenant colonel. Conwell maintained that he was severely wounded at the Battle of Kennesaw Mountain on June 27, 1864, but no evidence exists of his presence on McPherson's staff or at the battle, other than his word. One simply does not know what to make of the contradictions. Conwell possessed photographs of himself in the uniform of a lieutenant colonel, and in speeches he frequently referred to his role as a staff officer in the war. Later in life, according to several sources, Conwell sought treatment for a recurring war wound that could not have been imagined.

Conwell often said he was so moved by Johnny Ring's devotion to duty and to his God that he decided to devote his life to being a minister. The decision to enter the ministry, however, was not confirmed until 1876. In the meantime Conwell lent his hand to journalism, filing a series of graphic stories depicting the horrors of war that earned him a position as a reporter and a round-the-world trip as correspondent for the *New York Tribune* and *Boston Traveler*. In 1869 he revisited the Civil War battlefields and described the battles in a series of reports and vignettes later assembled by Temple professor Joseph C. Carter and published as a book.

The statue of Johnny Ring was sculpted by Boris Blai, founding dean of Temple's Tyler School of Art, and placed in the garden setting north of Mitten Hall and west of Beasley Walk (formerly Watts Walk). The statue commemorates Conwell's Civil War orderly, whose piety and devotion Conwell credited for his work ethic of sixteen-hour days—"eight hours for himself and eight hours for Johnny Ring who died for me."

One thing is certain about Conwell's Civil War service: He never abandoned his love of books and learning. He carried books with him everywhere, studying the law and the classics every spare moment. Conwell earnestly believed that "there are no real scholars but those who have fought with circumstances while they studied books." Returning home, Conwell read the law with a local lawyer, entered law school at the University of Albany, and earned a bachelor of laws in the spring of 1865.

That summer he married Jennie P. Hayden, his childhood sweetheart, moved to Minneapolis, and was baptized in the First Baptist Church. He practiced law, worked as a correspondent for the *St. Paul Press,* published two weekly newspapers, ran a real estate business, and served in a host of local civic organizations. When a devastating fire burned his home and all of his possessions, including his voluminous library, Conwell, his wife, and their two small children returned to the Boston area and settled in Somerville, where he practiced law, served as a Baptist lay preacher, and wrote articles for the *New York Tribune*. In 1872 Conwell's wife, Jennie, died suddenly. The stricken Conwell immersed himself in theological studies, mission work, and his law practice.

Two years later Conwell married Sarah F. Sanborn, a devout Baptist and member of a patrician Boston family. They formed a strong, purposeful union, melding common sense and duty with

Russell H. Conwell (1843–1925)
Soldier, journalist, lawyer, minister, orator on the
Chautauqua circuit, and founder of Temple University.

the virtues of their faith. Meanwhile, Conwell's law practice thrived. He was admitted to the bar and served as counsel to banks and railroads. Yet these successes gave him small satisfaction. In 1876 he formally committed to the ministry, becoming the full-time pastor of a frail Baptist church in Lexington, Massachusetts, immediately reviving it and putting it on its feet financially. Conwell was formally ordained in 1879 at the Newton Seminary.

Many elements contributed to his decision to enter the ministry, but Conwell frequently singled out Johnny Ring's devotion and sacrifice as the reason for his decision, pledging to rededicate his life in compensation for Ring's death. Conwell retold his version of the Ring story countless times. It became officially enshrined in Temple University's lore in 1964 when a statue of Ring sculpted by Boris Blai, founding dean of the Tyler School of Art, was placed in a garden just north of Mitten Hall, thereafter to be called Johnny Ring Garden.

In November 1882 Russell Conwell accepted the pastorate of the Grace Baptist Church in Philadelphia and moved his family into the parsonage at 2004 North Park Avenue (now the site of Peabody Hall). The congregation was small, with only ninety persons, and it carried a heavy debt from a new building at Berks and Mervine streets, where the courtyard of Gladfelter Hall now stands. Conwell's energy, organizational skills, and gifted oratory attracted many new parishioners, and soon there was not enough room to accommodate all who wished to worship at the church and to listen to the brilliant, entertaining, and motivating pastor. He had barely arrived before the parishioners were discussing the need to build yet another, larger church.

Conwell and his wife Sarah (née Sanborn) married in 1874 in Massachusetts. Sarah was instrumental in Conwell's Philadelphia Baptist ministry, which he began in 1882. From this position he extended beyond the spiritual needs of the community into the intellectual and medical well-being of his congregation and neighborhood. At one time Sarah served as head of the Women's Department in the young college.

The Speech

By the time Conwell arrived in Philadelphia he had gained fame as a lecturer on the Chautauqua circuit, a traveling tent show that visited towns in America's heartland, presenting musical performances, plays, political speeches, and spellbinding orations, such as Conwell's "Acres of Diamonds" lecture, part sermon, part dramatic recitation, part autobiographical recounting, and always entertaining. By Conwell's count he gave the speech 6,152 times, a fact included in *Ripley's Believe It or Not.* Tirelessly delivered in conversational style, "Acres of Diamonds" was a morality tale of the value of education, devotion to the Protestant ethic, and the importance of family and community service.

In 1870, while traveling near Baghdad along the Tigris river in what is modern-day Iraq, Conwell heard the tale of a wealthy Persian farmer, Ali Hafed, who spent years wandering in search of a mythical field of diamonds. Ali Hafed died far from home a disillusioned pauper. Soon after, the acres of diamonds were discovered in his own land. "Your diamonds are not in far distant mountains or in yonder seas," Conwell concluded, "they are in your own back yard, if you but dig for them."

Conwell molded the tale of Ali Hafed to fit modern times and urged listeners to "do what you can with what you have where you are today." Greatness, he insisted, "consists not in holding some office; greatness really consists in doing some great deed with little means, in the accomplishment of vast purposes from the private ranks of life. . . . To be great, one must be great here and now in Philadelphia. He must give to this city better streets and sidewalks, better schools, more colleges, more happiness, more civilization, more of God."

Conwell believed that Christian living would surely yield material success. Money, Conwell often repeated, was not evil, only the love of money was. "I say you ought to be rich; you have no right to be poor. To live in Philadelphia and not be rich is a misfortune, because," as he put it, "Philadelphia furnishes so many opportunities. . . . Money is power, money has powers; and for a man to say, 'I do not want money,' is to say, 'I do not wish to do any good to my fellowmen.'"

Conwell's speech reinforced much of the contemporary wisdom of the day. He endorsed the doctrine of the secular calling, the obligation to serve both God and community through a chosen profession or simply through hard work. He also espoused the then-fashionable tenets of the "Gospel of Wealth," as articulated by Andrew Carnegie, the steel-magnate-turned-philanthropist who urged that wealth not be passed on to heirs but be used, instead, to accomplish great things for the common good. He promoted the ideas of democratic capitalism and the theory of the

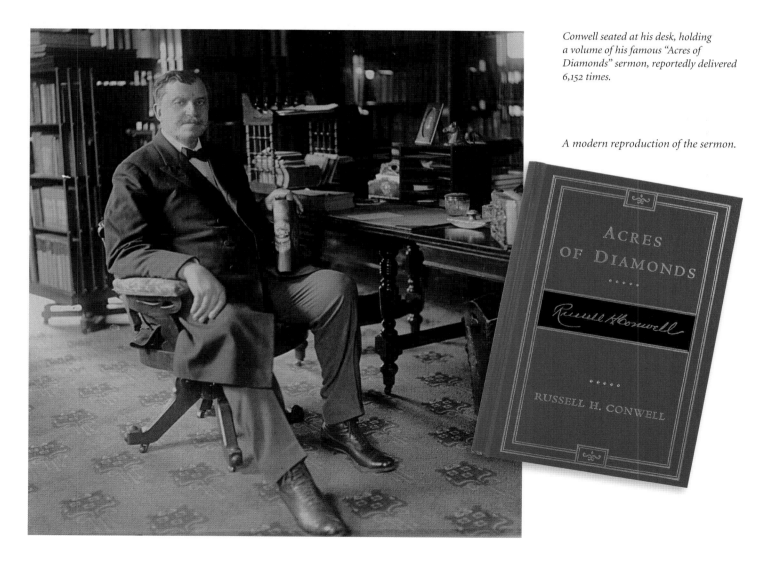

Conwell seated at his desk, holding a volume of his famous "Acres of Diamonds" sermon, reportedly delivered 6,152 times.

A modern reproduction of the sermon.

self-made man made popular by Horatio Alger's "rags to riches" novels. Truly great people, he said, were simple, approachable people of common origins. Mixed in with all of these beliefs was an unabated sense of progress and national destiny.

Conwell's message had a larger purpose transcending contemporary wisdom. The pathway to personal success, he stressed, was largely education. Educated persons, in turn, were obligated to serve the less fortunate and to help them realize their full potential. Further, it was the duty of all to meet the needs of the community. "We must know what the world needs first," said Conwell, "and then invest ourselves to supply that need, and success is almost certain." To meet those needs Conwell initially used his church to reach out to all peoples of North Philadelphia— many of them poor and many of them recent immigrants—offering spiritual sustenance, recreation, social life, economic assistance, and instruction in basic life skills. Gradually he channeled his energies into meeting what he considered the foremost of those needs, namely education.

Conwell's Philadelphia

Conwell arrived in 1882 to a thriving, throbbing Philadelphia, known then as the Workshop of the World. Philadelphia and the United States were in the midst of a huge industrial expansion. Philadelphia's expansion differed from that of other large industrial centers whose huge plants produced mass quantities of steel. The city focused instead on mid-sized industries engaged in flexible specialization, relying on batch and custom operations rather than mass production.

At the heart of this specialized production process was the skilled worker, making hats, glass, linoleum, pianos, or other custom goods; cutting fabrics; rolling cigars; stitching baseballs; working in a machine shop; assembling locomotives and ships; brewing beer; or tanning leather. Conwell's new church lay near what amounted to the western border of an industrial village that housed a large segment of working-class Philadelphia; the areas east of the church teemed with industry and with the homes of skilled workers and their families.

Textiles was the city's largest industry, with 60,000 jobs and 800 mills at its peak. Broad and Lehigh was the textile center of the United States. Frankford and Kensington housed mills and factories of varied descriptions. The Baldwin Locomotive Works, at one time the region's largest single

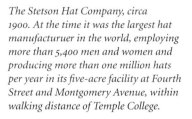

The Stetson Hat Company, circa 1900. At the time it was the largest hat manufacturuer in the world, employing more than 5,400 men and women and producing more than one million hats per year in its five-acre facility at Fourth Street and Montgomery Avenue, within walking distance of Temple College.

The Pennsylvania Railroad North Broad Street Station, circa 1895.

employer, was located at Broad and Spring Garden streets. The Baldwin production process did not rely on mass production techniques; instead the company used skilled craftsmen to build and assemble each part of the locomotive, relying on an apprentice-training program to enlarge skill levels for custom work. Henry Disston & Son Saw Works was at Front and Laurel streets. John B. Stetson operated the nation's largest nonunion hat business at Fourth Street and Montgomery Avenue. Nicetown was home to the Midvale Steel Works. All were within walking distance of Grace Baptist Church.

Philadelphia was called a paradise for skilled workmen whose abilities were highly respected. Most of the skilled workers were of northern European, Irish, or Anglo descent, with ancestors who immigrated to America generations earlier. The worst jobs, the most dangerous and deadening unskilled industrial jobs, went to the "new" immigrants from southern and eastern Europe, who received the lowest pay and the least respect. Between the time of Conwell's arrival in Philadelphia in 1882 and the onset of World War I in 1914 approximately one million "new" immigrants arrived in the United States each year.

By 1920 Philadelphia was the third-largest metropolis in the United States, with two million people. However, it never became the center of new immigrant life comparable to New York or Boston. Unlike New York, Philadelphia did not concentrate its population in tenements or high-rise multi-family buildings. Known as The City of Homes for its proportion of single-family and owner-occupied homes, Philadelphia possessed relatively inexpensive land and accessibility that permitted the construction of low-rise housing and single homes. It also featured the row house, which multiplied prodigiously after the Civil War.

In the late nineteenth and early twentieth centuries the areas around Conwell's church (and the future Temple campus) blended the best and the worst of living conditions. The industrial village stretched from around Tenth and Berks streets eastward toward the Delaware River into Northern Liberties and Kensington to the mills, shops, and factories that served as the backdrops for block after block of workers' row houses. Westward, however, the scene changed dramatically to one of elegant row houses and impressive, well-constructed town houses with brick facades, mansard roofs, and granite stoops, such as those buildings still standing on Temple's campus along Park Avenue (now Liacouras Walk). Just beyond lay the grand tree-lined boulevard that was North Broad Street, home until the 1920s of Philadelphia's new business and professional classes and many nouveau riche entrepreneurs.

When Conwell arrived, the old-money Philadelphia elite lived in a pocket of grandeur around Rittenhouse Square. In the 1870s center city congestion, combined with the demand for larger showcase homes of conspicuous consumption, brought new-money classes to build magnificent mansions and palatial four-story town houses along North Broad Street. Two of Philadelphia's richest men, the street railway and trolley car magnates P.A.B. Widener and William Elkins, lived at Broad and Girard in splendid mansions across the street from each other. Henry Disston, who owned the mammoth saw works in Tacony, built a mansion at Broad and Jefferson. In 1892, as a sign of his growing status and success, Conwell moved to a larger, more luxurious home at 2020 North Broad Street (across the street from where Johnson-Hardwick Hall currently stands).

Russell Conwell's relationships with the wealthier classes and the working classes are critical factors in understanding the contexts within which Temple University originated. Conwell arrived in Philadelphia in the midst of a redefining moment in the city's social and cultural history. The huge Centennial celebration had just concluded, and cultural institutions were preparing for the 1887 Constitution Centennial, just as immigrants poured into the city. Philadelphia's affluent classes promoted an image of the city as a cosmopolitan center of cultural and historical importance; they were wedded to its historical imagery, to its importance to the national character and the nation's meta-narrative. In those days the belief was widespread, as historian Gary Nash revealed, that "historical memory would nourish sacred values, that remembrances of the dead white heroes would sustain a country of immigrants." Such images benefited and sustained the identity and importance of Philadelphia's dominant white majority and its cultural and political leaders.

In reality, though, such images and remembrances resonated weakly among immigrants and the working classes, because they stood in marked contrast to the stark reality of the industrial city, differing as they did with the desperation and starkness of the lives of the working-class families, new immigrants, and migrating Southern blacks, the city's working-class backbone.

Conwell found himself caught in the tension between Philadelphia's old elite—the remnants of the founding Quaker oligarchy and the old established commercial crowd that dominated Philadelphia

1919 Mervine Street was the first building in which Conwell conducted class meetings when the number of students grew to overflow the capacity of his study.

Row houses on Park Avenue, now Liacouras Walk, were once working-class homes, then classrooms and office spaces for Temple. They have been refurbished for administrative offices and commercial properties as part of "Temple Town."

economic and cultural life for more than a century—and the new, defiantly un-elite class of working men, skilled craftsmen, and immigrants striving for ascendancy. Conwell was philosophically and sentimentally aligned with the working classes, yet reliant on the elites for donations and social acceptance. For the working classes, his sermons on the "success gospel" fed their dreams and aspirations; for the affluent classes, those same words were taken as license or rationalizations for keeping what was theirs.

Conwell donated the proceeds from his "Acres of Diamonds" lectures to Temple College and spent his remaining years appealing to the affluent elites, beseeching them for money and approval. Conwell proved marvelously adroit at fund-raising among the middle and business classes, but he was not nearly as successful with the truly super rich and the old-line Philadelphia elite. He won their personal appreciation and esteem, but rarely their ultimate approval in the form of institution-shifting, large-scale philanthropic gifts. His hopes for substantial gifts to the college, he often said, were pegged on elevating Temple's students into the middle class, where they in turn would help their alma mater.

Temple College

One Sunday evening in 1884, Charles M. Davies, a young printer, approached Conwell to ask for advice on preparing for the ministry. Davies had little money or formal education. Conwell offered to teach him. Davies brought along six friends, and Conwell tutored them all in his study. Shortly after, the number grew to forty. Conwell found volunteer teachers and moved classes from his study into the church basement. Extensive tutorials or short courses continued until the fall of 1887, when Conwell announced from the pulpit the official formation of Temple College and set a formal schedule of classes.

Oddly enough, given all that transpired later, the name *Temple College* was not Conwell's idea. According to a reliable account provided many years later by Orlando T. Steward, one of the first students to seek tutoring in Conwell's study and later the secretary of the Baptist Union of Philadelphia, it was the students who first suggested that what they were experiencing ought to be thought of as "college." As Steward remembered, "We began to call it a 'college' and felt it should have a name." They decided to name the college after the new church building, which, although not yet built, they knew would be called The Temple. And for this reason, said Steward, "the name 'Temple College' was selected." Conwell suggested another name, but "[h]e finally yielded to our desire," said Steward, "and Temple College it was called."

With the aid of pamphlets prepared by Davies, word was sent throughout center city and the working-class neighborhoods describing Grace Baptist Church and Temple College as within "easy walking distance to factories employing 30,000 workmen" and within a half hour's ride by horse car from where "180,000 working men and working women" were employed. Two hundred prospective students signed up in the first month.

A temporary board of trustees, drawn mostly from the membership of Grace Baptist Church, elected Conwell president. Conwell then invited representatives from Philadelphia's thirty-two Baptist churches to join the effort. However, they insisted on restricting admission to Baptist men and to limiting the courses to preparation for the Baptist ministry, which Conwell rejected. He did not envision a college based exclusively on Christian principles like so many of America's existing sectarian liberal arts colleges. Conwell doubted that instruction based exclusively on Christian ethics and piety could sustain colleges if they failed to prepare young people for success in the real world. Sensing the temper of his times, realizing what motivated and concerned young working-class people, Conwell set out to create a non-denominational college to open the way for social and economic advancement and awaken the untapped talents and potential of all citizens, especially those for whom higher education was otherwise beyond reach.

On May 14, 1888, Temple College was chartered and incorporated by the state. Its stated purpose was "the support of an education institution, intended primarily for the benefit of Working Men." In 1891 the charter was amended to read "primarily for the benefit of Working Men; and for men and women desirous of attending the same." "The regular tuition," according to the college catalogue, "is free." Moreover, "No special grade of previous study is at present required for admission, as the purpose of the faculty is to assist any ambitious young man, without especial reference to previous study." Free tuition and open enrollments attracted more than the basement of the Grace Baptist Church could accommodate. Some classes were moved to the two houses next to the church on Mervine Street, one rented and one owned by the church.

No distinct legal connection existed between Temple College and Grace Baptist Church, but they were closely linked. The church publicly acknowledged taking a "special interest" in Temple College. Indeed, the college could not have survived in its early years without the support of the church. But within just three short years of Conwell's arrival, both the college and the church were in desperate need of space. Together they resolved to meet those needs.

The Temple (aka the Baptist Temple)

Conwell's popularity as a mesmerizing lecturer and sermonizer was so great and the crowds so large that the congregation resorted to printing tickets for Sunday services. The Grace Baptist Church simply could not hold all who wanted to attend. The church wanted to move from Berks and Mervine to Broad and Berks streets, up on the main thoroughfare and nearer to the center of residential wealth and influence, but it lacked money enough.

Ever the innovator and opportunist, Conwell contrived several ingenious methods to raise funds for the new church. The most often cited example of that prowess is the story of Hattie May Wiatt. One Sunday, as Conwell tells it, he encountered Hattie outside the church. She had been denied entrance into the Sunday school because it was filled. Children were being turned away. Conwell said, "I took her up in my arms, lifted her to my shoulder, and then as she held on to my head—an embrace I never can forget—I carried her through the crowd in the hall." The next day, according to Conwell, he met Hattie on the street and told her, "Hattie, we are going to have a larger Sunday school room soon," one "large enough to get all the little children in."

Hattie May Wiatt died soon after. She had saved fifty-seven pennies in a small purse, which Hattie's mother gave to Conwell after the funeral. Conwell auctioned off each of the pennies, raising $250, which was used to buy the house next door to the church on Mervine Street to serve initially as a Sunday school and eventually as the place where Temple College first organized. When fifty-four of the pennies were returned to Conwell, he persuaded the owner of the lot at Broad and Berks to accept the fifty-four cents (along with other funds and collateral) as a down payment on the lot.

In 1886 the land was acquired, and a year later Thomas P. Lonsdale was selected as the architect. Ground was broken in 1888. William Bucknell, a prosperous real estate and utilities investor,

Hattie May Wiatt was the subject of Conwell's "Fifty-seven Cents" sermon, which he delivered numerous times in fund-raising for the new church. Her fifty-seven cents were auctioned off penny by penny by Conwell to raise additional funds for what became The Temple.

Conwell's Temple in 1926.

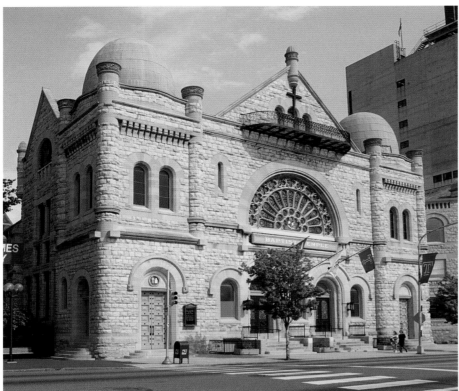

Conwell's Temple, circa 2005.

contributed $10,000 to the campaign on condition that the building would not be dedicated as a church until the mortgage was paid. To comply with Bucknell's wishes, Conwell designated the new building as simply "The Temple," and until the mortgage was paid it was technically only the meetinghouse of Grace Baptist Church. The power and simplicity of the name *The Temple* appealed to Conwell, and so, even after the mortgage was paid, he declared, "It will always be known as The Temple."

Conwell intended The Temple to be a multi-purpose spiritual, educational, and community facility where "entertainments" could be held for the "mutual and spiritual advantage" of the people of Philadelphia and also for help in paying off the mortgage. He was once warned: "Russell, you'll never make a success of this Temple as a religious and educational institution." To which Conwell the showman replied, "If we don't make it a success as a Temple, we'll turn it into a theater."

The building opened March 2, 1891, to a joyful and spectacular day of services, addresses, and musical performances. The *Philadelphia Inquirer* reported that 15,000 people flocked to the church for one or another of the services held throughout the day. Considered an architectural marvel of its time, The Temple sanctuary was designed with four support columns and the balconies were hung by cables, thus affording clear sight lines to the choir loft and pulpit from virtually every one of the 4,108 seats. With the addition of camp chairs the total seating capacity could be expanded to 4,600, giving The Temple the largest seating capacity among Protestant churches in the United States.

The building's exterior is a fine example of the Romanesque Revival style in America. The most prominent feature of the front, or west-facing, facade is the stained-glass half-rose window, thirty feet in diameter. Beneath the window, THE TEMPLE is carved in relief. By 1894 the building was commonly referred to as Grace Temple (Baptist). Sometime thereafter (date uncertain but after Conwell's death), the carving of THE TEMPLE on the front of the building was covered over by a metal sign reading The Baptist Temple, which was how the building came to be known to almost everyone. In 2008 the metal sign was removed, restoring the original appearance.

The Temple soon became a Philadelphia landmark, a popular and frequent venue for major civic meetings, musical performances, and cultural events, including Russell Conwell's delivery of "Acres of Diamonds" for the 6,000th time on October 25, 1921. The Temple attracted visitors and tourists; its likeness even appeared on postcards and travel circulars.

The Temple was Conwell's personal showcase. Sunday services were extravaganzas with Conwell at center stage. The productions featured the huge, booming Robert Hope-Jones organ and a spirited choir (sometimes with a hundred or more trained voices), framed in theatrical lighting, with every element of the program produced and directed by Conwell. Conwell's majestic stentorian baritone resonated throughout the hall in this pre-loudspeaker era. His large physical presence and animated antics charmed and captivated congregants. "He was a big man," Kathryn F. Bovaird, a church member, recalled, "large of frame with rather unruly black hair, which stayed black until he was an old man.... His voice was rich and deep." Conwell's granddaughter, Jane Conwell Tuttle, later wrote that the baptismal ceremony in particular "was something no one ever forgot." Her grandfather, she said, had a special hold on the audience: "Personally, I have always felt he was a combination of psychiatrist, magician, and hypnotist."

The Temple met the needs of the Grace Baptist Church, but what of Temple College? The church had already provided temporary space for classes, raised money to aid the college, loaned money to meet the monthly payroll, and paid Conwell's salary. Prodded by Conwell, the church offered to sell its old building at Berks and Mervine to Temple College. But the college, still in its infancy, lacked the funds and the credit to follow through on the purchase. The church needed to recover some of its investment in the old building, and so it sold the original church at Berks and Mervine streets to the Christian Church. Again encouraged by Conwell, the church purchased land on Broad Street immediately south of The Temple and deeded it to the college corporation as a site for its own building.

The Temple (aka the Baptist Temple and Grace Baptist Temple) also became a regular venue for Temple College events, including the first commencement in 1892 and all thereafter until 1932, when the graduating classes became too large for the church auditorium to accommodate and commencement exercises were transferred to the Municipal Auditorium. Even then, mid-year commencements, convocations, and other special events were held in the Baptist Temple well into the 1960s.

In 1951 the Chapel of the Four Chaplains was installed in the west end of The Temple's lower level. The multi-denominational chapel was constructed to honor the heroism of four World War II army chaplains of different faiths (one of whom was the son of Grace Baptist Church pastor the Rev. Daniel K. Poling) who gave up their life vests to save others on a sinking army transport ship, the USAT *Dorchester*, which had been torpedoed off the coast of Greenland. The chapel was officially dedicated in 1951 by President Harry Truman. It remained until the 1980s, when the officers of the chapel decided to end their relationship with Temple University and move away, first to Valley Forge, Pennsylvania, and subsequently to the naval yard in South Philadelphia.

President Harry S Truman is shown here with General William J. Donovan at the unveiling of the mural painted by Nils Hogner for the 1951 dedication of the Chapel of the Four Chaplains within Conwell's Temple. The four chaplains gave up their life vests when the USAT Dorchester was sunk off the coast of Greenland by a German submarine on February 3, 1943.

Over the years many distinguished figures visited the Baptist Temple, including President Franklin D. Roosevelt, General Dwight Eisenhower (when he was president of Columbia University), the Rev. Martin Luther King Jr., the Rev. Billy Graham, presidential candidate Senator George McGovern, anthropologist Margaret Mead, and Anne Sullivan and her famed pupil Helen Keller. Alistair Cooke and Edward R. Murrow delivered commencement addresses at the Baptist Temple.

By the 1970s the congregation of Grace Baptist Church had dwindled, and in 1972 the church trustees voted to relocate to Blue Bell, Pennsylvania. In 1974 they sold the building to Temple University for $550,000. The university continued to use the building as an auditorium and for academic offices for another few years. However, in the 1980s the truss system supporting the roof failed, causing a great deal of water damage to the building's interior. Scaffolding and emergency repairs paid for by the commonwealth stabilized the building, but it was effectively condemned and unusable thereafter. A 1983 university planning study recommended renovating the building and converting it to a performing arts center. In 1984 the Philadelphia Historical Commission certified the Baptist Temple as a historic building.

Two years later the board of trustees voted to demolish the building, citing the high cost of renovation, finding no clear reuse for it, and declaring its inadequacy as a performing arts space. The Historical Commission denied the demolition request. In 1998 the university performed further work to stabilize the building. Shortly after his arrival at Temple, President David Adamany declared in his 2001 "Self-Study and Agenda" that "this historically important and aesthetically fine building should be carefully studied both for potential University uses and for historic preservation." Major repairs to fix the roof and facade and to correct structural deficiencies were begun in 2002. Plans were once again developed for the restoration and adaptive reuse of the building as a performing arts center. In 2003 the American Institute of Architects designated the structure a landmark building, recognizing its historical significance, its contribution to the architectural character of North Broad Street, and the work of its architect, Thomas Lonsdale.

Exciting new plans call for $29 million in expenditures to resurrect and completely renovate the building, expected to reopen in 2010 with room for a 100-piece orchestra and flexible seating for as many as 1,200 people. When completed, The Temple will again take its place as one of Philadelphia's premier venues for arts and cultural productions, international speakers, and symposia. As a northern anchor of Philadelphia's Avenue of the Arts, the new Temple will reclaim its place as a magnificent setting for education and entertainment, reviving and restoring Russell Conwell's grandest aspirations.

The "Temple Idea"

Temple College was more than a place, more than just a gathering of teachers and students: It was a bold new idea, a transforming concept. "The Temple Idea," Conwell explained, is to educate "workingmen and workingwomen on a benevolent basis, at an expense to the students just sufficient to enhance their appreciation of the advantages of the institution." Benevolence, said Conwell, "was the motive when 'the Temple College idea' was conceived and from its foundation to its present fame every step has been governed by this one central idea."

When Conwell saw a need, he stepped forward to fulfill it. He understood that the skilled crafts necessary to propel the Workshop of the World and to move Philadelphia's commerce depended on continuing education. He also knew that the aspirations of the working classes for themselves and their children could ultimately be met only through more education. "Everywhere the call for some useful education to aid in the daily toil of the people was loud and sincere. Into that duty," wrote Conwell, "the Temple College rushed with promptness and care."

The gist of the Temple Idea was summarized in an early advertisement, which stated, "Temple College is the pioneer in the work of providing an education for working people. In the evening from 7:45 to 9:45 it provides thorough instruction in all branches of practical education." The advertisement summarized the mission of Temple College thusly: "Temple College does not exist as a private enterprise for the purpose of gain but as a 'Peoples' University' to give all possible help to those who enter its walls."

Open admissions and free tuition brought increasing numbers into Temple's walls but cost the college the respect of the state accrediting agencies. But like many of his entrepreneurial breed who risked all to realize their visions, Russell Conwell accepted the risks and operated with little regard for government or public opinion. In many respects, as one historian noted, higher educa-tion during the Gilded Age was the "ultimate unregulated industry." In 1891 Conwell bypassed the state education agencies and went to the Court of Common Pleas, which granted Temple College the authority to award degrees. The first commencement was held in June 1892. Eigh-teen graduates of Conwell's class in oratory were awarded the bachelor of oratory. Four women were among those receiving degrees. The college also received authority to award honorary degrees, and one of the earliest recipients was Conwell, who received doctor of divinity and doctor of laws degrees.

An early advertisement for Temple College, showing the Temple College Academies located throughout the Philadelphia area and also in Camden, New Jersey, and South Worthington, Massachusetts (Conwell's hometown). A "nominal fee of $5 entitles a student to the privileges of any three branches for the entire year."

By 1893 the Temple faculty had grown to forty, almost all of whom were personally recruited from students and recent graduates of the University of Pennsylvania, the Philadelphia school district, or area businesses. Early in Temple's history the majority of faculty members were volunteers. Very few, if any, during the college's infancy relied exclusively on Temple for employment. Conwell called them "self-sacrificing philan-thropists." Faculty salaries were very low, no more than token honorariums. Moreover, Temple's chronic financial problems meant the faculty members were underpaid and sometimes not paid at all. There was no gradation in faculty ranks; all faculty members were "professors." None were recognized as noted schol-ars, but all were able teachers. Because of negative public opinion about evening schools and Temple's non-accredited status, highly credentialed, well-pub-lished, and accomplished faculty trained at accredited universities shied away. The majority of classes were conducted on weekday evenings, and most of the faculty taught classes after working at their day jobs. Governance and the setting of academic policy were strictly the purview of Conwell and the board of trustees and did not involve faculty.

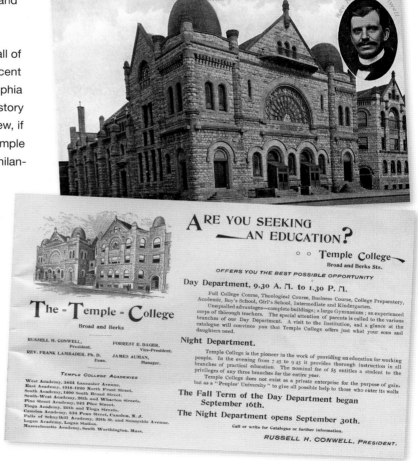

As enrollments increased and Conwell's ambitions for the college grew, he needed help managing its affairs. Conwell was not a detail person, and so the position of dean was created to recruit and manage the faculty, keep records and accounts, solicit funds, and prepare reports. The dean was expected to arrive early and attend to administrative duties from 3:00 to 5:00 P.M. before teaching evening classes. Five deans came and went between 1888 and 1891. When Conwell threatened to resign in 1891, the board of trustees changed the dean's job description to shift more of the administrative burdens away from Conwell. Dr. Frank Lambader accepted the position under those terms, joined by James M. Lingle, the business manager, and a bright-eyed, young Philadelphia schoolteacher named Laura Carnell, who took care of just about everything else.

The range of academic programs offered in the early years of Temple College ran the educational gamut. No curricular planning was evident. Courses were developed on the basis of need and interest. Laura Carnell was under orders from Conwell to provide classrooms and teachers for any group of six or more students who wished instruction in any subject, no matter what it was. This approach required a remarkable amount of flexibility and energy. Conwell himself offered classes on an astounding array of subjects, including Greek, Latin, French, German, rhetoric and logic, surveying, newswriting, English composition, and Bible training.

By 1891 the outlines of a liberal arts program appeared, along with the first day classes. To earn a baccalaureate degree, students were required to pass examinations in the following subjects: Greek (Homer's *Iliad* and Xenophon's *Anabasis*), Latin (Cicero's *Oration*, Virgil's *Aeneid* and *Bucolics*), German or French (general written correspondence), logic (a comprehensive review), composition (a comprehensive review), geography and history (ancient and modern), elocution (general examination), geometry (plane and solid), and hygiene. Clusters of theology and business courses were added in 1893. A group of education courses were organized into a kindergarten training department in 1894. That same year a ladies' department opened with Mrs. Sarah F. Conwell as principal; this led to a department of household science that offered courses in cooking, embroidery, millinery, and dressmaking.

College Hall, circa 1895.

By 1893, close to 3,000 students of all grades, kindergarten to college, attended Temple College. Enrollment increases meant additional demands for classroom space. After the Grace Baptist Church was sold, the college moved some classes into The Temple basement and also rented row houses at 1831–1833 Park Avenue (now Liacouras Walk). Still growing, it rented two large halls, one at 1235 Columbia Avenue (now Cecil B. Moore Avenue) and one at 2107 North Broad Street. When those spaces proved insufficient, the only alternative was to build on the lot next to The Temple. And so Conwell again hired Thomas Lonsdale as the architect and launched the first capital campaign for Temple College. Unable to secure a large lead gift from a benefactor, Conwell gladly accepted any and all contributions, regardless of size. Two of the largest came from John B. Stetson (owner of the hat company) and Charles E. Hires (maker of root beer); they each gave $1,000 toward the total building costs of $100,000.

College Hall was dedicated on May 3, 1894, with the governor and other dignitaries in attendance. The building contained thirty-five classrooms, a large lecture hall known as the Forum, and a gymnasium in the basement. A passageway above the street connected the building via a bridge to The Temple. In fairly short order the Forum was taken over by the Library, where it remained until 1936. The opening of College Hall encouraged Conwell to think again of expanding the Temple Idea.

Conwell, like his counterparts in industry and big business, sought always to expand. He proposed to extend the Temple Idea to create a totally comprehensive educational institution with instruction from kindergarten through professional schools. In business parlance, he sought to "vertically integrate," from the bottom to the top, and thus control a significant portion of the market. A bold step was taken in 1894 when he opened "Temple Academies" spread across the region—to the west on Lancaster Avenue, to the east on Frankford Avenue, to the south on South Broad Street, Wharton Street, and Pine Street, and to the north at Twentieth and Tioga streets—enrolling approximately 2,000 students in rented classroom facilities. The academies were basically high school–level evening programs for adults. The intention, as Conwell explained, was for the academies "to act as feeders for the college," receiving any person of any grade. Conwell once considered placing a Temple academy in each of the city's wards, thus creating a kind of shadow secondary school system to supplement the school district.

Conwell's exuberant haste to fill an education need with the Temple Academies was one instance in which he should have taken greater care before rushing in, for the demand on Temple College was too great. Tuition was too low (five dollars per year) and the costs too high for the college to support. With no alternative, Conwell closed the academies. Still, his experiment with them demonstrated the existence of a huge demand among immigrants and working adults to commence or complete their high school educations. Moreover, Conwell's initiative brought the city school district to respond to those needs by opening the first evening schools.

Conwell's experiment in secondary education left Temple with "a most dangerous debt," which, according to Conwell, was paid by "some enthusiastic friends" who "gave all their property to enable the college honorably to draw out of the academies and pay all bills." Conwell also had no other option than to begin raising tuition. Tuition started at five dollars per year for the evening division (for those employed during the day) and at fifty dollars for the day division. By 1907 those fees increased respectively to forty dollars and seventy-five dollars "for the whole year of nine months."

In founding Temple College, Conwell had hoped to strike a blow, as Douglas Perry wrote, "to free higher education from the fetters of the aristocratic ideal." Conwell worried that unless the working classes "could be educated further, the wealthy classes alone would form an educational aristocracy dangerous to our American democracy." Yet, in many respects Conwell's association with Philadelphia's working class bound him and the college to a mission resisted by the well-born and moneyed classes. The large, spectacular philanthropic gifts thrust at other institutions eluded Temple for all its early history.

Looking back, Conwell regretted that there were "no large donations in the first thirty years of the college life." But he regretted most "the gifts that never came," the pledges of prospective donors that were not kept. Conwell's neighbors who lived in the mansions and luxury town houses along Broad Street may have occasionally worshipped in Conwell's church, but by and large they sent their children and their money to other colleges.

College Hall / Barrack Hall

Recently refurbished and refitted to include a new turreted entryway, the interior of College Hall has been reconfigured for use by the Law School, providing classrooms, seminar rooms, lounges, and administrative offices. Renovations were made possible by a $2.5 million gift from university trustee Leonard Barrack, a Law School graduate, and his wife, Lynne Barrack, who earned a degree from the College of Education. In January 2002 the building was renamed Morris and Sylvia Barrack Hall in honor of Leonard Barrack's parents.

At times Conwell seemed to doubt whether Temple College could be more than a momentary social experiment, a seed for others to cultivate and nurture to fruition. He ignored taunts that Temple was a "sham" college, and he stoically dismissed those who called it "Conwell's Folly." But at various times when facing dire financial straits he attempted to coax others into assuming Temple's responsibilities and debts. Among others, he tried offering Temple College to the Baptists, the Philadelphia School Board, and the Commonwealth of Pennsylvania.

Conwell desperately tried to persuade men of great fortunes to endow Temple College with enough funds to guarantee its continuation. He and his fellow captains of erudition—William Rainey Harper (University of Chicago), David Starr Jordan (Stanford), G. Stanley Hall (Clark), Andrew White (Cornell), Seth Low (Columbia)—all became "honorable beggars" in search of large-scale philanthropic gifts. By 1900 most major donors became less inclined to undertake the building of a new campus; there was recurrent worry that American higher education had become overextended with too many immature institutions. The super rich sought new strategies to influence higher education; one such means was the philanthropic foundation.

All of this must have been greatly frustrating to Conwell because he knew many men of means capable of such gifts. For example, he spent years attempting to bring the like-minded, seemingly sympathetic John Wanamaker to support Temple College with a large gift. Wanamaker, the creator of the modern department store and a civic activist and philanthropist, sometimes attended Conwell's services, even though he was a Presbyterian. Conwell wrote a flattering biography of Wanamaker, who spoke glowing praise for Conwell's church and educational work, but to Conwell's disappointment, Wanamaker never offered a substantial gift.

Anthony J. Drexel, head of Drexel & Company, so appreciated Conwell's idea of serving the unmet educational needs of the city and was so moved by Conwell's passionate advocacy of the Temple Idea that he decided to emulate it. Drexel put more than $2 million toward establishing the Drexel Institute of Art, Science and Industry, now Drexel University. On the one hand, Drexel's decision was a great symbolic victory for the Temple Idea, but on the other hand, it was yet another rebuke by the affluent establishment.

Fellow Baptists John D. Rockefeller and William Bucknell were at the top of Conwell's prospect list. Rockefeller contributed $35 million to revive the University of Chicago, but he ignored two decades of appeals and detailed proposals from Conwell. Finally, he sent Conwell a check for $1,000 as a personal gift. When Conwell sent Rockefeller a note acknowledging the gift on behalf of Temple University, Rockefeller sent another $1,000 check, pleading, "Won't you keep this for yourself this time?"

William Bucknell's large donation saved the University at Lewisburg from financial ruin in 1881, and so in 1886 the Lewisburg trustees changed its name to Bucknell University. In 1889 Conwell offered to change the name of Temple College to Bucknell University of Philadelphia if William Bucknell would assume Temple's debts. Bucknell contributed $10,000 to The Temple, but his death in 1890, with nothing bequeathed to Temple, ended the matter.

Temple also suffered by comparison with the University of Pennsylvania. A preeminent university during Revolutionary times, Penn had declined in stature. Except for its Medical and Law schools, still among the most prestigious in the country, Penn had slipped, and by 1870 it was described as hardly more than a "parochial academy for the more conservative Old Philadelphians." But in

1872 Penn purchased part of the Andrew Hamilton estate (the Woodlands), sold its center city campus at Ninth and Chestnut, and moved to its current location in West Philadelphia, experiencing a brilliant "academic blossoming" with new buildings and inspired leadership, plus a huge infusion of donations.

Conwell and all of his Temple successors have since faced inevitably unflattering comparisons of their school with the powerful Ivy League university "across the river." However, one seminal study of the distinctions between American colleges and universities in the 1880 to 1910 era indicates that prospective students may not have differentiated between Penn and Temple in terms of a hierarchy of prestige. Affordability was an issue but not reputation. American higher education had not yet crystallized into "universities versus colleges." Back then, Philadelphia students behaved as consumers who opted for one program over another for varied, pragmatic reasons, rather than differences in reputation and prestige. Temple's rise to university status in 1907 both helped attract more students and contributed to a rise in status.

Until 1910, when interest in and demand for college admission increased, few universities (Temple included) did much planning; when demand increased, universities (Temple included) simply admitted more students. Some universities instituted entrance (more properly placement) exams to screen applicants and place them in majors, but few applicants were turned away. As the lure of collegiate life descended on America's middle class, entrance exams began to be used to exclude applicants. It is at this point that the hierarchy of prestige among American colleges took hold; thereafter the reputational differences between Temple and Penn were more often noticed and asserted.

By World War I the most materially successful colleges, such as Penn, catered to the urban Protestant upper and upper-middle classes, drawing on their new wealth to build institutions for them. These colleges successfully positioned themselves to place students on the path to the most desirable professional opportunities in business, medicine, and law. Temple University found itself struggling to compete in that market. But one sweet, ironic consequence Conwell observed from offering a "thorough university training" to "busy people" was that "many sons of wealthy men who could not be spared" from their offices or businesses found it convenient to enroll at Temple in the evening. "So that the institution which was founded for the poor," Conwell said with undisguised satisfaction, "soon became a university for all classes."

Looking at Temple within the broader context of American higher education leaves one all the more impressed by Russell Conwell's daring. Founding a college in nineteenth-century America, according to one distinguished historian of American higher education, "required courage and vision, if not foolhardiness." No European precedent existed for creating small institutions of higher education; this was truly an American enterprise. Many colleges, however, were doomed to fail or become secondary schools. Temple's situation was more precarious than most since it benefited from neither the Morrill Act, which fostered the establishment of the great land-grant universities (Cornell, Penn State, Michigan), nor large-scale philanthropy, yet Conwell somehow managed to keep Temple afloat. The future was by no means guaranteed and the most difficult of times lay ahead, but Conwell had plans to make Temple College into Temple University.

The 1910-1911 School of Pharmacy basketball team. University athletics started in 1894, but many early records were lost or destroyed as offices moved from College Hall to Conwell Hall in 1923. Temple's first director of athletics was Charles M. Williams, who graduated from Springfield College and coached all sports at Temple. The first collegiate basketball opponent was Haverford College, whose team defeated the Owls 6–4 on March 23, 1895. Temple's home court was the College Hall gym.

Chapter 2
Growing Pains, 1907–1928

Russell Conwell described this period in Temple's history as its "Martyr Age" for the extensive personal sacrifices of Laura Carnell and others who guided Temple on the path to credibility and respectability.

TEMPLE UNIVERSITY TIMELINE

1907
Temple College becomes Temple University.

1910
An amendment to the original Charter of Incorporation acknowledges a merger of the Samaritan and Garretson Hospitals into Temple University.

1915
Trustees appoint James Henry Dunham dean of the College of Arts and Sciences.

1922
College of Liberal Arts and Sciences is fully accredited.

1926
Charles Ezra Beury becomes Temple's second president. A General Alumni Association forms.

1927
The School of Business creates a Department of Journalism. A football stadium opens in the West Oak Lane neighborhood.

1928
A new nursery school offers education and practical experience to pre-school teachers.

The official seal of Temple University.

Over the span of two decades Temple University fought through major financial crises; diversified its programs, adding new ones to accommodate changing times, meet new expectations, and serve the community; survived the impact of World War I; established a second building program; and developed a distinct style and enhanced reputation that earned grudging respect in some quarters, outright admiration in others. Standing before Temple were many daunting barriers. None were easily hurdled, especially the new professional accreditation bodies.

Temple began its dramatic transformation in 1907 when it incorporated as a university and the next year when the Pennsylvania College and University Council listed Temple as one of the state's higher-education institutions. Finally recognized as a bona fide postsecondary institution, Temple University set a new course, one heavily influenced by the burgeoning interest in formal training for the new professions, such as education, business, and health, and formal training for and licensing of the established professions of law, medicine, and dentistry as the appeal of freestanding professional schools vanished.

Temple Becomes a University

What is a university? Why did calling Temple a university instead of a college matter? At the turn of the twentieth century there was little agreement among educators as to what constituted a university. Unlike in Europe, the system of higher education in America was unregulated and devoid of central planning. Most states, including Pennsylvania, resisted urges to plan or to create an overarching vision. Free to innovate, many institutions called themselves universities.

Temple in its infancy was a patchwork of programs and departments, an experimental quilt of course offerings covering a wide array of subjects and grade levels. By 1907 Temple entered its adolescence exuberant, full of life, teeming with unbridled ambition and a desire to reach higher in the educational firmament.

Johns Hopkins University (founded in 1876) was universally acknowledged as the prototype of the modern university for the quality of its advanced scientific research, high level of faculty expertise, and rigor of its graduate and professional programs. To meet these standards to which all universities—Temple included—granted obeisance, universities were expected to support graduate and professional education and faculty members were increasingly expected to have earned the PhD or terminal professional degrees and to be engaged in research, creative, or scholarly activity in addition to their teaching duties.

PhD training and professional education quickly concentrated among a select group of private universities and a burgeoning group of state land-grant colleges. The Morrill Act of 1862 provided each state with public land grants to endow state colleges to support agricultural and mechanical education. In 1863 the Commonwealth of Pennsylvania designated the tiny Agricultural College of Pennsylvania in Centre County as the sole land-grant college in the state, changing its name to the Pennsylvania State College. Unable to benefit from the Morrill Act or to match the large gifts that flowed into Penn's coffers, and thus compete in costly PhD programs, Temple instead sought credibility and stability by educating working-class students for entry into the rising professions.

Impetus for the creation of universities sprang in part from the new professions' absorption of the progressive temperament. The period from 1890 to 1920 is known in American history as the Progressive Era, during which the prevailing intellectual impulse was to create order out of the chaos of the Industrial Age. Part of the *Search for Order*, as historian Robert Wiebe labeled the progressive impulse, was manifested in an emphasis on organizational structures to eliminate inefficiencies and restore social and economic equilibrium. Driven by this organizational impulse, the professions sought acceptance and cachet through associations with universities and through the creation of professional organizations, such as the American Medical Association (AMA), American Bar Association (ABA), and American Dental Association (ADA). These national organizations set internal guidelines, performance standards, and codes of conduct to regulate their practitioners and to control the flow of new people into the profession.

Temple's designation as a university followed a chain of pivotal events that included the founding of Samaritan Hospital, the creation of Temple's Medical School, and Temple's merger with the Philadelphia Dental College.

Samaritan Hospital and Temple Medical School

In 1891 neighbors in the Broad and Tioga section asked Russell Conwell to help reorganize a failed community hospital. Conwell immediately agreed and called on a member of his church, Ida Hamilton, to coordinate the effort. She and Conwell raised the down payment for the purchase of a three-story Victorian house at 3403 North Broad near Ontario Street, oversaw its renovations, and recruited volunteer good Samaritans, for whom she named the charity hospital. Dedicated on January 30, 1892, Samaritan Hospital had only twenty beds, two full-time staff members, and a horse-drawn ambulance, courtesy of an undertaker and the gift of two horses from P.A.B. Widener.

Samaritan Hospital soon expanded. A second building next door was purchased in 1898 and named Greatheart Hospital for use as a maternity department and later as a nurses' residence. The state appropriated funds in 1901 for a three-story administration building and in 1905 for another wing, plus a power plant and dining facility.

3403 North Broad Street (near Ontario Street) was the site of Samaritan Hospital. Russell Conwell was appointed president of the twenty-bed facility, which was designed to provide care for anyone in the neighborhood regardless of color, creed, or nationality.

Dr. W. Wayne Babcock operating, Samaritan Hospital, 1916.

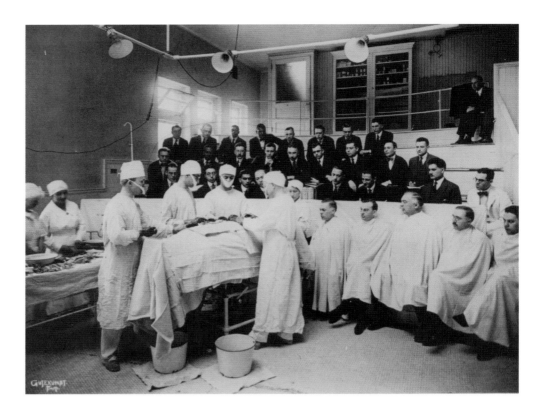

Philadelphia physicians, realizing that their traditional apprenticeship method of instruction no longer met the demands of contemporary medical science, saw formal medical education as the answer. By 1900 the city already had four medical schools: the University of Pennsylvania, Thomas Jefferson, Hahnemann, and the Women's Medical College of Pennsylvania. A group of young working men asked Conwell to open a fifth. Existing medical schools, they complained, were too expensive, restricted admissions to full-time day students, and too often adhered to a tacit discriminatory code, excluding blacks, women, Jews, new immigrant groups, and working students. It was the kind of challenge Conwell could not resist. He consulted with a group of Philadelphia physicians (many of whom vehemently opposed the idea) and educators (one warned, "It will kill Temple"). Conwell, as was his wont, plowed ahead.

Samaritan Hospital ambulance, circa 1930.

And so in September 1901 Temple opened a medical school. To mesh with student work hours, courses met in gaslit classrooms six days a week from 7:00 to 10:00 P.M. for nine months of the year. Quickly dubbed the "midnight medical school," it was Pennsylvania's first coeducational and first evening medical school. All academically qualified students were admitted, regardless of gender, religion, color, or ethnic background. Tuition was set at $125 a year for the evening school. Classes were held initially at College Hall, and medical students were given hands-on practice at Samaritan Hospital, which formally merged with Temple in 1906. The first dean, Dr. W. Wallace Fritz, devised a five-year program of part-time study, matching the number of instructional hours offered in day programs at other medical schools. Reactions within the medical community were negative. Many physicians feared that Temple was creating a "diploma mill" and that Temple's lack of endowment and poor facilities would "cheapen the medical degree."

The first year, twenty volunteer faculty members received thirty-one students. Faculty salaries were a problem: If the salaries were too low, the reputations of both the professors and the Medical School would be harmed. Temple's board of trustees agreed to an extraordinary arrangement, turning over to the school 90 percent of the net income, after expenses, for distribution to the faculty. Several of the early faculty made significant contributions to medicine. I. Newton Snively, who succeeded Fritz as dean in 1903, was the first to administer diphtheria antitoxin in Philadelphia. Edward W. Holmes, chief of surgery, authored a standard text on surgery. W. Wayne Babcock, who served forty years on the faculty, earned an international reputation as an inventor of surgical instruments, developer of spinal anesthesia, and user of steel-wire sutures.

In 1904 the Medical Council of Pennsylvania approved the quality of instruction and recognized Temple's MD degrees. Two women, Sara Allen and Mary E. Shepard, were among fourteen graduates in 1906. The 1908 class included Agnes Berry Montier, the first African American woman to receive an MD degree from Temple. Pennsylvania's legislature, under pressure from the older medical schools, the state licensing board, and the AMA, changed medical licensing requirements in 1907, effectively banning evening medical schools. Day classes and a four-year medical curriculum were organized in 1907.

Eighteenth and Buttonwood Campus

The Kornberg School of Dentistry that we know today started when Temple accepted the offer of the Philadelphia Dental College to merge. After the merger, Temple officially reincorporated as Temple University on December 12, 1907.

The Philadelphia Dental College retained its name until 1913, when it became the Temple University School of Dentistry. Founded in 1863 and the second-oldest U.S. school of dentistry, the Philadelphia Dental College and its Garretson Hospital for Oral Surgery (founded in 1878 and the first facility devoted exclusively to oral and maxillofacial surgery) were located in a cluster of buildings at Eighteenth and Buttonwood streets near Spring Garden Street (adjacent to the current location of Philadelphia Community College). Because the main building (erected in 1897) was relatively new, modern, and spacious, the Schools of Medicine and Pharmacy also moved there, followed in 1915 by the School of Chiropody.

Pharmacy

Pharmacy courses appeared in Temple bulletins as early as 1891. When the university trustees authorized formation of the Medical School in March 1901, the motion included provisions for a department of pharmacy. Established initially as a two-year program, the pharmacy curriculum offered a wide array of courses in medicine, pharmacy, and the liberal arts. At first, pharmacy students took courses alongside Medical School students in the same classrooms, all in the evening. Students sometimes referred to themselves as the "Night Owls." The first degrees were conferred in 1904.

The next year the Temple School of Pharmacy was founded, with its own staff of six part-time professors and ten part-time instructors. Classes were held in College Hall and then moved to

Conwell holding a new delivery in Temple's maternity ward.

Eighteenth and Buttonwood in 1907. The first dean of pharmacy, Dr. John R. Minehart, started a day division, closed the evening division in 1918, and extended the curriculum to three years. In 1928 Temple became a member of the Association of American Colleges of Pharmacy (AACP), which oversaw standards of pharmaceutical education. In 1932 the AACP ruled that pharmacy colleges should institute a mandatory four-year bachelor of science degree as a minimum for entry into the profession, and Temple complied.

Dean H. Evert Kendig, who succeeded Minehart in 1932 and served until 1950, established a master of science program, stimulated faculty research and participation in scientific meetings, and obtained external support for students. Kendig's attention to detail and professional standards paid a substantial dividend when in 1939 the School of Pharmacy received full accreditation from the American Council in Pharmaceutical Education. Kendig also persistently complained to the Temple administration about the poor facilities at Eighteenth and Buttonwood and pleaded for a new building. His pleas were partly answered in 1947 when the School of Pharmacy moved, along with the School of Dentistry, to the Packard Building at 3223 North Broad Street.

Chiropody

In September 1915 Temple University's School of Chiropody (later Podiatric Medicine) opened in response to a request from the Chiropody Society of Pennsylvania, which agreed to provide teachers if Temple provided space in Garretson Hospital. It was only the second chiropody school in the nation and the first attached to a university. Frank A. Thompson, MD, was named director. The first class consisted of three men and one woman. Courses were offered in the Rittenhouse Building, patients were treated at the Garretson Hospital at Eighteenth and Buttonwood, and a separate clinic for practical training was established nearby. Originally only a one-year program, it was increased to two and eventually four years. Anatomy, chemistry, surgery, and hygiene and sanitation were among the courses offered. First diplomas were awarded in 1916; three African American graduates were in the 1919 class.

Control over the program gradually became a sore point between the university and the Chiropody Society. The insistence of the Chiropody Society and its national association's Council on Education went largely unnoticed by Conwell, but President Charles Beury, elected Temple's second president in 1926, found the group difficult to deal with. In 1933 the council threatened to drop the School of Chiropody to a Class C rating unless Temple immediately updated equipment and facilities at a cost of $25,000. Guessing the threat was inspired by his own faculty, Beury instructed Dean Ralph R. Willoughby to ignore the council.

Somehow Beury found the funds to provide enough equipment to satisfy the National Association of Chiropodists, and the school received full accreditation. The School of Chiropody moved several times within the Eighteenth and Buttonwood campus, finally locating clinics and classrooms in the same building on Spring Garden Street. Chiropody managed to hang on until June 1960, when diminished enrollments and rising costs forced Temple to close it. However, the school revived and reconstituted itself and thirty-eight years later rejoined Temple as the School of Podiatry.

Accreditation Miseries

Medicine

Chiropody's accreditation fight was a minor skirmish compared with the protracted battles waged by the Medical School. Throughout the years at Eighteenth and Buttonwood, each of the health science programs experienced various problems as a result of inadequate facilities. Both the School of Medicine and the School of Dentistry faced major accreditation crises caused largely by the university's financial situation, which would not permit greater support for these two important units.

The Medical School phased out evening classes in 1911, but other problems persisted, including a lack of full-time faculty and inadequate laboratory, classroom, and office facilities. The space problem eased in 1907 when Temple acquired the Garretson Hospital and its seventy-five beds. When added to those available at Samaritan Hospital, they almost doubled the clinical space and the number of patients available to the Medical School. Many changes accompanied the move, including additional volunteer faculty, modifications to the clinical program, and an internship program. Nonetheless, in 1909 the AMA Council on Medical Education withheld its A rating.

In April, 1923 Conwell reestablished the Greatheart Hospital at 1810–12 Spring Garden Street as a maternity hospital for Temple University. Shortly afterward, renamed the Garretson-Greatheart Hospital, it gained a reputation as one of the most advanced maternity hospitals in the East. The gates were installed to enhance the property and served as an entrance to Temple's Buttonwood campus. Eventually, the medical classes, as well as the Pharmacy, Dental, and Chiropody schools were located here. The gates were moved in 1960 to the Main Campus entrance at Broad and Berks streets.

With no full-time medical faculty, limited resources, and a penchant for admitting students with less than a high school education, Temple's Medical School, in the words of Dr. Abraham Flexner, had "absolutely no future." A famously harsh critic, Flexner, in his first book, *The American College* (1908), criticized many aspects of American higher education. As a result, the Carnegie Foundation for the Advancement of Teaching selected the Louisville physician to lead a series of studies of professional education and the way doctors were trained. Flexner, in his 1910 report, concluded that, except for Johns Hopkins, none of the other medical schools in the United States and Canada provided truly sound medical training. The Flexner Report mandated that medical practice be linked to advanced scholarship in the biological sciences and that medical schools be affiliated with and integrated into a university structure. The ideal professional education involved full-time study beyond the bachelor's degree, with strong ties between scholarship and practice. The AMA took charge of enforcing the Flexner standards. Temple's Medical School, like many across the country, struggled over the next two decades to attain and hold full accredited status.

Many marginal medical schools—43 out of 160, according to one report—closed their doors after the Flexner Report. Dr. Frank C. Hammond, appointed Temple's dean of medicine in 1910, urgently asked Conwell and Temple's trustees to provide adequate funding to meet the Flexner Report criticisms. The trustees agreed to appoint five full-time faculty members; but they set salary limits ridiculously low, deterring qualified applicants and none were appointed. World War I postponed further AMA action, but in 1919 the association dropped the Medical School's rating to C, effectively halting further licensing of Temple's graduates. The AMA informed Hammond that Temple could improve its rating only if the university appointed twelve full-time professors and spent hundreds of thousands on specified equipment and facilities.

Anatomy class, circa 1908.

In 1932, Temple University's School of Medicine left the Eighteenth and Buttonwood campus and moved into the splendid new, AMA-compliant Medical School Building at Broad and Ontario streets opposite Temple University Hospital.

Discussions of a merger with Thomas Jefferson failed because neither school was financially stable. Wearied by years of uncertainty, the faculty at first voted to close the school. Students pleaded to keep it open. A direct, personal appeal to the AMA by Dean Hammond and Charles E. Beury, then one of Temple's most active trustees, was rebuffed. Hammond and Beury then appealed to Pennsylvania Governor William C. Sproul and state legislators, emphasizing Temple's education of physicians who practiced in Pennsylvania and the school's service to Philadelphia. Appalled by the situation, the governor and legislature promised to add $100,000 to Temple's biennial appropriation to aid the Medical School. Upon learning of the state's deep interest in the school, the AMA relented in 1921 and granted a B rating.

Some of Temple's trustees, according to Temple journalism professor Douglas Perry's early account, wanted to close the school. Conwell wondered aloud in a 1921 note to Hammond, "I am trying to decide whether to go on or to stop." But then the president of the Medical School alumni association, William N. Parkinson (MD MED 1911), stepped forward and firmly inserted himself into the situation, organizing a fund-raising campaign for a new Medical School building and serving as assistant dean, then dean. By the end of nearly four decades of service to Temple, he had totally transformed both the Medical School and the hospital.

By the time of the 1927 AMA accreditation visit, Temple had raised Medical School tuition, covered some of its debt with the state appropriation, added a three-story brick building called "The Main" to Samaritan Hospital, made several other improvements at the hospital, converted Garretson Hospital into a basic sciences laboratory building, and improved clinical teaching enough to gain the A rating. But many issues remained unresolved to the AMA's satisfaction, including

Dr. William N. Parkinson became vice president in charge of the university's Medical Center in 1953. He was credited with its emergence as one of the nation's leading medical education institutions.

the effectiveness of a part-time dean, the lack of a governance role for the faculty, the absence of an endowment, and the need for a modern Medical School building next to the hospital.

William Parkinson was appointed director of Samaritan Hospital in February 1929, and in April he replaced Hammond as dean of medicine. He immediately set about reorganizing both institutions, pulling them together as one. He began by gaining approval to change the name of Samaritan Hospital to Temple University Hospital. In June 1930 the cornerstone was laid for the impressive new $1.5 million Medical School building at the northwest corner of Broad and Ontario, containing research laboratories, student lockers and lounges, faculty offices, conference rooms—indeed, all the facilities necessary to meet the AMA concerns and to allow the Medical School to move from Eighteenth and Buttonwood. The Medical School immediately admitted another 100 students.

Parkinson followed up with an ambitious renovation plan that by 1940 raised Temple Hospital's capacity from 350 to 500 beds. He now envisioned a new "Medical Center," similar to Columbia's in New York City, with the Medical School as its nucleus. Parkinson told Temple President Charles Beury that he must elevate the Medical School into a central role if Temple University were to ever hope of becoming one of the "great National Universities."

FACT

The Kornberg School of Dentistry at Temple University receives 4,500 applications per year for 125 available slots.

Dentistry

In the early twentieth century, American dental schools went through a torturous period of assessment and accreditation similar to that of medical schools. In 1910 the American Dental Association (ADA) joined the Dental Education Council of America, the national organization of dental faculties, to collaborate in unifying standards for the educational requirements of dentists and the accreditation of dental schools. The rating and assessment of dental schools done by the ADA's Council on Dental Education began in 1917. Temple received a B rating. Seven years later, William J. Gies conducted a comprehensive study of American dental education sponsored by the Carnegie Foundation for the Advancement of Teaching. Gies hoped to strengthen educational standards for dental education as Abraham Flexner had done for medicine.

Although Temple's dental school was one of the largest and seemingly most successful, it received a B rating from Gies and the Council on Dental Education in 1924. They cited overcrowding, an inadequate library, a lack of faculty research, and the absence of a graduate program as the school's major shortcomings. Temple had forty-seven teachers, five of whom were full-time faculty, to instruct 600 students. Salaries were low, however, and the huge student demand, combined with the school's limited financial resources, forced Dean I. Norman Broomell to teach several courses himself.

Broomell's years of service from 1918 to 1941 brought advancements in the quality of instruction and a substantial increase in the number of graduates who passed the State Board examinations. He and the dental faculty also anticipated national trends by requiring students to have at least two years of pre-dental college instruction and extending the dental curriculum itself to four years. The American Association of Dental Surgeons insisted that the "two-four" plan be in place by 1937, but Temple endorsed the plan in 1932 and put it into effect in 1935. As a consequence, Columbia University and Temple were among the elite to receive Class A ratings in 1934.

Law

One morning in May 1895, Henry S. Borneman, a twenty-four-year-old lawyer and lecturer in the Business Department, went to Conwell recommending establishment of an evening course of study in the law. Borneman argued that a theory-only legal curriculum of the kind provided in most law schools was inadequate preparation for the next generation of lawyers. A practical law curriculum at Temple, he asserted, would mitigate that concern. Conwell, a lawyer himself, was initially resistant to the idea. Finally, Conwell said, "All right. Go ahead. If it is a success, it is your success; if it is a failure, it is your failure."

Borneman chose the name Philadelphia Law School of Temple University and hired two attorneys to teach legal courses that fall in collaboration with the Business Department. Classes were held in the new College Hall. Forty-six students registered, paying twelve dollars in tuition for the first year, escalating to thirty-six dollars for the fourth and final year. Not yet ready to appoint deans, the board of trustees named Borneman principal of the Law Department in 1896, but three years later the board minutes referred to him as dean. The first graduating class of sixteen students received their bachelor of laws degrees in 1901. In an unusual concession, the trustees permitted the Law School to hold a commencement apart from that of Temple College.

The Law School boasted that all of its graduates passed the bar examination, because it would not grant the degree until after students passed the exam. In 1905 the trustees stopped the practice and began awarding students their degrees at the completion of course work, and until 1920 every graduate continued to pass the bar anyway. In 1907 the Pennsylvania Board of Law Examiners formally recognized the program, and in 1911 the name was changed to the Temple University School of Law.

Francis Chapman, dean of the Law School from 1906 to 1939, played a most important role in shaping the school's culture and character. Under Chapman's leadership, enrollments steadily increased and he lifted the law school's prestige and strengthened relations with prominent figures in Philadelphia's law community. In 1927 he established the *Temple Law Quarterly,* and in other ways throughout his tenure he encouraged student and faculty scholarship.

The Law School moved many times during its formative years. Cramped for space in College Hall, it moved downtown in 1909 to be closer to the courts, libraries, and city offices. For ten years the school was located in the Wilson Building at Sixteenth and Sansom streets. Then it moved to 1521 Locust Street, a building that coincidentally housed Temple's Music School. Five years later the Law School moved to the Public Ledger Building on Independence Square.

In 1933 the issue of accreditation suddenly arose. Members of the bar noted that Temple was not on the approved list of the ABA's Council on Legal Education. The task of seeing the Law School through accreditation fell to Associate Dean John G. Hervey. He and Dean Chapman were concerned about accreditation because some states, including Delaware, had begun to permit only students from approved schools to sit for the bar exams. To meet the ABA standards, Temple created a day division, hired more full-time faculty, increased faculty salaries, tightened admission requirements, and tried dropping weak students (to increase the percentage of graduates who passed the State Board examinations). The latter stratagem backfired somewhat when trustees, responding to student and parent protests, objected to allowing law faculty to fail fourth-year students. Still, the Law School was fully accredited by the ABA in 1933 and two years later received membership in the prestigious Association of American Law Schools (AALS).

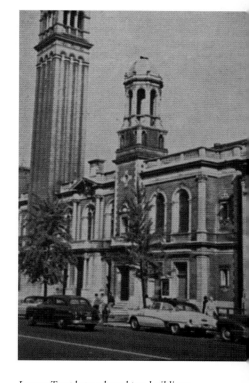

In 1953 Temple purchased two buildings from the Keneseth Israel (KI) Synagogue at 1715 North Broad Street for use of the peripatetic Law School. One building, dedicated in 1954, became Reber Hall and the other, dedicated in 1959, became the Charles Klein Law Library. (The Klein Library was destroyed by fire in 1972. In 1994 Reber Hall was renovated as a music recital hall and renamed Rock Hall in honor of Dr. Milton Rock and Mrs. Shirley Rock.)

Forced to move again in 1938, the Law School relocated to the thirteenth floor of Gimbel's department store on South Ninth Street, where it remained until 1953. Dean Chapman died in 1939, and a series of acting deans guided the school during the war years, when enrollment plunged to fifty-six students. By 1944 the faculty was reduced to three full-time members plus adjunct lecturers even though the AALS required at least four full-time faculty members. Fortunately, a member of the Business School faculty who taught business law was loaned to the Law School to satisfy the association's requirement. After the war, enrollments rebounded and a new dean, Benjamin Franklin Boyer, brought a number of changes, including a graduate program and a student legal aid society. Most important, he persuaded Temple's president and trustees to make space on the Main Campus.

Taking the lead was Judge Charles Klein. A trustee and alumnus of the Law School, Klein had earned his law degree at night while working on the day shift at Baldwin Locomotive Works and Midvale Steel, and in 1941 Klein became the youngest man ever to receive a judgeship in Philadelphia. The move became possible when J. Howard Reber (LLB Law 1900) bequeathed $300,000 to the Law School and when Congregation Keneseth Israel (KI) decided to follow its congregants to the suburbs. KI's two properties, a synagogue sanctuary building and a classroom building only a half block south of Conwell Hall, were purchased by the university for $250,000.

Klein raised funds to refurbish the interiors. In 1953 the Law School moved into the former KI classroom building, renamed Reber Hall in 1954. Denoting the Law School's enhanced stature, the honored speaker for the dedication ceremony was Chief Justice Earl Warren. Not done, Klein raised an additional $250,000 for remodeling the old synagogue building (built in 1891) and transforming it into a magnificent law library. When the building was completed, the alumni insisted on naming it the Charles Klein Law Library.

A Silver Lining

Conwell once dreamed of providing all comers with free education funded by philanthropic gifts. But the large-scale philanthropic gifts never materialized. And he learned from the financial fiasco forcing the closing of the Temple Academies in 1896 that he must charge tuition and that tuition must pay for an increasingly large proportion of the total operating costs. Yet, despite higher enrollments, whatever Temple took in from tuition during its years of growing pains was never enough to cover its costs. Operating on a shoestring, charging little or no tuition, relying mostly on volunteer faculty, and depending on contributions to stay afloat, Temple faced chronic financial problems. In 1909 matters reached a crisis. The board of trustees had borrowed from banks, issued bonds, and made public solicitations in newspaper ads; the trustees even insured Conwell's life to secure loans and mortgaged his Broad Street home. A 1902 benefit performance by John Philip Sousa's band added to their troubles by leaving a deficit of $1,185. A complete audit of the books in 1909 revealed a deficit of nearly $340,000. Emergency requests to alumni and friends were to no avail. The situation worsened, and in December 1910 Conwell considered selling College Hall and virtually all of the university's holdings to clear the debts.

Conwell made a desperate proposal that changed Temple's future. He offered to relocate the university and asked the state legislature for money for a new building to be built on the New Boulevard (now the Benjamin Franklin Parkway). On June 13, 1911, the governor signed a bill appropriating $110,000 to Temple—$100,000 for operating expenses and $10,000 for a building. The size of this first appropriation made very little difference as far as the huge debt was concerned, but it signaled the commonwealth's willingness to share in the university's responsibility to educate working men and women and the less advantaged. The state would come to Temple's rescue on other occasions, particularly on behalf of the hospital and Medical School, and by the time of Conwell's death in 1925, Temple was receiving a biennial appropriation of $270,000.

Growth of the New Professions

Conwell and Carnell set up every course and every program to meet a specific need. This left Temple's curricula a smorgasbord of offerings in the early years. Laura Carnell was under orders from Conwell to provide classrooms and teachers for any group of six or more students who wished instruction in any subject, no matter what it was. The 1897 catalogue listed "schools" of Domestic Sciences and Art, Music, Nursing, Oratory, and Theology and a School of Industry for Women. Most of them, in fact, were programs rather than legitimate schools with dedicated faculty, curricula, and deans. Within a few years, however, several programs evolved into schools and colleges of the more familiar kind, including Business, Education, Liberal Arts and Sciences, Music, and Theology. These programs principally served an ever-expanding need to train and educate students either in preparation for advanced training in the professional schools or for direct entry into the new and emerging professions, many of which required college degrees or college-level preparation for entry, certification, or licensure.

Business

Today's Fox School of Business and Management traces its roots back to 1884, when Conwell arranged student tutorials in commercial education. Temple College offered its first business course in 1893, a class in bookkeeping. The following year a Summer School of the Business Department offered classes in shorthand, typewriting, bookkeeping, and penmanship. A "College

The cornerstone for Conwell Hall, on the northeast corner of Broad Street and Montgomery Avenue, was laid in 1922, and the building was formally dedicated by Conwell on January 23, 1924. Known initially as "Unit No. 1" —the first in a series of connected buildings in the proposed "Temple of Learning"—it was named Conwell Hall in 1926. It was originally a six-story structure, with a fifth-floor gymnasium and basement swimming pool; a seventh floor was added in 1926. A connecting twelve-story building, "Unit No. 2," was completed in 1930 and named Carnell Hall.

Conwell Hall, circa 2005.

of Business" appears in the 1898 catalog, advertising a "full college course" and stating, "Business as a profession is rapidly being reduced to a Science, and the requirements necessitate a higher, broader, and more liberal business education," if one is to succeed. For whatever reasons, the college failed to take hold and was quietly abandoned.

The program's fortunes changed with the arrival in 1899 of Milton F. Stauffer, who answered a newspaper ad for the job "Professor of Stenography." Stauffer remained at Temple for nearly four decades in a number of positions, including Conwell's secretary and administrative assistant, Temple's government relations man in Harrisburg, and dean of the School of Commerce. In 1902 Stauffer was named "Principal" of Temple's Business Department "at a salary of $1,200 a year, plus carfare."

Stauffer organized a Department of Commercial Education in which students could complete two years of business courses plus two years in the Teachers College and receive a bachelor of science in education. A second attempt to organize a business school succeeded in 1918, when Stauffer became dean of the School of Commerce. Conwell decided to make the Commerce School a "leading feature of the University work." The first degree was awarded in 1922, and by1925 the school had awarded ten bachelor of science degrees in business. Gradually, Stauffer became drawn to other university duties and less involved in the School of Commerce.

Most administrative responsibilities of the school were progressively assumed by Dr. Harry A. Cochran, a genial, unpretentious man from a small town in upstate Pennsylvania who had earned a doctorate in education from Temple. Almost single-handedly Cochran built a quality faculty and modernized the curriculum. He sought accreditation from the American Association of Collegiate Schools of Business (AACSB), but it was initially denied because of the school's unclear leadership situation. Stauffer was elevated to assistant to the president in 1934 and Cochran appointed dean. And so the AACSB granted full accreditation. Cochran, too, eventually wore many hats for the university before retiring as vice president in 1960.

Education

In the early twentieth century, the professional education and certification of schoolteachers usually occurred in "normal schools" dedicated to teacher training; instead of granting a bachelor's degree, they conferred a certificate or license to teach. Normal schools emphasized curricular development and pedagogy as a science. With the advent of compulsory school attendance, however, education became the fastest-growing professional field and colleges and universities soon undertook the education of teachers.

The beginning of teacher education at Temple is traceable to 1894, when a course in kindergarten theory was first offered. Classes for teachers in vocal music and physical education soon followed. Dean Laura Carnell is credited with starting the first serious teacher-education programs at Temple. Responding to a request from the Philadelphia school district, she organized afternoon and Saturday classes for prospective and current Philadelphia teachers beginning in 1901, with a model school and a Department of Pedagogy soon after. Dean Carnell emphasized the need to train teachers for various specialized fields of study, such as home economics, art, music, physical education, and commercial subjects. A bachelor's degree in physical education was first offered in 1910, and by 1917, twenty courses were organized into six divisions.

Seeking a semblance of coherence, Carnell recommended in 1919 that the existing departments be "amalgamated into a single school and general administrative responsibility...centralized in

The Iron Gates

The trademark iron gates containing the university seal were created and installed in 1929 at Eighteenth and Buttonwood streets, where the Health Science Campus was then located. In 1960 the gates were moved to the Main Campus entrance at Broad Street and Berks Mall, between the Baptist Temple and Mitten Hall.

Students from Temple's two-year normal school program for elementary teachers posing during a 1912 outing in Atlantic City. Temple's Teachers College was founded in 1919.

an officer bearing the title of dean of the teachers college." George E. Walk, appointed first dean of the Teachers College, served until 1948, making several changes along the way. An experienced teacher and administrator with a PhD from New York University, Walk phased out two-year programs, established a four-year baccalaureate degree program with more stringent standards, and introduced master's and doctoral programs. In 1925 the New York State Board of Regents fully accredited and registered the Teachers College as an approved school of education.

Home Economics, one of Temple's oldest units, began in 1894 with classes in "Scientific Cooking." Soon there was a Department of Household Science, later to be called the Women's Department, at one time headed by Sarah Conwell, wife of the founder, and later by Laura Carnell. Courses offered in the initial one-year program included food preparation, sewing, textiles, family economics, and general homemaking. The program was expanded to two years, a diploma awarded, and the name changed to the Departments of Household Art and Household Science in 1913. It was gradually folded into the Teachers College and became known as Home Economics, offering a four-year bachelor of science degree to train young women and men for careers in both teaching and business.

Liberal Arts

The exact date of the founding of the College of Liberal Arts and Sciences is uncertain. References to a "College Department" appear as early as 1891, when a day department was established, but the first bachelor of arts degree was not awarded until 1901. The first dean, Albert E. McKinley, was elected by the trustees in 1903. A recipient of Temple's first degree, the bachelor of oratory, in 1892, McKinley earned a PhD from the University of Pennsylvania. After twelve years as dean, McKinley left Temple to accept appointment to the Penn faculty in its History Department—not an uncommon occurrence in those early years when richer universities frequently "raided" the faculties of lesser-endowed institutions such as Temple.

Temple's undergraduate programs in the arts and sciences closely approximated those offered at traditional institutions such as Princeton, Yale, and Penn, both in the range of offerings and particularly in the quality of instruction. Sticklers for academic standards, Liberal Arts and Sciences faculty insisted that prospective students complete admissions examinations in English, mathematics, history, and at least one foreign language. Applicants with a facility in Latin were permitted to enter the curriculum leading to a bachelor of arts degree. Those who chose French or German had to be content with the less highly regarded bachelor of science path. The liberal arts courses in the languages, philosophy, history, English, mathematics, and the basic sciences were known for their discipline and rigor. Many Temple graduates went on to study for advanced degrees. From this early date and continuing for many decades after, the liberal arts faculty thought of themselves as keepers of the standards for Temple. They were also concerned about quality instruction and teaching loads.

When James Henry Dunham became dean in 1915, he was dismayed to find some faculty members routinely assigned to lecture thirty-one hours a week. He decreed that it be no more than twenty, yet demanded that all classes begin and end precisely on time. Dunham, who served as dean until 1942, was a well-known scholar who published several important books on philosophy. Also a believer in democracy and shared faculty governance, he created the College Executive Committee (still in existence today), which had representation from each of the departments to share decisions on curricular matters and other issues of importance. "Teaching," he emphasized, "is the first function of a member of the College faculty." Dunham strengthened the college's reputation by recruiting accomplished teachers who were also excellent scholars.

Largely because of Dunham's successful blending of scholarship and superb teaching across the faculty, the College of Liberal Arts and Sciences became fully accredited in 1922, securing the approvals of the Association of Colleges and Preparatory Schools of the Middle States and Maryland, plus the New York State Board of Regents. Looking back, we see that the College of Liberal Arts and Sciences was the first to reshape the hodgepodge of undergraduate courses into an organized form and to lay claim to students, budget, and space.

Music

Conwell loved music and enjoyed gathering the congregation for hymns and joining impromptu harmonizing on street corners with neighborhood boys. It was not a surprise, then, to find fourteen persons listed as instrumental and voice instructors in the earliest Temple College bulletins. Professor Lyman S. Leason was hired in 1897 as a teacher of music, and in 1901 the trustees' minutes refer to "The Philadelphia School of Music of Temple College, Lyman S. Leason, Dean." Leason was reelected dean with the understanding that he was to assume the rent and janitorial service of the music hall and pay the college treasurer 10 percent of the gross receipts.

FACT

The doctoral program in music therapy at Temple University was the first of its kind in the United States.

How did the owl come to be Temple's mascot?

Professor C. Douglas Perry discovered that on April 28, 1893, trustees of the Grace Baptist Church decided that major activities of the church should be impressed on the public by identifiable symbols. For the church they selected the eagle. For Samaritan Hospital they chose the gentle dove. For Temple College their choice was the wise-looking owl. One day soon after at student convocation, the Rev. Forrest E. Dager, an Episcopal priest and a friend of Conwell's, presented Conwell with the stuffed carcass of an owl. The mascot of Temple College, Dager expounded, was honored in Greek mythology as sacred to Athene, the goddess of wisdom. Conwell accepted the stuffed bird and placed it on his office desk for all to see. Soon students were referring to themselves as the Owls. The public and the press followed suit.

Such arrangements generated a rapid turnover of Music School deans. In 1903 Leason resigned and the school moved downtown to a location on Chestnut Street near Fifteenth and changed its name to the Philadelphia School of Music. Thaddeus Rich, concertmaster of the Philadelphia Orchestra and closely associated with Leopold Stokowski, became dean in 1913. Rich also taught at the Curtis Institute of Music and traveled widely, affording little time to the School of Music, which declined precipitously during the Depression. In 1943 President Robert L. Johnson reluctantly closed the school. A program in music education in Teachers College continued on. Twenty years later the School of Music experienced a rebirth.

Theology

Surprisingly perhaps, the one fatality of growing pains was theology. Six of the first seven students to approach Conwell for instruction in 1884 entered the ministry. However, formal instruction in theology did not begin until 1893. Before then Conwell resisted all signs of sectarian instruction. Earnestly avowing a non-denominational approach, Conwell once said, "It is our belief that no man should have a creed." When the churches are willing to give up their creeds, he said, "then will we unite in one great church."

Conwell's ecumenical spirit extended to his selection of members for the Temple College Board of Trustees and to his choice of friends. Rabbi J. Leonard Levy was a Temple trustee and also taught Hebrew in the theology program. Rabbi Joseph Krauskopf of nearby Congregation Keneseth Israel borrowed a page from Conwell's book and in 1896 founded the National Farm School in Doylestown (now known as Delaware Valley College), both as a place where young men from disadvantaged neighborhoods could learn agricultural skills and as a living example of how Jewish agrarian roots could be reawakened in America. Conwell was gratified and delighted by Krauskopf's extrapolation of the "Temple Idea," but his Baptist colleagues were not. They would have preferred that Conwell use his talents to advance Baptist causes.

Notwithstanding, Conwell insisted, as he put it, on a "Theological Department of a purely undenominational nature." He set the course of instruction at two years, some of which could be completed via correspondence courses. By 1901, both day and evening classes were offered and the program requirements were increased to five years to earn a bachelor of divinity degree. Conwell frequently changed the curriculum and the school's name. At one time it was called the Divinity School and then the Philadelphia Theology School, before the Temple University School of Theology was settled on. Its first dean was the Rev. Forrest E. Dager, an Episcopal pastor and close friend of Conwell's who agreed that a pastor's leadership must reach into the community, working among the sick, the poor, the uneducated, and the unchurched. Conwell called it the "total ministry."

After Dager came the Rev. John Gordon, a Scotsman who had studied at the University of Chicago and whose pastorate was the Second Baptist Church in Germantown. During Gordon's service as dean from 1903 to 1909, the trustees, in an attempt to increase enrollments, reduced entrance requirements and cut back the course of study from five to four years. Under the Rev. Walter B. Shumway, who followed Gordon and served until 1927, efforts were made to broaden the appeal of the program to include all kinds of Christian activity and to attract interested laypersons.

Two graduate degrees (master of sacred theology and doctor of sacred theology) were added by Dean Floyd J. Zimmerman in 1933. The library, however, was totally inadequate to support graduate programs, and the school struggled for several years. The Rev. J. S. Ladd Thomas, pastor of the First Methodist Episcopal Church of Germantown and a former Temple trustee, agreed to attempt to revamp the school, focusing on the graduate program. Thomas patiently pleaded the school's case before the Association of American Theological Schools (AATS). But the AATS withdrew accreditation in 1944, and then restored it, before finally withdrawing recognition in 1958, mostly because of an insufficient number of full-time faculty. Efforts to revive the school failed and it closed in 1959. Conwell's ecumenical intentions ultimately prevailed in 1961 with the establishment within the College of Liberal Arts of the Temple Department of Religion, one of the first religion departments to be organized at a public university.

Today, Conwell's name is attached to the Gordon-Conwell Theological Seminary in Boston, Massachusetts. In 1889 the Rev. A. J. Gordon founded a missionary training school inspired by motives similar to Conwell's for forming Temple, but Gordon's school was built within a strong evangelical and denominational framework. Later renamed the Gordon Divinity School, it merged in 1969 with remnants of Temple's Theology School (aka The Conwell School of Theology), through the efforts of philanthropist J. Howard Pew, Dr. Harold J. Ockenga, and the Rev. Billy Graham. Beyond the use of Conwell's name, the Gordon-Conwell Theological Seminary has no connection to Temple University.

Temple and World War

When America entered World War I in 1917, enrollments dropped at Temple and most colleges. The patriotic fever, building for years, brought many to volunteer even before the United States declared war. Many American students volunteered for the ambulance service in France. Several members of Temple's dental faculty volunteered in 1914 to work in the American Hospital in Paris. Temple students gave a benefit musicale and promenade to raise money for Belgian refugees. Basketball (1918–1919) and football (1919–1921) seasons were canceled as men enlisted or were drafted.

Temple's Student Army Training Corps line up for inspection on Broad Street, 1918.

The government turned to universities for on-campus training programs for cadets and officers. President Woodrow Wilson established the Student Army Training Corps (SATC) in July 1917, and eventually 540 colleges participated and 125,000 men were inducted. Participating institutions received funds to house, feed, and instruct student trainees. Almost exactly 500 Temple students served in the war, and someone (perhaps Laura Carnell) compiled a handwritten list to be left in the archives. Temple's Medical School organized a Medical Cadet Corps to give "special instruction" to juniors and seniors on "sanitary and military tactics" to prepare them for commissions in the armed forces and to manage hospitals and deal with infectious diseases. Russell Conwell advised every soldier from every walk of life to do as he had in the Civil War and to carry a book and devote every spare minute to reading and to preparing to succeed in life after the war. When "normalcy" returned in 1920, Temple greeted 6,000 students that fall, including 346 World War I veterans.

Temple and the Collegiate Ideal

What did it mean to "go to college"? Was Temple in its early years truly a "college"? A typical response may be that of Helen Williams Hodgens, who earned two Temple degrees (BA 1918, MD 1925). Fifty years later, Hodgens recalled parties in College Hall attended by Russell Conwell, who chatted with students and was "friendly and talkative." Asked about the extent of campus life

in her time at Temple, she laughed. "Our campus didn't amount to anything in those days. There was one big building next to the church."

Temple in 1925 was far from the then-prevalent notion of an ideal college campus and college life. Early in the twentieth century, while Temple struggled to establish itself, the ideal construct of collegiate life became embedded in America's commercial and popular cultures. College for most adolescents became a coveted life experience, a combination of socioeconomic mobility and rite of passage. "College going," as one historian noted, "became fashionable and prestigious."

"College" was a place, as well as an experience. The archetypical college became the private liberal arts college. Yale and Princeton became America's colleges, the places where collegiate life and atmosphere came together like no other, fostering a sense of lifelong attachment. Social and athletic traditions were the binding elements of this process. So also was the architecture. American college architecture favored Gothic style; what was old was considered more permanent, more collegiate, more a symbol of a living heritage. New colleges, like Temple, aspired to look traditional—thus the neo-Gothic styling of its first buildings.

Loyalty to alma mater required the creation of distinguishing institutional symbols. These included mottoes, mascots, school colors, team names, school songs, distinctive dress and argot, official processions, Founder's Day, commencement, homecoming, yearbooks—all intended to unify and codify the college experience. Temple eventually added all of these, many of them associated with Temple's rich tradition in intercollegiate athletics, which are reviewed in a later chapter.

The idealized "college life" often evoked images of arrogance, irresponsibility, and perpetual adolescence. And that had to alienate and offend the average Temple student. College life for most Temple students consumed the time left over at the end of the workday. The vast majority worked their way through school. One perhaps extreme example was that of a young man who worked in a foundry from 7:00 A.M. to 6:00 P.M. and then went to classes at night, usually not getting to bed until 1:00 A.M. Temple students often sacrificed greatly for their educations, as many were forced to skip meals, walked to save money, and dressed in worn clothes. Russell Conwell both empathized with and celebrated such circumstances. His thirst for education and his painful confrontation with social elitism at Yale may well have led him to create the antithesis of Yale, a version of the modern college that relied on merit rather than social status.

All of this is not to suggest that Temple lacked a college life. A vibrant sense of school spirit made up for what the college lacked in student amenities and facilities. Student field trips—especially one to New York and another to Conwell's birthplace in Massachusetts—proved popular. After the opening of College Hall, space was available for celebrations and special events. Founder's Day in 1906 was celebrated with an informal convocation at which students presented Conwell with a gift of a fishing outfit. Group games drew many participants, as did promenades in the gym and hayrides. Fraternities soon formed, as did exercise, walking, choral, and athletic clubs. College fund-raisers included watermelon parties, trolley rides to Angora with ice cream and cake included, chicken suppers, talent shows, rummage sales, and bake sales.

The first student yearbook, *The Record,* appeared in 1901, with this salute to Temple: "To her we owe a debt that the books cannot record and that money cannot pay. Let us revere her name, honor her memory, and consecrate ourselves to the advancement of her welfare." Alumni associations had formed within various schools and colleges in the 1890s. To bond students to Temple after graduation, an alumni magazine first appeared in 1898 as *The Temple Magazine.*

Shortly after his inauguration as Temple's second president, Charles Beury established the Temple University General Alumni Association (GAA) as an umbrella organization to serve all of the schools and colleges. President Beury declared it his "happy privilege" to address himself for the first time in June 1926 to all the alumni and alumnae in the initial issue of the *Temple Alumni Bulletin* (later the *Temple Review*). Raymond L. Burkley (BS EDU 1928), a teacher and housemaster at Girard College, volunteered to organize the effort. In 1931 he was hired part-time as director of the GAA, and two years later he took the job full-time and remained in it until 1966. Needing an office and a place to welcome back alumni, Burkley established Alumni House in a Broad Street row house next to Mitten Hall, where it was located until 1966.

Dean Laura Carnell (seated at center) posed with faculty of the Teachers College, circa 1922. Dean George Walk is at her left. Dean Carnell established a Department of Pedagogy in 1902, which was the forerunner of Temple's Teachers College and College of Education.

End of an Era

Those who knew and admired Russell Conwell tended to use the same words to describe him: "perfectly natural—human to the core," "never pompous or egotistically important," possessed of a "boyish sense of humor" with a sincere laugh. Although always genial and friendly toward students, Conwell was not a social lion gifted with small talk or immediate ease with strangers. Will McCurdy, his associate pastor, said Conwell lived well and earned a generous salary, owning his home on North Broad Street and the family home in Massachusetts. Conwell employed his own secretary, nurse, and housekeeper. He traveled first-class, said McCurdy, "tipped handsomely, and gave generous gifts."

Indeed, his comfortable lifestyle and entrepreneurial flair led some to see Conwell as little more than a showman and shrewd businessman. After his death, the *American Mercury* magazine, known for H. L. Mencken's lambasting rants against American icons, attacked Conwell's "Polly-anna economics and saccharine sentiments," charging that his books and lectures were nothing more than "gaudy buncombe." Yet, regardless of one's perspective, it is impossible to dismiss the astounding amount of hope and opportunity Conwell offered to countless thousands of men and women in his lifetime. That hope and opportunity remain today so firmly a part of the Temple mission. John Wanamaker succinctly summarized Conwell's contributions: "A man dies, but his good work lives."

Conwell died December 6, 1925. He was interred next to his wife, Sarah, in the elegant Monument Cemetery, with its stately gatehouses facing the Baptist Temple. Later, Temple acquired Monument Cemetery to use for parking and athletic facilities, and Conwell and Sarah were moved temporarily to Laurel Hill Cemetery and then returned to Temple on May 11, 1959. They were buried with full honors in a small courtyard next to Conwell Hall. In 1968 the remains were quietly removed and reburied in a lovely pocket garden in the center of campus, a class of '67 gift now called Founder's Garden. The grave lies behind a large bust of Conwell sculpted by Boris Blai.

Laura Carnell—"Dean of Deans"

After his death, Conwell's "right hand" remained. Laura Carnell, the unseen power behind the growth of Temple University, carried on. Together, she and Conwell had lifted a small experimental college into the ranks of important universities. Called the "dean of deans," Carnell held several official titles, including dean of the corporation and secretary of the board of trustees, but she was effectively both Temple's first chief academic officer and chief administrator. Each of Temple's first eleven schools was started, organized, and developed by Carnell with no funds other than small tuition revenues and, before College Hall, only the use of row houses and makeshift facilities.

In Laura Carnell's day, few if any coeducational universities accorded a woman the status and power equal to Carnell's. Several colleges and universities matched Temple's record for welcoming women students, but most pigeonholed or restricted the rise of women in faculty and administrative ranks. In retrospect, Laura Carnell was one of the lone voyagers of her era, a reluctant pioneer of women's rights by her pure example and deed. Credit must be given to Conwell for seeing and using Carnell's rare talents. He believed a woman should be respected as a woman and honored for her achievements. "If we want to civilize men," Conwell wrote in 1909, "we must give the women a place in the church and society. There is no influence so powerful."

Laura Carnell (BA 1898, Hon. LDD 1902), Temple University's "dean of deans," organized and administered each of Temple's first eleven schools. In Conwell's final year of life, she was given the title of associate president, with full discretion over university affairs.

Only twenty-six when she gave up her job as a teacher in the Philadelphia public schools to join Conwell's staff in 1893, Laura Carnell worked during the day, attended classes at night, and earned a bachelor of arts degree in 1898. Soon after, Conwell appointed her principal of the Women's Department, but she was involved in virtually everything that was Temple. She taught art history classes for twenty-three years and was an energetic member of the Liberal Arts and Teachers College faculties. In 1902 Temple awarded her an honorary doctorate of literature. Totally dedicated to Temple, Carnell never married and lived with her mother on North Camac Street. Active in dozens of community organizations, she was a member of the Philadelphia Board of Education.

All great institutions, Russell Conwell wrote, endured a "Martyr Age," when "persons unknown to history sacrificed all to keep them alive." Dean Carnell, he said, "lived through all that toil without reward." Such sacrifices and consecrated devotion were necessary in order to lay the foundation of Temple University. "She was a leader," Conwell said of Carnell. "Without praise, with small pay, no recreation and no recognition; she sped on with no thought of honor or fortune."

By 1923, when Conwell turned eighty and his health declined, Carnell assumed many of the president's duties. In October 1925, when the trustees learned that Conwell's illness was terminal, they gave Carnell the title of associate president and full discretion over the university's business. When the time came to select a second president, Carnell's name was one of three brought to the board of trustees. After one candidate withdrew, Carnell reputedly said, "It's a man's job," and presented the name of Charles E. Beury and requested the board's support for him. Whether or not the board would have named Carnell president if she truly wanted the post can only be conjectured. Beury graciously acknowledged Carnell's indisputable qualifications for the position of president and continued to rely on her and call her associate president.

On February 15, 1929, Temple dedicated a new building next to Conwell Hall. Known initially as Unit 2, it was intended as the second building in a proposed block-long "Temple of Learning" to extend from Conwell Hall to College Hall. Not long afterward, Carnell died unexpectedly at the age of sixty-two. On February 12, 1930, university trustees, by a unanimous vote, named the building Carnell Hall. A school in Philadelphia on Devereaux Avenue is also named for her.

In recognition of Laura Carnell's inestimable importance, her portrait hangs today in Sullivan Hall's presidential portrait gallery, deservedly according her equal honor alongside Temple's presidents.

FACT

The founder of Temple University, Russell H. Conwell, and his wife are buried in the Founder's Garden on the Main Campus.

Chapter 3
Depression and War, 1929–1945

The stock market crash of October 1929, signaling the beginning of a long economic decline, had little immediate effect on Temple University. Indeed, enrollments held steady in 1930, and tuition revenues were ample to meet operating expenses. By 1931, however, many Temple students found it difficult to remain in school. Temple's Placement Bureau cited increased difficulty in finding part-time jobs for students, and the job markets for recent graduates were glutted.

Samaritan Hospital changes its name to Temple University Hospital.

1929

The Medical School moves to 3401 North Broad Street.

1932

President Franklin Delano Roosevelt dedicates Sullivan Hall.

1936

O. Spurgeon English, MD, professor of psychiatry, and Edward Weiss, MD, open the first clinic for psycho-somatic medicine.

1939

1931

Department of Theater starts. Mitten Hall is dedicated. Oak Lane Country Day School merges with Temple University.

1935

The estate of George and Stella Elkins Tyler becomes the site of Temple's Tyler School of Fine Arts. Temple plays in the inaugural Sugar Bowl on New Year's Day.

1938

Men's basketball team wins the first-ever National Invitational Basketball Tournament.

1941

Robert Livingston Johnson becomes Temple's third president.

Temple University Student Handbook, 1932—1933.

FACT

Temple University opened four state-of-the-art facilities devoted to business, medicine, art, and music during 2009.

Temple extended financial aid ("Work Scholarships") and offered students a deferred tuition payment plan. A shortfall of 1,000 students, combined with Governor Gifford Pinchot's 10 percent reduction in the commonwealth appropriation, left Temple facing a substantial deficit. No one at the time suspected these conditions would prevail for more than a year or two, but economic recovery required more than a decade.

Surprisingly, Temple and most of America's universities proved remarkably resilient, emerging from the Depression, if not stronger, at least more confident. Generally speaking, the 1930s was a period of growth for higher education in America. Colleges had gained a secure place as cultural institutions, and a college education was now regarded as essential to a young person's prospects for upward mobility in American society. Many institutions, consciously or not, followed the "Temple Idea" of making higher education more accessible, less of an elite experience. In the years between the two world wars college enrollments nationwide increased fivefold. Fewer than 5 percent of the eighteen- to twenty-year-olds had attended college in 1917, but by 1937—despite the Depression— the number had increased to 15 percent.

The federal government's New Deal economic recovery programs did not directly support universities' operating budgets, but they assisted students through the Employment Relief Act and with part-time work through the National Youth Administration (NYA). No federal program of need-based student financial aid existed, and so Temple and other universities instituted programs of their own. Temple, as we shall see, received timely assistance for its building program through the Public Works Administration.

Commonwealth support, despite the initial cutback from Governor Pinchot, actually increased during the Depression, as President Beury proved an able advocate before the governor and legislature. An important ally was Thomas S. Gates, president of the University of Pennsylvania. Beury and Gates developed a cordial relationship, accepting the differing missions of their universities and agreeing to work together on issues of mutual interest. Gates, who was also a director of the Pennsylvania Railroad, enjoyed the privileges of a private railway car and frequently invited Beury to join him for the ride to Harrisburg. They often met jointly with the governor and legislators.

Beury's argument in support of Temple's appropriation request was basically the same every year: Temple, compared with other universities receiving state appropriations, was treated inequitably, given the number of its full-time enrollments in degree programs. Temple's 1937 request listed universities (their enrollments) and appropriations: Penn State (5,623 students), $3,708,000; University of Pennsylvania (6,378), $1,485,000; University of Pittsburgh (6,323), $1,118,000; and Temple University (6,375), $750,000. Partly persuaded, Governor George H. Earle signed a bill holding biennial appropriations steady for the other universities but increasing Temple's to $900,000, exclusive of hospital subsidies.

Temple also had good fortune from time to time. In 1938 the Philadelphia School Board, forced to make drastic cutbacks, eliminated the Philadelphia Normal School, which trained students to fill teaching vacancies caused each year by age, death, matrimony, and other factors. The School Board asked Penn and Temple to absorb the enrollments into their Teachers Colleges and the Board would pay each student's tuition. Penn declined the invitation but Temple accepted. The tuition revenue from the School Board helped Temple make it through a very difficult time. The resulting program promoted a close relationship between the university and the public schools that has grown stronger over the years.

Temple, like all institutions of higher education, increased tuition during the 1930s. A relative bargain at $275 a year for tuition and fees and between $130 and $200 for room and board (available only to women), Temple's rates were well below the Ivy League rates but still a substantial sum for working-class families. While prestigious institutions became more and more out of reach for all but a small percentage of American families, Temple attempted to hold the line on affordability, raising tuition and fees only slightly (to $290) by the end of the war. To save money, Temple reduced program duplications and instituted a corporate operating style. As for the students, many resorted to cooperative living arrangements, rented rooms in cheap boardinghouses, or lived at home. Many skipped meals and endured significant hardships to pursue their dreams of a college degree. Part of America's "Greatest Generation," they embraced the spirit of Temple's motto and persevered.

"Beury the Builder"

Charles E. Beury, elected Temple's second president in January 1926, was well prepared for the office. Having served on Temple's board of trustees for fifteen years, he was already intimately involved with the university's financial management and physical planning. His contacts in the legal and banking communities afforded him access to Philadelphia's influential circles and involvement in major philanthropic causes. The son of a well-to-do coal operator, Beury grew up in Shamokin, Pennsylvania, and graduated from Princeton University and Harvard Law School. A worldly man, Beury traveled widely, belonged to the proper clubs, and played a major role in Philadelphia's civic community. Tall, erect, and of gentlemanly bearing, Beury had handsome features that radiated authority and confidence.

Charles E. Beury, second president of Temple University, served from 1926 to 1941.

Known as Beury the builder, Temple's second president brought substantial change. Most noticeable were the array of new buildings and the physical expansion of Temple. Dramatic changes also occurred within the university as Beury imposed a business approach on its organization and management, bringing greater efficiencies and cost savings, largely through greater centralization of administrative procedures.

The 1920s was an era during which many American institutions of higher education launched major building programs. Universities surrendered to urges to build large football stadiums and to create monumental campuses. Campus planning was like planning a small city; it required a broad range of technical skills, plus the acumen of a real estate developer and a politician's ingenuity. Charles Beury brought those skills to the presidency, along with a distinct vision of Temple's future and a profound commitment to elevate Temple's reputation among American universities. During Beury's fifteen years as president, Temple added a floor to Conwell Hall, constructed four new buildings (Carnell, Mitten, Sullivan, and a medical school), renovated the Eighteenth and Buttonwood campus, and acquired two substantial suburban properties. He also built a football team and a football stadium (discussed in Chapter 6).

Mitten Hall

In the 1930s, while real estate prices were depressed, Temple purchased the four-story row houses along the east side of Broad Street from Montgomery to Berks, using them for classrooms and offices. Row houses along Park Avenue were purchased and converted to dormitories and classrooms. As enrollments in day classes increased, more and more students found moments to spare on campus. A few fraternities and sororities sprang up and student organizations soon proliferated. Left to their own devices, students sometimes behaved as adolescents are wont, raising concerns among administrators. In this era the college served as in loco parentis and Temple felt obliged both to protect students and to engage them constructively in extra-curricular activities. To organize and control student life, Temple appointed Gertrude D. Peabody as dean of women and J. Conrad Seegers as dean of men. Needed even more was a student activities center.

Temple's sidewalk campus afforded few amenities or places for students to gather either casually or formally. The overtaxed facilities in College Hall and the awkward commingling of offices, classrooms, and gymnasia in Conwell and Carnell halls offered students no space of their own. President Beury proposed building a "social laboratory" for students, a place dedicated to their social activities and interests. Construction cost $633,000, of which $250,000 came from contributions made by employees of the Philadelphia Rapid Transit Company (RTC) and Yellow Cab Companies at the urging of RTC president Thomas E. Mitten, whose efforts on behalf of his employees earned their respect. Mitten died before the building opened. It was named and dedicated in his honor in February 1931.

One of the finer student unions of its time, Mitten Hall compared favorably with others, including Houston Hall at Penn, which was the country's first. Mitten Hall's Great Court, balconied auditorium, dining facilities, lounges, alcoves, recreation spaces, and meeting rooms have served Temple students well through the years—and it continues to serve the university even today. With students eager to use the building, two dances and a basketball game (against Purdue) were held before the official dedication. Mitten's neo-Gothic exterior and handsome ornate interior, with decorative leaded glass windows, ornamental sconces, polished flagstone floors, and imposing rooms trimmed in heavy oak, all bespoke sturdy permanence. Temple was looking and behaving like an idealized version of a college. And, except for the lack of a green quadrangle and open campus design, it was beginning to look like one. No longer just a sad cluster of row houses, Temple had the feel of a "college."

Sullivan Hall

Temple desperately needed a stand-alone library, having long since outgrown makeshift space in College Hall. That need was answered with the Sullivan Memorial Library. Begun with a gift of $275,000 in bonds from Thomas A. Sullivan, a warehouse owner and Conwell admirer, the building went up at the corner of Berks Street and Park Avenue directly behind The Temple. Construction was completed only with the assistance of a twenty-year loan of $550,000 guaranteed by the Emergency Public Works Administration (PWA), one of President Roosevelt's New Deal economic recovery programs. Officially designated PWA Project No. 1,326, the project provided steady work for 180 men for nine months. Sullivan's brother, the nationally known journalist Mark Sullivan, gave the dedicatory address on Founder's Day on February 22, 1936.

The main attraction, however, was the president of the United States, Franklin D. Roosevelt. FDR accepted the invitation at the behest of Trustee Albert M. Greenfield, the real estate mogul and Democratic Party power, and J. David Stern, publisher of the *Philadelphia Record*. The first visit of a U.S. president to Temple received the full attention of the national media. Although many hailed FDR's presence as a grand coup for Temple and a fitting capstone to Beury's first decade in office, others viewed it differently.

Founder's Day, February 22, 1936, in Mitten Hall. President Franklin Delano Roosevelt praised Russell Conwell and his successor, Charles E. Beury. Dr. Beury was in his tenth year as Temple's president. Roosevelt was visiting to help dedicate Sullivan Hall, Temple's first freestanding library.

Sullivan Memorial Library

Sullivan Memorial Library (PWA Project 1326) opened in 1936 as Temple's first freestanding Library. It was built with a bequest from Thomas D. Sullivan, a local warehouse owner, and with federal funds from the New Deal Emergency Relief Act. During the Christmas holidays in 1935, books and equipment were moved from College Hall to the new facility at Park Avenue and Berks Street. President Franklin Delano Roosevelt attended the dedication ceremonies in February 1936. They were held in Mitten Hall to permit a larger audience and easier access for the president. In 1965 the university library moved one block east to its new and current home at Paley Library. Sullivan Hall now houses the executive offices of the president, provost, and senior officers of the university, plus Alumni Affairs and the Charles Blockson Collection of African American history and literature.

The Reference Reading Room in Sullivan Memorial Library.

For weeks before and after FDR's visit Beury received angry letters chastising him for honoring "that man." Many of the upper crust regarded FDR as a "traitor to his class" and considered work-relief programs like the PWA to be "communistic" or worse. Obviously distraught, Beury showed a few of the letters to Charles A. Wright, a Temple journalism professor. "Some of these people," Beury told Wright, "have been good friends of mine and have contributed liberally to Temple. Now they say they won't give another dime." With heavy Secret Service protection and extraordinary support from the Philadelphia police, the president's visit came off splendidly. FDR received an honorary doctor of jurisprudence and delivered an inspirational speech praising Conwell and Beury before an overflow crowd in Mitten Hall. No noticeable drop-off in contributions occurred after Roosevelt's visit.

Much was built during Beury's years. Even more intriguing is what was not built. Beury imagined raising enough money from alumni and civic leaders to build a landmark skyscraper, a "Temple of Learning" approaching the scale of the University of Pittsburgh's "Cathedral of Learning." Pitt Chancellor John Bowman began construction of a forty-two-story multi-purpose building in 1926. When it was dedicated in 1937, one historian described it as the "prime example of 'girder Gothic' and civic pride." Beury's proposed Temple of Learning would have connected Conwell Hall to College Hall with buildings ultimately reaching over twenty stories.

Beury anticipated naming the central building of this complex The Curtis Tower of Learning to honor Cyrus H. K. Curtis. The founder of the publishing empire that included the *Philadelphia Public Ledger*, the *Saturday Evening Post*, and the *Ladies' Home Journal*, among others, Curtis donated $100,000 to Temple in 1926 just after Beury took office. Curtis then became a member of the board of trustees and made several additional donations, bringing the total to $625,000 by 1930, making him the largest Temple benefactor up to that time. Curtis died in 1933 and the Tower of Learning idea was scrubbed soon after. Later, the university attached the Curtis name to a general classroom building on Montgomery Avenue dedicated in 1956.

The Temple of Learning, planned in 1927 as a fitting memorial to Russell Conwell, was to consist of five units fronting 400 feet of Broad Street and extending back 150 feet to Watts Street, with capacity to accommodate 20,000 students. The mid-point building, a 350-foot tower, according to the Philadelphia Record, *was to be equal to a thirty-four-story office building.*

Temple High School

The Depression did not deter Temple from engaging in a number of innovative learning and teaching initiatives, as well as reconsidering existing programs such as the Temple High School. Many of Temple's offerings in the early years were high school–level college preparatory courses, for at that time a secondary school education was all that was needed for entrance into professional schools. At one point Conwell combined the high school–level courses into Temple Academies (no more, really, than high school evening programs) that he envisioned establishing across the city. That experiment, as described in Chapter 1, failed and the Temple Academies closed in 1896, replaced by Temple High School, which became a unit within Temple College. Early enrollment reports for Temple College often confusingly mingled high school and college registration numbers. Designed for educating adults (over the age of seventeen) deprived of schooling in their youth, the Temple High School prepared students for further academic work, on either the collegiate or technical school level. Until 1912, classes were held in many locations before being consolidated in a building at 1417 Diamond Street.

In 1930 Temple briefly considered converting the high school into a laboratory-demonstration school for the Teachers College. With this in mind, Millard E. Gladfelter was brought in as director, but then another option was found, Gladfelter was appointed registrar of the university, and the high school continued its original mission under the direction first of Charles E. Metzger and then of Hugh E. Harting. In 1945 it moved to Broad and York streets on the former site of Gratz College, where it helped accommodate college-bound veterans in a special accelerated program. Enrollments averaged around 860 students at the Gratz site. In 1960 the high school relocated to Stauffer Hall, then standing on the southeast corner of Broad Street and Columbia Avenue (now Cecil B. Moore Avenue). Conwell's aspirations to have Temple serve all educational levels ended on June 18, 1968, when Temple High School held its closing commencement exercises in the Baptist Temple. The program lost its connection to Temple, moved to the Central Branch of the YMCA, and assumed a new name, Penn Center Academy.

Oak Lane Country Day School

Flourishing enrollments in the Teachers College during the late 1920s led the university to consider establishing a laboratory-demonstration school as a facility for enhancing teacher training and for researching and experimenting with new learning methods. A seemingly perfect opportunity presented itself when the Oak Lane Country Day School suggested a merger. Incorporated in 1916 by a group of parents who followed John Dewey's progressive educational philosophy, the Oak Lane Country Day School sat in a thirty-acre compound on Oak Lane in Cheltenham Township. One of its several buildings was a nursery school, a gift from Leopold Stokowski.

When the economic downturn left parents unable to sustain the school, they turned to Temple. Trustees approved the acquisition in April 1931. Controversy revolved around the school for the next thirty years. Former supporters and patrons of the school reduced or ceased donations when Temple took over. Enrollments dropped sharply. Plagued by management issues and recurring deficits, the trustees tried twice to close the school. Only last-minute reprieves from the governor kept it open in 1937 and again in 1939. The trustees recommended elimination of the Upper School (or high school) and continuation of Oak Lane as the lab school of Teachers College for children aged four to thirteen. Under those conditions it survived another twenty years, gaining attention for the quality of the school programs and for its value as a teacher-training facility. When the deficit reached $128,000 in 1960, the board of trustees finally closed the school.

Tyler School of Art

Temple profited unexpectedly from the educational experiment at the Oak Lane Country Day School. Boris Blai, who joined the Oak Lane faculty in 1927 and remained on after it was acquired by Temple, was the inspiration for one of the most significant, transforming gifts in Temple's history. Stella Elkins Tyler, a neighbor of Blai's, had shown considerable talent as a sculptor and she asked Blai to become her tutor. Under his guidance Tyler's creative skills fully developed and her works were exhibited widely. Grateful for Blai's assistance, she made a gift of her nine-acre Elkins Park estate to Temple University "for the advancement of art education." Included was the Georgian mansion valued at $1 million that had been a wedding gift to her from her father, William L. Elkins, when she wed George F. Tyler.

In April 1935 the board of trustees established the Stella Elkins Tyler School of Fine Arts and installed Boris Blai as director. The school opened in September 1935 with twelve Temple students working in the art facility at the Oak Lane Country Day School. Blai meanwhile moved a trailer onto the Tyler estate, where he lived while directing renovations to the mansion to create classrooms, offices,

FACT

The Tyler School of Art at Temple University is ranked No. 14 in the United States, with its painting and drawing program at No. 7 and its sculpture program at No. 8, according to *U.S.News & World Report.*

and studios. For ten years the art school's degrees (BS, BFA) were offered through the Teachers College. Mrs. Tyler served on the Temple University Board of Trustees from 1940 to 1960, and at her urging, in 1945 the Tyler School of Fine Arts was established as an independent school and Blai was named the first dean. President's Hall, a multi-purpose building, was constructed in 1951, allowing Tyler room to grow.

Few Temple faculty members were ever as accomplished or flamboyant as Boris Blai. Born in Russia, he studied in Kiev and St. Petersburg and at the Ecole de Beaux Arts in Paris and apprenticed with Auguste Rodin. He came to the United States in 1917, the year of the Russian Revolution. Volatile, opinionated, and temperamental, he did not believe art history should be studied in an art school, because dependence on great examples hobbled the artist's creative spirit. His international reputation as a sculptor and his vast circle of acquaintances in the art world allowed him to build the Tyler faculty by drawing upon a selective group of daring and inventive artists.

Blai believed the role of the artist was to interpret the civilization of his time; that meant blending study of the fine arts with the liberal arts. His lifelong dream, Blai often said, was to create "a new kind of art school, where the student finds himself in an environment of many artistic media, learning the techniques of all before specializing in one or two"—a philosophy that persists in the Tyler School of Art curriculum to this day. Blai wanted the artist first to attain maturity as a personality and then to gain mastery of many expressive media. Requiring students to prepare their own canvases, grind their own paints, and cast their own sculpture, Blai sought the complete integration of an artist's inner conceptual power with the physical and technical processes necessary to express it. In twenty-five years as dean, Blai placed an indelible imprint on the school, shaping Tyler into one of the finest visual arts centers in the country.

Charles Le Clair succeeded Blai as dean in 1960. Le Clair increased enrollments, added more faculty members, gained approvals for a master of fine arts degree, and expanded Tyler's curriculum, adding more offerings in graphic design to meet the growing demand for those skills in the workplace. In 1966 Le Clair gained trustees' approval to change the school's name to the Tyler School of Art. The Tyler Campus was improved with construction of a residence hall and two studio/classroom buildings. Believing a European experience was "a must" for artists, Le Clair became the driving force behind the creation in 1966 of the Tyler Study Abroad program in Rome—Temple's first overseas program.

Through the years and under the gifted leadership of several deans, Tyler nimbly responded to new definitions of art-making and the role of art in society. New programs in and modern facilities for design, ceramics, glass, metals, and photography were added. Today the Tyler curriculum continues to address contemporary needs by incorporating digital technology, video, installation, and performance media. Tyler developed the Art and Art Education Department and the Art History Department to serve majors seeking the bachelor of arts degree in art or art history, the bachelor of science degree in art education, as well as electives to meet non-majors' interests.

As the years passed and the wear and tear on the Tyler facilities mounted, it became necessary to decide whether to expend large sums to restore and enhance the Tyler Campus in Elkins Park or to relocate the school to the Main Campus. After years of deliberations beginning in the 1980s, the entire Tyler School of Art was relocated in January 2009 to a sparkling new 236,000-square-foot facility adjoining the Boyer College of Music and Dance on Temple's Main Campus. (See Chapter 9 for details and pictures.)

Academic Innovations

Boris Blai was not the only academic innovator at Temple in the 1930s. One man who seemed in the middle of almost everything was Joseph S. Butterweck. He arrived at Temple in 1926 as an assistant professor of education, having earned a PhD from Columbia University's Teachers College and been nurtured on John Dewey's fashionable progressive approaches to education. For the learning process to be effective, said Butterweck, it must directly involve the students, and part of the education of students had to be devoted to firsthand experience with whatever interested them. Butterweck believed Temple could do more to challenge its students, particularly the increasing number of academically gifted students who were selecting Temple in the 1930s.

A shortfall in enrollments in 1931 was followed by an upsurge that brought more and better-qualified students. As middle- and working-class households were hit by the economic downturn, many more of their children were drawn to Temple because of its affordability. Growth in applications was so great that Temple's board of trustees decided in 1932 to begin requiring scholastic aptitude tests, noting that "the number of students is so greatly in excess of the ability of Temple to take care of them adequately that there must be a more rigid limitation in numbers and quality." Demand intensified for Temple's scholarships, many of which were available only through competitive examinations.

To attract the best students, Butterweck began an experimental program he called the X-Group. Almost every aspect of the program was an unknown quality, hence the name. For his first group Butterweck carefully selected a keenly motivated group of forty high school students with exceptionally strong academic records who had also survived a battery of qualifying exams. Once admitted, X-Group students were given a wide range of freedom to learn. Class attendance, assignments, and exams were optional. Butterweck expected faculty to allow his X-Group students to have a part in classroom presentations, ask questions of the instructor, and even set up problems for study. Dr. Eugene Udell, the first dean of Temple's Ambler Campus, was a member of the X-Group, as was Dr. Eunice Clarke, retired associate vice president for research. Clarke, who had earned a PhD at the University of Pennsylvania, years later fondly recalled the X-Group experience and praised Butterweck's learning experiment.

Founder's Day 1932 coincided with mid-year commencement, at which Helen Keller received an honorary doctor of humane letters. Processing up Broad Street to The Temple, where graduation services were held, Miss Keller is accompanied by her secretary, Miss Polly Thompson, and her friend and tutor, Mrs. Anne Sullivan Macy.

Butterweck's program released students from conventional discipline and encouraged unconventional attitudes, causing serious debate among the faculty. Faculty reliant on the lecture method and passive, note-taking students were especially distressed. The exemptions, selective instruction, special tuition, and distinct privileges granted to X-Group students all carried costs. When some X-Group students became involved in "radical" (i.e., anti-war) activities and when it was learned that teachers in the program received extra compensation, several faculty members protested to the president. Butterweck had hoped to use the program to break away from the traditional way of looking at college education. But Temple was not yet ready and the program was abandoned. In some respects the X-Group was a precursor to the highly successful University Honors Program put in place in 1988, when the faculty was decidedly more receptive to change.

Beury's Corporate Model

Change of another kind occurred at Temple in the 1930s. Threatened by fiscal insolvency at the onset of the Depression, Charles Beury sought to modernize and streamline Temple's organization and management by applying business principles and by modeling the administration after a corporation. To increase revenues, reduce costs, and create savings through greater efficiency, Beury both sought advice from within the faculty and brought in a new group of administrators to manage the university. He simultaneously encouraged innovation and experimentation. This "corporate model" and its many innovations sometimes produced unintended consequences, including faculty alienation.

On a 1927 brochure cover Temple identified itself with the "imperial theme." For the fiftieth anniversary celebration the 1934 Alumni Review cover used the same image.

Beury appeared in step with national trends. Studies by the Rockefeller and Carnegie foundations urged universities to eliminate program duplications, institute internal financial controls to make professors' work both countable and accountable, and change the composition of their boards to recruit leadership from the business, legal, and financial worlds. Knowingly or not, Temple followed these guidelines during the Beury years and beyond. The Temple Board of Trustees that initially comprised Conwell's congregants and friends from the ranks of the clergy was gradually altered during these years with the addition of men like Edward G. Budd (president of the Budd Company), John A. Stevenson (president of Penn Mutual Life Insurance), Albert M. Greenfield (real estate), James Nolen (construction and architecture), Judge Charles Klein, Charles Erny (construction), and many others from the legal, banking, and business communities.

Almost all of the university business went through Beury, sometimes creating awkward logjams. In time, he came to depend on Millard Gladfelter to break up those jams. Gladfelter was originally hired in 1930 to direct the high school, but circumstances led him to accept the position of registrar instead. Responsible for student applications, admissions, registration, catalog preparation, course numbering, room assignments, and other functions, Gladfelter restored order and cohesion to many routine administrative processes that had fallen into an untidy state of affairs after Laura Carnell's death. Before coming to Temple, Gladfelter was supervising principal of the public schools in West York, Pennsylvania. A modest, direct man without pretension, he quickly gained the respect of faculty, staff, and trustees. Gladfelter's trusted assistant was a University of Pittsburgh graduate named John M. Rhoads. Together they moved up the ladder until Gladfelter was president and Rhoads vice president.

Part of emulating the corporate model included the management of public perceptions. Beury deliberately built a football team to draw attention to Temple. And ever conscious of Temple's public image, he hired John St. George Joyce, a crusty veteran newspaperman, to oversee the university's public relations, with the goal of obtaining favorable press coverage.

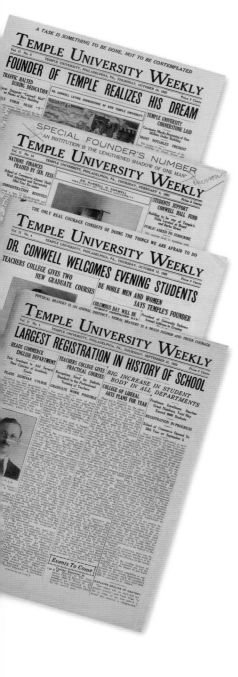

Beury never tried to find a replacement for Laura Carnell to serve as "dean of deans" or a provost with the authority to oversee academic affairs. Change in academic affairs came slowly, in part because of President Beury's reluctance to delegate authority and in part because of the entrenched power of the undergraduate colleges and their intense competitiveness.

At the beginning of Beury's presidency, each college handled its own admissions, course offerings, and faculty hiring. Liberal Arts set the most rigorous admission standards. Dean James Dunham personally interviewed each prospective student, often telling unacceptable applicants, "Why don't you try the School of Commerce? It's right down the street." Dunham's notion of a liberal arts curriculum varied little from the one he had completed when a student at Princeton and in place at Temple since the late 1890s. He resisted incorporating the "new" social sciences into the liberal arts. He refused, for example, to accept sociology as a legitimate discipline, and it did not move from the Teachers College into Liberal Arts until after he retired. Similarly, political science and economics remained in the School of Commerce until years later.

To sort out differences between the schools and colleges, Beury relied tentatively on faculty committees and from time to time assigned bright, energetic faculty to perform selected tasks. Beury, for example, detested the duplication of courses and programs resulting from the intense competition between Liberal Arts, Commerce, and Teachers College. Faculty in the School of Commerce and Teachers College believed the introductory liberal arts courses were too difficult, and the liberal arts professors were biased against students with vocational interests. And so commerce and education created their own basic science courses and separate departments of English, history, mathematics, and modern language. These courses were absent the "unnecessary profundity and detail" of the introductory courses in the College of Liberal Arts and Sciences. Beury ended this duplication of instruction with a simple directive: departments in the School of Commerce and Teachers College offering instruction in subject matter taught in Liberal Arts were closed and such instruction referred to the College of Liberal Arts and Sciences.

In search of further cost savings, Beury appointed Charles A. Ford (chairman of Psychology) as his administrative assistant, with instructions to comb through the university organization looking for departments, procedures, and positions that could be transferred, reorganized, or abolished to reduce costs and increase efficiency. Ford's 1936 report set standards for class size and teaching loads. The standard teaching roster was defined as fifteen academic hours a week, with eighteen being the maximum load and requiring added compensation. Courses had to be self-supporting or absolutely essential. Ford cut duplicate and excess courses and created some savings, but many of his recommendations went unheeded.

Professors nationwide often said the advocates of the corporate model were either ignorant or contemptuous of "faculty values." They countered corporate, top-down governance with proposals of their own through the American Association of University Professors (AAUP). Mostly about efficiency and control, the corporate model lacked a clear vision for the role of the American professor, whose expertise university presidents both envied and distrusted. Perhaps for the best, the corporate model was slow to take hold in the 1930s because it lacked respect as a result of the economic collapse.

Faculty

Temple prided itself on its excellent undergraduate teaching and the quality of its graduates. After a 1936 examination was given in Philadelphia to screen applicants to teach history in the senior high schools, results revealed that only 40 out of 280 passed the test. Yet not only did every Temple candidate pass the test, but four were among the top ten on the list. The Chemistry Department disclosed that seventy-five of its graduates since 1927 had gone on to earn PhD degrees. Temple's Medical School accepted an unusually high proportion of applicants from Temple's Liberal Arts College, knowing that the rigorous education they received prepared them well for medical school. Given the heavy instructional loads, a surprising number of Temple's faculty engaged in research and published. One survey indicated that between 1929 and 1935 Temple's undergraduate faculty produced thirty-seven books and contributed articles to forty-eight different scholarly journals. At Temple and most universities in the 1930s and 1940s, publication was not a job requirement, as it is today. Faculty published mostly for the satisfaction of advancing knowledge in their respective fields and for peer approval. Publication, however, was virtually the only vehicle for moving up the ladder or gaining employment at a more prestigious institution.

Faculty members were afforded few amenities and accorded little support during the Depression years. The parsimonious attitude of the administration shocked newer, younger faculty who were recruited from older, well-established universities and expected private offices, telephone service, and secretarial support. Telephones were available only to department heads and full professors. Offices were open six days a week, but only department heads received secretarial service, and even then only once a week for half a day during the standard six-day workweek.

Despite trying conditions, a notable sense of loyalty to Temple and its values was evident within the faculty during the Depression. Many faculty members remained at Temple through their entire careers, kept there for reasons other than money. Professors' salaries were low; many found they could not afford to marry and raise families, turning instead to a life of teaching and study. There was no job security or tenure beyond the annual letter of appointment, and no retirement or pension fund. Yet members of the faculty looking back on those years recalled an easy informality and a mutual trust existing between them and the administration.

Temple was one of only a few universities or colleges that avoided cutting salaries or furloughing full-time faculty during the Depression. Through the dark years the annual contract letters sent to faculty included a clause authorizing the trustees to reduce salaries by 15 percent if conditions warranted. That clause was never invoked. In fact, the university usually managed to include a small salary increment, usually no more than $100 or $200. Temple also established a group life insurance plan in 1930, paying half the premiums for faculty and staff.

There were still problems, however. Faculty complained of Beury's remoteness and seeming aloofness. In fact, he rarely met with faculty members or took part in academic programs, mostly because he was so busy raising money for the university. Whatever the reasons, faculty found him inaccessible and their deans often unapproachable. No person or group had the right or authority to demand that Beury and the deans hear their concerns. The local chapter of the AAUP attempted to be both emissary and spokesperson, but to no effect. What was needed, faculty members realized, was a forum where they could discuss issues and where the president would come and listen.

The Temple University Faculty Senate was established in May 1937 by a vote of the faculties of the College of Liberal Arts, Teachers College, and School of Commerce. President Beury approved the concept of a Senate forum with the understanding that it be advisory only, with the president presiding. After much discussion, a proportional representation plan was agreed to among the three large undergraduate schools. In relatively short time the Senate won acceptance by the president

Temple University NEWS

The *Temple University News* had much of interest to report during the 1930s, including guest speakers such as the Rev. Fulton J. Sheen (1931), aviatrix Amelia Earhart (1935), First Lady Eleanor Roosevelt (1936), and poet Carl Sandburg (1936), to name a few. Beginning in 1938 each freshman co-ed at Temple was taken under the wing of a senior woman who adopted her as a "baby sister" and helped her through the tribulations of the first year. In 1939 four fraternity brothers organized themselves into a guard to protect the library's goldfish from gulpers. Edna Shanis (Tuttleman) in 1942 became the first female to be elected a class president at Temple. And then there was Raye Timmins. She had the campus buzzing in 1940 when she became the first female in Temple history to wear slacks to class.

and trustees. In 1938 the president agreed to share some of the issues within the budget, and in 1941 the board of trustees recognized the Senate as the "official body representing the faculty."

The Senate became the sounding board for critical issues, including debate on faculty benefits, which were few. Except for the group life insurance plan adopted in 1930, faculty members had no other benefits. Working through the Faculty Senate, the trustees approved a formal sick-leave policy in 1939. Years of prolonged debate within the administration over a retirement and pension plan came to a head in 1937 when three distinguished members of the faculty—Napoleon Heller (mathematics), Thaddeus L. Bolton (psychology), and Robert Burns Wallace (English)—were given notices of mandatory retirement by Beury. The president arranged for each to receive a "gift" of $100 a month for ten months of the year. Bolton was fairly well-off and he bequeathed funds to endow the Thaddeus Bolton Chair in Psychology. But Wallace (an especially pathetic case) and Heller were impoverished in retirement, and their pleas to Beury for part-time work or a larger pension went unheeded. Still, Beury's "gifts" had set a precedent; they were extended to twelve months and offered thereafter to retirees until, finally, in 1946 a formal pension and retirement system went into effect.

Toward the end of the 1930s, as several authoritarian regimes abroad were strangling free speech and making dissent a capital crime, concerns arose in America over the extent to which students and faculty were free to explore ideas without restrictions or fear of retribution. For leadership on matters of academic freedom, the faculty turned to the AAUP; its *1940 Statement of Principles on Academic Freedom and Tenure* was accepted by Temple and incorporated into the *Faculty Handbook*. Briefly and broadly summarized, the AAUP statement said professors were entitled to full freedom in research and publication of their work, subject to adequate performance of their other academic duties, and entitled to freedom in classroom utterances, provided they were careful not to introduce unrelated controversial matter; finally, professors had special obligations to the community, but they were also citizens and when they spoke or wrote as citizens they should be free from institutional censorship or discipline. Thus, gradually and almost imperceptibly the Temple faculty gained in status and respectability.

Campus Life

Temple was often described as a "commuter college." But how and from where did students commute? Philadelphia's trolley car system was not established until six years after Temple's 1884 founding, and so the first students lived or worked nearby and walked or rode bicycles to Temple. In the 1890s, when students were unable to come to Temple, Temple went to them, opening branches around the city. When the Philadelphia subway system opened in 1928, it became the principal form of transportation to and from the Main Campus through the Columbia (now Cecil B. Moore/Temple University) Station. To reach the Eighteenth and Buttonwood campus, health sciences students rode the subway to Spring Garden Station.

Temple students and others boarding the double-decker C bus in front of Conwell Hall.

A few students and faculty traveled on the railroad into North Philadelphia Station and walked down Broad Street to Temple. Additionally, the C bus conveniently stopped directly in front of Conwell Hall. Hitchhiking must also have been a common means of commuting, because in 1931 Temple's Student Council granted a charter to a local chapter of the "Registered Collegiate Thumbers," an organization designed to protect the interests of students who "thumb" their way in automobiles. Wide streets around Temple provided ample parking for those few who drove their own automobiles, but their numbers dwindled even further as a result of gasoline rationing in World War II.

Once on campus, what did students do during their spare time? By the mid-1930s a growing number of students lived on or near campus. Temple purchased and renovated several row houses along Park Avenue (now Liacouras Walk) for use as dormitories (initially available only to women) to accommodate upwards of 400 students. The university also maintained a list of approved off-campus boardinghouses. Wiatt Hall, located at 1830 North Park Avenue and named for Hattie May Wiatt, and Williams Hall, a series of connected row houses along the 1800 block of Park Avenue, served as women's dormitories for several decades. Life in the women's dorms was rather austere, as the 1937 rules attest: "Shades must be drawn when the lights are on; typewriters and radios may not be used after 11 P.M. or before 7 A.M., lest others be disturbed; pressing may be done for 10 cents an hour in an ironing room."

Popular images of American campus life in the 1930s were hardly positive. Some colleges other than Temple became notorious for the hedonistic behavior of students and alumni. In the mind's eye of the average person, virtually every college function—homecoming, reunions, proms, fraternity gatherings—was coupled with alcohol, gambling, or loose sexual standards. Indeed, Temple's student life administrators, Dean Seegers and Dean Peabody, were greatly challenged during Prohibition. When students insisted on smuggling liquor into dances, plainclothes detectives were hired to confiscate and empty flasks. Young people had to prove their status by misbehaving in ritualized ways, such as concocting bathtub gin, gulping goldfish, enduring fraternity hazing, or snake-dancing down Broad Street after a football victory.

"Flaming youth" included the archetypal "college woman" who exhibited the misbehavior associated with the flapper, or the "new woman" of the 1920s. Perhaps it was no surprise, then, that Dean Peabody reported in 1930 being shocked by the "wholesale and unabashed love-making" on the

FACT

Temple University surgeon W. Emory Burnett performed the first human lung removal in Philadelphia in 1938.

A well-dressed audience looks on as the annual freshman tug-of-war gets a cooling down, 1941.

Of unknown origins, the annual flour fight required freshmen to ingeniously conceal packets of flour in their clothing or on their persons and for the sophomores to search the freshmen, open all of the packets, and empty them on the freshmen. If any packets went undiscovered, the freshmen won. The result was a flour blizzard.

front steps of the dormitories each night as she enforced a curfew and shooed the young women inside. In 1931 Temple freshman Hilda Leaf scored highest in the nation on a psychological test; she smoked cigarettes, adored jazz, and said she did not consider modern youth "flaming."

Disappointed over the conduct of Temple students, President Beury directed the establishment of courses on student deportment, declaring, "One of the greatest shortcomings of student bodies is lack of politeness. Some are careless, some thoughtlessly selfish, and many are ignorant of what constitutes good form." What he and Deans Seegers and Peabody encountered was a virtual revolution in manners and morals that spread across all of American society in the 1920s and did not spare college life. Youth of that era delighted in rejecting what they considered antiquated and restrictive formalities and in accepting the less disciplined, more energetic forms of expression, whether in language, music, art, literature, or simple common courtesies.

No one knows for sure what Beury thought of the annual "flour fight" between sophomores and freshmen or the tug-of-war in the middle of Broad and Berks streets. Nor is there record of official reaction to the giant "toga party" at which 300 women students celebrated Greek culture by wearing short togas and performing pyrrhic dances. But Beury spared little in terms of funding student organizations and providing special services, such as freshman orientation, intramural sports, and vocational guidance. More than 100 student organizations were created, including a student council, glee club, choir, and debate club, as well as various student publications. To meet the proliferating needs of sororities and fraternities, a Pan-Hellenic House was established in a row house at the southeast corner of Broad and Norris streets. Traditional hazing, however, was banned by Temple's Student Council as "undignified and archaic."

Academic life for most students in the 1930s was at odds with the self-indulgent image purveyed in the media. Indeed, many students were deeply concerned about international affairs. Beginning at Oxford University in England where students took the Oxford Oath, refusing "to fight for King or country," a movement swept America's campuses, including Temple's, opposing policies leading America toward war. Organizations such as the American Student Union, which had a charter on Temple's campus, urged students to take an American version of the Oxford Oath. Student organizations also mocked and parodied patriotic organizations, such as the Veterans of Foreign Wars, by creating the Veterans of Future Wars (started at Princeton), demanding pre-payment of the bonuses their families would receive upon their deaths in the next war. A Women's Auxiliary of the Veterans of Future Wars demanded early payment of the death benefits of future husbands so they could visit their husbands' future grave sites in France. A VFW protest march down Broad Street was led by a drum major twirling a crutch. "More Scholarships, Not Battleships" was painted on the stone walls bounding the cemetery opposite Mitten Hall.

Such conduct spawned a wave of negative publicity and cries that Temple was a "communist hotbed." Actually, a considerable element of conservative sentiment was also evident among the student body. A large "Peace Meeting" organized by the American Student Union on April 23, 1936, ended when detractors on Carnell Hall's upper floors hurled rotten tomatoes, sacks of flour, and containers of water down on the guest speaker and his listeners gathered beneath. A Faculty-Student Committee on Controversial Issues formed in 1937 in an effort to protect the civil liberties of student protesters while simultaneously limiting the damage to Temple's public image.

First class to wear the green academic hoods, representing the profession of chiropody, June 1934.

Partly responsible for shaping that image was the student newspaper, first printed in 1921 as the *Temple University Weekly*. In 1925 it was placed under the editorship of Charles A. Wright, a former reporter for the *Philadelphia Evening Bulletin* who gave students byline credit and greater leeway in the production of the paper. In 1927 its name was changed to the *Temple University News*, and it appeared twice, and later three times, a week. Independent-minded and somewhat free-spirited, the *News* was buffeted by criticisms of its editorial content and slant of the news reporting, which seemed to echo the American Student Union line. In 1937, editorial direction was placed under the Journalism Department in the School of Commerce. The department faculty took control of editorial policy, appointed the student editor, and restricted staff membership to journalism students. After World War II an influx of returning veterans took charge of the *Temple News*. Their experienced, mature perspectives allowed the Journalism Department to back away and to return management of the newspaper to students and oversight to the dean of students.

Beury's Demise

Financial problems beset the university once again in 1940, leading to a major public crisis of confidence in Temple's leadership. Over the years Temple had maintained solvency often by borrowing from the banks to cover operating expenses while awaiting the frequently delayed commonwealth appropriation and the payments of student tuition. Beginning in 1937 Temple's banking creditors asked hard questions about the university's finances and began setting stricter terms for granting loans. The Philadelphia banks demanded unanimous approval of the board

before granting additional loans because they were concerned about rumors of dissension within the board of trustees.

In October 1940 those rumors became front-page headlines in Philadelphia's newspapers. Charges and countercharges flew, as speculation over the causes accelerated. Some said it involved a faction intent on ousting Beury and replacing him with Medical School Dean and Vice President William N. Parkinson, who was also a member of the board of trustees. An opposing board faction issued public statements openly criticizing Parkinson, claiming that the Medical School's success was "achieved at the cost of the imbalance of the university." Others more prudently attributed differences among trustees to disagreements over how to resolve the financial crisis. Still others said it was nothing more than the routine refreshment of board leadership. When the controversy ended in January 1941—after three tortuous, disputatious months—four trustees were gone, including Parkinson, who remained dean of medicine and director of the hospital.

Three days later, Beury resigned, effective August 31, 1941. The board elected him president emeritus and began the search for a successor. At the height of the crisis the *Temple University News* wisely editorialized, "The University is still here. It will be here next year, ten years from now, one hundred years hence. Founded by a great personality, it has grown beyond the stage where it can be affected by the conflict of personalities within its organization."

By the end of Beury's presidency, Temple's total head count exceeded 12,000, the size of the faculty had doubled, a solid coterie of professional administrators was in place, every academic program that required accreditation was accredited, and the commonwealth biennial appropriation had increased to $900,000. In addition, Beury could claim credit for the incredible building boom and physical expansion started when he was a trustee and carried through his presidency.

Robert L. Johnson was formally inducted as Temple's third president just three days before the Japanese bombing of Pearl Harbor. The announcement of his selection caught many by surprise. Johnson had no academic background. In fact, he did not have a college degree. Johnson had dropped out of Yale at the end of his junior year in 1917 to serve as an artillery officer in France during World War I. After the war he went into advertising and was best known as one of the three founders of *Time* magazine—Henry R. Luce (president), Britton Hadden (editor), and Robert Johnson (vice president and advertising director). The *Time* publishing empire soon included *Life* and *Fortune* magazines. A millionaire by the mid-1930s, Johnson sought to give back through various public-service activities, including directing Pennsylvania's Public Assistance Department by appointment of Governor Earle in 1935.

Johnson came to Temple's attention through his impressive circle of friends, who included Wendell Willkie, the 1940 Republican candidate for president of the United States. Willkie credited Johnson with successfully orchestrating his nomination at the Republican National Convention in Philadelphia. During a meeting with Judge Charles Klein, chairman of Temple's board of trustees, Willkie recommended Johnson as Beury's successor. Johnson's business acumen, vast range of contacts, and standing in financial circles persuaded the selection committee. On September 18, 1941, the board formally ratified its choice. Johnson, then only forty-seven years old, and his wife, Peggy, moved to Philadelphia the next day.

Faculty members were initially unimpressed by the choice. They wondered aloud about Johnson's motives. Knowing of his connections to the Republican Party hierarchy, they suspected that Temple was only a layover on the way to a political appointment or elected office. Because he was without a degree, they questioned his knowledge and commitment to higher education. Johnson disarmed faculty by excusing himself at times, saying "I'm still a freshman here. I know I have to move cautiously." Although a talented writer and speaker, he wisely sought faculty counsel, inviting (and compensating) at least two, and possibly more, members of the faculty to offer drafts of his inaugural speech, word of which soon circulated.

Only a few days into his presidency and before his induction, Johnson met with the Senate to discuss abolishing annual contracts and his willingness to establish a tenure process, as well as a retirement system. Pearl Harbor and the war put most of these plans on hold, but Johnson immediately created a small faculty research-incentive fund, taking money from his own salary and expense accounts. Johnson also tossed a party for the faculty and their spouses. The first ever hosted by a Temple president, it was a grand affair at the Barclay Hotel that included dinner, dancing, and an open bar. "You know," said Herbert Webster, professor of English, "He treated us [as] though we were business men."

The Philadelphia business community was greatly impressed by Temple's selection of Johnson as president. Well known in Republican circles, he possessed a long list of "very old and very dear friends," as he called them. Early in his administration he paid a visit to the president of the Pennsylvania Company, one of Philadelphia's largest banks; this led to a meeting with the vice president in charge of loans. In a single afternoon Johnson restored Temple University's credit rating in the Philadelphia banking community.

World War II

On December 8, 1941, more than 1,600 students jammed into Mitten Hall to hear FDR's radio broadcast asking Congress for a declaration of war. President Johnson urged students to remain in school and await the call, but many rushed out, as he had done in 1917, to join the service. Approximately 1,600 men from the 1941 freshman class enlisted immediately. The war instantly touched the campus when word came two days after the Pearl Harbor attack that Doris M. Yetter (Nursing 1930) had been captured by the Japanese on Guam. Large drums of sand were placed atop university

Band leader Artie Shaw performed at the 1939 Junior Prom in Mitten Hall.

As war broke out in Europe, Betty Talbott (SBM 1940) became Temple's first aviatrix.

buildings to fight anticipated incendiary bombs. Temple University Hospital blacked out its operating rooms and arranged for nearby churches to be used as hospital facilities if necessary.

In a span of one month, twenty-five doctors and forty nurses left Temple Hospital for war duty. A year after Pearl Harbor, 633 Temple University medical and dental students wore U.S. Army and Navy uniforms. To meet the increased demand for nurses, Temple participated in the federally funded U.S. Cadet Nurses Corps, graduating 225 nurses by war's end. Hard pressed to find the necessary classroom space for the nurses' training program, Temple renovated basements in one of the Park Avenue buildings and at the Allegheny House, a student residence at Fifteenth and Allegheny. As young men rushed to war and many women turned to working in war industries, Temple enrollments dropped precipitously and financial exigencies loomed, to be somewhat relieved by the vast amount of contract teaching done for war industries. Charles E. Metzger, who would serve Temple for nearly four decades in a number of administrative positions, directed Temple's War Training Office, which provided 100 short courses to train a total of 25,000 employees in 543 plants and offices. One project that gained a lot of publicity was sponsored by the Philco Radio and Television Corporation of America, training sixty young women to serve as laboratory technicians. Known as the Philco Radarettes, the young women were selected from among the very top high school students in the region, enrolled at Temple, with all university expenses paid by Philco, and trained for jobs in Philco's research and production laboratories.

Faculty members contributed in various ways to the war effort, with approximately two-thirds volunteering for additional wartime duties. Lloyd Bohn, a professor of physics, directed a civilian pilot training program under the sponsorship of the Civil Aeronautics Authority. A total of 619 civilians took courses at the Oak Lane Country Day School and received flight training in Pottstown. Medical School faculty conducted research directly related to the war effort, including studies of combat

Rear Admiral John R. Beardall and President Robert L. Johnson congratulate graduates J. Howard Wildowson and Morris Snyder at the June 12, 1942, commencement.

By May 1944, 7,241 Temple students and graduates were serving in the military. Forty-six had given their lives. Four faculty members contributed to the war effort with their discoveries involving the use of chlorophyll in healing wounds and burns, and the use of blood plasma to repair ruptured livers. Temple also played host to two major international conferences: the Institute for Post-War Planning and the International Labor Conference.

infections and environmental diseases, air sickness, new methods of skin grafting, improvements in penicillin, and other advancements.

Dean Boris Blai of the Tyler School of Fine Arts had fought for France during World War I and knew firsthand the horrors of war. To do his part, he went to New Jersey's Fort Dix and offered his services in providing art therapy to wounded soldiers. By the war's end Blai, his fellow faculty members, and students had instructed more than 2,000 persons in painting and sculpture at Fort Dix. Blai also taught special courses in camouflage at Fort Dix.

The war years were not without profound ironies. Temple enrolled four American-born Japanese American students who were forcibly relocated from the western internment camps to Philadelphia. One of them, Kenneth Murase, won second place in a Temple essay contest titled "What Are We Fighting For?" And commuter transportation to Temple was disrupted in August 1944 by a street car trolley strike when riders refused to ride trolleys with black motormen. The situation became so tense that President Roosevelt ordered the army to take over and operate the Philadelphia transportation system. Temple students riding the trolleys were accompanied by Philadelphia police officers until the strike was settled.

Temple made many wartime adjustments. Because the war siphoned off hospital personnel into the armed forces, Temple Hospital accelerated its internship period to make more practitioners available. Mitten Hall was all but taken over by domestic war efforts; bandages were rolled by Red Cross volunteers in the club room, and sewing machines were set up in the east alcove to make cloth articles for the armed services. Mitten's auditorium was converted into sleeping and studying quarters for men taking pre-dental and pre-medical training under the army's Specialized Training Program and its counterpart in the navy, the V-12 program.

Rationing and shortages forced Temple to adapt. Janitors scavenged for rubber in the trash to aid the rubber drive. Founder's Day Dinner was canceled because of food rationing. *The Owl* magazine suspended operations in October 1943 because of the paper and manpower shortages. By 1943 male students were in such short supply that there were three women for every man enrolled at

Philco contracted with Temple to educate its women employees on radio technologies.

Temple. Young women found it so difficult to get dates that the dean of students set up an official "date bureau." Coeds filled out information cards for male students to use as "leads." Because of the lack of men, the annual tug-of-war was made up of women students. The sophomore women pulled freshmen women through a shower of water.

Temple voluntarily suspended varsity athletic programs. Jack Sugarman, who scored Temple's winning touchdown in the Villanova freshman game in the fall of '41, joined the Marines and became a hero at Guadalcanal, saving the lives of nine officers. By 1944 there were 981 Owl athletes in the service and 23 percent had seen combat. Jean Shiley Newhouse (BS EDU 1933), captain of the 1932 U.S. Women's Olympic team and a gold medal winner in the high jump, joined the WAVES. Football star Mike Jarmoluk, six foot five and 280 pounds, had to wait two months at the New Cumberland induction center until special uniforms could be made for him.

When the war was finally over—when VE Day and VJ Day were celebrated—a grateful university looked back with pride at what it had accomplished but with anguish over its cost. On VJ Day President Johnson convened an assembly in the Baptist Temple and asked students to pause and reflect on the sacrifices made by their fellow students. Temple was represented in the armed forces by 8,344 men and women, 299 of whom were decorated for gallantry in action, extraordinary achievement, or meritorious service. Major William Benn (Commerce 1932), who had developed a "skip bombing" method used in the South Pacific, was awarded the Distinguished Service Cross. Not to be forgotten, 152 former students, graduates, and faculty members lost their lives in the war, including George Benjamin Jr., killed in action at Leyte in the Philippines and awarded the Congressional Medal of Honor. Special memorial services were held in 1946 for Benjamin and all the war dead.

Temple University proved remarkably adaptive, adjusting as necessary to wartime circumstances and ably contributing to the war effort. Special wartime training programs with corporations and government agencies, plus the expertise contributed by Temple's professors in a variety of fields, provided the impetus and rationale for future partnerships between the federal government and universities that flowered after 1945.

Boris Blai, dean of the Tyler School of Art (shown here giving a thumbs-up sign to a student), offered art courses as therapy to soldiers and spouses during World War II.

The S.S. *Temple Victory,* launched from Portland, Oregon, on March 27, 1945, was one of twenty-two such ships named after U.S. schools. With its 455-foot keel and 62-foot beam, it could carry a day's supply of C rations for three million men. Because of wartime travel restrictions, Temple President Robert L. Johnson was represented by Dr. A. L. Strand, president of Oregon State College, at the dedication. Temple students donated an onboard library of 1,200 books.

Chapter 4
Middle Passage, 1945–1965

The end of World War II brought rapid and substantial changes across America and throughout American higher education, particularly to Temple University. Over the course of twenty postwar years Temple was transformed into a modern university, not totally unlike others, yet continually inspired by its distinctive mission. Change came so quickly after the war that normally restrained voices used the word *revolution* to describe the significant transformations occurring in American society.

1945
Returning veterans flood the campus.

1948
Temple Community College opens at Eighteenth and Buttonwood streets.

1953
Law School moves back to Main Campus.

1959
Millard Gladfelter becomes fourth president.

1963
Temple wins the GE College Bowl.

1947
Dentistry and Pharmacy move to Broad and Allegheny.

1951
Men's soccer team wins national championship.

1956
Curtis Hall is dedicated.

1960
John F. Kennedy speaks on campus.

1965
Temple University is designated a state-related institution.

Page 72 *Students leaving Temple's Eighteenth and Buttonwood campus, circa 1946.*

The nexus of change was America's economic transformation from an industrial to a postindustrial society, a change wrought largely by the de-industrialization of America's cities and the growth in its place of a new service economy accompanied by dramatic innovations in the organization of business (the Managerial Revolution) and the way Americans receive and process information (the Information Revolution). Inside higher education, changes occurred regarding faculty and student relationships to their universities, and by 1965 observers spoke knowingly of an Academic Revolution. These forces required Temple to reevaluate and adapt to society's changing needs.

In 1949 Harry Truman was president, South Pacific *opened on Broadway, and George Orwell published* 1984. *The Phillies finished third in the eight-team National League but showed flashes of brilliance. Led by their twenty-two-year-old center fielder, Richie Ashburn, the "Whiz Kids" advanced to the World Series a year later. In those years Conwell Hall was a multi-purpose building and students dressed more formally.*

The first of Temple's many postwar challenges was to accommodate the thousands of returning servicemen and servicewomen who poured onto the campus even before the war ended. In 1944 Congress passed the Serviceman's Readjustment Act, better known as the GI Bill. Intended to keep returning servicemen out of the job market until industry could retool and the economy could recover, the GI Bill guaranteed each veteran unemployment benefits for one year. Almost as an afterthought, the act contained a provision for generous educational benefits, including allowances for tuition, fees, books, and supplies to be paid directly to the university. Veterans were also given a subsistence allowance—an enticing package, all considered.

In short order America's college campuses were flooded with veterans. By the fall of 1946 GI enrollments nationally exceeded one million and by 1950 surpassed two million. Almost immediately Temple received nearly 3,300 war veterans, and within a year total undergraduate enrollments increased 50 percent. To handle the large influx, Temple's registrar, John Rhoads, streamlined the admissions and evaluative procedures to admit students more quickly and move them through the system faster.

More worldly and experienced than traditional-aged students, veterans tended also to be pragmatic, hardworking, and in a hurry to complete their degrees. Still, many of the veterans at Temple enjoyed the college life, joined clubs, and participated in sports. Returning GIs also influenced the course offerings, as many of them opted for courses and majors in employable fields such as business and engineering. Temple's largest problem, however, was where to put them all.

Temple's undergraduate campus simply could not accommodate the growing student population. In 1946 the trustees authorized construction of a new classroom building but lacked funds to proceed. Having already rented or bought all of the available and usable row houses on Broad Street and Park Avenue, Temple looked elsewhere. To relieve the crush of freshman and sophomore students, two small satellite campuses were established—one at Olney High School and a second at the Brookline Square Country Club in Havertown, Delaware County. Regular full-time faculty members were assigned to teach at the two sites, which each attracted over 500 students.

Students and instructors found the Olney High School facility unsuitable, and after two years the program was transferred to the grounds near Temple's football stadium in the Cedarbrook community just inside the city along Cheltenham Avenue. Pre-fabricated war surplus buildings from the U.S. Army housed temporary classrooms. Both the Havertown and Cedarbrook facilities served their purposes well, acting as feeder units to the larger Main Campus. The postwar surge in enrollments continued until 1950. But enrollments fell sharply after the U.S. entry into the Korean War.

In the fall of 1951 the university closed the Havertown unit and classes at the Cedarbrook Center were moved to Broad and Montgomery.

Location Is Destiny

The most difficult postwar challenge facing Temple was the accelerated physical and population changes occurring in North Philadelphia. De-industrialization was a national phenomenon, with the percentage of jobs in manufacturing declining from 35 to 19 percent between 1946 and 1968, and it brought a great transformation to the areas near Temple as businesses and industries surrounding the university closed their doors, abandoned warehouses, factories, and offices, and left behind anguish and decay. Some industries moved operations to the suburbs, where business costs and access were more favorable. Workers in the abandoned industries, accustomed to living near their work, moved to the suburbs or to other parts of the city where they could gain work. Shuttered industries left behind a crumbling infrastructure. As a result of "white flight" to the suburbs, many houses were soon filled by newcomers, among them recent African American migrants from the South searching for better opportunities in Philadelphia.

The relocation or closure of industries left huge holes in the residential fabric around Temple. African Americans who moved into the abandoned industrial villages were often held solely to blame for creating the physical decay and urban blight. But research by Temple professors Carolyn Adams, William Yancey, David Elesh, and their colleagues demonstrated that it was the presence of industry and jobs—not the presence of ethnic enclaves or their incumbent institutions—that produced neighborhood cohesion and stability. Although the new arrivals lived close to the fading North Philadelphia industries, they were denied jobs in those industries because of prejudice and forced to work elsewhere in the city. In the new postindustrial economy, substantially sized North Philadelphia neighborhoods became disconnected from what social scientists call the "structures of opportunity." Without jobs to hold residents and anchor neighborhoods, they soon fell into neglect.

As industrial production declined across the region, the service, information, and construction industries boomed, drawing people to the suburbs and attracting whites from the city. The shift of population from the city to the suburbs was noticeable as early as the 1920s, but it accelerated rapidly after 1945. Between 1955 and 1960, 12 percent of Philadelphia's white population moved to the suburbs, compared with only 2 percent of the black population. By 1960 the suburbs contained approximately half of the region's residents, and by 1980 the proportion had grown to two-thirds of the total.

Temple considered joining the move to the suburbs. Opportunities presented themselves as early as 1931, when President Beury received an offer to buy the William M. Elkins estate in Cheltenham for $400,000. He rejected it, writing, "It would not fit with our plans." Neither did the university have the funds to afford it. A 1939 offer to purchase the Cedarbrook Country Club, a 173-acre expanse above Cheltenham Avenue running along the west side of Route 309, was given serious consideration by the board of trustees. Trustee Charles Erny, who had financed construction of the nearby Temple football stadium, agreed to finance the project without cost to the university. Board sentiment was mixed, with some members vehemently opposed. When a motion to reject the move was narrowly defeated, Erny sensed the intensity of the opposition and withdrew the proposal.

When the 252-acre Widener estate in Cheltenham Township went on the market in 1944, President Johnson was initially enthusiastic. Erny again supported the idea and put his checkbook behind it.

TEMPLE NOTABLE
Johnny Young

A North Philadelphia–Temple University success story. Seven-year-old Johnny Young left Savannah, Georgia, in 1947 under tow of his "mom," an aunt who made a deathbed promise to Young's mother to care for him. They settled into a North Philadelphia housing project. Young excelled in school, worked days in a South Street women's wear shop, attended Temple at night, earned a BS in accounting (SBM 1966), and became chief accountant for a city department. Fascinated by international affairs, Young handily passed the Foreign Service exam and launched a distinguished career as an American diplomat. He served as U.S. ambassador to Sierra Leone (1989–1992), Togo (1994–1997), Bahrain (1997–2001), and Slovenia (2001–2004).

But Johnson changed his mind. As it happened, Johnson was more eager to acquire Hunting Park, an eighty-seven-acre tract of trees, grass, and walkways located just east of North Broad Street at the juncture of Hunting Park Avenue and Roosevelt Boulevard. Negotiations with the Fairmount Park Commission, Mayor Bernard Samuel, and other city officials were supportive. But the residents of Nicetown, Logan, Olney, Mayfair, and Frankford became indignant when stories broke in the newspapers that Temple planned to take their park. Johnson withdrew the petition.

The Cedarbrook Country Club property went back on the market in 1949 and, again, trustees gave the offer due consideration. Opposition this time came from the Cheltenham Township manager and commissioners, who objected to removing the property from the tax rolls, and homeowners and country club bond holders filed suit to block the sale. Temple again withdrew.

Temple came closest to moving when in 1950 it purchased the Randall Morgan estate, an eighty-acre property situated in Chestnut Hill at Stenton and Willow Grove avenues, along with a twenty-acre site adjacent to Wyndmoor Station. Announcements were made of a "new campus" and articles published with photographs of students strolling verdant pathways of the future home for Temple's undergraduate programs. A survey committee, chaired by Provost Millard E. Gladfelter, considered all contingencies and concluded that moving anywhere would involve severe logistical problems. The "problem," as committee member Sterling Atkinson admitted, was "providing for the necessary services to maintain an effective educational center at the new location but at the same time avoiding a needless pyramiding of University costs."

University officers realized that renovating the Wyndmoor property and moving the undergraduate colleges were beyond their reach. But something had to be done to stem the erosion of Temple's reputation, which had declined along with the physical deterioration of the neighborhoods, "bringing city slums to the doors of the University," as board chairman Frederick P. Corson recalled. President Johnson acknowledged that the area next to Temple was the "[n]umber one slum area in Philadelphia." Temple's reputation nationally suffered. A February 1951 issue of *Saturday Evening Post* featured an article on Temple's president, Robert Johnson, hailing his accomplishments. However, students were not flattered by the *Post's* references to the "subway divers" who attend the "poor man's university" in the "semislum" area of Philadelphia.

Fortunately, the publicity accorded Temple's plans to move reached City Hall, which was aware of two things: Temple had no room to grow at Broad and Montgomery, and Temple's presence in North Philadelphia was an important counterweight in slowing the progression of urban blight. After lengthy consideration, which included substantial input from Temple, the City Planning Commission and Redevelopment Authority joined forces and in March 1953 certified for the use of Temple University the area bounded by Broad Street, Columbia Avenue (now Cecil B. Moore Avenue), Twelfth Street, and Diamond Street, creating an Institutional Development District and setting aside funds for acquisition and demolition costs. Temple quietly sold the Wyndmoor property.

Robert L. Johnson

President Robert L. Johnson presented "The Case for Temple University" in a speech before the American Newcomen Society in 1954. Johnson began by describing Temple's students: three out of four were commuters, 60 percent lived in Philadelphia proper, 80 percent earned all or part of their college expenses, just less than half were from families in which one or both parents were foreign-born. He pointed with pride to the ethnic and racial diversity of Temple students, noting the balance of religious affiliations and the number of African Americans (6 percent, or double the national average attending college). Students selected Temple, he said, because of "its spirit of tolerance and democracy." No other Philadelphia institution fulfills such a role, and "That is why," Johnson announced, "Temple University is not moving out."

Johnson pledged that Temple would stay, because "[f]or seventy years we of Temple University have taken the community's sons and daughters, kept them with us for a while, then returned them to give to Philadelphia and its environs better homes, better schools, better health, more happiness, more civilization." It would take a while for the process to begin, but the commitment was made: Temple's destiny was tied to its location.

Robert Livingston Johnson, president of Temple University from 1941 to 1959.

Robert L. Johnson was dedicated to the mission and purpose of Temple and especially to its students. Johnson said that his goal each year was to make the personal acquaintance of 200 Temple students. He was known to visit with students and accept potluck dinner invitations in students' apartments. No one will ever know the number of students who received their first job after college because of a phone call or letter from Johnson. Charles F. (Chuck) Schalch (BS SBM 1955), winner of the Sword Award for student leadership, remembered President Johnson casually suggesting that he stop by after graduation to discuss his future plans. A few years later, when Chuck's service commitment was completed, he called Johnson and reminded him of his offer. The president invited Chuck to join him for lunch at the Union League and afterward made several calls on his behalf that landed him the position that became his career. Similarly, All-American basketball player Bill Mlkvy (DDS 1955)—the "Owl Without a Vowel"—easily recalled several personal kindnesses extended him by Johnson, who always had the time to chat and to catch up on Bill's progress toward his ultimate goal of becoming a dentist.

Johnson devoted a great deal of his attention to public outreach and fund-raising. He hired Robert V. Geasey (SBM 1929), a former newspaperman and sportswriter, to head an Office of Public Information. Geasey was instantly endeared to the Temple family, and after his premature death in 1953 new student playing fields were named Geasey Field. To establish Temple's first regular development effort, Johnson hired William W. Tomlinson, a Swarthmore alumnus and former Scott Paper executive. In 1943 Tomlinson organized an Acres of Diamonds Fund and an Annual Giving Fund; both began modestly, but as higher-education costs escalated and competition for available resources intensified, fund-raising could not remain on the periphery.

Temple University Hospital, circa 1953.

Temple and all universities were changed by the federal government's decision to build on the relationships begun with universities during the war and to continue to expand its funding of pure scientific research. Given the success of the wartime programs that yielded such results as the atomic bomb, the architects of the postwar policies guiding federal support of science asserted that the "best science" was "Big Science." That meant a system of competitive grants awarded to university scientists who submitted proposals for large-scale projects that were then selected through peer review to carry out government plans. The system, however, was inherently inequitable: a closed system reserved almost exclusively for the premier universities and a select group of powerful, well-endowed research universities. Unfortunately, Temple was not among them.

The federal government became the largest patron of and contractor for basic scientific research, far surpassing and largely replacing philanthropic foundations, which turned their efforts to supplementing the big science federal initiatives. To distribute federal funds, a series of federal agencies were established, including the National Science Foundation, National Institutes of Health, Atomic Energy Commission, and Departments of Defense and Agriculture. Eventually a university's total academic reputation was affixed to its record for attracting federal funding for scientific research. Temple's undergraduate programs in the basic sciences, although featuring excellent instruction and a few distinguished researchers, were not in a strong position to compete in federal grantsmanship contests for lack of adequate facilities. The Main Campus would not have a building dedicated exclusively to science until 1960. The Medical School, on the other hand, was well prepared.

Medical School

Opposite page *The Medical School building, dedicated in 1930, served the university well during its middle passage from 1945 to 1965. Demands for a larger, more modern facility were answered in 2009 with the opening of the new Medical Education and Research Building.*

The infusion of federal funds had a particularly profound impact on medical schools. Johns Hopkins University immediately became the leader in the field, having successfully linked medical education to advanced scholarship in biological sciences. Other university medical schools, including Temple's, followed suit. Scientists with PhDs in the natural and physical sciences joined the clinical faculty and research staff, leading to the development of increasingly sophisticated medical research departments.

The growing strength and reputation of Temple's Medical School were owed chiefly to the visionary and forceful leadership of William N. Parkinson (MD MED 1911), who served concurrently as dean of the Medical School, medical director of the hospital, and university vice president. At one time also a member of the Temple Board of Trustees, Parkinson led the Medical School to new prominence

during the postwar years. Hard-driving, totally dedicated, and often controversial, Parkinson left an indelible mark with his legendary, single-minded devotion to Temple Medicine.

Determined to elevate Temple's medical center to national preeminence and equally insistent that it be independent from the university, Parkinson methodically engineered the establishment of major research centers, recruited an impressive group of top-notch researchers and clinicians, and succeeded in directing university and commonwealth resources toward the building of a new Temple Hospital and supporting facilities.

Parkinson's quest began with two substantial gifts. In 1945 Dr. Theodore L. Chase arranged to bequeath a substantial sum to establish a surgical research foundation at the Medical School in memory of his wife, Agnes Barr Chase (MD MED 1909). An accomplished artist and illustrator, Agnes Barr Chase collaborated with her husband in compiling a highly regarded atlas of surgery. A second breakthrough occurred a year later when Parkinson gained an affiliation with the Samuel Fels Institute. The Fels Foundation appropriated $400,000 to build an additional floor on the Medical School building to house the Fels Research Institute and voted an annual sum for its maintenance. Dr. Harry Shay, a gastroenterologist and cancer researcher, known for his development of therapies for treating leukemia, was Fels's first director. The Fels Institute attracted top scholars to Temple, including Dr. Sidney Weinhouse, who received the first grant ever awarded by the National Science Foundation, and Dr. Michael Shimkin, whose research helped establish the link between cigarette smoking and cancer.

Parkinson's goal was to build a strong faculty of proven professionals, people with established records and high accomplishments. His intensity and persuasive manner lured many prominent physicians and researchers away from leading universities. The examples are many. Parkinson persuaded Dr. John A. Kolmer, known worldwide for the serologic test for syphilis that bears his name, to bring his Research Institute for Cutaneous Medicine to Temple, along with an endowment of $475,000. Dr. Walter Ivan Lillie, an expert neuro-ophthalmologist, left the Mayo Clinic and the University of Minnesota to join Temple's staff.

Parkinson also recruited Dr. W. Edward Chamberlain from Stanford to head Temple's Radiology Department and bring it to national prominence. Chamberlain is credited with developing a long list of radiological techniques, including the first stereoscopic X-ray machine, making possible television viewing and three-dimensional effects in X-ray diagnosis. Along with Professors George Henry and R. B. Taft, Chamberlain developed the electrokymograph, which recorded the movements of the heart's chambers to aid in the early detection of heart disease. Electromyography (EMG) is still used clinically for the diagnosis of neurological and neuromuscular problems, as well as in research laboratories.

In 1950 the AMA Council on Medical Education review cited the school for its excellent research. Dr. O. Spurgeon English, a renowned psychiatrist, wrote two popular books—*Fathers Are Parents Too* and *The Emotional Problems of Living*—and with Dr. Edward Weiss he was a pioneer in psychosomatic medicine. Dr. Chevalier Jackson, professor of bronchoesophagology, developed instruments that saved children and others from death caused by blockage of air and food passages. He and his son, Dr. Chevalier Lawrence Jackson, taught physicians from all over the world the techniques they had perfected. Dr. Ernest A. Spiegel published approximately 250 scientific papers, wrote extensively about the brain and nervous system, and edited the annual review *Progress in Neurology*. Dr. Thomas Durant served as chair of Medicine from 1956 to 1966. The consummate diagnostician, he also made notable contributions in electrocardiography, contrast visualization, and the dynamics of circulation and respiration. Among other honors, Durant was president of the American College of Physicians.

Managing this talented collection of clinicians and researchers as well as the hospital required enormous dedication and organizational skills. No detail was too small for Parkinson. His overbearing management style required virtually every decision to come through him, and he tolerated no violations of the chain of command. Parkinson consulted rarely, if ever, directly with faculty, only with the department heads. The medical faculty met infrequently, and they took very little role in governance and administration. In 1950 the AMA Council on Medical Education examiners suggested that faculty interest in the school would be increased if faculty were allowed greater participation. Parkinson rejected the suggestion and the examiners backed down.

Dental School

The Dental School hit a low point in its history in 1943. Ten years earlier it had received a Class A designation, but in the interim the aging facilities at Eighteenth and Buttonwood deteriorated beyond repair and the Council on Dental Education rated the Dental School's plant in the lowest tenth of all physical accommodations for dental colleges in the country. The new dean, Gerald D. Timmons, who had been the executive secretary of the American Dental Association, inherited a seemingly insurmountable task. But, with the assistance of Provost Millard Gladfelter and university trustee James A. Nolen, he persuaded the university to acquire the Packard Building on Broad Street just north of Allegheny Avenue, only a block from Temple Hospital.

With $2 million in university funds, space was now provided for classrooms and labs, operating rooms, offices, and storage ample enough to accommodate both the Dental School and the Pharmacy School. They moved into the building in October 1947, permitting the Dental School to

In 1947 Temple's Dentistry and Pharmacy schools moved to the Health Sciences Center. The four-story building provided five acres of floor space fronting more than 300 feet on Broad Street at Allegheny Avenue.

reacquire good standing and ending the health sciences' forty-year presence at the Eighteenth and Buttonwood campus.

In 1962 Dean Charles L. Howell succeeded Timmons as Dental School dean. Howell instituted a number of advanced education programs in areas such as oral pathology, oral pediatrics, orthodontics, and periodontics, which were put in place within five years. He also emphasized a closer correlation of basic sciences and oversaw a 50 percent expansion of the clinical facilities, affording an increased program of community service. A new Department of Community Dentistry furthered education in dental health, dental epidemiology, ethics, and jurisprudence.

Pharmacy

Pharmacy shared Dentistry's excitement over the move from Eighteenth and Buttonwood to North Broad Street. Settling into their new quarters, the Pharmacy faculty revived graduate-level courses with a new fusion of energy and resources, gaining approval in 1958 to offer a PhD program. In response to national standards set by the American Council on Pharmaceutical Education, the requirements for the bachelor of science degree in Pharmacy were amended in 1961, adding a fifth year allocated to pre-professional education and the inclusion of courses in the social sciences and humanities.

H. Evert Kendig stepped down as dean in 1950. To honor his service, which extended back to 1932, the school dedicated the H. Evert Kendig Memorial Museum. Originally on the first floor of the Dental/Pharmacy Building, the museum was relocated in 1974 to the fourth floor of the Allied Health/Pharmacy Building at 3307 North Broad Street. Dr. Joseph B. Sprowls succeeded Kendig and served until 1967.

At the dedication of the H. Evert Kendig Memorial Museum, April 10, 1957, in the Dental/Pharmacy Building, Provost Millard Gladfelter chatted with Dr. Kendig's four daughters, Mrs. S. Logan Kerr, Mrs. S. Palmer Skoglund, Mrs. Richard W. Chirchman, and Mrs. Josephine K. Costello.

Pharmacy, like Medicine, enjoyed relative autonomy at the Health Sciences Campus. Independent of the Main Campus, students and faculty created their own social and cultural programs, generating a special sense of attachment to the school. Intramural sports programs, student organizations, and even theatrical productions invigorated student life at the School of Pharmacy. Students began staging theatrical performances in 1952, offering such fare as *A Rx for Love*, written by Joseph Brakin (BPharm PHR 1952) and Sydney Lisken (BPharm PHR 1952), which included the song "This Is Bio-Chemistry." Pharmacy instructor Fred B. Gable directed the popular performances, which were staged in the first-floor auditorium of the Dental/Pharmacy Building. A formal amateur theatrical group formed, adopted the name Mortar and Pestle Players in 1961, and offered performances until the school moved into new facilities in 1974.

Temple University Hospital

At the center of the health sciences complex lay the hospital, directed by William Parkinson. A deft and demanding manager, Parkinson was also a savvy political operator who usually got his way, whether in the corridors of the state capitol or in the Temple boardroom. A former member of the board of trustees, he was the only dean invited to board meetings whenever anything concerning his school or the hospital was discussed. To remain close to the trustees, he formed an advisory group called the Medical School and Hospital Committee that included five trustees. He used that leverage, immediately after the war ended, to begin to lobby for the construction of a new hospital.

There were many competing needs, including the need for a new classroom facility at Broad and Montgomery. Overcrowding on campus had reached the dire stage with the influx of returning veterans. Parkinson nonetheless persuaded the trustees that the needs of the Medical School and hospital must come first and must be met completely. Parkinson presented data and outside agency reports demonstrating that Temple University Hospital was the most overcrowded in the region and that fewer than half of the people seeking admission as patients could be accepted. Independent estimates placed the costs for replacing the hospital at $11 million, including an outpatient building, ancillary building, X-ray facilities, and clinical laboratories; all, he emphasized, were urgently needed. The board agreed in 1950 to authorize construction as soon as funds became available. It fell to President Johnson to inform the undergraduate faculty that their long-delayed classroom facility — approved in principle by the board in 1946 and estimated to cost only a fraction of what Parkinson demanded—had to be put on hold until funds first were raised for the hospital. The Faculty Senate protested, as did the Temple chapter of the American Association of University Professors (AAUP), to no avail.

When funding was finally in place, Parkinson directed the expenditure of almost $11 million to bring the new hospital into existence. In 1956 three buildings were added to the medical center: Parkinson Pavilion, a ten-story, 600-bed inpatient building; a two-story ancillary building for radiology, surgical operating rooms, and clinical laboratories; and an eight-story outpatient building with clinics, laboratories, and offices. The same year the Skin and Cancer Hospital became a unit of the Department of Dermatology.

Parkinson liked the autonomy afforded by the distance from the hospital to the Main Campus. The Medical School faculty, after all, had little in common with the undergraduate faculty; they taught a minimal amount and spent most of their time with private patients and set their own fees. Parkinson was deliberately aloof in his relations with other schools, refusing to cooperate unless personally directed by the president.

Above *Aerial view of Temple Hospital and Medical School, circa 1965. Clockwise from the top: the old Medical School (1930), Medical Research Building (1963), Parkinson Pavilion (1956), Ancillary Services and Out-Patient Building (1956), and the old "main" hospital building (originally Samaritan Hospital), razed in 1986 to make way for the new Temple University Hospital.*

Parkinson enjoyed excellent dealings with Robert Johnson, who admired and defended Parkinson. His relationship with Provost Millard Gladfelter was not as smooth. When Johnson signaled his intention to step down in June 1959, Parkinson accepted the appointment of Robert M. Bucher (MD MED 1944) as associate dean, with the understanding that he would succeed Parkinson as dean of Medicine after a year. Parkinson stayed on as vice president until 1961. Bucher and Gladfelter wanted to bring Dentistry and Pharmacy into close association with the Medical School by creating a new unit called the Health Sciences Center.

Below *In 1961 Dr. Leroy E. Burney, former surgeon general of the United States and a thirty-year veteran of public health service, was named the first vice president of Temple's Health Sciences Center.*

With all of the principal health sciences schools and programs located near each other and with Dean Parkinson retired, President Gladfelter proposed that Medicine, Pharmacy, and Dentistry, together with the hospital, form a new university division, responsible to a vice president. On July 1, 1961, Dr. Leroy E. Burney, former surgeon general of the United States, took office as vice president of the Temple University Health Sciences Center.

Dean Bucher and Dr. Burney picked up where Dean Parkinson left off, and in September 1962 saw through the construction of Jones Hall, a ten-story, $3 million residence for women at the Health Sciences Center. Named in honor of Edith Bolling Jones, founder and president of the Medical Center Auxiliary and a trustee for twenty years, Jones Hall was air-conditioned, with recreational facilities and laundry rooms on every floor. And in 1963 a new medical research building opened. It was constructed adjacent to and just north of the old medical research building built in 1930 and on the former site of the Tioga Baptist Church that Russell Conwell helped found in 1891 and the university purchased in 1960 after the congregation moved. The new Medical Research Building—constructed without windows to precisely control light, sound, and temperature—was financed, in part, by a $1.5 million grant from the U.S. Public Health Service and by the Fels Institute, to which two floors of the building were dedicated for cancer research.

Millard E. Gladfelter

The first Temple president to come to the office with a background in and training as an educator and the first with an earned doctorate, Millard Gladfelter (everyone called him Gladdy) began as a teacher in country schools. At age twenty-five he was teaching history and serving as principal in West York High School. He earned a bachelor's degree from Gettysburg College, a master's degree from the University of Wisconsin, and a PhD from the University of Pennsylvania in education. Gladfelter arrived at Temple in 1930, when he was only thirty years old. Originally appointed as director of the Temple High School, he became the registrar, gradually assuming expanded responsibilities and gaining the confidence of board members and faculty alike. Robert L. Johnson promoted Gladfelter to vice president in 1941 and in 1946 added the title provost to distinguish him as the senior academic officer in the university.

Gladfelter's appointment was widely welcomed by the faculty and staff, as he was seen as a benefactor in arranging salary increases, a retirement plan, and other benefits while serving as provost. After becoming president on July 1, 1959, Gladfelter continued to be sympathetic toward faculty and their issues. Gladfelter's gentlemanly demeanor and amicable bearing belied a tough inner spirit and a keen appreciation for the political arts. If he was capable of guile, it never showed. Although born on a farm and possessed of the taciturn temperament of his Amish neighbors when growing up, Gladfelter became an adopted son of North Philadelphia. He worked well with community organizations and after retirement served as president of the North City Corporation, an association that brought housing, investment, and job opportunities to North Philadelphia. Gladfelter believed that urban universities were duty-bound to help solve their neighborhoods' economic and social problems.

Gladfelter's principal contribution to the history of Temple was his unerring and indefatigable labor on behalf of securing Temple's state-related status with the Commonwealth of Pennsylvania. The decision changed the university as no other has since the founding. It opened up a period of fantastic growth and expansion, both of which are discussed in the following chapter. By the time of Gladfelter's retirement in 1967, Temple's enrollment had grown to 38,000, the faculty increased to 2,361, and the budget reached $57 million.

Some measure of the man and the esteem with which he was held are reflected in just one of the scores of letters sent to Gladfelter on the occasion of his retirement. "You were a major reason why I and the others so thoroughly committed ourselves to the University," wrote Professor William Rossky. "Your own dedication inspired by example our commitment."

Main Campus Building Plan

The undergraduate colleges finally received their new classroom facility ten years after the board approved the construction of a classroom building at a cost not exceeding $350,000. When the

FACT

Temple University alumnus Joseph Torg (MD MED 1961) saved thousands of athletes from serious knee injuries with his research leading to today's athletic shoes with shorter cleats.

board in 1954 finally authorized actual expenditures, $1.3 million was budgeted for construction, the amount to be financed by mortgaging certain university properties, including the football stadium. The building went up on the northwest corner of Montgomery Avenue and Thirteenth Street. On February 16, 1956, Temple President Robert L. Johnson and Common Pleas Court Judge Curtis Bok laid the cornerstone for Curtis Hall, using a silver trowel and mortar. Bok was the grandson of early Temple benefactor Cyrus H. K. Curtis, former head of the Curtis Publishing Company, after whom the building was named.

Curtis Hall was a welcome addition when it opened for classes in the summer of 1956. A simple, rectangular building of unimposing design, it contained no offices, laboratories, lounges, or auditoriums—only classrooms. The first air-conditioned building on Temple's campus, it made a great difference when built, shifting the campus's center of gravity toward Thirteenth and Montgomery and providing quality teaching space. Faculty and student survivors of the days when classes met in row house bedrooms, kitchens, or parlors could only marvel at the change. Curtis Hall served Temple well for more than fifty years until torn down to make way for the magnificent Alter Hall, home of the Fox School of Business and Management, which opened in January 2009.

Curtis Hall, the first modern air-conditioned building on Temple's campus, opened in 1956 on the northwest corner of Montgomery Avenue and Thirteenth Street. It was razed to make room for Alter Hall, which opened on this site in 2009.

A virtual blizzard of demolition and new construction followed the opening of Curtis Hall, because in 1956 commonwealth legislation was passed permitting the General State Authority (GSA) to acquire ground and put up buildings for state-aided institutions. Temple University, the University of Pittsburgh, and Penn State University were invited to file with the GSA six-year plans for their facilities' needs. Each school conveniently requested $40 million. In the prior ten years Temple had spent $16 million on capital improvements (only a small amount on the main academic center), funded by borrowing and large gifts. Top priorities for the years ahead were for the sciences—physics, chemistry, biology, and geology—areas in which Temple had fallen behind in providing adequate instructional and research facilities.

In April 1960 Temple's undergraduate Physics and Chemistry departments were elated by the dedication of Barton Hall, named in honor of Dr. Samuel Goodwin Barton (BA CLA 1903). Barton, a professor of physics at the University of Pennsylvania, noted astronomer, and prolific science writer, gave Temple approximately $300,000 to equip the building. The GSA appropriated $4 million for construction of a building located along Park Avenue (now Liacouras Walk) north of Berks Street. Governor David Lawrence attended the dedication of the first building constructed by the GSA for a state-aided institution.

A second much-needed science building followed in 1964, as Temple attempted to keep up with the swiftly changing requirements for modern scientific education and to provide facilities for scientific research. Beury Hall on Thirteenth Street, just north of Berks Street, became the home of Chemistry and Geology. Named for Temple's second president, Charles E. Beury, the building included fifty laboratories, twenty-two classrooms, and four large lecture halls.

During these years Temple acquired a number of properties close to Broad and Montgomery. The Park Avenue Methodist Church at 1940 North Park Avenue (now Liacouras Walk) was purchased by Temple in 1942. Originally named Thatcher Hall in honor of William D. Thatcher, one of the original seven students whose interest led to the founding of Temple College, it was initially reserved for the use of the Theology School (closed in 1959). Thatcher Hall was renamed and rededicated in 1947 as Thomas Hall in memory of the parents of Morgan H. Thomas, who was active in Philadelphia charities and president of the Garrett Buchanan Company, a large twine wholesaler. Thomas Hall was used mostly thereafter by the Colleges of Music and Communications and Theater before being taken down in 1998 to make way for the construction of a new dormitory simply called 1940.

Another church on campus, the Christian Science Church located on Park Avenue (now Liacouras Walk) just south of Sullivan Hall, was purchased in 1950 and named Stauffer Hall, honoring Dr. Milton F. Stauffer, dean of the School of Commerce (now the Fox School of Business and Management), who served Temple from 1899 to 1942. The building was later renamed Park Hall. For several years from the late 1960s until the mid-1970s, the building housed the university's computer center. In 1997 Park Hall was completely renovated and renamed Shusterman Hall in honor of Law alumnus Murray Shusterman (BA CLA 1933; LLB LAW 1936).

Turngemeinde Hall, a German social and athletic club located on the east side of Broad Street at Columbia Avenue (now Cecil B. Moore Avenue), was purchased by Temple in 1946. Renamed South Hall, the building housed physical education activities, a swimming pool dedicated mostly to community use, and a gym where Temple's basketball team occasionally played. South Hall was torn down to make way for a new park and the renovated Cecil B. Moore subway station, which opened in 1983.

With the addition in 1954 and 1959 of the two Keneseth Israel buildings—Reber Hall (now Rock Hall) and the Keneseth Israel synagogue (later the Klein Library and eventually the Law Center of the James E. Beasley School of Law) — save for a gasoline station at the corner of Broad and Montgomery, the Temple campus by 1959 filled the block on the east side of North Broad extending from Columbia Avenue to Montgomery Avenue.

In 1955 Temple acquired the Monument Cemetery on the west side of Broad Street opposite Mitten Hall. The remains in the cemetery, including those of Russell Conwell and his wife, Sarah, were removed and relocated. The grounds were converted into a parking lot and intramural athletic fields. Ornamental gatehouses stood on either side of the Berks Street driveway and were used for a time as offices by Campus Recreation and Intercollegiate Athletics until razed in 2000.

Temple was the successful bidder when the Hardt Building on the southeast corner of Broad and Columbia went up for auction in December 1958. Named for Milton Stauffer and formally dedicated in 1960, the ten-story building was variously occupied by the Temple University High School, Temple's Technical Institute, and Campus Information. Built in 1901, the structure was condemned and torn down in 1980 and became a visitors' parking lot.

As more Temple students made known their interest in living on campus or spending more time after classes, Temple responded. Three new student dormitories were planned and built. Financed on borrowed money, the facilities had to be self-sustaining, generating revenue to pay the mortgages. Peabody Hall, constructed on the site of Russell Conwell's first Philadelphia home, was

Pete's Tavern, a popular campus hangout for the over-twenty-one set, was located on the northeast corner of Thirteenth Street and Montgomery Avenue. The site was cleared by the Redevelopment Authority of Philadelphia in 1956 to make way for a parking lot and eventually for the construction in 1999 of the Tuttleman Learning Center.

Students leaving the subway, circa 1970, and entering Temple's campus in front of South Hall (on the right).

named in honor of Temple's first dean of women, Gertrude Peabody, and opened in the fall of 1957 as a women's dormitory. Johnson Hall, named for Temple's third president, Robert L. Johnson, was erected in 1961 on Broad Street near the corner of Norris. Costing $3 million, the 500-bed men's dormitory was financed by a loan from the Federal Housing and Home Finance Administration. In 1967 Hardwick Hall, a companion women's dormitory, was built next door and dedicated to Ida Seal Hardwick, late wife of Aaron W. Hardwick, a Philadelphia businessman who gave $300,000 for its furnishings and equipment. In addition, an annex to Mitten Hall, doubling the square footage of usable space for student activities, was dedicated in February 1964 and available for use that fall.

Senior class gifts added texture and elegance to the campus. The class of 1962 gift went toward planting trees along Berks Street, east of Broad Street to Thirteenth Street, starting an annual custom

Right *Barton Hall under construction in 1959. The Redevelopment Authority of Philadelphia cleared more than four acres of land for Temple's expansion.*

Below *Barton Hall was completed and opened in 1960. The first building in Temple's three-building science complex, Barton Hall housed classrooms and laboratories for the Physics Department and included an electrically shielded nuclear lab, a rooftop weather station, and a planetarium.*

of adding greenery to the campus. Markers along the Berks walkway indicated succeeding class plantings. Johnny Ring Garden, north of Mitten Hall, was a gift of the class of 1964. The garden featured a bronze statue of Johnny Ring (sculpted by Boris Blai, dean of the Tyler School of Art), a gift of the class of 1948 (see photo, page 4 of Chapter 1).

Over several decades, from the 1920s to the 1950s, Temple gradually purchased all of the row house properties on both the east and west sides of Park Avenue, extending from Columbia Avenue (now Cecil B. Moore Avenue) to Diamond Street. As Park Avenue filled in with university buildings, it was closed off from vehicular traffic in 1962 and over time made into a pedestrian mall (Liacouras Walk). With the building of Barton Hall in 1960, the streets and sidewalks from Berks to Norris were leveled, repaved, and named Park Mall. Flagpoles added at the north end of the mall were the gift of the class of 1963 and dedicated in May of that year.

The Temple campus master plan and virtually all of the architectural work completed during these years was done by Nolen and Swinburne, architects and developers known for their designs of government buildings in Washington, D.C., and also for the Pennsylvania State Office Building at Broad and Spring Garden. James A. Nolen Jr., son of the firm's founder, was a longtime Temple trustee. The plan included landscaped plazas, grass plots, and pocket gardens spaced between new buildings replacing densely packed row houses and providing students small retreats and faculty a place for an occasional outdoor class in fair weather.

The Academic Revolution

By the mid-1960s observers noticed many changes occurring within America's institutions of higher education. Two particularly adept analysts, Christopher Jencks and David Riesman, summarized those changes in a 1969 book titled *The Academic Revolution*. In the course of two decades since the end of the war, American society had come to rely on and accept the expertise of colleges and universities, indicative of an "information society" whose foundation was a "knowledge industry." Student enrollments as a proportion of total population had grown, widening access and democratizing universities, but analysts noted that attending college had become less about learning and more about certification and socialization into an upper-middle-class orbit. Within universities, as the professoriate became more professionalized, there was a generally diminished concentration on educating undergraduates and an increased emphasis on graduate and professional education with a concomitant rise in specialization. Higher education had also become big business, with annual operating budgets and capital assets resembling those of major corporations.

Temple University to one degree or another experienced all of these transformative trends, particularly changes within the faculty. By the 1960s the cohort of largely homegrown faculty who had joined Temple circa 1930 were retiring, replaced by faculty from the outside, many of whom were already established scholars and experienced teachers. As the personal worth and esteem of individual faculty members enlarged, some faculty, as Faculty Senate debates attest, questioned whether Temple was on the right track. The vast majority of the Temple faculty hired after the war received their advanced degrees at America's most prestigious institutions. Many consequently thought that Temple ought to be more restrictive, forsake those who lacked the native ability to earn a first-rate college education, admit only the highest-qualified students, increase tuition, and concentrate on research and graduate education. Some faculty members said Temple should aspire to be a "Harvard on the Delaware."

Temple Enrollment Grows

By 1957 Temple enrollment reached 17,842, with 8,034 full-time and 9,808 part-time students. Penn State by comparison had 14,689 full-time and only 1,356 part-time students. Just eight years later, on the eve of becoming state-related, Temple University enrolled 28,285 students, making it the fourth-largest private university in the country, behind New York, Columbia, and Boston universities. In 1965 most of Temple's students (62 percent) worked part-time, almost half (13,836) were part-time students, and more than 11,000 students were registered for evening classes. Nearly half of the Evening Division students already had a college degree.

President Gladfelter and thought leaders within the Temple faculty attempted to redirect the energies of this elitist approach toward fulfilling the Conwell ideal of maintaining broad access combined with the goal of achieving higher levels of scholarly attainment, among both students and faculty. The tensions between the two faculty points of view revealed themselves in several ways, including voicing differing perceptions of Temple's reputational standing and lengthy debates over what all students ought to learn.

A university's academic reputation rests, in large part, on the quality of its liberal arts programs. Temple's Liberal Arts dean, James H. Dunham, retired in 1942 to be succeeded by another Princeton graduate, Dr. William T. Caldwell, chairman of the Chemistry Department, who served until 1961. Where Dunham had been a staunch traditionalist on matters of curriculum and academic standards, Caldwell by comparison was inclined toward curricular innovations, more willing to listen to and follow faculty recommendations and less inclined to intercede in department affairs.

Under Caldwell's guidance the College of Liberal Arts began as early as 1945 to broach the issue of general education requirements for freshmen and sophomores, asking critical questions about what all properly educated persons ought to learn. Over the next fourteen years a series of costly grant-supported studies and dense reports failed to generate a consensus or to bridge the critical issue of the respective sovereignties of the undergraduate schools. In short, the conflict within Liberal Arts between orthodox traditionalists and innovators, combined with the reluctance of the faculties in the other undergraduate schools and colleges to surrender prerogatives, provoked a stalemate on the subject of general education.

Just after President Gladfelter assumed office he assigned his new provost, Paul Anderson, the task of developing a common curriculum to bring the undergraduate schools together for the first two years of each student's college life. After much discussion and consultation across the faculty over a two-year period, agreement was reached on the obligation of finding a common course of study for all freshmen and sophomores in the undergraduate schools. In December 1961 the board of trustees approved in principle the "common elements" approach. The following fall Gladfelter persuaded the Faculty Senate to act as a joint faculty of the university and resolve the problem.

When it was done, the Senate approved the concept of the common elements and resolved that all undergraduates enroll in Liberal Arts for the first two years of their college work.

Soon the moniker "Basic Studies" was attached to the collection of courses deemed essential for a Temple-educated person. The next step, the determination of which courses belonged among Basic Studies, involved a seventy-four-member committee and exhaustive deliberations and negotiations before Basic Studies finally went into effect in the fall semester of 1964. The Basic Studies Program brought together faculty from all of the colleges and helped break through the distrust that for so long had divided the College of Liberal Arts and the other undergraduate colleges. However, by 1966 most of the Basic Studies courses in Liberal Arts and Education were taught by instructors and graduate assistants, a distinct change from "the old Temple," where full-time faculty and Temple's best scholars took pride in teaching undergraduates.

The use of teaching assistants, however, was a by-product of the growing emphasis on faculty research and the development of graduate programs, two baseline criteria for attaining modern university status. Dr. Rhoten Smith, who assumed the College of Liberal Arts deanship in August 1961, defended the practice. Arriving from New York University, where he had been a professor of politics, Smith called immediately for a shift of the college from its long-time emphasis on teaching toward becoming a more research-oriented college. Smith recruited liberal arts faculty much the way William Parkinson recruited medical faculty, seeking and hiring professors of national eminence with established scholarly records. He also insisted that chairs be selected and faculty tenured and promoted largely on the basis of the quality of their research and writing.

Academic reputation by the 1960s and thereafter was disproportionately weighted toward the institution's effort in doctoral programs and externally sponsored research. Adding new doctoral programs and securing professors with existing grants and with access to the federal grants arena became the name of the game. The wave of federal assistance began to level off in the mid-1950s but was sparked anew by the political response to the launching of Sputnik by the Soviet Union in 1957 and to the furthering of Cold War tensions in the early 1960s that led to substantial increases in federal spending on research to advance national security.

Graduate instruction at Temple had gone forward for some time—the first master's degrees were awarded in 1925—without much concern for university standards and consistency and without guidelines and basic standards. Master's degree programs in Business, Education, and Liberal Arts began to proliferate. To alleviate the problem, in 1946 Temple established a University Graduate Council (later renamed the Graduate Board) with authority to develop policies to cover graduate education within the entire institution. Initially the president appointed its members, and the provost chaired the Graduate Council. The first PhD proposals came from English and Chemistry (1947), then Physics (1948) and Psychology (1949).

One of the first tests of the Graduate Council's power came in 1958 when the Medical School proposed to create a PhD program but Dean Parkinson insisted that it be independent of the rest of the university and not subject to Graduate Council oversight. Finally, President Johnson had to step in and tell Parkinson that either his program came under the Graduate Council or there would be no program.

In June 1955 commencement speaker Vice President Richard M. Nixon received an honorary degree from Temple president Robert L. Johnson.

Carl Sandburg, winner of Pulitzer prizes for poetry and biography, was surrounded by admiring students and faculty during a campus visit in 1949, when he delivered a convocation address in Mitten Hall auditorium.

The Middle States evaluation in 1956 called for a number of reforms in the way Temple offered and supervised graduate education. When inaugurated in 1959, President Gladfelter promised to strengthen graduate affairs further. In March 1960, at his recommendation, the trustees authorized the establishment of the Graduate School of Temple University. The Graduate School's mission was to encourage new programs, provide basic standards for graduate programs, and assign responsibility for policy formulation, without threatening the autonomy of the schools and departments. The Graduate School was assigned responsibility for coordinating and administering graduate affairs. Its first dean was Dr. George H. Huganir (BA CLA 1938), a professor of sociology who had earned his PhD at the University of Pennsylvania.

The Graduate Council was replaced by the Graduate Board, which included elected representatives of all schools engaged in graduate instruction. By 1965 more than 6,600 graduate students, almost all part-timers, were enrolled at Temple; that number surpassed 9,500 by 1969. A 1967 Middle States team complimented Temple for its vigor in pursuing doctoral programs, increasing teaching assistant appointments, and improving library holdings.

Faculty

Doctoral programs required tenured full professors. Of course, the more published, more highly accomplished, and more marketable faculty demanded higher salaries. Senior scholars also demanded released time for research and reduced course loads with fewer students. And they preferred to teach only advanced undergraduate courses or, ideally, small doctoral seminars. All required more funding and drove up institutional expenditures dramatically. In the 1960s these needs meant an increasing reliance on teaching assistants or adjunct instructors and part-timers to teach lower-level courses.

Faculty gains—increased incomes, greater prestige, and protections—were substantial from 1945 to 1965. Faculty marketability notably rose as Temple and other institutions desiring to enhance their national reputations sought experienced, accomplished faculty members. Added to that were generous levels of support from the state and federal governments through the 1960s. President Robert Johnson spoke often of the need to increase Temple faculty salaries and benefits, and the record indicates that he and Provost Millard Gladfelter succeeded.

Faculty salaries were frozen in 1941 because of the war, but by 1959 the average salary for a full professor had tripled and then doubled again by 1973. A comparison of faculty salaries in 1973 showed that faculty salaries at the University of Pennsylvania were slightly higher than at Temple, but according to the *Temple Faculty Herald*, those at the University of Pittsburgh and Penn State University were not.

Faculty pensions were first discussed in 1925 and some "gifts" were doled out selectively in the late 1930s and early 1940s, but entering the postwar era Temple faculty had no dependable plan. As the number of faculty and employee retirements increased, the need for a consistent plan became more evident. In 1946 the board of trustees offered the first pension plan, setting "normal" retirement at age sixty-five and making employees and faculty eligible after five years. Faculty and employees were required to contribute a portion of their base pay, matched by the university. The maximum benefit, however, was $3,000 a year. Improvements to the plan came in 1957, 1961, 1963, and 1965—retirement was permitted at sixty-five but compulsory at sixty-seven. The maximum annuity was dropped, and the university, faculty, and employee contributions were increased. The Teachers Insurance and Annuity Association described the plan as "one of the very best in the nation." In addition, in 1950 the Social Security Act was amended to make its old-age pension provisions available for the first time to university personnel, and Temple immediately joined the plan.

Unlike most colleges and universities, Temple did not provide for periodic faculty sabbaticals or paid leaves for intellectual refreshment or retooling. Instead, Temple's administration favored a program of competitive study leaves, in which full salaries were paid for a one-semester leave or half salaries for a full year's leave, upon the submission of an approved plan of study. Only faculty with an approved research plan were granted time off from teaching.

Faculty governance remained a persistent issue. After the war the Faculty Senate's influence declined. Senate bylaws called for the university president to preside at Senate meetings, but he was often absent. Moreover, the Senate had no parliamentarian and its procedures were quite loose. Some faculty felt the proceedings were manipulated by faculty "politicians" and not worth the effort to participate; still others saw the Senate as a debating society with no real power or function. English professor Ernest P. Earnest chaired a committee to study the situation, and its report called for a complete reorganization of the Senate. A new constitution was approved in May 1949. It enlarged membership to include all professors of all ranks who had served three years on the undergraduate faculties. Instructors were represented by two persons of that rank selected by the instructors. Each professional school and the Community College elected a representative. The president, provost, deans, and librarian were ex officio members, which muted some of the criticism.

In 1961 Temple's ROTC unit led the homecoming parade up Broad Street.

Real gains were made when criteria for promotion and tenure were codified in a faculty handbook drafted by the Personnel Committee and approved by the president and when faculty were consulted in the selection of administrative officials above the rank of dean. However, the board of trustees frequently turned down expressed concerns of the faculty and refused to surrender any of its rights, powers, or prerogatives to the faculty. In 1957 the Senate asked the board to invite a committee of faculty to sit with the board as non-voting members. The board refused, but a few years later, of its own volition, began inviting two faculty members to be its guests at regular meetings.

The Korean War

The invasion of South Korea by North Korean forces in June 1950 and the U.S. entry into the war put Temple and the nation back on a wartime footing. Student elections went on as usual; campus clubs and sororities and fraternities remained active, but by December these activities were tempered by the gravity of world events. ROTC cadets drilled with a new earnestness, and students lined up in Mitten Hall to donate blood to the Red Cross. Christmas wreaths adorned Mitten Hall and the A Cappella Choir and the Chorus, under the direction of Elaine Brown, performed their annual Christmas concert, but campus life was hardly normal.

Concerned about world affairs, a delegation of Temple student leaders journeyed to the United Nations in New York City and received a personal briefing from former first lady and U.S. delegate Eleanor Roosevelt. By 1951 almost 400 Temple men had received their pre-induction notices and nearly 100 had been called up when their reserve units were activated.

Cold War Jitters

The growing importance of higher education, combined with America's deepening fear of international communism and the Soviet Union, made the personal loyalty and conduct of professors an issue of national security. In addition, the infusion of federal and state funding brought greater surveillance of university conduct and speculation about its mission. At Temple this tension was manifested in the name of one man, Barrows Dunham.

Cold War jitters and fears of communist conspiracies brought state legislatures and the U.S. Congress to investigate faculty teaching, publications, and political associations. Senator Joseph R. McCarthy (R-WI) and others in Congress sought to rid the government, schools, universities, and motion picture industry of persons of known or suspected radical leanings. Many states responded by requiring teachers and professors to take loyalty oaths as a condition of employment.

When such a bill was introduced in the Pennsylvania General Assembly, Temple students immediately organized in protest and 800 students signed a petition opposing the bill, believing its provisions would intimidate their professors. Others at Temple, including the university trustees, did not see the harm in requiring faculty to affirm their loyalty. In December 1951 a jam-packed Mitten Hall was the scene of a heated debate that presented both sides of the question. Afterward, the *Temple University News* said the debate "reaffirmed our faith in the integrity of the University."

As finally enacted, the Pennsylvania Loyalty Act (known as the Pechan Act) did not require faculty loyalty oaths but it did require the university to certify annually that no one on the payroll was a "subversive person" and to list exceptions. A report to the governor in effect determined whether Temple would receive an appropriation for the year.

Professor Barrows Dunham, chairman, Department of Philosophy, in 1950.

Professor Barrows Dunham was summoned in February 1953 to appear before the U.S. House Un-American Activities Committee (HUAC). Dunham, like his father James Dunham, retired dean of the College of Liberal Arts, was a respected and well-published philosopher. Before testifying, he freely admitted to Temple officials that from 1938 to 1945 he had been a member of the Communist Political Association and had resigned because he ceased to believe in the economic promises of the Communist Party, a legal political party when Dunham joined. Neither he nor anyone associated with Dunham thought he was a radical subversive. But Dunham regarded the HUAC hearings as an inquisition and believed they only wanted him to "name names" and implicate others. When called, he refused to answer any questions, invoked his Fifth Amendment rights, and was cited for contempt of Congress.

Two days later, President Johnson suspended Dunham. At a May hearing before the Temple Committee on the Loyalty Act, Dunham affirmed his loyalty and vigorously denied that he would contribute by word or deed to any kind of revolutionary violence. Dunham's students, past and present, rallied to his cause. None believed that a man of his learning and charm could be a menace to the Republic. "Far from leading his students to believe in Communism," said a spokesperson for a group of his students, "Dr. Dunham has inspired them to think and to lead themselves."

Fearing the loss of the state appropriation, the board of trustees fired Dunham in September 1953. In 1955 the U.S. District Court ruled that Dunham had been within his rights in invoking the Fifth Amendment and acquitted him of the contempt charge. But the trustees refused to reconsider.

Twenty years and three books later, Dunham bore Temple no ill will. That year a group of Temple faculty and administrators took up the Dunham case again, sparked by Fred Zimring, a member of the Academic Advising staff in Liberal Arts. Over the next several years the Temple Faculty Senate repeatedly urged the president and trustees to reinstate Dunham, arguing that Dunham's defense of his own constitutional rights preserved and strengthened the constitutional rights of every citizen.

Finally, in July 1981 the trustees acknowledged that Temple had erred in dismissing Dunham twenty-eight years earlier and, acting upon the recommendation of President Marvin Wachman, agreed to reinstate Dunham as professor emeritus with a lifetime pension. The reinstatement, Wachman told the Faculty Senate, "removes a painful vestige of McCarthyism, that sad and bitter period in our history." It also removed Temple from the AAUP censure list, where it had been since Dunham's firing. Dunham returned to Temple in November 1981 and before a packed audience delivered a gracious, erudite lecture—"The Tradition of Tenderness in American Culture." He reminded listeners of Russell Conwell's noble vision for Temple and urged listeners to be ever mindful of "how close this University lies to the hearts of the people of this Commonwealth." On April 19, 1982, the Faculty Senate welcomed Dunham back to the University with a special tribute to an extraordinary man of character who was the conscience of american society during one of its most troubled times.

Campus Life

Beginning in 1948 and continuing through the 1950s, freshman orientation was held away from campus, usually at a summer camp location in the suburbs where the students engaged in team sports, campfire songs, and faculty lectures and generally got to know each other. The goal was to develop a sense of team spirit and welcome fledgling owls into the flock.

Clubs, sororities, and fraternities participated actively in campus life, building floats for the annual homecoming parade down Broad Street, joining fund-raising activities to aid local charities, and leading special programs put on by Student Affairs. The Panhellenic House was home base for

TEMPLE NOTABLE
Richard Brooks

A journalism major at Temple in the 1930s, Richard Brooks is shown here directing film stars Burt Lancaster and Shirley Jones in *Elmer Gantry*. Known at Temple as Reuben Sax, he was told by his first boss, the editor of the *Kansas City Star*, "From now on you are Richard Brooks, Mr. Sax." Brooks wrote several novels and successful screenplays, including *Brute Force*, *Key Largo*, and *Brick Foxhole*. He later became a movie director and directed and wrote such films as *The Brothers Karamazov*, *Blackboard Jungle*, *Something of Value*, and *Cat on a Hot Tin Roof*. He won an Academy Award for *Elmer Gantry*.

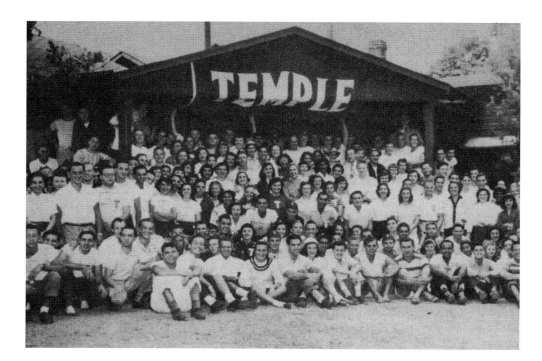

In the fall of 1949, 130 members of the class of 1953 attended freshman camp. Gertrude Peabody, dean of women, developed freshman orientation camps, which started in 1948 at Camp Hilltop in Downingtown, Pennsylvania. Freshman camp was replaced in the early 1960s with on-campus summer orientation sessions.

sorority women, providing a chapter room for each sorority for meetings and small social gatherings, plus three living rooms for general use.

A 1961 survey of the composition and motivation of Temple students revealed that over 11,000 of Temple's 28,000 students took courses in the fully accredited Evening Division of the university, attending classes from 6:30 to 9:30 P.M., Monday through Friday. Half of the evening students were between the ages of twenty-three and thirty-four; almost all of them were employed full-time. "They dress well and own cars," reported the *Temple Review*. More than half already held college degrees and were seeking advanced degrees or teacher certification. "Many of them," the *Review* found, "have made down payments on modest homes in the suburbs."

Right *Students studying in a Temple dormitory room, circa 1965.*

Below *Spring 1954 marked the tenth anniversary of the Penny Preakness, an annual contest between Frosh-Junior and Sophomore-Senior classes. The team with the longer line of pennies won. Proceeds of the contest were donated to the Salvation Army.*

DAVID ROSS L. GOLDSTEIN D. O'LENIK CURT NOEL

CAPTAIN

TEMPLE UNIVERSITY

GE College Bowl champions, 1963: Temple's College Bowl team is pictured here in the first and toughest of its matches, a 280–235 victory over Yeshiva University. The team went on to win five matches and retired undefeated, earning a place in the College Bowl Hall of Fame.

A survey a year later found that 62 percent of the full-time undergraduate student body worked part-time. Typically, students worked as supermarket checkers, waiters, clerks, typists, or even bus drivers. Some of the more unusual part-time positions included hand model (Pat Darwin); veterinarian's assistant (Jerry Hershovitz); barber (Rick Grabfelder); Moscow monitor, listening to Radio Moscow (Richard Subin); magician's assistant (Dorothy Lerner Richards); puppeteer (Eva Schultz-Herda); and, most famously, comedian (Bill Cosby). Then a sophomore physical education major, the "Coz," as his classmates called him, earned upwards of sixteen dollars a night entertaining in center city nightclubs.

Temple undergraduates David Ross (pre-med major), Leonard Goldstein (team captain, English major), Dolores O'Lenik (English major), and Curt Noel (history major) represented Temple in the General Electric College Bowl in the spring of 1963. The nationally televised show, broadcast live from New York City, pitted teams of four from each college against each other. Contestants matched wits in a rapid-fire quiz requiring them to buzz in electrically to answer questions before their opponents. Temple's College Bowl team was expertly coached by Dr. Sidney Axinn, chairman of the Philosophy Department. Temple earned a place in the College Bowl Hall of Fame by defeating five opponents—Yeshiva University, University of Alaska, St. Mary's College, University of California at Santa Barbara, and Bucknell University—retiring undefeated, and bringing home $9,000 in scholarship money for Temple.

By 1965 more students were remaining on the campus after classes. With the addition of new dormitories—Peabody, Johnson, and Hardwick halls—the campus began to acquire a real residential life. An addition to Mitten Hall gave students more space and places for commuter students to relax between classes. With the availability of South Hall, students also had more locations for swimming (besides the pool in the basement of Conwell Hall) and participation in vigorous intramural athletic programs.

Presidential candidate John Fitzgerald Kennedy addressed thousands of Temple students on Park Avenue (now Liacouras Walk) behind Curtis Hall in October 1960.

Students attending Temple in the fall of 1960 vividly recall the day when Senator John F. Kennedy of Massachusetts visited the campus during the presidential campaign. Wearing a rain slicker and his famous toothy smile, he addressed a throng of the curious and the partisan along Park Avenue (now Liacouras Walk). All also surely remember where they were just three short years later on November 22, 1963. The gift of the class of 1965 created a small garden (since covered over by Alter Hall) to commemorate JFK's 1960 visit.

Chapter 5
Vehicle for Social Change, 1965–1982

The years from 1965 to 1982 were among the most flourishing and eventful, yet also the most trying and anxious, in Temple's history. For America these years were memorable for the simultaneous collision of major social developments, including the rediscovery of poverty in the midst of plenty, the civil rights revolution, changing gender roles, anti-war fervor, and youth demands for participatory democracy—all of which left lasting imprints on Temple.

TEMPLE UNIVERSITY TIMELINE

1965
Temple becomes a state-affiliated institution.

1966
Paley Library opens.
Temple Rome opens.

1967
Paul Anderson is named Temple's fifth president.

1969
The College of Engineering and the School of Social Administration are established.

1973
Marvin Wachman becomes Temple's sixth president.
Temple University Center City (TUCC) opens at 1619 Walnut Street.

1980
President Jimmy Carter holds a town meeting in McGonigle Hall.

1982
Peter J. Liacouras becomes Temple's seventh president.
Temple University Japan opens.

For Temple these years opened with high expectations, booming enrollments, unprecedented growth, and physical expansion brought by state affiliation. But they closed on a dark note as the harsh realities of sudden enrollment declines, community turmoil, student unrest, faculty dissatisfaction, and unpredictable political and economic fluctuations tested Temple's confidence and left the university facing yet another financial crisis.

Temple's middle passage gradually redirected the university away from thinking of itself as a private institution dedicated to the public interest and toward serious consideration of formal state affiliation as a means to accommodate the growing demand for higher education and to open the door to a larger, more ambitious future. The final step, however, was neither easy nor uneventful. It brought many consequences, some of them unintended.

Having made the decision to stay, Temple sought a permanent foothold in North Philadelphia. But its credibility and legitimacy were frequently challenged by turmoil stirred within the decaying inner city and the revolution of rising expectations. At the same time Temple was challenged from within by the growing momentum of student activism and faculty uneasiness. At times Temple seemed at war with itself. But the collective impact of seemingly perpetual tension left the university more attuned to itself and its many constituencies, more in sync with the changes occurring around it, and re-dedicated to its role as an instrument for social change.

The Sixties

American higher education was changed in the 1960s by the growth in student enrollments and the direct impact of social changes occurring across America. America was now an information society, its economy and public life driven to a great extent by a knowledge industry based in its colleges and universities. But Temple did more than react to society's changing educational needs. Temple was stirred to a new awareness of its broader obligations.

The sixties witnessed rising government involvement in higher education. Federal support of higher education, first proposed by President John F. Kennedy and instituted by President Lyndon B. Johnson, meant greater availability of student financial aid and more direct support for the university, along with expanded involvement in the university's internal affairs. But for Temple the most significant impact was its growing dependence on the Commonwealth of Pennsylvania for student financial aid, operating costs, and capital expenses, culminating in the 1965 agreement to become state-affiliated and a part of the Commonwealth System of Higher Education.

State Affiliation

Temple's enrollments rose in the immediate postwar years, dropped off slightly in the early 1950s because of the reduced 1930s' birthrates, increased dramatically in the early 1960s with the arrival of "war babies" born during the war, and then surged with the infusion of the baby boom generation, the unparalleled explosion in America's birthrate in the immediate postwar years. Temple's campus and virtually all of America's universities filled to capacity.

More than rising birthrates contributed to Temple's enrollment increases, however. By the 1960s, access to higher education had become the principal gateway to upward social mobility. Many of Temple's students continued to be the first in their families to attend college, brought there because of fast-growing changes in the American economy and consequent changes in the nature of the American Dream—and often because their parents willingly sacrificed to help their children get ahead.

Temple projected that enrollment would increase by approximately 900 students each year beginning in 1961 and continue through to the exhaustion of the baby boom generation, adding about $800,000 in annual costs. One alternative for raising additional revenue was to institute a large tuition increase, but Temple historically had kept tuition low because such a large proportion of its students

Temple's impressive iron gates holding the university seal were created and installed at the Eighteenth and Buttonwood campus. In 1960 they were moved to the Main Campus and re-installed at the Broad Street entrance to Berks Mall, linking the Baptist Temple and Mitten Hall.

came from financially strapped families and circumstances. Another option might have been to draw on the endowment, except that Temple's minuscule endowment was of no consequence. Neither could the university rely on large philanthropic gifts. In short, Temple required commonwealth support to meet Pennsylvania's higher-education needs in the Philadelphia region.

President Millard Gladfelter was determined to increase the state government's responsibility for Temple's obligations either through a state relationship or by conveying Temple to the commonwealth. He began meeting in 1960 with key people in Harrisburg, including legislative floor leaders, the budget director, and the governor's staff. That year, state budget officials asked state-aided colleges and universities if they would be interested in a program whereby tuitions would be reduced and enrollments expanded in conjunction with increased financial support and commonwealth representation on the institutions' boards of trustees.

Temple immediately consented. In return for additional funding, the university agreed to seat trustees appointed by commonwealth officers and to set differential tuition for resident and non-resident students. The arrangement enabled Temple to cut tuition by $100 for over 7,000 full-time undergraduate Pennsylvania residents and to add 900 students. Gladfelter proposed to Governor David Lawrence a "closer relationship" between Temple and the state, one that ensured lower tuition for Pennsylvania residents, expanded enrollment, and an increased appropriation to cover higher costs. Lawrence responded by recommending that Temple's 1962–1963 appropriation be increased 74 percent. The governor's January 1962 address to the General Assembly noted that 82 percent of Temple's students were Pennsylvania residents. Lawrence therefore requested the legislature to bring Temple "more closely into the Commonwealth's higher education system, making it more comparable to Penn State than to the other state-supported schools."

Lawrence, a Democrat, soon left office, replaced by William W. Scranton, a Republican. A Yale-educated lawyer, banker, and congressman, Scranton was hesitant to follow through on Lawrence's commitments. Gladfelter sent Scranton a letter, insisting "It is too late to retreat." Additional faculty and staff had been recruited and program commitments already made. Former president Robert L. Johnson, a close friend of Scranton and still a major factor in Republican circles, appealed to Scranton, stressing the benefit of what he called an "ideal" public-private partnership in shared responsibility. If not supported by the state, Johnson told Scranton, Temple would have no choice but to raise tuition, curtail services, and reduce its commitment to Pennsylvania's most populous region.

In the fall of 1964 the Council of Higher Education held hearings in Philadelphia. Testifying for Temple were Gladfelter and Professor Leon Ovsiew, chairman of the Faculty Senate Steering Committee. Both men urged that the council write the basics of the Temple proposal into its master plan to clarify the state's provisions for higher education. Both also stressed Temple's role and contributions as an urban university. Gladfelter itemized Temple's contributions to the community in the form of health clinics, legal aid, and help with psychological problems, recreational resources, and organizational support for community groups.

Gaylord P. Harnwell, president of the University of Pennsylvania, joined Gladfelter in urging immediate action on Temple's proposal. Unlike in Boston, where each of the major universities — Harvard, MIT, Boston College, Boston University, Northeastern University, and Tufts—worked out a formal compact to carve out a distinctive mission aimed at a specific constituency, Philadelphia's largest

FACT

Temple University is the third-largest private employer in the city of Philadelphia.

higher-education institutions—Temple, Penn, and Drexel—never signed a compact or worked out a formal agreement, preferring instead to work together informally.

The alternative to making Temple a state-related institution was for the commonwealth to build a new state university of the scope and size of Penn State somewhere in the Philadelphia region. Such an institution would require an enormous expenditure in state funds and take many years to establish. Meanwhile, the immediate need for higher education in the region would go unmet. Gladfelter argued that designating Temple a state-related institution would give the people of the state the immediate benefit of an established institution.

Legislators agreed, and a bill moved through the Pennsylvania House in the spring of 1965. Consultations and reconciliations occurred throughout the summer, with Temple's president and trustees directly involved. In November the bill cleared the General Assembly. Governor Scranton invited Gladfelter and others to watch him sign into law the Temple University Commonwealth Act on November 30, 1965. The act designated Temple a "state-related" institution and an instrumentality of the Commonwealth System of Higher Education to provide higher-education opportunities to Pennsylvania citizens, effective July 1, 1965.

On November 30, 1965, Governor William W. Scranton signed Act 355, making Temple University a state-related institution. Scranton is flanked by Millard E. Gladfelter, president of Temple (left), and Judge Charles Klein, chairman of the board of trustees (right).

Temple's state relationship, basically the same as Penn State's, specified that Temple's board of trustees be composed of twenty-four university trustees and twelve commonwealth trustees—four appointed by the governor, four by the president pro tempore of the Senate, and four by the Speaker of the House. Temple, like Penn State, remained a private corporation "invested with a quasi-public character and charged with certain public responsibilities."

At about the same time, several other recommendations of the Council of Higher Education went into effect. The fourteen state-owned teachers colleges were transformed into state colleges (later universities) broadly based on the arts and sciences and governed under the state System of Higher Education. Funds were appropriated to assist counties in creating community colleges to provide two-year programs. Penn State University was given financial support to open additional centers in areas of greatest need. And the University of Pittsburgh and Lincoln University joined Temple and Penn State University as state-affiliated universities within the Commonwealth System of Higher Education. To meet Pennsylvanians' growing demands for student financial aid, the General Assembly established the Pennsylvania Higher Education Assistance Agency (PHEAA). Beginning as a small student loan guarantor in 1964, PHEAA expanded into one of the largest full-service financial aid organizations in the nation and by 2008 managed approximately $80 billion in total assets to assist Pennsylvania residents in attending the college of their choice.

Affiliation Aftermath

The impact of state affiliation on Temple was immediate. A boost in the annual appropriation to $11 million allowed Temple in the fall of 1967 to reduce tuition for Pennsylvania residents from $920 to $450. Non-residents were charged $1,350 a year. By 1968–1969 the annual commonwealth appropriation jumped to $33.4 million. It rose more slowly and unevenly thereafter, enough so that the university soon complained of an "Appropriations Gap" between Temple's requests and the actual allotment. Still, over the next six years, average faculty salaries for professors doubled, the university's annual contribution to faculty and staff retirement funds increased, faculty teaching loads decreased, university-supported research doubled and re-doubled, and library holdings doubled. Increased state funding permitted the recruitment of additional faculty, the creation of new doctoral programs, additional funding for research, and the additions of academic journals, a university press, a new library, and Temple's first overseas program.

Under the terms of the state-affiliation accord and the Master Plan for Higher Education, Temple agreed to focus on baccalaureate, graduate, and professional education. Among other things, that meant jettisoning the Temple High School and the Temple Community College, two vestiges of past attempts at comprehensive responses to the community's educational needs. The Temple High School, in existence since 1894, held its final graduation in 1968 and its programs were relocated to the central YMCA.

The Temple Community College had opened in September 1948 in response to faculty surveys that indicated a substantial unmet need in Philadelphia for two-year vocational-training programs. Under the direction of Dean Charles A. Ford, the Community College was the first in the state to offer two-year associate's degrees in business, technology, and the arts, with several specialties, including a program in mortuary science offered jointly with the Eckels College of Mortuary Science. The Community College and Temple's Technical Institute—Temple's evening school technical arm since 1921—were joined in 1948 and moved into the recently vacated buildings at Eighteenth and Buttonwood streets. In 1952 they relocated to the Cedarbrook Center at Sedgwick Street and Cheltenham Avenue next to Temple Stadium in four buildings erected initially to handle the overflow of returning veterans after World War II.

Flourishing for a time, Temple Community College had its own library, student organizations, newspaper, intramural athletics associations, and at its peak twenty-seven full-time faculty instructing 2,200 students who were not required to meet Temple's regular academic admission standards. Operating somewhat independently from the university, the Community College was separately accredited by the Middle States Association and its basketball team competed against other teams in the Pennsylvania Junior College Association.

In compliance with the Commonwealth Master Plan for Higher Education, President Gladfelter announced in December 1966 that the Community College would close, effective June 1968. The Master Plan charged Temple to focus on four-year programs and beyond, leaving two-year programs to be offered in locally sponsored state-funded community colleges, such as Philadelphia Com-

1965

A Year to Remember

Temple enrolled a record-breaking number of freshman students, Muhammad Ali (aka Cassius Clay) won the heavyweight boxing championship, Sandy Koufax pitched a perfect game, Bill Cosby won an Emmy as best actor for *I Spy*. As the refrain of the Rolling Stones' "I Can't Get No Satisfaction" echoed across the land, America fretted over the escalation of the war in Vietnam, a race riot in the Los Angeles ghetto of Watts, the brutal suppression of a civil rights march at Selma, Alabama, and the assassination of Malcolm X in Harlem. Students pictured above gathered to hear Jane Fonda speak.

munity College, which opened in 1965. Temple's Technical Institute relocated to the Main Campus in Stauffer Hall (since demolished). In May 1969 the trustees merged the Technical Institute into the new College of Engineering Technology.

Closing the high school and community college freed additional resources for Temple to improve its stature as a center of academic excellence. In the eight years following state affiliation Temple established eighteen new academic departments and three new schools and colleges, increasing the number of full-time faculty by almost 50 percent. The overall quality of the faculty improved, as 76 percent of the Temple faculty held doctorates in 1973, compared with only 54 percent in 1967. Experienced and accomplished faculty members were recruited away from prestigious institutions to staff Temple's new departments and create or expand graduate programs and research centers.

In short order a dozen new PhD programs and nearly fifty new master's degree programs were in place. Many of the new programs were within the College of Liberal Arts, which attracted a sizable number of eminent scholars, particularly to its newly formed Religion Department and to its Philosophy, English, Political Science, and History departments, which already claimed many productive scholars. Liberal Arts also boasted the addition of several prestigious academic journals, including *Publius* (the publication of the new Center for the Study of Federalism); the *Journal of Ecumenical Studies*, edited by Leonard Swidler; the *Journal of Modern Literature*; and the *Journal of the History of Ideas*, which Temple attracted away from Johns Hopkins University.

New graduate programs spurred externally funded research. To coordinate Temple's research efforts, Dr. Edwin P. Adkins, former vice president and dean of faculties at Indiana State University, was brought in as director of the Office of Research and Program Development. Three important research centers were added: the Center for the Study of Federalism, the Institute for Survey Research, and the Higher Education Center, headed by Dr. Earl J. McGrath, former U.S. commissioner of education. Adkins's efforts raised Temple's total research budget in 1965–1966 to over $11 million—a vast difference from 1942, when President Johnson took $8,000 from his own pocket to fund research—but still far short of the sums raised by Temple's cross-state peers, Penn State University and the University of Pittsburgh.

Temple University Press

The idea for establishing a university press at Temple surfaced in the early 1940s when Temple made agreements, first with the University of Pennsylvania and then with Columbia University, to use their facilities to publish books under the Temple University imprint. The Publications Committee of the Faculty Senate, chaired by Hughbert Hamilton, professor and chair of psychology, selected and evaluated manuscripts for publication, but the awkward, costly arrangement often meant that the prestige garnered by successful books tended to go to Penn and Columbia instead of Temple.

Temple's aspirations for attaining a place in the upper tier of research universities led the Faculty Senate in 1965 to recommend the formation of a university press as a publishing outlet for the expanding faculty and as a means of broadening Temple's academic reach. The board of trustees subsequently approved creation of the Temple University Press, and in 1969 Maurice English, senior editor at the University of Chicago Press, was appointed director. The first books complemented Temple's urban mission, focusing on communications, world literature, and social, ethnic, and urban history. Among the first university presses to recognize the scholarly value of publications on women's studies, African

A sampling of recent Temple University Press publications.

American studies, Asian American studies, and the study of race, Temple University Press won early election to full membership in the Association of American University Presses.

Maurice English was succeeded by David M. Bartlett, who lifted the academic reputation of the Press. One 1983 publication ranked Temple University Press as the third-best university press, behind only Harvard and Princeton. Hard times followed, however, and mounting losses necessitated leadership changes and even threatened the continued existence of the Press. Yet the Press maintained high scholarly standards and won many awards. Temple's publications in Asian American studies virtually reshaped the discipline, earning a Lifetime Achievement Award from the Association for Asian American Studies. Temple made a fresh commitment to the Press with the arrival of Alex Holzman, who left Cambridge University Press to assume Temple's directorship in 2003. Each year since, two or more Temple University Press books have been named by *Choice* magazine as Outstanding Academic Titles, adding luster to Temple's academic reputation.

Paley Library

Temple needed a first-rate library to support its elevated emphasis on graduate studies and faculty research. Temple's first library, which developed around Conwell's personal book collection, was established in 1892 in a row house at 1833 Park Avenue (the present site of Speakman Hall). Two years later, it moved into College Hall (now Barrack Hall) and then in 1936 to Sullivan Hall. Despite its charm and impressive Gothic beauty, Sullivan Hall proved inadequate in meeting the demands of a modern university research library and the needs of faculty and student populations that quadrupled between 1936 and 1966.

Paley Library opened in 1966 on land purchased and cleared by city and state agencies just south of Berks Street between Twelfth and Thirteenth streets. Construction costs of $5,350,000 were financed by the General State Authority (GSA). Equipment and furnishings were paid for with a $1 million grant from the Samuel Paley Foundation. Samuel Paley once owned the Congress Cigar Company at Third and Spruce streets in Philadelphia, reputedly the largest in the world. Paley's son, William S. Paley, chairman of the board of the Columbia Broadcasting System, delivered the dedicatory address in October 1966.

Paley Library, circa 1969.

The new library featured open stacks; study carrels; separate rooms for maps, micromaterials, and the Hausdorfer Rare Book Room; student lounges; a lecture hall; and the Conwellana-Templana Collection, with its rich assortment of materials dealing with the founding and history of Temple. Within just a few years, Paley Library, under the energetic direction of Arthur T. Hamlin, increased its holdings to over one million volumes.

Gifts from the Samuel Paley Foundation also permitted construction of a campanile, a freestanding bell tower set within a plaza in front of the library. Encased under glass at the foot of the 105-foot-tall bell tower was a collection of rocks from Pakistan, purportedly one of the places of origin of the "Acres of Diamonds" legend. The campanile included a carillon, with five bells cast in Holland's Van Bergen Foundry and electrically controlled to chime the Westminster hour and to play the Temple alma mater each day at noon and 6:00 P.M. The landscaped bell tower plaza separating Paley Library

Above left *In 1981 the card catalogs and circulation desk dominated the ground floor of Paley Library.*

Left *In 2009 computer terminals assist students in their searches for books and documents.*

Above *Students relax on Beury Beach.*

and Beury Hall quickly became the most popular meeting place for pep rallies and other student events. In warm weather, students gathered for impromptu Hacky Sack or Frisbee games or sunned themselves on the lawns known as Beury Beach.

Paul R. Anderson

Taking stock in 1966, Millard Gladfelter could look back with satisfaction over his thirty-seven years of service to Temple University. His principal contribution was his unerring and indefatigable labor on behalf of securing Temple's state-related status, a decision that changed the university as no other since its founding. Temple's total number of part-time and full-time enrollments stood at just over 31,000, the number of faculty at more than 2,300, and the budget at $57 million. Moreover, extensive plans for physical and programmatic expansion were firmly in place on July 1, 1967, when Gladfelter turned over his presidential office to Paul Russell Anderson.

Paul R. Anderson, Temple's fifth president, served from 1967 to 1973.

Anderson, a philosophy professor, author of notable works such as *Platonism in the Midwest*, and an expert on Henry James, came to Temple as vice president for academic affairs in 1960. Before that he was president of the 600-student, all-female Chatham College in Pittsburgh for fifteen years. Anderson's succession to the Temple presidency was expected, long before the trustees made it official. Soon after his arrival, former president Robert Johnson confidently introduced Anderson to a social gathering as "the next president of Temple University."

Anderson's unfailingly calm public demeanor masked a sturdy, forceful management style. An inveterate pipe smoker, the bespectacled president seemed the archetypal college professor, but he managed Temple's administration in a firm, no-nonsense manner. A writer for *Philadelphia* magazine saw him as "heavy-handed" and "inconsistent." George Ingram (BS SBM 1962), the former News Bureau director who worked closely with Anderson, described him as "a flinty native Ohioan who could, when necessary, display toughness more in keeping with a corporate board room than the ivied walls of Conwell Hall."

Anderson's presidency—seen initially as an opportunity to consolidate gains made during the Johnson and Gladfelter years—immediately collided with several massive forces sweeping across American higher education. Most notably, students disputed university authority and faculty challenged university governing systems. These actions were compounded by anti–Vietnam War protests and stunning transformations in the balance of power within Philadelphia and the neighborhoods surrounding Temple that soon spawned an all-out confrontation between Temple and the African American community. The immense, simultaneous impact of these issues made Anderson's presidency one of the most trying and difficult in Temple's history. Out of it, however, came lasting, beneficial changes.

Physical Expansion

The Anderson years, from 1967 to 1973, included the most substantial period of physical expansion in Temple's history. During those years more than 2.6 million square feet of new facilities were completed or nearly so. John G. McKevitt was brought in from the University of Michigan as associate vice president for campus planning, responsible for carrying through on ambitious plans laid years earlier.

Most of those plans were initiated back in 1954 when trustees approved a multi-million-dollar program to modernize the Main Campus. By then the Dental and Pharmacy schools were ensconced at the Health Sciences Center, funds and plans for a new medical center and hospital were in place, and plans were solidified for the long-awaited Main Campus classroom facility (Curtis Hall).

108

Temple University: 125 Years of Service

In addition, the City Planning Commission and the Redevelopment Authority had set aside a thirty-eight-acre Institutional Development District (IDD) at the Main Campus.

Even thirty-eight acres of campus development seemed ambitious in 1954, but within a few years, as the Redevelopment Authority purchased and cleared more land, even grander plans were drawn up to expand Temple's Main Campus to 140 acres and, then, ultimately to 207 acres by the 1990s. It was never to be, of course, but plans once existed on drawing boards to expand Temple's Main Campus in North Philadelphia to more than twice the size it would be in 2009.

To provide a workable blueprint for such grandiose plans, Temple's trustees commissioned the architectural firm of Nolen & Swinburne Associates to develop a Master Site Plan. Unveiled in 1954, the plan proclaimed that Temple had entered its "golden age." Published reports in 1955 stated that only Conwell, Carnell, College, Mitten, and Sullivan halls would remain after the removal of the "blighted area around the present campus." The "squeeze of the slum area is becoming intolerable," reported the plan's framers, making it necessary "to wipe the slate clean from the ground up." Ten years later, the summer 1965 issue of the *Temple Review* featured pictures of smiling donors such as Mr. and Mrs. Walter H. Annenberg flanking President Gladfelter as they ceremonially sledgehammered row houses standing in the path of Temple's progress.

The Master Site Plan called for the closing of several streets to provide "room to grow." Park Avenue, Berks and Norris streets, and "many of the small streets" intersecting the campus were destined, according to the plan, to "disappear from the campus area." In place of demolished row houses the plan envisioned a classic campus quadrangle, an assemblage of buildings defining the campus edges and framing an interior of walkways, cloister gardens, and lawns.

With encouragement from city and state officials, Temple's expansion plans by 1965 encompassed an area extending from Columbia Avenue (now Cecil B. Moore Avenue) on the south, northward to Diamond Street, eastward to the Reading Railroad tracks (now the SEPTA Regional Rail tracks), and westward to Eighteenth Street (four blocks west of Broad Street). Plans called for two phases of development: 1965 to 1967, with five buildings costing $27 million planned for construction, and 1968 to 1970, when an additional nine buildings totaling $77 million were scheduled to be built.

Expansion began in earnest in 1965. A $4.6 million Federal Urban Renewal grant to the city's Redevelopment Authority was used to acquire and clear land bounded by Twelfth and Thirteenth streets, Diamond and Norris streets, and Columbia (now Cecil B. Moore) and Montgomery avenues.

Ritter Hall, the first building to be erected by the GSA, was located on newly cleared land south of Montgomery Avenue between Park Avenue (now Liacouras Walk) and Thirteenth Street. The new structure housed the College of Education, whose offices and classrooms for decades had been crowded into Conwell and Carnell halls and scattered among several row houses. Governor Scranton made the principal dedicatory address in October 1965. The $3 million building was named in honor of Rolland Ritter, a university trustee and founder of the Ritter Finance Company who contributed generously toward equipping the building. Parts of Ritter Hall dedicated to the first three deans of Education were the George E. Walk Auditorium, J. Conrad Seegers Student Lounge, and D. William Zahn Instructional Media Center. In the summer of 1974 Ritter Annex was completed to accommodate College of Education growth and to be used by the School of Social Administration.

Speakman Hall, located between Thirteenth Street and Park Avenue, opened in September 1966 for classes and use by the School of Business Administration (now called the Fox School of Business and Management). The $3.3 million, four-story building included a computer center and state-of-the art soundproof classrooms. The building was named to honor Frank M. Speakman, who taught insurance and business economics at Temple from 1913 to 1916 and who died in 1956, bequeathing over $1.7 million to Temple. Speakman Hall was entirely constructed and equipped from private funds, including more than 9,000 separate contributions from individuals, businesses, labor organizations, and private foundations.

The appearance of bulldozers and cranes was seen as a welcome sign of progress by Temple but not by the community surrounding Temple. Pressure first came from African American community residents and leaders west of Broad Street. A November 1967 study reported that Temple's expansion program was operating, according to Herman Niebuhr Jr., associate vice president for urban affairs, "as if the community doesn't exist." At this point President Anderson halted plans for nearly $20 million of construction in the area extending west of Broad Street to Eighteenth Street and from Columbia Avenue (now Cecil B. Moore Avenue) north to Diamond Street.

Expansion continued east of Broad Street. Within a five-month span in 1968 the GSA completed three buildings costing $7.5 million clustered on the northeast and northwest corners of Norris, between Twelfth and Thirteenth streets. Presser Hall, built on the east side of Thirteenth Street, north of Norris, became the home of the College of Music. Named after Theodore Presser, the music publisher and founder of the Presser Foundation, which contributed funds to equip the building, Presser Hall was dedicated in August 1968.

A month later, the new home of the School of Communications and Theater was dedicated across the street from Presser on the northeast corner of Thirteenth and Norris streets. The building was named for Walter H. Annenberg, president of Triangle Publications and a gigantic force in the communications industry, who contributed $500,000 to equip the building. He was so touched by remarks made at the dedication ceremony complimenting him for his generosity that Annenberg pledged another $250,000. Annenberg Hall housed the departments of Journalism and Radio-Television-Film, plus the university radio station, WRTI-FM. A companion structure, Tomlinson Theater, was dedicated three months later and named for Vice President Emeritus William Tomlinson and his wife, Rebecca, who provided $350,000 for equipping the facility. Just a few days later, Randall Laboratory Theater was named to honor Professor Paul "Pop" Randall for his thirty-seven years of distinguished service to Temple's theater program.

More land was cleared and three state-constructed buildings sprang up in quick succession and opened during the summer of 1969. Temple's science complex was completed with the addition of the $7 million Biology–Life Sciences building on the west side of Twelfth Street between Berks and Norris streets, adjacent to and with connecting walkways to Barton (physics) and Beury (chemistry and geology).

Two physical education buildings, Pearson and McGonigle halls, were erected on the northwest corner of North Broad Street and Montgomery Avenue. Pearson Hall, intended for classes in physical education and recreation, was named for Albert ("Reds") Pearson, captain of the 1930–1931 basketball team and owner of a successful sporting goods store. Pearson Hall contained a swimming pool, gymnasia, exercise rooms, and other much-needed space for instruction and intramural recreation. McGonigle Hall, named for university trustee Arthur T. McGonigle, adjoined Pearson to form a single complex. Designed to accommodate several of Temple's varsity athletic teams, McGonigle included a sports arena seating 3,900 for basketball games, with expandable seating to accommodate

Above *Joe Brown (BS EDU 1931) stands next to his sculpture,* Two Athletes, *installed in front of the Pearson-McGonigle complex in 1969. Brown (1909–1985) entered Temple in 1927 on a football scholarship, shifted to the boxing team, which he captained in 1929, then turned professional, winning nine-straight bouts before being injured and deciding that "there must be a better way to make a living." Brown took up sculpting, and his work, mostly of sports figures, won immediate acclaim and many prizes. From 1938 to 1962 he coached boxing at Princeton University, where he also held appointment as a full professor of art from 1939 until his retirement in 1977. Brown's work is on display in the National Art Museum of Sport.*

Right *McGonigle Hall, part of a 225,000-square-foot athletic complex that includes Pearson Hall, was designed by Nolen & Swinburne Associates and opened in 1969. This 1969 Evening Bulletin photo contrasts the growth of the university with the neighborhood of row houses and high-rise public housing then standing to the north and west of the campus.*

another 1,000 for convocations and special events. The front entrance of the $8 million complex featured a striking sculpture, *Two Athletes*, designed by Temple alumnus Joe Brown.

By 1971 Mitten Hall was forty years old. Although stable and still functional, the formidable Gothic structure was neither large nor modern enough to meet increasing student demands. In June a new Student Activities Center opened on the southeast corner of Thirteenth Street and Montgomery Avenue. Immediately the center of gravity of student life shifted toward SAC, as it has always been known. The $4 million structure housed a variety of student organizations, student services, the *Temple News*, the campus bookstore, a cafeteria, and a host of support functions.

To persuade businesses to locate near Temple and to provide needed services for the faculty and staff, Temple encouraged and supported private developers, who put up three buildings during the expansion phase. One developer built a four-story, 84,000-gross-square-foot commercial building at 1700 North Broad Street on the northwest corner of Columbia (now Cecil B. Moore) Avenue, opening for occupancy in 1967. The ground floor was occupied over the years by various retail establishments, including a bookstore and fast-food restaurants. Known originally as the Seltzer Building, it was later named Vivacqua Hall, after John J. Vivacqua (DEN 1943). The upper floors have been occupied by various Temple units. From 1967 to 1983 the building's fourth floor housed the Faculty Club, a private dining and entertainment facility for Temple faculty and staff. Before that the Faculty Club was housed for several years in a gray stone row house, once a funeral home, in the 1900 block of North Broad Street. In 1983 the Faculty Club was renamed the Diamond Club and moved to the ground floor of Mitten Hall.

Temple negotiated with a private developer to build Cooney Apartments, a three-story building on the south side of Columbia Avenue that was leased back to Temple for graduate student and staff housing. Dedicated in October 1967, the building was named in honor of Russell Conwell Cooney, grandnephew of the founder and for many years a trustee and university general counsel. Cooney Apartments were razed in 1999 to make way for a modern new undergraduate dormitory known simply as 1300 for its address on Cecil B. Moore Avenue.

The University Services Building, a four-story, 115,000-gross-square-foot commercial building on the northeast corner of North Broad and Oxford streets, opened in November 1973. Because the building was a partnership venture with a developer, the first floor was designed for commercial rentals. But there were few takers after the first few years and the university eventually occupied all of the building, providing space for such offices as Human Resources, Purchasing, Temple University Press, copying services, and the News Bureau.

Temple needed a first-rate conference center. That need was answered in 1969 when the Greenfield Foundation donated Sugarloaf, the verdant thirty-two-acre estate of the late Albert M. Greenfield at Bells Mill Road and Germantown Avenue in Chestnut Hill. At the same time, F. Eugene Dixon Jr. gave Temple his childhood home, the Eleanor Widener Dixon House, located on Crefeld Street a few hundred yards from Sugarloaf. Temple renovated the thirty-room Dixon House and constructed a two-story, sixty-four-room lodge next to the Greenfield mansion; together in 1971 they became the Albert M. Greenfield Conference Center of Temple University. Over the next thirty-three years the conference center hosted hundreds of Temple meetings, corporate conferences, and social events. However, the costs of maintaining a residential conference center in a very competitive market eventually proved prohibitive. The university closed the conference center, sold the Dixon House, and returned Sugarloaf to the Greenfield Foundation in 2005.

TEMPLE NOTABLE
F. Eugene Dixon Jr.

F. Eugene Dixon Jr., shown here in 1980 with President Jimmy Carter and Temple president Marvin Wachman, began his long association with Temple with the gift of the Eleanor Widener Dixon House as a conference center. Soon afterward, the philanthropist, sportsman, and heir to the Widener fortune accepted an offer to join Temple's board of trustees. For thirteen years he played key roles as board chairman and chief fund-raiser, donating millions of dollars to the university, including funds for the construction of two buildings at the Ambler Campus. In his honor the Alumni Association established the Fitz Eugene Dixon Jr. Inspiration Award to honor the non-alumnus, who had provided support, encouragement, and inspiration to Temple's student athletes and the intercollegiate athletics program.

In 1972 fire destroyed the Klein Law Library. Only a few hundred of the 150,000 volumes were salvaged, despite the valiant efforts of law students, faculty, staff, and volunteers.

The final phase of state-funded construction on the Main Campus was scheduled for completion by 1970. However, student protests, steady resistance from the African American community, and diminished city support slowed and then stopped construction in 1969, before it again lurched forward into the mid- and late 1970s. When completed, four of the buildings were different in design and location than originally intended.

Twin office and classroom towers—one for the social sciences and one for humanities—were completed by the GSA and turned over to Temple in April 1973. Located on the east side of Twelfth Street on either side of Berks Walkway, the two buildings finally allowed the bulk of the growing Liberal Arts faculty to move out of row houses and makeshift accommodations into modern offices and classrooms. The social sciences building was dedicated in April 1976 and named in honor of Millard E. Gladfelter, Temple's fourth president. The humanities building, the southern half of the pair of towers, opened shortly after Gladfelter Hall but was not dedicated until 1984, when it was named for Temple's fifth president, Paul Anderson.

On July 25, 1972, fire destroyed the Klein Law School Library, housed since 1959 in the former Keneseth Israel building. Fortunately, plans were in place to build a new, permanent law school at the southeast corner of Broad Street and Montgomery Avenue (on the former site of a gasoline station). The GSA turned over the building to Temple in March 1973. Two years later the building was dedicated and formally named the Charles Klein Law Center.

With the opening of Weiss Hall in the summer of 1974 on the northeast corner of Thirteenth and Columbia (now Cecil B. Moore) Avenue, the Speech and Psychology departments at last had dedicated spaces. The trustees named the building after Helen Weiss and Abram Weiss, chairman of the Colonial Service Mortgage Company, whose contributions paid for the building's equipment and furnishings. In 1978 the high-rise Computer Activity Building went up at 1805 North Broad Street adjoining Carnell Hall. In 1996 the building was dedicated as Wachman Hall, named after Temple's sixth president, Marvin Wachman. And, finally, after many delays, the Engineering and Architecture building opened in September 1978 at the southeast corner of Twelfth and Norris streets.

The GSA-designed buildings constructed in 1973 and thereafter—Gladfelter, Anderson, Weiss, and Wachman halls; the Klein Law Center; and the Engineering and Architecture building—all transmitted an institutional starkness, both in their parsimonious designs and in the barren simplicity of their poured-concrete construction. Architectural tastes notwithstanding, the framework of Temple University's Main Campus was in place by 1978, and the facilities' modernization program entered a lengthy hiatus.

Student Unrest

All the while that Temple was physically expanding, student and community unrest simmered. Part of the unrest was spawned by the social-cultural forces sweeping across America in the 1960s. The sixties' spirit of change, as manifested on college campuses, embodied an awakening of social justice concerns mixed with the rejection of arbitrary, authoritarian power in favor of a new sense of personal empowerment, openness, and self-direction. The university was at once the fount of these new feelings, the wellspring of new ideas and stimulating approaches to dealing with social problems, and at the same time the target of movements that sought symbols of authority to oppose. During these troubling times virtually every administrative decision evoked intense criticism or bitter recriminations from one quarter or another. Commonplace campus protests, demonstrations, and counter-demonstrations led some to question the university's mission and purpose.

F A C T

The Sol Sherry Thrombosis Research Center at Temple University, the largest of its kind in the world, was founded in 1971.

University campuses in the 1960s became hothouses for social causes—civil rights, women's rights, anti–Vietnam War movements—along with growing student and faculty disillusion over their inability to shape and influence the important decisions within their universities. These movements combined to produce anger and frustration, turning Temple and other universities into pressure cookers. Many Americans, not the least being Philadelphia's obstreperous police commissioner Frank Rizzo, believed the country was facing violent revolution and that the source of these revolutionary ideas was to be found on its college campuses.

For whatever reasons, President Paul Anderson bore the brunt of Temple student protests, literally from the opening minutes of his administration. Students picketed his inauguration ceremony. One group marched out of the Academy of Music carrying "Anderson Must Go!" placards. The *Temple News* openly and frequently criticized Anderson, as did the *Temple Free Press,* an underground campus tabloid that resorted to obscenities and gratuitous attacks on Temple administrators. No attempt was made to censor either publication, but Anderson countered the evident bias of the *Temple News* by publishing a twice-monthly in-house paper, the *Temple Times*. Anderson also hired James M. Shea, a Brooklyn native and former director of university relations at the University of Oregon, to become vice president for university relations. Shea's abiding sense of humor and solid rapport with students soothed many contentious moments.

Anderson was caught in the middle: The most outspoken students considered him a hard-liner, yet more than a few legislators and alumni criticized his management and accused Anderson of coddling student protesters and appeasing community activists. The focus of attention on the university's president was not uncommon during this era; presidents were the most convenient and accessible human objects of frustration on a university campus. The norm for presidents of this period, as one scholar of American higher education observed, was early retirement, heart attacks, and disbelief that these contentious groups, numerically so small, had come to exert such a disproportionate influence on the image and reputation of the campus.

At the heart of the matter was the complex transformation in the way universities looked at their students. For most of the history of American higher education researchers and educational practitioners viewed students in one of two ways: how their background characteristics—academic preparation, gender, race, or special qualifications—contributed to the university's culture or how students were shaped and influenced by the university and how they fit socially and economically into society at large. Until the 1960s little or no thought was given to students as sources of institutional change.

Students in the sixties, whether part of organized protests or not, demanded that Temple treat them differently from the way students were treated in the past. The logic of the legal contrivance of in loco parentis (the university as surrogate parent) simply no longer made sense, neither in a deadly serious era of expanding civil rights, at a time when eighteen-year-old youths could be drafted and die before they could legally vote or buy a beer, nor in a highly competitive higher-education marketplace in which students demanded to be treated as consumers. Although in loco parentis was undergoing a speedy demise in the courts and as a legal precept, some critics of student protests persisted in attributing them to adolescent immaturity, pranks by attention-seeking adolescents, and displaced aggression against parental authority. Sympathetic Temple faculty, such as speech professor Herbert W. Simons, categorically rejected such arguments. Simons and other faculty members embraced

Temple students and faculty march from the campus to Independence Hall in silent protest over the murder of the Rev. James J. Reeb during the Selma, Alabama, civil rights march in March 1965.

the new student activism, argued on students' behalf, urged colleagues and administrators to treat students as adults, and invited students to participate in policy making directly affecting them.

Student activists reacted to the impersonality of university bureaucracy and resented the technology used to manage large enrollments, especially the omnipresent IBM data cards that became symbols of bureaucratic indifference. Instructions on Temple registration cards read, "Do not bend, fold, spindle, or mutilate"; otherwise the cards could not be machine processed. Feeling they were being bent, folded, spindled, and mutilated by the bureaucracy, students found the administration an easy and convenient target. From this initially sprang polite demands for smaller classes, curricular reforms, and a role in university governance. Before long, however, tensions mounted, other issues intervened, and often minor complaints exploded into major confrontations.

Student activists may have been disappointed or disillusioned, but they were true believers in higher education. "They do not want to run the University," as Professor Simons insisted in 1966, "they want to be treated as junior partners." Temple eventually obliged, inviting students to participate in a committee that in 1968 evolved into the Temple Plan for University Governance, which included roles for students on university committees, such as the University Disciplinary Committee and search committees for positions in student affairs. Students also were invited to participate in negotiations regarding cafeteria food and vendor contracts. And students were given a voice in governance through non-voting membership status on several standing committees of the board of trustees and the Faculty Senate. Some academic departments also found ways to involve students more effectively. A new student code of conduct redefining students' rights and establishing disciplinary procedures was established, along with a Student Senate, intended as a parallel forum to the Faculty Senate. The Student Senate proved short-lived, as students preferred debating the faculty and administration rather than debating amongst themselves. All considered, Temple students made the faculty, administration, and trustees take notice; pay attention to their demands for better services, amenities, and facilities; and treat students as valued partners in the academic enterprise and as concerned adult citizens. Those changes were felt across the university thereafter.

Canadian prime minister Lester B. Pearson (left) received the university's 1965 World Peace Award, a bronze statuette sculpted by Raphael Sabatini, professor and chairman of the Sculpture Department in the Tyler School of Art. The award was created in memory of former Temple student Lawrence C. Kline by his mother, Reba Kline (center). Extending the statue is President Millard Gladfelter. To the right of Gladfelter is Judge Charles Klein, chairman of the board of trustees; to the left of the prime minister is the Honorable James H. J. Tate (LLB LAW 1938), mayor of Philadelphia.

Student protest organizations first attracted national attention in 1962 with the formation of Students for a Democratic Society (SDS), an umbrella organization advocating participatory democracy but often characterized as radical. SDS never gained much traction on the Temple campus, despite the presence of a national organizer after 1969. Nationally, the student movements accelerated and coalesced after 1965 with the escalation of American involvement in the Vietnam War and tended to focus principally on opposition to the war and the expansion of the military draft.

Temple students and faculty—most notably religion professor John C. Raines, who was among the original Freedom Riders in 1961—were involved in the civil rights movement and went into the South to participate in voter registration drives or Freedom Summer (Mississippi) in 1964. Some Temple students participated in SNCC (Student Non-violent Coordinating Committee), known on campuses as Snick. Martin Luther King Jr. spoke at Temple to support and encourage further direct-

action participation in the civil rights cause. Students volunteered to help the disadvantaged and were quick to demonstrate against injustice.

To be sure, intense, active, and prolonged participation in such movements was limited and confined to a relatively small number of students and campuses. The majority of students and faculty, as one researcher put it, "remained markedly conservative and predictable." Most students were neither bomb throwers nor radicals, but virtually all were concerned about the war, racism, and social justice and wanted to do something about those issues.

Temple's student protests were not typical. Yes, Temple had its share of sit-in demonstrations and public protests—the ROTC program was a frequent object of both student and faculty protests—but unlike what happened at some of the large residential universities, there was little or no damage done to the campus and no significant class time was lost because of protests. Temple students, who were mostly commuters, were principally concerned about their studies, jobs, and getting home or to work after class. Moreover, the faculty and administration usually did not react aggressively or punitively against protests, knowing that over-reaction only worsened matters.

Philadelphia police were called to handle Temple protests only as a last resort. Anderson preferred instead to use internal disciplinary procedures and court injunctions to break up sit-ins and other disruptions. Anderson firmly believed that Temple's campus police and the common sense of the students kept situations from getting out of hand.

Moreover, Temple prided itself on creating open forums in which all sides of an argument could be heard. At many universities disagreements between students and administrators began and

Temple experienced its share of sixties student demonstrations and counter-demonstrations. Some, however, had a comedic tint, as when student anti-war demonstrators decided to "capture" a tank when an Army Reserve tank unit thoughtlessly drove down Broad Street past the campus.

escalated over students' rights of self-determination in hosting campus speakers, such as the Free Speech Movement at the University of California Berkeley. But presidents Gladfelter and Anderson insisted that the university must be an open forum for examining and defending ideas from all sides, within constitutional limits. "We couldn't have a Free Speech Movement here," said Jon Cutler, one of the leaders of a Temple group called Conscience, "because the University allows complete freedom of speech."

Indeed, Temple faculty and administrators intensely defended freedom of speech and the maintenance of the university as a free marketplace of ideas. The Faculty Senate, for example, condemned anti–Vietnam War protesters who shouted down an opposing speaker's presentation, declaring the act "contrary to the very idea of a university, which requires the free exchange of all ideas." Paul Anderson avowed that the "Rule of Reason" must always prevail. Yet, his was an unenviable position, as he was forced to walk a thin tightrope between maintaining openness and maintaining campus order. In an April 1969 open letter to students, staff, and alumni, Anderson wrote, "Temple will continue to be a campus open to discussion, debate, and to peaceful demonstration and protest."

He acknowledged, however, "that there are a few who are not willing to accept normal procedural means for resolving issues but instead resort to threats, intimidation and forms of coercion." The university, Anderson declared, would "not respond to dictation, to coercion, to intimidation, or to the disturbance of the orderly processes of the institution."

Anderson's open letter had several purposes: to reiterate his stand on free speech, to draw clear lines regarding what would be tolerated from student activists, and also to assure legislators and alumni who were alarmed by news reports of student protests and demands at Temple. Each heavily publicized protest and each Temple demonstration produced public rejoinders from legislators, threatening to reduce or eliminate Temple's commonwealth appropriation. Moreover, alumni giving had slowed to a trickle. Anderson's Annual Fund appeal letters were returned in empty envelopes with critical comments. "No $ for riotous students," read one returned form in the spring of 1969. "I am sending my contribution to Notre Dame," wrote one alum. "They know how to handle protestors."

A racial divide was evident among Temple's student activists. To begin, African American students insisted in 1966 that they no longer be called Negroes. Preferring instead, at least at that time, to call themselves and be referred to as blacks, they created their own set of demands and negotiating agenda and published their own leaflets and publications that voiced distrust of their "long-haired, pot-smoking" white brethren. Few African American students were involved in the anti-war protests, focusing instead on the issues of racism and the real and perceived inequities in the way Temple treated them and the black community around Temple.

A turning point occurred on March 17, 1969, when the fifteen-member Steering Committee for Black Students (SCBS)—an umbrella organization for black students that regularly channeled demands to the university administration—walked into Anderson's office and handed him a fresh set of demands. It began, "We the Black people attending Temple University." The SCBS demands included an Afro-Asian Institute (which evolved into the African-American Studies Department) and a special recruitment and admissions program for African American and Hispanic inner-city students unable to meet Temple's regular admission standards. Faculty Senate votes quickly approved both programs. The Special Recruitment and Admissions Program (SRAP) opened in the fall of 1969, directed by Curtis Leonard (BS EDU 1961; PhD CLA 1979), a professional social worker with a master's degree from the University of Pennsylvania. With the help of the SCBS, recent graduates from North Philadelphia high schools were recruited and provided a heavy concentration of supportive courses designed to upgrade their skills and prepare them to transition successfully into college-level courses.

The SRAP proposal gained immediate faculty approval, largely because it responded to a growing faculty concern that conventional measurement standards and particularly standardized test scores, such as SAT scores, were inadequate, even biased, measures of the academic potential of minorities. The faculty urged the university to waive or relax admission standards to accommodate these concerns; this led to the establishment in years hence of a wide array of programs for admission or pre-admission counseling of disadvantaged students and the creation of remedial programs, special counseling, and academic advising to prepare disadvantaged students to meet Temple's academic standards and ultimately to be matriculated and graduated.

President Lyndon Baines Johnson visited Temple University on October 30, 1964, and shared his vision of the Great Society. LBJ is pictured here with trustee Albert M. Greenfield, who arranged the president's visit. Johnson told the students, "Our country will become great because of young people like you with their eyes on the stars and their feet on the ground." Enthused by the crowd response, he told the students, "I wish I could change places with you," to which a chorus among the 10,000 swarming the presidential limousine answered back, "Oh, no, you don't."

A third proposal from the SCBS became the catalyst for an open dispute between Temple and the surrounding community. The SCBS demanded written assurance that Temple has "no intention of expanding anymore . . . unless approved by the Black community or its representatives . . . and unless provisions are made for the re-location in mass of Black communities and the retaining of Black communities in the area of future expansion." Temple's administration thought it was doing the right thing by clearing slum housing to make way for the noble purpose of higher education with the firm support of the city and the state. From the community perspective, however, Temple was an impersonal, sprawling giant moving relentlessly into its neighborhoods, taking homes, and disrupting families.

Community Unrest

The outburst of community unrest did not come unexpectedly or catch Temple flat-footed. Anderson and his predecessors were well aware of the swelling tide of resentment within the African American community. Temple's physical ascendance and obvious abundance became a convenient and proximate symbol for releasing the frustration and anger occasioned by the widening gap between rising expectations and the harsh realities of their deteriorating neighborhoods.

Mindful of the university's historic role in the Philadelphia community, President Gladfelter early in the decade had instituted several academic and service initiatives to maintain Temple's connection to the community. He explained the initiatives as part of an effort to "develop new dimensions of neighborliness."

Temple's hospital and the Medical School responded to Gladfelter's urgings with bold expressions of medical activism and social responsibility. A group of psychiatrists, psychologists, and social workers became enthused by the possibilities of extending emergency care, psychiatric, and community health services to the area. Plans to establish comprehensive Neighborhood Health Centers were launched but cutbacks in government funding ended the experiment.

With assistance authorized by the 1964 U.S. Community Mental Health Act, Temple opened a Community Mental Health Center in 1967, operating out of row houses on Ontario Street near the hospital. Soon afterward, however, a controversy erupted between the Health Sciences administration and a group of self-described "black power activists" who demanded control over the center. There followed hostile neighborhood meetings, picketing, threats of violence, and a sit-in at the center. Finally, the vice president of the Health Sciences Center, Dr. Leroy Burney, and acting dean of the School of Medicine, Dr. William Barba, negotiated turning the Mental Health Center over to a newly formed community health corporation.

Back at the Main Campus, Temple assisted community leaders in establishing an independent non-profit corporation, the Philadelphia Council for Community Advancement, to coordinate local social agencies. The following year Gladfelter established the Center for Community Studies, under the direction of Herman Niebuhr Jr., a clinical psychologist who arrived at Temple in 1957 and would be at the center of Temple-community relations for nearly two decades. Niebuhr coordinated the university's academic resources and collaborated with various government agencies and local organizations in joint efforts to improve North Philadelphia's social conditions.

Niebuhr directed a team of university researchers who worked with the North Philadelphia Program, an umbrella organization headed by Temple alumnus Samuel Dash (BS CLA 1947), a former Phila-delphia district attorney and later counsel to the Senate Watergate committee. One of the largest programs of its kind anywhere, the North Philadelphia Program was supported by $7 million in Ford Foundation and federal grants and charged with coordinating North Philadelphia's revitalization. Although unable to find a comprehensive solution, Temple and the North Philadelphia Program at least made a commitment to respond to community concerns.

After meeting with SCBS and community leaders in May 1969, President Anderson declared a moratorium on Temple expansion east of Twelfth Street, where the engineering, social sciences, and humanities buildings, along with a central steam plant, were scheduled for construction. Ander-son promised that the moratorium would remain in effect until Temple and the community worked out their differences. The SCBS, led by Clifford Jeffries, and Anderson agreed on creating a joint community-Temple steering committee from which sprang the idea to hold a *charrette* (a French architectural term to describe a process for resolving disputes).

Temple, community, and government representatives met in December 1969 at the Norris Homes housing project's community center near Eleventh and Norris streets. The Temple team appointed by Anderson included two trustees, two deans, two faculty members, four administrators, and two stu-dents. The dispute centered on six blocks of property between Twelfth and Tenth streets extending from Montgomery Avenue north to Susquehanna Avenue, all within the city-designated Temple Insti-tutional Development District. Temple agreed to forfeit use of land north of Diamond Street, assist in creating low-income housing, hire more community residents, and provide other services. Nothing, however, could placate or transcend community resentment over Temple's previous expansion or bring coherence to the community's segmented priorities. After three weeks of intense, frequently heated discussions the charrette collapsed, ending acrimoniously with no agreement.

Governor Raymond Shafer appointed three cabinet members to mediate the issues and imposed a settlement on both sides. An agreement was signed on February 6, 1970. Of the twenty-two acres in dispute, the community would control twelve and a half and Temple less than ten. Temple turned back four city blocks, including one originally designated for the engineering building, for community use. The community agreed to allow Temple to proceed with constructing the social sciences and humanities buildings, and Temple agreed to limit the heights of buildings on the campus perimeter. The Temple-Community Agreement of 1970 established a newsletter to keep community residents

During Labor Day weekend 1970, Temple reluctantly permitted the Black Panther Party to hold its national convention at McGonigle Hall. The event attracted many well-known radical activists, but no violence.

informed of Temple's development plans. But community leaders involved in the negotiations characterized the charrette derisively, declaring that Temple only intended to placate them. However, a key member of the Temple team, trustee Richard J. Fox, observed that the process itself was an important breakthrough, as Temple and its neighbors, for the first time, openly and frankly discussed their differences.

Black Panthers

On Labor Day weekend 1970 the university played reluctant host to the national convention of the highly controversial Black Panther Party. Earlier that summer a North Philadelphia clergyman had telephoned President Anderson to personally request use of the new McGonigle Hall gymnasium for meetings of the Philadelphia Coordinating Committee. Anderson granted approval, only later to learn that the group was actually coordinating the convening of the National Revolutionary People's Constitutional Convention, more commonly known as the Black Panther Party. Among those scheduled to attend and speak was Huey P. Newton, Panther minister of defense, out on bail pending retrial for a conviction for manslaughter in connection with the killing of an Oakland, California, policeman.

Temple administrators initially thought to revoke the permit because of the misrepresentations that led to its issuance. But North Philadelphia had become a tinderbox, capable of exploding over the slightest provocation. On August 30, just a week before the Panther convention was scheduled to begin, a police officer on duty in Fairmount Park was gunned down by a "black revolutionary," according to police. The shooting prompted a crackdown on the Panthers, resulting in many claims of police brutality from the African American community. Temple administrators agreed that it would be better to allow the convention than to risk an explosion by banning it.

Several state legislators publicly demanded that Anderson withdraw the permit. One Philadelphia legislator openly warned Anderson that "Temple may suffer the most serious consequences" if permission was not rescinded, warning of possible legislative investigations, demands for Anderson's resignation, and "questions about Temple's appropriation." Governor Shafer refused to intercede, stating "suppression of unpopular views is wrong." The two-day convention attracted 8,000 delegates and spectators, but no violence.

Social Service Agenda

Rather than pull back from the community and its obvious animosity, Temple in the years after the failed charrette pursued an even more aggressive social service agenda. It established new programs and found additional ways to reach out to those in need and to open the door further to those deserving persons of limited means who desired a Temple education.

Space does not permit listing and describing Temple's many programs and special efforts created to serve community needs since the late 1960s. Some programs cooperated with community organizations in delivering services, such as the College of Education, which worked with several community schools. A highly visible collaboration brought together the School of Business Administration and the Opportunities Industrialization Center (OIC), founded by the Rev. Leon Sullivan. OIC,

Temple's Community Mental Health Center opened in 1967 on Ontario Street near the Health Sciences Center. Unfortunately, in 1970 it became a casualty of financial crises and community misunderstandings. Temple eventually turned the center over to neighborhood activists to run.

which was headquartered at Nineteenth and Oxford streets near Temple's campus, had achieved worldwide recognition as a self-help vocational training center for African Americans that opened job opportunities formerly closed to them. In April 1970 Temple and OIC co-sponsored a high-level, three-day Mid-Atlantic Assembly on Black Economic Development that attracted leadership from several states to Philadelphia to discuss prospects for developing African American manpower and entrepreneurial training, sources of capital, and minority business enterprises.

Other Temple programs provided direct services to individuals in the community. Some examples of these services were the Legal Aid Clinic, free or low-cost dental care, a reading clinic, and art therapy. Temple also established new services to ensure that every effort was made to attract and hold minority students and those outside the academic mainstream. The Office of Affirmative Action was established to ensure that minority job applicants were given fair and equal consideration. A women's continuing education center advised returning female students on how to finish their educations. The Veterans Guidance Center offered psychological testing and vocational guidance for returning Vietnam War veterans referred by the Veterans Administration.

Additionally, university facilities were opened to civic and community groups. McGonigle Hall, for example, became a popular venue for North Philadelphia high school graduations and community events and the basketball arena the annual home of the Sonny Hill League, attracting top high school and college athletes from across the city. The recreational facilities in Pearson Hall were frequently opened to the community, and a swimming pool in the basement of South Hall was renovated and opened for exclusive use by neighborhood children and young people.

The Afro-Asian Institute, founded in 1969 directly as a result of the SCBS demands, later changed its name to the Pan-African Studies Department and then to the African-American Studies Department within the College of Liberal Arts. The transformation from a community advocacy organization to an academic department was not without incidents and tension. The program's demands for autonomy, including the right to select its own chair and to avoid the normal rigors of academic courses and scholarship, and its emphasis on advocacy for minority rights made it difficult at first to fit in with other departments. But the department gradually found its academic groove and a place within Liberal Arts. In 1988 it established the first doctorate in black studies to be offered in the United States. The department created a respectable undergraduate enrollment and graduated more than 100 PhDs who assumed various academic and professional appointments at major universities. Although the department was once thought to be a marginal program, African-American Studies faculty members have won numerous awards for their published scholarship consistently advancing Afrocentric normative theories.

To meet the African American community's needs for low-cost, non-credit continuing education, Temple in 1979 welcomed the Pan-African Studies Community Education Program (PASCEP) as a service of the College of Liberal Arts. The program, known initially as the Community Education Program, was founded in 1975 by Annie D. Hyman, a Temple graduate and North Philadelphia community activist who recruited Temple faculty volunteers to teach classes in schools, row houses, and community centers. With the support of the African-American Studies Department (known then as Pan-African Studies), Hyman gained Temple sponsorship, plus program and classroom space within university buildings. PASCEP courses taught by volunteers from Temple and the community offered instruction in basic skills, plus GED programs and personal enrichment courses. As it entered its third decade at Temple in 2009, PASCEP continued to embody the Conwellian self-help spirit and to be a marvelous example of the Temple-community connection.

FACT

There are 184 community outreach programs at Temple University.

Temple's most productive and successful community outreach program became the Center for Social Policy and Community Development (CSPCD), founded in 1969 by Seymour J. Rosenthal. Originally attached to the president's office, the CSPCD was created as a mechanism for reaching directly into the community and ensuring a two-way flow of resources, information, and goodwill. Before joining Temple, Rosenthal was chief of human resources for the federal Model Cities Administration and earlier head of the training section for the Office of Juvenile Delinquency. Over the next three decades at Temple, Rosenthal brought in millions of dollars in external funding and created scores of community service programs, reaching thousands within the North Philadelphia community. CSPCD eventually encompassed five departments, delivering professional development and continuing education programs to social workers, providing job training and literacy programs, evaluating social service organizations, and analyzing data on foster care families and children's services.

Temple's School of Social Administration (SSA) was established in 1969 as a direct response to national and local concerns to protect people, especially those least able to protect themselves, against poverty, technological change, urban blight, and racial and sexual discrimination. One of the first institutions in the nation to offer a bachelor's of social work degree (BSW), the School of Social Administration was intended to eliminate human suffering and social injustice and to promote human rights and social equality. Committed to educating, training, and certifying professional social workers in frontline, supervisory, managerial, and leadership positions, the School of Social Administration dedicated itself to the elimination of social, political, and economic injustices for the poor and oppressed populations.

SSA's roots can be traced back to 1938 and to the establishment of a graduate division called Social Group Work within the College of Education (then known as Teachers College), created for the purpose of certifying social workers. Dr. Everett DuVall started the program, which was discontinued in 1942 but resurrected in 1958 by Zelda Samoff. In 1965 the program became a department in the College of Education, and in 1969 the trustees approved its establishment as a separate school.

Dr. Simon Slavin was appointed the first dean of the School of Social Administration, with Dr. Willard Richan and Herbert Winston serving as associate and assistant deans. Emphasis within SSA was placed on the discovery and dissemination of practical, applied knowledge to be used to resolve problems between people and their social environments. A large part of the school's activities were devoted to public service to the community through collaborations and partnerships.

A building for the School of Social Administration was found in 1971 when the university acquired the former Burk Mansion, a three-story, twenty-seven-room house at 1500 North Broad Street. Standing at the corner of Jefferson Street, it was located appropriately enough just beyond the campus proper and close to the community. Built in 1907 by Alfred E. Burk, president of Burk Brothers, then the world's largest producer of glazed kid leather, the Burk Mansion included a large carriage house in the rear where a child care program was established in 1975 along with the university day care center. The day care center that served children of Temple students and staff, opened in 1970 in Mitten Hall, moved to the Baptist Temple after a few years and then into the Burk Mansion carriage house in 1975; there it remained until closed in 1995, following a fire in the mansion that also forced the CSPCD and the SSA to find other quarters.

The Council of Social Work Education fully accredited the School of Social Administration in 1972, just three years after its founding. SSA's programs were aimed directly at the community and

TEMPLE NOTABLE
Sister Mary Scullion

Reared in an Irish-immigrant household in Northeast Philadelphia, she attended Temple briefly before becoming a Sister of Mercy nun. Sister Mary began her service to the homeless in the 1970s and founded the Women of Hope residence for homeless women in 1985. In 1989 she and Joan Dawson McConnon co-founded Project H.O.M.E., which provides supportive housing, employment, education, and health care to enable chronically homeless and low-income persons to break the cycle of homelessness and poverty. Sister Mary studied part-time for five years to earn a master's degree in social work (MSW SSA 1987). Her advocacy on behalf of the homeless—"None of us are home until all of us are home"—has brought many accolades, including selection as one of *Time* magazine's "World's Most Influential People" of 2009.

its problems. Faculty members worked alongside community agencies, and students received hands-on practical experience working within and alongside community groups. To better serve the community, SSA began the New Career Ladders Program in 1975 to enroll persons out of high school for several years who were interested in human services careers.

Dr. Ione D. Vargus was appointed dean of the School of Social Administration in 1978, becoming the first African American woman appointed academic dean at Temple University. The next year SSA began offering programs at Temple University Harrisburg. In 1998 the SSA programs moved into new space at Strawberry Square in downtown Harrisburg and continued over the next decade to find a substantial demand for social work and human services training programs in the state capital. In 1994 Dr. Curtis Leonard became dean, and the school held a twenty-fifth-anniversary celebration.

The CSPCD officially joined the School of Social Administration in 1995, and Professor Rosenthal was named associate dean. The CSPCD united with several other institutes within SSA established to advance the school's research and public service agenda, including the Family Reunion Institute (a program created in 1990 to assist families in conducting family reunions) and the Institute on Protective Services (established at the Temple University Harrisburg Center to provide consultative services to the commonwealth agencies on aging and local law enforcement).

When Curtis Leonard retired in 2002, Dr. Jay Fagan filled in as acting dean for a year before Dr. Larry D. Icard stepped into the dean's position in 2003. That year the school introduced courses leading to a clinical concentration in social work. Dr. Linda Mauro, appointed acting dean in 2006, guided the school through a successful 2008 reaccreditation review by the Council on Social Work Education. In May 2009 the SSA was folded into the College of Health Professions, which was renamed the College of Health Professions and Social Work. By then—forty years after its founding—the school claimed more than 7,000 alumni serving worldwide in all facets of social work, with a significant concentration among the human services professionals in Philadelphia and Southeast Pennsylvania. The school's academic leadership and service to the North Philadelphia communities nobly exemplified Temple's mission as a vehicle for social change.

Marvin Wachman

At the height of the Temple-community conflict in January 1970, Marvin Wachman arrived at Temple ready to take up new duties as vice president for academic affairs after serving eight years as president of Lincoln University, one of the nation's oldest predominantly African American universities. His service at Lincoln and his friendly relationships with such African American luminaries as Thurgood Marshall, Ralph Bunche, Jesse Jackson, and the late Martin Luther King Jr. made him the perfect choice for the senior academic position during a time of community and racial strife. Wachman's steadfast good humor, pleasant demeanor, and gentlemanly manner served him well in all of the university venues, making him a natural choice for the presidency when it came time for Paul Anderson to step aside.

Controversy shadowed Anderson to the end of his presidency. When John M. Rhoads retired as vice president, Anderson selected James D. Logan, former director of the GSA , to be vice president for financial affairs. Rhoads had become the most powerful number-two person at Temple since Laura Carnell. He had an almost free hand in managing huge portions of the university's operations. On December 8, 1970, the trustees confirmed Anderson's choice of Logan to replace Rhoads. Two days later the Faculty Senate in an emergency meeting decried Anderson's failure to consult the Faculty

Senate on the Logan appointment, cited his lack of "genuine consultation" over many years, and voted to call for Anderson's resignation. A subsequent mail referendum sent to all 1,566 full-time faculty members revealed that Anderson held the support of 59 percent of the faculty.

Anderson held the full support of the board throughout the Logan contretemps, but then, the following fall, the Law School dean, Ralph Norvell, suddenly resigned, blasting the president for "repeated intervention" in the school's operation. Matters worsened when, for various reasons—not the least being Harrisburg politicians' dissatisfaction with campus protests and the seeming politicization of college campuses—the governor and legislature had second thoughts about funding higher education, particularly in the face of state revenue shortfalls. Governor Milton J. Shapp froze Temple's annual appropriation in 1971, providing a zero increase over the year before and leaving Temple to absorb inflationary costs and to have no room for growth or experimentation. Shapp subsequently rescued the state budget by instituting a flat, no-deductions income tax and a state lottery. But Temple gained small relief and began wondering aloud if the commonwealth truly intended to keep the promises embodied in the state-affiliation agreement.

President Anderson announced his retirement in March 1972, effective June 30, 1973, allowing ample time to select a successor. The search and selection process required little time. By May 18, 1972, the anticipated news of Marvin Wachman's unanimous endorsement by the presidential search committee and his unanimous election by the board of trustees was confirmed. Wachman had also gained the approval of every university constituency, including students, faculty, admin-

President Wachman chats with students at a popular lunch site, 1973.

istrators, and trustees, plus the endorsement of the community leaders invited by the presidential search committee to discussions of the candidates.

Marvin Wachman assumed the Temple presidency on July 1, 1973, but his formal installation was not until March 1974 in the ballroom of the Bellevue Stratford Hotel. To save money and avoid pomp and circumstance, Wachman combined his investiture with the annual Founder's Dinner and did not hold a formal inauguration. Taking the podium that evening, Wachman reaffirmed his belief in and support for the Conwellian mission of making higher education available to everyone with the basic talent and the will to work, regardless of social class. Wachman said that just as Temple had met the needs of the new immigrants in Conwell's time, Temple must continue to meet the educational needs of another generation of new immigrants—those from the American South and the barrios of Puerto Rico—and Temple must assist them in their struggle for upward mobility.

Wachman was himself the son of immigrants from Latvia and Belorussia. He grew up in Milwaukee, shining shoes, delivering the *Milwaukee Journal,* and running errands to supplement his family's meager income. A star tennis player in high school and one of the leading players on the amateur tennis circuit, Wachman entered Northwestern University on an athletic scholarship and worked at various odd jobs to pay for extras. He completed a PhD in history at the University of Illinois, defending his dissertation on the Socialist Party in Milwaukee the weekend before his induction into the army. Wachman served as an infantry sergeant and saw combat in Europe during World War II.

An intellectual with the common touch and proud to be called a liberal, Wachman believed ardently in the value of public service and the obligation of society's advantaged classes to protect and assist the disadvantaged. Inclined to see the better angels within almost everyone, as his memoir, *The Education of a University President,* demonstrates, Wachman was also a lifelong advocate of human rights and equal opportunity. He deeply appreciated Conwell's genius and vision and, like Conwell, spoke often of Temple as "The People's University," even though it irritated some faculty

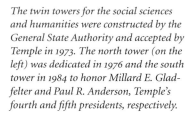

The twin towers for the social sciences and humanities were constructed by the General State Authority and accepted by Temple in 1973. The north tower (on the left) was dedicated in 1976 and the south tower in 1984 to honor Millard E. Gladfelter and Paul R. Anderson, Temple's fourth and fifth presidents, respectively.

and administrators who thought the phrase suggested open admissions. While some faculty would come to question his managerial skills, none doubted Wachman's genuine dedication to Temple's dual responsibilities of facilitating social justice while simultaneously delivering a superb education to all deserving students.

Where Paul Anderson had been ensnarled in the social turbulence of the sixties, Marvin Wachman became entangled in what University of California chancellor Clark Kerr called the "great transformation in higher education" occurring in the 1970s. From 1945 to 1970 higher education experienced high enrollments and generous support from the state and federal governments. But despite the appearances of growth and vitality, all institutions experienced difficult times between 1970 and 1980 when certain endemic problems manifested themselves as universities like Temple attempted to ascend too quickly into the ranks of the full-service, modern university. As a result, Temple, like many universities, found itself financially overextended, its meager endowments and operating budgets severely weakened. As the decade progressed, financial problems deepened to crisis proportions. The tide of goodwill that swept Marvin Wachman into the presidency ebbed completely by the late 1970s, leaving rancorous tidal pools of acrimony.

What went wrong? Following World War II Temple enjoyed almost twenty-five years of uninterrupted growth and expansion. But pervasive expansion became part of the problem. Across America the growing student demand led to a proliferation of new or expanded universities and new, larger state systems of higher education, along with new degree programs and fields of study—all of which led to wider, more intense competition for a shrinking student market by the mid-1970s. What had previously passed for strategic planning at Temple and most universities amounted to little more than vast spending plans for new facilities, new programs, and new faculty, presumably to be funded from perpetually expanding enrollments and a persistent flow of state funds. Neither, of course, was certain.

Several factors were to blame. The decline in college enrollments following the huge baby-boom surge was not unexpected. The task of projecting college enrollments is made simpler by the fact that we know how many people were born twenty years ago. Declining birth rates in the early and mid-1950s translated into fewer college-aged students beginning in the mid-1970s. Temple, however, defied the trend lines, at least for a few years. Enrollments in colleges and universities nationwide declined by 175,000 during the 1975–1976 academic year—the first drop since 1951—but Temple's total enrollments actually peaked in the fall 1977 semester when 36,339 students registered for at least one course. However, it would be another thirty years—the fall of 2007—before Temple's total enrollments again exceeded 36,000. The huge enrollments of 40,000-plus students projected by Temple back in 1961 never materialized. Unfortunately, the Temple University of the 1970s was staffed and configured for a much more prosperous future than the one that actually arrived.

Temple, like most universities on the rise during the 1970s, was determined to match or exceed in size and quality the programs and facilities of competitors and aspirant institutions. The standard for assessing a university's standing at the time was the Carnegie Commission on Higher Education classifications. First developed in 1970, the classifications sorted universities by defining empirical differences between them. Temple was classified as a Research II institution and sought to move up in the reputational standings to the top echelon, which was a Research I classification. Temple added many new programs in an attempt to imitate rivals and to be all things to all people. This produced what the educational planner Harold L. Hodgkinson labeled the "omnibus" university and

FACT

In 1973 professors of rehabilitation medicine and biomedical engineering at Temple University developed the first artificial arm that was fully mobile and operated on command from the brain.

what Clark Kerr called the "multiversity." Eventually the costs of trying to satisfy everyone caught up with Temple.

The national economy and state politics also played roles in Temple's gathering financial dilemma. Stagflation, the unusual 1970s phenomenon of double-digit annual inflation combined with declining economic productivity, wreaked havoc for Temple. Furthermore, a series of flat-line annual commonwealth appropriations reduced the buying power of Temple's funds. Net revenues declined or remained flat while Temple's costs escalated dramatically. The OPEC oil embargo in 1974 raised gas and oil prices and increased the costs of heating Temple's buildings, most of which were built in the 1950s and 1960s, when energy costs were low, and therefore were not energy efficient. Consequently, maintenance on Temple facilities was deferred, creating larger problems later on.

All of this was evident to only a few analysts early in the decade. By the end of the decade, however, the facts were inescapable. Adjustments in the university's expectations and belated attempts at austerity and strategic planning could not stave off retrenchment. A crisis mentality gripped the university at all levels as the leadership went into triage mode, focusing on and responding to problems in the order of their real and perceived seriousness.

The most pressing problem facing Wachman was the future of Temple University Hospital. Entering the 1970s rapid technological developments had increased the costs of basic patient diagnosis, treatment, and care. Inflation, coupled with increased salary demands from staff and unionized employees, added to the hospital's operating costs. Private patient admissions decreased because of the deterioration of the neighborhood, changing referral practices and bringing annual deficits to the Medical School's physicians' practice plan. But the major source of annual operating deficits was the cost of unreimbursed and under-reimbursed indigent care.

Temple's 530-bed hospital at Broad and Ontario streets served as family physician for 200,000 indigent and poor people in the surrounding area. Outpatient clinics recorded about 100,000 patient visits annually, most of them from people covered by Pennsylvania Medical Assistance (Medicaid), but the commonwealth refused to reimburse the hospital for the full costs of indigent care. Moreover, the emergency department—the city's second busiest—handled 45,000 cases a year. In 1964 Dr. Burney announced that Temple Hospital would be forced to diminish its volume of free care to achieve a balanced budget, bringing a storm of community protest and rescission of the order. At one point the hospital leadership threatened to close the emergency room. Frank Rizzo, then police commissioner, barged into the news conference, declaring that he would order policemen to "break down the doors" to get the sick and injured inside for treatment. There was no further talk of closing, but neither did the city provide real support for Temple Hospital (even after Mayor Rizzo later closed Philadelphia General Hospital in 1977).

Over the years the deficits mounted, threatening the hospital and the university. In the spring of 1974, when the accumulated deficit approached $30 million, Wachman launched a public relations campaign to inform the public of the scope of the problem. Then on May 1 he went to the Commonwealth General Assembly (Senate Appropriations Committee) and requested assistance in meeting the staggering debt, explaining that the hospital was going broke trying to meet the health care needs of poor people living in North Philadelphia. "Like the Biblical [Good] Samaritan, Temple Hospital still serves those in need," Wachman told legislators, who needed reminding of the name and original purpose of Temple Hospital. "Yet today it is the Samaritan, not the person he helped on the road to Jericho, that lies bleeding and beaten." He stressed that public health care "is a public responsibility."

Governor Milton Shapp agreed to meet with Wachman; A. Addison Roberts, chairman of the trustees; and Paul Kotin, vice president for Health Sciences. Wachman urged Shapp to take over operation of the hospital and the entire Health Sciences Center, but Shapp rejected the idea. A few days later, on May 21, 1974, John R. Bunting, chairman of the First Pennsylvania Banking and Trust Company (also a Temple alumnus and a trustee), informed President Wachman that Temple Hospital "has now reached the point where we must advise you that it will not be possible for us to renew your loans after the end of this calendar year." Other Philadelphia banks followed suit, refusing to finance deficits with bank loans.

Bunting's letter, along with a nicely timed press conference that detailed the hospital's plight, gained the attention of legislative leaders, who appointed a special Commonwealth Blue Ribbon Committee to work with Temple to solve the hospital's financial problems.

Unfortunately, at this crucial juncture neither the hospital nor the Medical School had the benefit of stable leadership. Dr. Paul Kotin, who succeeded Leroy Burney as Health Sciences Center vice president in 1970, resigned in May 1974. The Medical School was ably directed by acting dean Dr. Roger Sevy. But, in contrast to the Parkinson years, the Health Sciences Center lacked firm, central leadership. This left the management of the situation in the hands of President Wachman and trustee F. Eugene Dixon, who chaired the trustees' hospital committee.

Compounding matters, Leroy Burney and his successors at the hospital had persisted in the face of insurmountable deficits with plans for building a new hospital. Architectural plans were drawn in 1967 for what Burney described as a medical "megacenter with a social conscience." The legislature had agreed to fund a new building and appropriated $55 million, contingent upon a new, more realistic set of plans. In 1974 the state actually began preparations on the site, demolishing several buildings and excavating an enormous hole, the presumed foundation for the new hospital.

Meanwhile the Blue Ribbon Committee recommended a statute that was enacted on October 8, 1975, authorizing the state to acquire the hospital for $30 million (the total accumulated debt). Funds would be taken out of the $55 million bond issue previously authorized for construction of a new hospital, with the proviso that the hospital be leased back to Temple for one dollar a year and that Temple continue to manage its operations. The legislation also included provisions authorizing an additional $2.5 million annual appropriation to help cover the cost of unreimbursed health care, with funds to assist in renovating the hospital to meet accreditation standards. The complicated settlement further required Temple to establish a fifteen-member board of governors to oversee hospital operations. F. Eugene Dixon, who was active in the negotiations, became its first chairman. Years later, Dixon gave Governor Shapp much of the credit for the settlement, saying "the whole damn university might have gone down the tube."

Hospital officials proceeded with architectural plans and with raising funds for a new hospital, but when Wachman left office in 1982 the project had yet to be finally authorized by the trustees and the decision was left to the incoming Liacouras administration.

Besides the hospital crisis, Wachman faced the residual effects of racial unrest at Temple, weathering charges of institutional and personal racism and defending Temple's record of equitable treatment

FACT

More than 260,000 Temple University alumni live in all fifty states and 145 countries.

of African Americans and other minorities. While external evaluators, such as the Middle States accrediting team and the Human Relations Commission, found much to compliment about Temple's record, factions within the campus still found much room for improving Temple's minority and community relations—and Marvin Wachman was among the first to agree. He established the Office of Community Relations, headed by Thomas Anderson, to serve as a permanent liaison to the community. Wachman appointed Temple's first African American vice president, Dr. Bernard C. Watson, and dean, Dr. Ione Vargus. He also arranged with the city's Board of Education to lease Stauffer Hall to it for one dollar a year to establish a magnet school, the Carver High School of Engineering and Science, until a permanent building was found.

International Education

Temple's academic reach extended overseas for the first time when in 1965 the trustees approved a proposal from President Gladfelter and Dean Charles G. LeClair to open a Tyler School of Art program in Rome. A site was selected on the banks of the Tiber at the Villa Caproni to accommodate a maximum of sixty students, with library, gallery, lounges, classrooms, and professional studio. A junior year in Rome became an option for Tyler students and for a select few students from other institutions, widening Temple's reputation for innovation and academic excellence.

Marvin Wachman's interest in international education extended back to the latter months of World War II when he had taught college classes to GIs in Europe, returning later to teach through the University of Maryland and at the Salzburg Seminar. At one time he served as a specialist for African affairs advising the U.S. State Department. Wachman was also an inveterate traveler. In 1972 Wachman led an alumni tour to Greece, where he presented the Order of the Owl Award to U.S. Ambassador Henry Tasca (BS SBM 1934; LLD Hon. 1966). During Wachman's presidency and as a result of his urgings, Temple experienced a virtual explosion of new international programs, posting educational programs in business administration in Brazil, courses in liberal arts in Paris and Dublin, communications and Medical School programs in London, and Law School exchange programs in Ghana, Greece, and Israel.

FACT

Temple University Rome is one of the largest and longest-standing international programs in Italy.

Temple University Rome, as illustrated by Kevin Sprouls (BFA TYL 1977) in the portraiture style known as hedcut. Sprouls, who attended Temple Rome in 1976, introduced the concise engraving style to the Wall Street Journal *in 1979. He became the* Journal'*s first full-time artist and eventually the head of the illustration department. Sprouls donated the picture to Temple Rome for its fortieth-anniversary celebration.*

Wachman was successful in opening programs where few other American universities had ventured, including China, Japan, and Africa. The People's Republic of China began opening to foreigners after President Richard Nixon's historic visit there in 1972 and even more so after the death of Chairman Mao Tse-tung in 1976. With Wachman's help, Dr. Mann Chiang Niu, a Temple professor of molecular biology, was able to return to his native China and make a number of useful connections with the post-Mao reformist government headed by Deng Xiaoping. During Deng's highly publicized 1979 visit to America, Niu arranged for Wachman to present Deng with an honorary degree, conferred at the Blair House in Washington, D.C.

The next year President Wachman headed a nine-member Temple delegation that toured six cities in the People's Republic of China, establishing cultural and education exchanges with various institutions of higher learning. When Deng Xiaoping learned that President Wachman was visiting China, he summoned the Temple delegation to Peking's Great Hall of the People for a casual one-hour discussion. The Wachman journey ended with Temple signing "sister" relationships with Nankai University in Tianjin and with a teacher training school, Tianjin Normal College.

President Wachman very early saw the emerging importance of the Pacific Rim nations and recognized an educational need that Temple could fill in Tokyo, Japan. During the 1970s the Japanese were expanding economically and they realized that their lack of sound training in English limited their reach. After a year of negotiations Wachman succeeded in convincing authorities that a Temple

Temple University Main Campus, circa 1966, after the opening of Paley Library (top right) and during construction of Presser Hall (upper left). No longer merely a sidewalk campus along Broad Street, but not yet the thriving urban campus.

Temple's President Marvin Wachman and Chinese Vice-Premier Deng Xiaoping cordially discuss the American Civil War and the book Gone with the Wind *during Wachman's visit to China in 1980.*

FACT

Temple University Japan is the first non-Japanese university to be formally recognized by the government of Japan.

presence would not threaten Japanese educational hegemony. In June 1982 Wachman appointed William F. Sharp, professor of history and head of Temple's Honors Program, to direct the Temple program, known as TUJ. The program eventually expanded to include full-time instruction in liberal arts, art, business, and other courses and became Temple University Japan.

Two international programs were of major consequence in allowing Temple some flexibility in dealing with significant enrollment downturns between 1978 and 1981 that hit the College of Education particularly hard. Under siege because of steeply declining enrollments, the College of Education deployed faculty members to a teacher-training program in Nigeria at Abraka College in the rural Nigerian state of Bendel. Rather than have the Abraka teachers travel to the United States, members of Temple's graduate education faculty went to Abraka to present the coursework. In the summer of 1980, President Wachman, Dean Jay Scribner of the College of Education, and Trustee Henry Nichols traveled to Nigeria to visit the program. Years later, Scribner vividly recalled sitting in the back of a Land Rover with a goat as they journeyed from Benin into the bush to reach Abraka. There they participated in the first overseas commencement ever held by Temple University, conferring master's degrees on sixty-two proud Nigerian teachers.

In the late 1970s many of the soldiers in America's new all-volunteer army lacked basic education skills. To remedy the situation, Temple's College of Education received a $23 million contract to launch a program to teach basic reading and math skills to members of the U.S. Army assigned to NATO bases in Europe, extending from Great Britain to Greece. Temple sent graduate faculty to hire and train qualified teachers and to design educational tools to complete what American elementary and secondary schools had failed to do. The program, known as TEAM (Temple European Army Mission), offered Temple the opportunity to serve the nation and develop instructional methods to improve basic education at home.

Temple's faculty in the 1970s radiated a collective aura of reform and experimentation, tinged with advocacy. During the 1960s faculty members found it justified and convenient to separate from the administration on matters of student protests and student rights, sometimes openly siding with the protesters against the university administration. By the 1970s the university's problems were generally perceived by faculty to be those of the administration and trustees, not theirs. Feeling marginalized, the faculty sought a greater voice in university affairs.

In 1968 the Commission of the Faculty Senate recommended fundamental changes in faculty participation in university governance. A new Faculty Senate Constitution and Bylaws were adopted by the Faculty Senate on February 24, 1969, and recognized by the board of trustees on May 13, 1969. The Faculty Senate accepted the responsibility for and was given the right to advise the administration and the board of trustees on all matters of university policy, faculty relations, and administrative decision making in which the faculty claimed a reasonable role. The Faculty Senate was also welcomed to submit recommendations and reactions regarding policy decisions and acedemic programs.

Rejuvenated, the Faculty Senate created a host of committees—thirty-eight by 1973—intended to encourage greater faculty participation in university affairs. However, one result of the academic revolution of the 1960s was increased faculty independence and mobility. Faculty with national reputations found the one way to advance in rank and salary was through scholarly publication or movement from one institution to another. Some faculty "stars" became independent contractors whose services were available to the highest bidder; their first loyalties were usually to their professional organizations and peers within their disciplines, those who shaped their academic reputations. Loyalty and service to home institutions were of lesser consequence. Temple's Faculty Senate leadership often found it difficult to gather and hold faculty interest in Senate affairs.

At the same time that the faculty insisted on being accorded a larger partnership in the university, they also demanded higher salaries, improved benefits, and workplace protections of the kinds negotiated in collective-bargaining agreements. In the spring of 1971 the Faculty Senate Committee on Salaries failed to reach an agreement with the administration, resigned in protest, and urged the faculty to form a union. Three groups bid to organize the faculty: the American Federation of Teachers (led by Professor Leon Ovsiew of the College of Education); the National Education Association (led by Dr. Robert Llewellyn, a Chaucer scholar); and the American Association of University Professors, or AAUP (represented by Dr. Henri Amar, a physics professor).

The faculty vote was delayed a year by arguments before the Pennsylvania Labor Relations Board (PLRB) over whether the bargaining unit should comprise all faculty, including those from Law, Medicine, and Dentistry (who had elected not to join a union at that time), and whether department chairs should be considered administrators and therefore excluded. The administration lost the case, the Law School faculty subsequently voted to form its own union, and in the fall of 1972 the rest of the faculty, excluding those from Medicine and Dentistry but including department chairs, librarians, and academic professionals, voted to join the AAUP.

The first AAUP contract agreement was reached in 1974, making Temple the first major university in Pennsylvania to have a faculty union. The formalization of adversarial relationships and all that was necessarily a part of the American labor relations negotiating process created a lasting divide within the university. One perhaps unintended consequence from the faculty perspective was the simple designation of the adversaries in such negotiations. Professor David H. Webster, editor of the *Temple Faculty Herald,* remonstrated against President Wachman's public statements during negotiations in which he legally equated himself and the board of trustees with "Temple" and "the University," which legal documents and contracts between Temple and the AAUP (later the TAUP) would thereafter state. Webster insisted that Wachman was "the administration," an essential part of the university, to be sure, but not "*the* university" and politely requested, "Please move over a little so we can sit there, too."

The unionization movement at Temple was spawned by the commonwealth's Act 195, which granted almost all categories of employees in state-related institutions the right to organize. Where Temple had only three unions in 1970, by 1977 there were fourteen unions with collective-bargaining agreements with Temple. With the unions came additional costs for legal fees and another layer of bureaucracy to administer personnel and union matters. Walter Powell, an executive with First Pennsylvania Bank, was hired by Wachman as vice president for personnel (later known as human resources).

Financial Adversity, 1977–1982

The Temple-faculty agreement came into play in 1979 and again in 1982 in a way neither side hoped it ever would. It began in the summer of 1977 when the Pennsylvania General Assembly engaged in a partisan deadlock and could not agree on a commonwealth budget. No funds were authorized for state-related and state-aided institutions of higher learning. Temple was forced to rely on tuition revenues (never enough at any point in its history to sustain the institution) and borrowed funds from banks to pay expenses while the commonwealth remained deadlocked. By the end of October Temple paid thousands of dollars a day in bank interest.

As the crisis deepened, Wachman issued a special message to faculty, staff, and alumni: "I must tell you candidly that the possibility of payless paydays, cuts in programs and even the closing

Students join faculty, administrators, and President Wachman at the Bell Tower on October 12, 1977, to demonstrate their joint concerns over the legislative stalemate provoking a state funding crisis.

of the University is a very real one." This, he said, was the "greatest crisis" in the history of Pennsylvania's colleges and universities. Eventually the commonwealth authorized a budget, but not before Temple had exhausted its reserves and paid hundreds of thousands of dollars in interest payments, which the commonwealth refused to reimburse. The commonwealth's irresolution had weakened Temple financially, almost fatally. Temple survived the 1977 crisis, thanks in large part to record enrollments in the fall of 1977, but by the fall 1982 semester total university enrollments had dropped by 17.5 percent.

Temple's budgetary problems worsened, being caused by inflation, rising energy costs, and declines in state aid and exacerbated by plummeting enrollments. After pursuing all other remedies, Wachman and John Rumpf, vice president for academic affairs, decided in 1979 to follow the provisions of the faculty contract, which required the administration to provide eighteen months' notice before retrenching faculty. Letters of "provisional retrenchment" (potential layoffs) were sent to twenty-three tenured faculty in schools and colleges that had experienced the most severe enrollment declines. However, that fall, twenty-one of the termination letters were rescinded after new assignments or improved situations made it possible to retain the faculty members.

The situation worsened three years later, and on February 18, 1982, Wachman addressed the Faculty Senate on the "financial status and future of the University," stating bluntly: "It is very clear that because of our income situation, life cannot go on as usual at Temple. . . . Without personnel cuts, the total deficit next year could be about $8 million or more, the second year double that, and in the third year, triple." The faculty leadership questioned Wachman's dire analysis, as well as his personal judgment. On March 5 the Collegial Assembly of the College of Liberal Arts (CLA) passed a resolution protesting Wachman's "arrogant disregard for established academic procedures" and his "administrative display of unreason. . . . There clearly is a crisis at Temple University, but it is a crisis of confidence in the leadership of President Wachman and his associates." CLA demanded full disclosure of the non-academic cuts and faculty participation in the decision process, as well as the involvement of president-elect Peter Liacouras. (Liacouras had been elected president on December 18, 1981, to succeed Wachman, effective June 30, 1982.)

Liacouras thought it inappropriate for him to be involved, and Wachman believed it irresponsible to leave the staffing and financial problems to the next administration. And so in April 1982 Wachman sent out fifty-eight termination letters under the retrenchment clauses of the AAUP contract; fifty-two letters went to tenured faculty. Wachman and Rumpf, working with the deans, attempted to find alternative assignments. By October 1983, when the eighteen-month notification expired, only four of the fifty-eight faculty members were actually let go. The retrenchment action led the national AAUP offices to place Temple University on its list of censured institutions.

Looking back, the era began with high hopes brought by swollen enrollments, infusions of government funds, and expectations of substantial growth from state affiliation. Within a few years Temple's expansion plans ran headlong into the conflicting aspirations of neighbors emboldened in part by the civil rights movement and empowered by Philadelphia's fluid politics. Temple survived the community ferment chastened and humbled but stronger for the experience and more committed to serving as a vehicle for social change. Inside the campus the relationships of students and faculty to the administration underwent substantial change, generating an air of near-constant tension. Out of it all, however, came a reshaped, slimmer, more focused institution, whose leaders were determined to revive and enliven the campus and to enlarge Temple's reputation in American higher education.

Chapter 6
Temple's Ambassadors

Temple and other universities, much like sovereign states, send ambassadors into the world as exemplars of their missions and values. Now, surely it is important for Temple to have eloquent and persuasive leaders and professional spokespersons, but their impact, as significant as it may be, ultimately is offset by the cumulative weight of the tens of thousands of student athletes and performers who, by dint of their brilliance on the playing fields or in concert halls, theaters, and studios, speak volumes about Temple University.

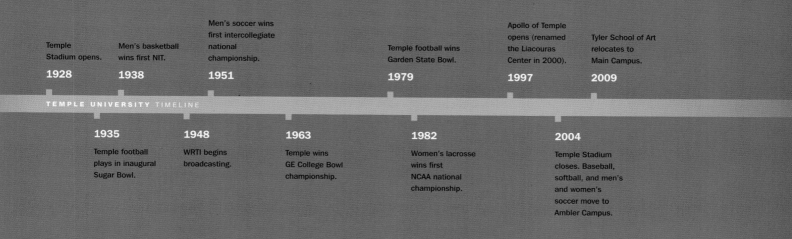

TEMPLE UNIVERSITY TIMELINE

Temple Stadium opens.
1928

Men's basketball wins first NIT.
1938

Men's soccer wins first intercollegiate national championship.
1951

Temple football wins Garden State Bowl.
1979

Apollo of Temple opens (renamed the Liacouras Center in 2000).
1997

Tyler School of Art relocates to Main Campus.
2009

1935
Temple football plays in inaugural Sugar Bowl.

1948
WRTI begins broadcasting.

1963
Temple wins GE College Bowl championship.

1982
Women's lacrosse wins first NCAA national championship.

2004
Temple Stadium closes. Baseball, softball, and men's and women's soccer move to Ambler Campus.

For all that may be written about the quality of Temple's academic programs or the strength of its faculty, the university is known through its public representatives, by those students approved to perform, compete, or speak on behalf of the university and by those alumni whose Temple-honed professional skills brought them success and lasting identification with their alma mater.

Like an ambassador credentialed to represent his or her country before a foreign sovereign, Temple's athletes and performers are accredited ambassadors to the world. They are the persons Temple wants the rest of the world to see and know. These are the men and women whom Temple's coaches and faculty entrust with wearing the Temple name across their athletic tunics, with carrying the Temple name to perform in Carnegie Hall, and with representing Temple in North Philadelphia, across the region, or in foreign lands. Throughout its history Temple has taken enormous pride in the athletic and artistic excellence of its student ambassadors. Whether at an exciting championship gymnastics meet or a moving chamber music presentation, a thrilling Big Five basketball game or a stirring performance of a Eugene O'Neill play, Temple's athletes and performers have exuded that singular combination of spirit, pride, discipline, and integrity that is the Temple hallmark.

All of Temple's schools and colleges have produced students who grandly achieved and were celebrated and honored for their accomplishments, but this chapter singles out those programs whose students represent Temple before the public, those programs that prepare students as performers, athletes, and public communicators. The privilege of publicly representing Temple carries with it a lasting responsibility. Temple students and alumni bear that responsibility with pride.

Wherever they go in life and in whatever arena they perform, Temple graduates are judged, and so, also, is Temple. Many of Temple's alumni remain active representatives, credentialed by their diplomas as Temple's ambassadors plenipotentiary to the world. Temple takes great pride in the successes of all of its graduates. This chapter attempts to capture and acknowledge, as much as space will allow, the historical contributions of our performance-based programs and the gifted students, faculty, staff, and alumni who have served as Temple's ambassadors through the years. We begin with the performing arts.

Boyer College of Music and Dance

Temple established a School of Music in 1893 but suspended operations in 1943 because of unrelieved budget deficits (see Chapter 2). However, courses continued to be offered in the Department of Music Education in Teachers College (now the College of Education), the purpose being to produce teachers of music rather than performers. Dr. David L. Stone was appointed director in 1951, and the program began to grow and to turn, once again, toward performance training. By 1960 the program enrolled nearly 650 graduate and undergraduate students. In 1961 Stone secured approval for a bachelor of music degree to be offered to students interested in music performance and theory. The new degree prepared the way, with Millard Gladfelter's assistance, for the creation of a new college.

In 1962 Temple's trustees approved the creation of the new College of Music and David Stone was appointed dean. Stone, who held a Harvard PhD and studied at Juilliard Graduate School, was an intense, no-nonsense New Englander who left few people wondering where he and they stood. "When he hired me," Jeffrey Cornelius recalled, "David said, 'If I don't like you, this is a one-year job, and if you don't like me, this is a one-year job.'" Cornelius stayed and eventually became dean.

To build a strong conservatory-type faculty, Stone hired the best available teacher-musicians from the Philadelphia Orchestra, the New York Philharmonic, and the Metropolitan Opera in New York. Music education was continued, but Stone designed programs primarily for gifted student performers seeking advanced study under private teachers. Programs were eventually established in choral activities, composition, history, instrumental studies, jazz studies, keyboard, theory, therapy, voice, and opera. The college gained membership in the National Association of Schools of Music in 1964 and received high marks from evaluators for the quality of its students, faculty, and instruction.

College offices were located initially in row houses on the west side of Broad Street, and classes were held in South Hall (since demolished). Student performances were held in Mitten Hall, McGonigle Arena, and Thomas Hall (since demolished). The program required space of its own if it was to grow. Stone successfully lobbied the administration to include a music building in the commonwealth's capital budget plan. He gained the support of the Presser Foundation to equip and furnish the new building. Presser Hall opened in 1968 (see Chapter 5), with the offices, classrooms, and practice and rehearsal areas necessary for a first-line university college of music.

Maestro Luis Biava, artistic director of the Temple Symphony Orchestra, conducted the symphony's debut at Carnegie Hall in April 2008.

Music Festival/Music Institute, 1968–1980

Stone sought to enhance the stature of the college by creating an "eastern cousin" to the prestigious Aspen (Colorado) Institute, a program to bring gifted young musicians and established artists together in residence for a summer of study and performances. The result was the Temple University Music Festival and Institute that opened in the summer of 1968 at Temple's Ambler Campus. Stone was the overall artistic director, but the festival and institute operated separately. The festival featured stellar attractions from every variety of musical expression, such as pianist Van Cliburn, classical guitarist Carlos Montoya, Duke Ellington's jazz orchestra, the German opera sensation Elizabeth Schwartzkopf, and popular singers such as Ella Fitzgerald, Judy Collins, and Joan Baez. Beginning in 1969 with the Zagreb (Yugoslavia) Philharmonic Orchestra, each year an orchestra was in residence for six weeks, performing and conducting master classes for the 200 nationally recruited institute students who resided at the Ambler Campus.

The festival proved extremely popular. To accommodate overflow crowds, Temple constructed a 1,000-car parking lot and a large amphitheater (since destroyed by fire and in 2004 converted into the Temple women's varsity softball complex). Big-name acts were expensive, and according to trustees' minutes, the festival incurred an annual operating deficit of $250,000. In the spring of 1980 Temple terminated an affiliation with the Pittsburgh Symphony Orchestra, which had been in residence since 1970. A few months later it closed both the festival and the institute. The university could not justify the deficits at the same time it was moving to retrench tenured faculty. Over thirteen seasons the festival attracted more than 1.3 million attendees, mostly from the suburbs, to see performers such as opera star Beverly Sills, composer Aaron Copland, and jazz greats Benny Goodman and Dave Brubeck.

Community Music Program

The College of Music did not neglect Temple's home turf in North Philadelphia. Since its earliest years the college extended its musical resources and talents into Philadelphia communities, offering free instruction to children of disadvantaged circumstances. Beginning in 1967 with a Rockefeller Foundation–funded three-year experimental program offered through the Settlement Music School and developing into a permanent Community Music Program, Temple teachers have given thousands of children in neighborhoods across the city the opportunity to play a musical instrument.

The program soared under the magical touch of Nancy Hess (M.Ed. MUS 1970). Appointed director of Temple's Music Preparatory Division in 1980, she expanded the free Saturday morning instrument lessons, launching additional music appreciation programs, adding pre-school and early childhood programs, and founding the Center for Gifted Young Musicians. She also established a cultural exchange with young musicians in Puerto Rico and created a children's choir and the Youth Chamber Orchestra. Music Prep alumni include renowned violinist Sarah Chang, jazz bassist Christian McBride, and scores of professional musicians. Hess retired in 2004, leaving an immeasurable legacy of joy and goodwill, but the college remained committed to extending its reach into the community, offering the healing power of music.

Continuity and Change

David Stone stepped down as dean in 1975, accepting the position of director of Temple Rome. Dr. Allen Garrett served as acting dean until 1978, when Helen Laird, division head and director of opera theater at the College-Conservatory of Music at the University of Cincinnati, was appointed dean. Laird brought many years of experience to Temple, including ten years as the lead soprano with opera theaters in Basel, Switzerland, and Mainz and Kassel, Germany. She guided the college through a number of significant changes.

The most important of those changes occurred in 1985 when alumna Esther Boyer Griswold (BA CLA 1927) endowed the college with what was then the single largest gift in Temple's history. As a Temple freshman in 1923, Boyer was inspired by one of Russell Conwell's sermons, probably one of his many variations on the "Acres of Diamonds" theme. Later in life, after she had married Earle Griswold and accumulated a tidy fortune, Mrs. Boyer Griswold selected Temple to receive a gift valued between $4 million and $5 million. In recognition of the gift and in her honor, on April 4, 1985, the College of Music was officially renamed the Esther Boyer College of Music.

Then, in March 1987 the New School Institute of Music, a Philadelphia conservatory widely known for excellence in string and chamber performance training, and its faculty, students, programs, and library were merged into the Esther Boyer College of Music. New School president Richard Brodhead joined the Temple faculty. Temple acquired the New School Institute building on South Twenty-First Street and subsequently sold it to help fund renovations to provide a suitable, medium-sized performance space for the college and for the New School Institute chamber musicians. To meet those needs, Temple renovated Reber Hall, the former Keneseth Israel building once used by the Law School.

Following $6 million worth of renovations, the building reopened in 1994 and was rededicated as Rock Hall, named in honor of Dr. Milton Rock (BA CLA 1947; MA CLA 1948) and his wife, the late Shirley Rock (SBM 1943), whose gifts funded a substantial portion of the renovations. Milton Rock served as a Temple trustee and chairman of the boards of both the Curtis Institute of Music and the Pennsylvania Ballet. Rock Hall housed a 325-seat chamber music recital hall, the Alice Tully Library, computer labs, practice rooms, and the string/chamber music programs of the New School Institute. Peter Dobrin, a *Philadelphia Inquirer* music reviewer, described Rock Hall as "a near-perfect hall that will likely outclass other chamber music venues in town." Rock Hall also fit Temple into Philadelphia's then-new Avenue of the Arts, a plan since implemented to extend cultural venues along the Broad Street corridor.

Dean Laird retired in 1993, and Dr. Jeffrey Cornelius was appointed dean. Under Cornelius's direction the New School Institute settled into the college, the Rock Hall renovations were completed, and noteworthy enrollment increases occurred. Cornelius served until 2001, followed briefly by Dr. Richard Brodhead as interim dean. Then, in 2002 Dr. Robert T. Stroker was appointed dean, coming to Temple from the Meadows School of Music at Southern Methodist University, where he served as associate dean. Dean Stroker has since overseen a number of innovations, including the establishment in 2004 of the Arts and Quality of Life Research Center to promote interdisciplinary research demonstrating the unique role of the arts in making a difference in people's lives.

In October 2007 the college received yet another stunning gift when Mrs. Joy Valderrama Abbott (BS EDU 1952) made a provision in her estate to bequeath her share of rights and future royalties earned by theater productions authored by her husband, George Abbott. Those rights were valued

TEMPLE NOTABLE
Esther Boyer Griswold

An honor roll student, vivacious performer in student dramas, and hugely popular on campus, Esther K. Boyer was fondly known to her classmates as "Toots." After graduating in 1927 she taught high school before taking an executive secretary's job in New York City. There she met and later married Earle Griswold, who would become the manufacturing genius behind Tampax (now Tambrands, Inc.). In addition to endowing the College of Music, the Griswolds contributed to the new plaza at Temple University Hospital named in their honor. She later helped fund the Temple University Children's Medical Center and in 1997 made a lead gift in support of the construction of the Apollo of Temple (the Liacouras Center). The Esther Boyer Theater was named in her honor. Esther Boyer died in March 1999. By then the spirit of giving that she inspired had grown stronger, sparking a new culture of generosity at Temple.

Paul "Pop" Randall, founder of Temple's theater program, directs Joy Valderrama in a 1951 student production. Valderrama went on to a career in the theater and married the celebrated playwright and producer, George Abbott. In 2007 she endowed the Joy and George Abbott Center for Musical Theater at Temple University.

at more than $6 million. The purpose of the gift was to establish the George and Joy Abbott Center for Musical Theater at the Boyer College of Music and Dance and to create a BFA degree in musical theater. George Abbott, winner of four Tony awards and a Pulitzer Prize, authored and produced such well-known Broadway plays as *The Pajama Game, Damn Yankees, On Your Toes,* and *The Boys from Syracuse.*

The arts at Temple—always one of the university's strengths—underwent a renaissance in the first decade of the new century with the relocation of the Tyler School of Art to the Main Campus. Its new home is next door to Presser Hall and across the street from Annenberg Hall and the School of Communications and Theater. The growth of the Boyer College of Music and Dance necessitated a major expansion of Presser Hall begun in 2007, funded in part by the commonwealth, and aided substantially by a grant from the Presser Foundation. A new addition to Presser Hall was completed in the fall of 2009, adding new classrooms, teaching studios, practice rooms, and a recording studio for the music programs. The project further expanded the thriving arts enclave along Norris Street between Broad and Twelfth streets, encompassing the new Tyler School of Art building, the Boyer College of Music and Dance, the School of Communications and Theater, and the magnificently restored Baptist Temple.

Musical Ambassadors

Many extraordinarily talented graduates of the Boyer College of Music and Dance have risen to stardom, among them Hugh Panaro (B.Mus. MUS 1985), who studied voice at Temple and went on to become a top Broadway star with lead roles in *The Phantom of the Opera, Lestat,* and *Les Misérables.* Marietta Simpson (B.Mus. MUS 1981), the talented, much-sought-after mezzo-soprano, debuted at Carnegie Hall in 1988 and has since performed at New York City Opera, Atlanta Symphony, New York Philharmonic, Lyric Opera of Chicago, and houses across Europe. Pianist and composer Marc-Andre Hamelin (B.Mus. MUS 1983; M.Mus. MUS 1985) won the 1985 Carnegie Hall International Competition of American Music, the 2004 international record award in Cannes, and the 2008 Juno Award for Classical Album of the Year. Derrick Hodge (B.Mus. MUS 2001), the remarkable bassist, composer, and musical producer, studied jazz composition and performance at Temple, where he played in the Temple University Jazz Band and was the first jazz major to participate in the Temple University Symphony Orchestra.

Building on David Stone's firm foundation, the Boyer College of Music and Dance has attracted outstanding faculty through the years. Many, such as Grammy-winning pianist Lambert Orkis, harpsichord virtuoso Joyce Lindorff, talented composer Richard Brodhead, and celebrated cellist Jeffrey Solow, are world-renowned artists. Temple has a long, illustrious tradition of producing outstanding concert choirs under iconic directors such as Elaine Brown (M.Ed. EDU 1964), the first American woman to conduct the Philadelphia Orchestra; Robert Page, who made Grammy-winning recordings with Eugene Ormandy and the Philadelphia Orchestra; and, more recently, director Alan Harland, known worldwide for his collaborations with leading conductors, including Riccardo Muti, Zubin Mehta, and Wolfgang Sawallisch.

Maestro Luis Biava, artistic director of the Temple University Symphony Orchestra since 1986, spent four decades with the Philadelphia Orchestra, including two as conductor-in-residence. In 2008 Biava conducted the Temple University Symphony debut at Carnegie Hall. Eduard Schmieder, professor of violin, has performed at major concert venues around the world. In 1991 Schmieder founded *iPalpiti* (Italian for "heartbeat"), sometimes known as the Musical Peace Corps because all of the orchestra's players (aged nineteen to thirty) are winners of prestigious international awards and they represent twenty countries worldwide. Temple University's Jazz Band (TUJB) has flourished since the 1990s under the brilliant artistic leadership of Terrell Stafford, an immensely talented trumpeter who has recorded more than sixty albums. In recent years the TUJB has played and recorded with many of the biggest names in jazz, including Wynton Marsalis and Clark Terry, and at venues such as the Kimmel Center and the Kennedy Center for the Performing Arts.

Dance

The dance program began in the mid-1950s as an activities course within the College of Education. With the arrival in 1967 of Edrie Ferdun and then Hellmut Gottschild and Sarah Alberti, the program gathered momentum. They recruited students and built a curriculum, leading in 1970 to a dance major within the College of Education. In 1974 an M.Ed. program in dance was accredited. To provide a performance outlet for their students, several faculty members established independent dance companies and held performances in Mitten Hall, McGonigle Arena, and Tomlinson Theater.

In 1974 the Dance Department was folded into the new College of Health, Physical Education, Recreation and Dance (HPERD) and Joseph Oxendine was named dean. John Gamble joined the faculty as chair of dance in 1975 and established the Conwell Dance Theater on the fifth floor of Conwell Hall in a former gymnasium converted into a black box theater. The bachelor of science degree was changed in 1978 to the bachelor of fine arts (BFA) to reflect the shift from producing dance educators to a performance-based curriculum. The program also won approval for an MFA degree shaped by the artistic vision of Hellmut Gottschild, Eva Gholson, and Ann Vachon, each directing the professional companies of Zeromoving, Sybil Dance Co., Seminole Works, and Dance Conduit. In 1980 Sarah Alberti Hilsendager was elected the second president of the Philadelphia Dance Alliance, just one indication of how the Temple dance faculty had become a vital artistic presence. Performances in the Conwell Dance Theater drew increased attention and won favorable reviews from dance critics.

D. Brenda Dixon joined the dance faculty in 1982 and took the lead in developing the doctoral studies program. Dance students then had their choice of pursuing degrees concentrating on performance (leading to the BFA and MFA degrees), education (M.Ed.), or research and teaching (PhD). Beginning with the first accreditation review in 1980, all of the dance degrees received full national accreditation status for each periodic review thereafter.

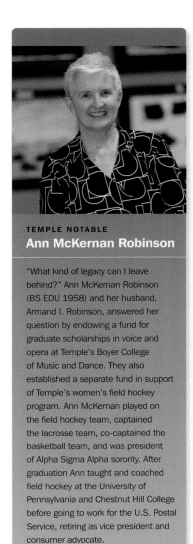

TEMPLE NOTABLE
Ann McKernan Robinson

"What kind of legacy can I leave behind?" Ann McKernan Robinson (BS EDU 1958) and her husband, Armand I. Robinson, answered her question by endowing a fund for graduate scholarships in voice and opera at Temple's Boyer College of Music and Dance. They also established a separate fund in support of Temple's women's field hockey program. Ann McKernan played on the field hockey team, captained the lacrosse team, co-captained the basketball team, and was president of Alpha Sigma Alpha sorority. After graduation Ann taught and coached field hockey at the University of Pennsylvania and Chestnut Hill College before going to work for the U.S. Postal Service, retiring as vice president and consumer advocate.

Taking dance into the community. Students of the Kariamu & Company: Traditions are shown here in a 2008 performance. Directed by Dance Department chair Kariamu Welsh, the company offered a traveling stage show called the "'I See You!' Dance Mobile" to bring performances of dance traditions from the African and Latino diasporas to underserved urban communities.

Philadelphia Dance Collection

A GUIDE TO THE PHILADELPHIA DANCE COLLECTION
IN THE SPECIAL COLLECTIONS DEPARTMENT

Mindful of the richly diverse and historically important place of dance in Philadelphia's cultural history, Temple University in 2001 established the Philadelphia Dance Collection. Housed in Temple's Paley Library, the collection sustains and extends the legacy of Philadelphia dance art by preserving documents, oral histories, performance videos, and other vital information essential to the legacies of Philadelphia's premier dance companies and their contributions to the movement phenomenon.

The College of HPERD was dissolved in 1998, and the Dance Department was moved into the Esther Boyer College of Music. In 2001 the college name was changed to the Esther Boyer College of Music and Department of Dance. In 2004 the Dance Department was incorporated into the college, necessitating another name change, this time to the Esther Boyer College of Music and Dance, subsequently shortened to the Boyer College of Music and Dance.

Several faculty members in Temple's dance program are known for their national and international contributions as teachers and performers. Dr. Kariamu Welsh, professor and department chair, was the founding artistic director of the National Dance Company of Zimbabwe. Eva Gholson conducted master dance workshops in modern dance, jazz, and choreomusical analysis in Greece, Germany, Hong Kong, and Taiwan. Merian Soto received six Choreographers Fellowships from the National Endowment for the Arts and in 2000 received the New York Dance and Performance BESSIE Award for sustained choreographic achievement.

The Boyer College of Music and Dance has prepared students for careers as educators, performers, composers, choreographers, and scholars. The college annually offers 300 on-campus student performances, master classes, and faculty and guest artist recitals. In addition, Boyer students perform at venerable venues such as the Lincoln Center, Carnegie Hall, Kimmel Center for the Performing Arts, and Jazz at Lincoln Center. The Boyer College of Music and Dance has integrated the best in conservatory-level arts training with a challenging academic curriculum. Graduates of the Boyer College can be found in major orchestras of the world, including the Philadelphia, Chicago, Cleveland, Los Angeles, and San Francisco symphony orchestras. In 2009 nine graduates performed with the Metropolitan Opera Orchestra, rated as one of the finest opera orchestras in the world. Whether serving North Philadelphia or the world at large, the Boyer College of Music and Dance has a long, proud history and a grand future lies ahead.

The School of Communications and Theater

Temple's School of Communications and Theater (SCT) is a relatively young independent unit. Nearly all of the integral parts of the school have histories as parts of other units within the university. When officially formed in 1967, the school brought together programs in theater, journalism, and communications (radio-television-film). Each began as a separate program in other schools.

Journalism, the oldest of the three programs and one of the oldest in the nation, started in 1927 as a four-year program in the School of Commerce (see Chapter 3) under the chairmanship of Henry E. Birdsong. Elsewhere, journalism was either a separate school or a department in liberal arts. But the Temple liberal arts faculty looked on journalism with some disdain, turning down petitions from the department to allow liberal arts students to take journalism courses for liberal arts credit, mostly because many of the instructors, although skilled professionals, lacked advanced degrees. Still, the program met an important need and it gained in popularity. Between 1927 and 1967 about 1,400 journalism degrees were awarded to Temple graduates.

Theater was a student-directed extra-curricular activity until Paul E. "Pop" Randall arrived in 1931, fresh from completing his MFA at Yale. Randall crafted a curriculum, formalized instruction, and directed students in professional-quality theater productions. The theater program began as part of the English Department in the Teachers College. When President Beury united the English departments of Liberal Arts, Commerce, and Teachers, the action swept both the theater and journalism programs into the English Department within the College of Liberal Arts.

The communications (radio-television) program came into being in 1947 when Walter Annenberg's Triangle Publications presented Temple a grant to create a program in radio and television. The radio-television program was placed in the College of Liberal Arts, and in 1948 Temple became the first college in the United States to offer a bachelor's degree in broadcasting. Eventually, radio-television, journalism, and theater courses appeared in a new liberal arts division named the Department of Radio, Speech, and Theater, with John B. Roberts (Radio), Gordon Hostettler (Speech and Journalism), and Paul Randall (Theater) directing respective majors within the department.

The theater and radio-television programs never found an intellectual niche in the College of Liberal Arts, whose faculty denied students credit for theater or journalism courses toward a liberal arts degree. They regarded the radio-television sequence as a vocational encroachment that lessened the college's reputation. Indeed, Phi Beta Kappa cited the presence of the radio-television program in the College of Liberal Arts as one of its reasons for initially withholding the establishment of a Temple chapter. In 1949 J. Douglas Perry, then chairman of the Journalism Department, began a communications curriculum that combined journalism with electives in radio and television. In search of a more comfortable home and more compatible colleagues, radio-television and journalism asked to be shifted to the School of Business and Public Administration. With the help of Dean Harry Cochran, the programs were joined in 1951 to form the Department of Journalism and Communications. That department eventually merged into the Department of Communications with a division of journalism and a division of radio-television. The program produced hundreds of graduates who found success in advertising, broadcasting (radio and TV), and public relations.

In 2002 the university constructed a three-story atrium to cover the open court in Annenberg Hall. The atrium provides newfound space for presentations, lectures, a video library, student lounges, and a café. The bold, modernistic entryway serves as a visual connector dramatically linking the School of Communications and Theater to the adjacent Tyler School of Art and Boyer College of Music and Dance.

The School of Communications and Theater began functioning informally in the fall semester 1965 under the direction of an interim committee made up of representatives from the three departments—John Roberts (Radio-Television), J. Douglas Perry (Journalism), and Paul Randall (Theater). In 1967 Temple's trustees formally established the School of Communications and Theater, authorizing it to grant bachelor of science degrees in journalism, theater, and radio-television-film (film was added in 1967) and a master's degree in journalism. Professor Perry was named acting dean until a national search brought in Kenneth Harwood to take over in 1968. Before coming to Temple, Harwood had been chair of the Department of Telecommunications at the University of Southern California and was widely known for his expertise in the emerging field of communications. Tomlinson Theater and Annenberg Hall were built to house the School of Communications and Theater and dedicated in 1968 (see Chapter 5).

Journalism

In June 1968 the first master's degrees in journalism were awarded, and the next year the department received full accreditation from the American Council for Education in Journalism. Between 1966 and 2009 the program produced nearly 6,000 graduates in all aspects of journalism and mass communications. Temple graduates have long dominated the Philadelphia region's media market, staffing newspapers, television newsrooms, and anchor desks. Many have gained high-level positions across the nation. Temple journalism graduates have claimed major awards, including three Pulitzer prizes: John L. Dotson Jr. (BS SCT 1958) in 1994 for Meritorious Public Service, Joby S. Warrick (BA SCT 1982) in 1996 for Public Service, and Clarence J. Williams III (BA SCT 1993) in 1998 for Feature Photography. More recently, Stephen M. Katz (MA SCT 2003) was named the 2009 Newspaper Photographer of the Year by the National Press Photographers Association.

Temple's distinguished journalism faculty claimed multiple winners of teaching awards, including Temple's Great Teacher Award (Ed Trayes), plus a three-time winner of the Messenger Award for Civil Rights Commentary (Linn Washington), the 2006 James W. Carey Media Research Award winner (Carolyn Kitch), and the 2006 winner of the Harold Innis Dissertation Award (Susan Jacobson). Since its inception the Journalism Department has included faculty members who are both accomplished practitioners and scholars, a carefully blended balance that in 2009 left the program as just one of two in Pennsylvania meeting all professional accrediting standards.

The immense expansion of the electronic media since the 1980s required the Journalism Department to make a number of curricular and instructional adjustments. For example, the public's growing reliance on commercial television led to the addition of broadcast journalism as a major in 1994. As the Journalism Department entered the new millennium it carefully developed niche expertise in urban journalism and multimedia reporting. The cornerstone of this endeavor was the replication of a modern multimedia newsroom environment at Temple's Center City Campus next to City Hall. The Multimedia Urban Reporting Lab (MURL)—with wireless networking, Internet access, digital recorders, access to the AP wires, and video cameras and recorders—became the foundation of the Journalism Department's mission to train students to the highest and best standards in the field and to fulfill the department's mission to better tell stories in the under-covered and under-served neighborhoods of Philadelphia.

Theater

For most of his thirty-eight years at Temple, Paul "Pop" Randall had few resources to work with when staging theatrical productions. Two undergraduate student organizations, the Templayers and Scores and Encores (the latter devoted to musical comedy productions), provided the early talent

TEMPLE NOTABLE
Clarence J. Williams III

Drawing upon skills acquired in the School of Communications and Theater and a strong social conscience honed while at Temple, Philadelphia-born Clarence Williams began as an intern for the *Philadelphia Tribune*, then became a staff photographer at the *Los Angeles Times*. His two-part 1997 feature series "Orphans of Addiction," documenting the plight of young children with parents addicted to alcohol and drugs, earned him the 1998 Pulitzer Prize for Photography. His many other honors include the National Headliner Award, the Robert F. Kennedy Photojournalism Award, and the National Association of Black Journalists award for Journalist of the Year.

for his stage plays. The old gymnasium in the basement of College Hall and the Mitten Hall auditorium served as makeshift theaters. After so many years of making do with inadequate facilities and equipment, Randall experienced bittersweet joy with the opening in 1968 of the Tomlinson Theater within the Annenberg communications complex (see Chapter 5). With 481 plush seats, a huge seventy-five-foot proscenium stage, a sleek lobby, and sophisticated lighting and sound systems, Tomlinson Theater provided everything Randall wanted. Regrettably, he produced only one play before reaching mandatory retirement in 1969. However, the Annenberg complex also included a small ninety-seat theater with all of the latest lighting and stage technologies. Quite appropriately, it is now known simply as Randall Theater.

Since Randall's day the Department of Theater has focused on the study and practice of the art, craft, and scholarship of theater. Based on the concept of a conservatory, the program has successfully prepared students for careers in acting, theatrical design, directing, stage management, and technical theater. The MFA in theater was first offered in 1967. A new two-year MFA in acting was introduced in 2009, intended to attract seasoned mid-career professionals interested in re-examining their craft with the goal of achieving personal growth as artists and teachers.

Leadership of the theater program was for many years in the hands of Robert Hedley, founder of The Philadelphia Company, a performing arts company, and nationally known playwright, director, and developer of new plays. In 2006 Hedley was honored with a Lifetime Achievement Award at the Barrymore Awards ceremony (the Philadelphia theater community's equivalent of New York's Tony Awards). Dr. Roberta Sloane, former artistic director/chair of the Theater Conservatory at the University of Central Florida, became chair in 2005.

Paul "Pop" Randall is shown (circa 1968) directing students in one of the first theatrical productions in Temple's Tomlinson Theater.

Hollywood Comes to Temple

The In Crowd, a motion picture that had major scenes shot at the university, premiered in Philadelphia in February 1988. Interiors for the movie were filmed at Tomlinson Theater in August 1986. Mark Rosenthal (BA CLA 1972) directed the movie. More than sixty members of the Temple community worked behind the scenes and in front of the camera.

Temple's theater program boasts many notable alumni, among them Robin Atkin Downes (MFA SCT 1994), one of the most sought-after voice-over talents in the industry with over 140 voice-over performances in major motion pictures; Kevin Del Aguila (MFA SCT 1994), author of the long-running Off-Broadway hit *Altar Boyz;* and Jason George (MFA SCT 1997), who appeared in principal roles in over thirty television series, including *ER*, *House*, and *Friends. Jason* Kolotouros (MFA SCT 1997) has appeared on *As the World Turns, Law & Order,* and *Sex and the City*; John Littlefield (MFA SCT 1995) served as co-host of ABC's *Extreme Makeover: Home Edition* and played featured roles on *Law & Order*, *The West Wing*, and *Roswell*; and Kunal Nayyar (MFA SCT 2006) starred in the hit CBS sitcom *The Big Bang Theory.* Corey Sorenson (MFA SCT 2006) performed at the world-renowned Old Globe Theater as Proteus in *Two Gentlemen of Verona* and Laertes in *Hamlet*; Josh Tower (BA SCT 1995) starred in two major Broadway productions, as Simba in *The Lion King* and in *Ragtime, the Musical.*

Responding to the complex and rapid technological changes in communications media occurring since the 1980s, the School of Communications and Theater made frequent adjustments in the school's array of majors and course offerings. Radio-television-film, for example, was divided between the departments of film and media arts and the more generic program in broadcasting, telecommunications, and mass media. In 2004 the Department of Journalism, Public Relations and Advertising split into the Department of Journalism, the Department of Advertising, and the Department of Strategic and Organizational Communication. By 2009 SCT was offering master's degrees in six areas and a PhD in mass media and communications.

In addition to theater and journalism, SCT programs were concentrated in departments of advertising (focusing on marketing communication for a high-tech and media-intense environment); broadcasting, telecommunications, and mass media (featuring media production, management, and comprehensive broadcast training); film and media arts (emphasizing independent film and documentary work); and strategic and organizational communication (combining rhetoric and communications and a comprehensive approach to public relations).

To foster intellectual exchange and broaden students' horizons, the School of Communications and Theater has offered a study abroad program in London, England, since the 1970s, affording Temple students career-building internship opportunities in British and American media and theater operations in an international context.

There have been relatively few leadership changes in the School of Communications and Theater since its founding in 1967. Robert Smith succeeded Harwood, became dean in 1978, and served until 1996, overseeing the development of new MFA programs, a post-doctoral program in communications, and substantial enrollment increases. Dr. Robert Greenberg served from 1996 to 2000, followed by Concetta Stewart, who remained until 2009, when she resigned to accept a position at the Pratt Institute. Associate Dean Thomas Jacobson was appointed interim dean.

An enrollment surge after 1999 created a demand for more rooms, leading to the construction in 2002 of a three story atrium to cover the open court in Annenberg Hall. The area provides a dramatic entrance from Thirteenth Street and additional programmable space for presentations, lectures, a video library, student lounges, and a café.

The School of Communications and Theater received a great deal of media attention from the establishment in 2001 of the Lew Klein awards in media excellence, which honored such luminaries as Chris Matthews, Ed Bradley, and Dick Vermeil. Lew Klein served the School of Communications and Theater as an adjunct professor for more than five decades. A seasoned professional who produced such landmark television programs as *American Bandstand*, Klein earned a reputation as a master teacher and wise mentor. Speaking of Klein, Bob Saget (BA SCT 1978) said: "One of the best things that I did was [to take a course with] Lew Klein, who has helped so many people. He got me an internship at the *Mike Douglas Show*, and so I worked for six months at the *Mike Douglas Show*, and it was like 'Wow! Show business.' That particular internship changed my life. . . . I never thought that I'd end up in television as an actor. . . . It was a really a special part of my life that . . . changed my path."

Recent Lew Klein awardees include Ed Cunningham (BS SCT 1969), best known as the unmistakable "voice of WHYY"; Suzanne Smith (BA SCT 1983), a three-time Emmy Award winner as director of CBS sports coverage for *The NFL on CBS*, NCAA Men's Basketball Championship, and the Olympics; Yair Stern (MS SCT 1970), former director general of Israel Television; Shirley Powell (BA SCT 1988), senior vice president of corporate communications for Turner Broadcasting System; Dr. Marilyn Lashner (PhD SCT 1979), the owner of Media Analysis & Communications Research and the first woman to earn a PhD in communications at Temple; Barry Levine (BA SCT 1981), executive editor of the *National Enquirer*; and Steve Capus (BA SCT 1986), president of NBC News and winner of four Emmy Awards and six Edward R. Murrow Awards.

WRTI

Temple University established the first college radio curriculum in the country and by 2009 could claim more graduates in the broadcast industry and in broadcast education than any other broadcast curriculum. The program was launched in 1947 by John B. Roberts, who recruited faculty, shaped the curriculum, and guided the program's destiny for forty-two years. A broadcast newsman and

For its first twenty years (1948 to 1968) WRTI was a student-managed radio station, featuring a wide range of creative programming, including live musical performances, dramatic presentations, and current events forums, plus recorded popular music, news, and sports reporting. Student-produced shows, such as the one pictured here, circa 1953, afforded Temple graduates unique opportunities for professional training and advancement during the golden age of radio.

weekend TV anchor, Roberts enjoyed a lengthy association with WFIL-TV and WFIL radio. Largely because of Roberts's involvement, WFIL provided a grant to start Temple's radio program and to begin building broadcast studios as teaching laboratories.

"I thought it was not enough just to sit in class," Roberts later recalled. He wanted his students to experience the irreplaceable, hands-on experience of working in an on-air environment. Roberts secured a license, WFIL and the *Philadelphia Inquirer* donated funds for modern equipment, and on Monday, March 15, 1948, at 4:30 P.M. WRTI—the call letters stood for Radio Teaching Institute—made its first test broadcast to the Temple campus. WRTI nurtured the careers of thousands of aspiring radio and television broadcasters; it is where young broadcasters such as Merrill Reese (BS CLA 1964), the voice of the Philadelphia Eagles, Norman Fell (BA CLA 1950), a star on the television show *Three's Company*, and world-famous comedian Bill Cosby received their starts.

WRTI was formed during the Golden Age of Radio as a campus-only station at 640 AM, broadcasting from the basement of Thomas Hall (at 1940 Park Avenue, since demolished to make way for a Temple dormitory). Quickly popular with students and faculty, the station received an FM license in 1953, operating on 90.1 FM. A new transmitter was installed atop Conwell Hall, broadcasting a playlist that included dramas, book reviews written by instructors from the English Department, and live performances by soloists from the College of Music.

When WRTI moved to the new Annenberg Hall in 1968, Dean Harwood decided to place the station in the hands of a paid professional staff assisted by student volunteers. At some time in the summer of 1969, under faculty director Bob Kassi, the station went to an all-jazz format. By 1970, WRTI was the number-one jazz station in Philadelphia. In 1972 the gift of an anonymous donor allowed the station to purchase a new transmitter and antenna that were relocated to the site of station WFLN-FM, then an all-classical music station in the Roxborough section of Philadelphia, thus allowing WRTI to extend its coverage significantly. WRTI in 1977 became the first public radio station to transmit printed text for the deaf.

For administrative clarity and sound business reasons, President Liacouras found it necessary in 1983 to move WRTI out of the School of Communications and Theater and place it under the office of Vice President H. Patrick Swygert within the University Relations Department. The all-jazz format continued with additional community involvement. With new professional management, repeater stations to extend its broadcast range, and an affiliation with National Public Radio, WRTI attracted new listeners, even though it continued to amass deficits.

Then, on September 5, 1997, WFLN's owners abruptly ceased broadcasting classical music. Classical music on Philadelphia's airwaves went silent for ten days. Peter Liacouras quickly seized the initiative, deciding that WRTI could fill the void by offering classical music during the day and jazz at night. The format change allowed former WFLN listeners to hear the voices that guided them throughout their classical music listening day, including personalities Jill Pasternak, Dave Conant, and Jack Moore. For nighttime jazz, WRTI hired longtime Philadelphia jazz host Bob Perkins and added Maureen Malloy as jazz music director.

On March 1, 2004, WRTI relocated to the new Entertainment and Community Education Center (ECEC) and began broadcasting from the 61,000-square-foot structure at the corner of Fifteenth Street and Cecil B. Moore Avenue. The new facility provided ten studios and control rooms, nineteen offices, a conference room, and a 400-square-foot music library with a capacity for 70,000 CDs and 9,000 albums. A live-performance studio and adjoining high-end multi-track control room were designed for live classical and jazz performances. In the first ten years of the dual classical and jazz broadcasting format, WRTI's audience more than doubled to 350,000 listeners per week. WRTI's signal extended west to Harrisburg and north to Scranton and Wilkes-Barre, also reaching listeners as far south as Dover, Delaware, and at the Jersey shore, making it one of the most listened-to public radio stations in the United States.

WHIP and WRFT

Students remained involved in WRTI as volunteers and interns, receiving exceptional training in state-of-the-art facilities, but after 1968 they took no role in managing the station. In 1997 a group of communications and business students decided to start their own student-operated station. They selected the call sign WHIP (We Have Infinite Potential) and decided on a format of rock, hip-hop, news, and sports. With the support of student services staff, WHIP finally went on the air in 2002, broadcasting on 91.3 FM from a studio in the Student Activities Center. WHIP shut down from 2004 to 2006 during building renovations, but in February 2007 the station moved into the first floor of the new TECH Center and went live again, this time with an Internet live-stream broadcast that attracted listeners from around the world. WRFT, a totally student-run station, has operated at the Ambler Campus for over twenty years, broadcasting an assorted mix of music to students within the campus.

Athletics

Temple University's intercollegiate athletics program has a long, storied, and proud history. Its teams and individual athletes have won national championships, gained international recognition, and engendered enormous pride in Temple. Temple University boasts nine national Hall of Fame coaches, in football, basketball, soccer, baseball, lacrosse, golf, and fencing. One of the first institutions in the United States to sponsor extra-curricular athletic activities for its students, Temple enjoyed a leadership role in the early years, having fabulous success through the 1930s in football and basketball. Temple's middle passage in the postwar years and through the 1980s brought continued success in many sports, especially men's basketball, but decline in others as Temple often found it difficult to compete nationally with the burgeoning, well-funded land-grant institutions and the sports-conscious, generously subsidized Sun Belt universities. In recent years, however, with the emergence of a highly successful women's program and the reinvigoration of several men's sports, Temple athletics once again are on the rise.

In April 1894, only ten years after Russell Conwell began tutoring students in his study, the trustees authorized the establishment of a Temple Athletic Association to be supervised by the dean of the faculty, Dr. Frank Lambader, and a board of control that included faculty representatives from all departments of the college. That year Charles M. Williams assumed the post of Temple's first director of athletics, coaching the football and basketball teams and overseeing several field sports, including cricket, baseball, lawn tennis, and croquet, that were played on a field at Seventeenth Street and Erie Avenue. Williams's first love was basketball. He was a recent graduate of Springfield College (Massachusetts) and a student of Dr. James Naismith, who was credited with inventing the game of basketball just three years earlier. Basketball quickly became Temple's most popular sport.

Williams lost little time in recruiting a basketball team to take advantage of the new gymnasium in the basement of College Hall, which despite its low eighteen-foot ceiling was considered one of best of its day because it was longer and wider than most and could seat more than 1,000 spectators.

TEMPLE NOTABLE
Marty Moss-Coane

Marjorie Moss (BA CLA 1973), as she was known during her Temple days, began a career in broadcasting as a part-timer in 1983, working her way up to become the host and executive producer of *Radio Times*, an award-winning daily two-hour interview and call-in program on WHYY (90.9 FM) radio, a National Public Radio (NPR) affiliate in Philadelphia. Since her debut in 1987 Moss-Coane has won critics' praise and many awards for her skills in producing intriguing, educational, and entertaining programs and for her unmatched ability to guide thought-provoking discussions on highly controversial topics in a fair-minded, balanced, and informative manner. Equally at home on television as the host and moderator of WHYY-TV community forums and candidate debates, Moss-Coane is one of the most respected figures in Philadelphia's broadcast community.

Temple played an intramural schedule its first year. The Owls' first recorded basketball victory came against the Purple Crescent Athletic Club, 3–1.

Temple inaugurated an intercollegiate schedule on March 23, 1895, losing 6–4 to Haverford College. The next season Temple began a brief but spirited rivalry with the University of Pennsylvania, sharing the distinction with Yale of being Penn's oldest foe. After three hotly contested games—Penn won two games 4–2 and 6–4 and Temple took the third, 3–1—the Temple-Penn rivalry was halted in 1898, when Penn dropped the sport for a few seasons, not to be resumed until the 1920–1921 season. That game, won by Penn 24–19, was marked by such bad sportsmanship on the part of both players and spectators that the series was broken off until the 1955–1956 season, when it resumed with a convincing 92–73 Temple victory led by Harold "Hal" Lear (BS SBM 1956) and Guy Rodgers (BS EDU 1958).

The low-scoring games in the early years were due to the rules (or lack of them) that counted only one point for a goal, prohibited close-in shots to the very shallow hoops, allowed close guarding and very rough play, and did not award free or uncontested shots after fouls. Coach Charles Williams helped evolve the game, establishing the five-man game in 1896 (seven or nine men played in the first games), defining fouls, and developing the first scoreboards and official scorecards. Williams coached the basketball and football teams until 1899, getting both programs off to promising starts. However, over the next decade both programs sputtered along, frequently changing coaches, periodically failing to field teams, or relying on pickup squads.

Whatever archives once existed containing materials related to the histories of the early years of Temple's sports teams were lost during a move from College Hall to Conwell Hall in 1922. But based on what history professor Lawrence O. Ealy (BA CLA 1934) was able to piece together in 1949 from the records of other institutions, we know that the intra-city basketball rivalry that later developed into the "Big Five" had a slow, intermittent beginning. Temple and La Salle first played in 1900 (won by La Salle 15–10), and the Temple–St. Joseph's series began in 1902 with a resounding 27–4 Temple victory. Temple and St. Joseph's met on a fairly regular basis thereafter. Villanova became a regular Temple basketball opponent beginning in 1915. However, annual round-robin scheduling of all Big Five schools—Temple, St. Joseph's, La Salle, Villanova, and Penn—did not commence until the 1954–1955 season.

Temple's competition in the early years was limited to club teams, some high school and prep squads, plus nearby colleges, such as Ursinus, Drexel, Muhlenberg, and Franklin and Marshall. Basketball was suspended for two years (1918–1919) during World War I, but the football team remained in hiatus four seasons. In 1920 Temple reorganized its athletics programs, placed control in the hands of a faculty-led Athletic Council, and applied for membership in the National Collegiate Athletic Association (NCAA). Deciding once more to boost its program of varsity competition, Temple hired Dr. Francis D'Eliscue to coach major sports and he succeeded in fielding a football team in 1921. In 1927 Earl R. Yeomans was appointed graduate manager of athletics (later named athletic director), and teams were organized in baseball, boxing, wrestling, soccer, fencing, gymnastics, swimming, cross-country, track, golf, and, of course, basketball and football. Many of Temple's men's and women's teams (after 1923) had greater success, but football—the king of American college campuses—received the majority of Temple's attention and the largest share of available resources.

Football

College sports in the 1920s were greatly influenced by the collegiate ideal—the notion of what a perfect college experience ought to entail. By the 1920s that ideal experience included attendance at a college boasting a successful football program playing games before large crowds, preferably in a huge stadium owned by the college or university. Football games in the 1920s became public spectacles, a part of mass media marketing. Too important and too lucrative to be left in the hands of student managers or professor-coaches, college football became big-time and was taken over by professionals. Power over collegiate sports shifted away from the faculty to the alumni, trustees, and athletic directors, plus the highly paid coaches they recruited. Walter Camp (Yale) became the prototypical athletic director, and his famous pupil, Amos Alonzo Stagg (University of Chicago), set the pattern, demanding and receiving administrative control over athletics and exemption from most university regulations. Big-time college sports became associated with crass commercialism and insinuations of a willingness in places to do anything, including bending the rules, to deliver football victories to please donors and alumni.

Temple was one of the first universities to participate in intercollegiate athletics, beginning with varsity football, shown here in 1894. Prior to 1928 and the opening of Temple Stadium, the football team played important games at Penn's Franklin Field and other games at Hunting Park or occasionally on high school fields.

Notwithstanding, Temple in the 1920s rushed headlong into the foray of major college football, but without much initial success. Between 1922 and 1925 the team won only two games and lost thirteen. Lack of proper facilities—games were played at Hunting Park and the teams practiced on vacant lots—became the accepted explanation. The trustees responded by increasing student fees to fund the purchase of a proper playing field. Two Temple trustees, Charles E. Beury (later president) and developer Charles G. Erny, spearheaded the move to acquire an eleven-acre site (later expanded to thirty-two acres) at Vernon Road and Cheltenham Avenue, almost eight miles directly north of the campus. A football field, clubhouse, and stands for 5,000 spectators were ready for the 1926 season.

The team immediately responded with an improved record. Henry J. "Heinie" Miller, an All-American at Penn in 1919, was hired as head coach in 1925. Miller quickly turned the Owls into a regional power. In just eight seasons he compiled a record of fifty wins, fifteen losses, and eight ties. During the 1927 season Miller led Temple to lopsided victories over Blue Ridge College (110–0) and Juniata (58–0), losing only to Dartmouth. The 1927 season also produced Temple's first win over an upper-echelon power, a 7–0 win over Brown, then the leading team in the nation's top conference, the Ivy League. When Temple pushed over the winning score against Brown, Laura Carnell, the normally reserved associate president, threw her arms around Beury in a rare display of emotion and elation. Temple football had won over the one recalcitrant voice in the Temple administration.

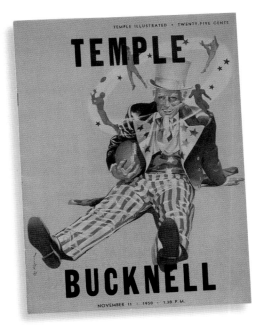

Above *Bucknell was Temple's arch-rival in football from 1927 to 1970. After World War II the winner of the game received the Old Shoe Trophy, a bronzed football shoe commemorating the sacrifices of football players from both schools who died during the war. The two schools last played in 1970, and the Old Shoe Trophy remains in Temple's possession.*

Opposite *Temple's 1934 football squad was undefeated (two ties) and received a bid to play in the inaugural Sugar Bowl in New Orleans.*

Charles Beury, who became president in 1926, believed that a big-time college program would pay dividends for Temple, bringing much-needed attention to a school that was hardly known beyond Philadelphia. By then, impressive stadia were de rigueur for universities with pretensions to greatness, "a symbolic rite of passage for an ambitious university," as historian John R. Thelin described them. Temple was unable to resist the temptation, particularly because the University of Pennsylvania had enjoyed splendid success since the 1895 construction of its own monument to greatness, the 30,000-seat (later 60,500-seat) Franklin Field.

In 1927 Charles Erny, an avid college football fan, presented Temple with a $100,000 gift and a promise to finance the balance of $300,000 necessary to build a new football stadium on the field at Vernon Road and Cheltenham Avenue. The stadium opened in time for the 1928 season, providing a maximum seating capacity of 34,200. The horseshoe-shaped stadium, built in a natural bowl, was known first as Beury Stadium, later as Owl Stadium, and finally as Temple Stadium. To help defray expenses, Temple occasionally rented the stadium to the Philadelphia Eagles for home games. To avoid directly competing against the University of Pennsylvania on Saturday afternoons, when college games were normally played, Temple experimented with game schedules, installed floodlights, and played some games at night. The largest crowd in stadium history was an estimated 40,000, which overflowed the stadium in November 1934 to see Temple defeat Villanova 22–0.

Heinie Miller's charges had great success in Temple Stadium and soon gained national respect, scheduling perennial powers such as Carnegie Tech, Drake, and Penn State. In 1931 Temple defeated Penn State at home and traveled west, winning against both the University of Missouri and the University of Denver. Yet attendance at the stadium lagged, and the plaudits and attention of the local media were all directed toward the powerful teams of the University of Pennsylvania. In 1932, despite Miller's excellent record, which included another win that season over Penn State, Beury decided Temple needed a big-name coach. After Knute Rockne died, none was better known than the inimitable Glenn Scobey "Pop" Warner, legendary coach of Jim Thorpe at the Carlisle Indian School and winner in the previous nineteen years of three national championships at Pittsburgh and Stanford universities. To the surprise of many, Warner accepted Beury's offer and took over Temple's program beginning with the 1933 season.

Warner's presence at Temple brought the media attention Beury and Erny expected, but at the cost of faculty uneasiness over the administration's willingness to pay Warner's extravagant salary during the Depression. In six seasons at Temple, playing against the best competition in the land, Warner's teams won thirty-one, lost eighteen, and tied two games. The 1934 season, Warner's second at Temple, was arguably the greatest in Temple's history. That year the team won seven games, lost none, and tied twice (Indiana and Bucknell). At season's end it earned an invitation to

1st ANNUAL
SUGAR BOWL Classic

NEW
YEAR'S
DAY
1935

NEW
ORLEANS

R
TEMPLE
— VS. —
TULANE

TULANE STADIUM OFFICIAL SOUVENIR

PRICE
25¢

COPYRIGHT 1935

DO SNIDER 34

FRANKLIN PTG. CO.
N.O. LA.

play on January 1, 1935, in the inaugural Sugar Bowl in New Orleans, where it lost to Tulane 20–14. Warner remained at Temple through the 1938 season.

From the 1939 season until 1963, Temple de-emphasized football and had only four winning seasons. President Robert L. Johnson simply believed the university had higher priorities. Between 1940 and 1948, Roy Morrison, former Vanderbilt All-American, coached with some success, ending with a 31–38–9 record. Three coaches—Albert Kawal, Josh Cody, and Pete Stevens, who captained the 1935 Sugar Bowl team—served between 1949 and 1959, rarely winning, although the 1950 team managed a 7–7 tie against Penn State. The team reached a nadir in the late 1950s, enduring a school record twenty-one-game losing streak from the last four games of the 1957 season and through the entire 1958 and 1959 seasons. George Makris arrived as head coach to start the 1960 season and restored competitiveness to the Temple program, compiling a ten-year record of 45–44–4. During most of Makris's tenure Temple competed in the University Division of the Middle Atlantic States Conference against teams such as Bucknell, Delaware, Gettysburg, and Hofstra, winning the conference title in 1967.

In 1969 President Anderson instructed athletic director Ernie Casale to upgrade the football program. Anderson believed that Temple's state-affiliated status required Temple to compete on all levels with Penn State and Pittsburgh, both of which fielded highly competitive football teams. Moreover, playing a minor-league schedule did nothing to enhance the university's reputation. Temple became an independent in football, scheduled the best teams in the East, and hired Wayne Hardin, who had coached two Heisman Trophy winners during his six successful years as head coach at Navy. Taking over in 1970, Hardin led Temple to an 80–52–3 record over twelve years. Temple went 9–1 in 1973 and 8–2 in 1974, winning fourteen straight games at one point over two seasons. Temple played two regular-season games in Tokyo, Japan, in what journalists called the Mirage Bowl, losing 35–32 to Grambling in 1977 and beating Boston College 28–24 in 1978. Always close to breaking through with a momentous victory, Temple faced its nemesis Penn State, suffering last-minute heartbreaking 31–30 and 10–7 losses in 1976 and 1978.

Hardin restored pride and respectability to Temple football. In 1979 the Owls won the most games (ten) in school history. The team opened the season with a 38–16 win at West Virginia and later beat Rutgers (41–20) and Syracuse (49–17). Temple's only losses during the regular season were to nationally ranked Pittsburgh (10–9) and Penn State (22–7). Finishing the season ranked seventeenth in the nation, Temple defeated the University of California 28–17 in the second Garden State Bowl before a crowd of 55,952 at Giants Stadium. Several of Hardin's stalwarts earned major awards, including guard Bill Singletary (BS EDU 1973), a first-team All-American in 1972, and Steve Joachim (BA SCT 1975; MBA SBM 1988), winner of the 1974 Maxwell Award as the top college football player and also a Walter Camp first-team All-America selection.

When Hardin retired in 1982, Temple brought in Bruce Arians, then only thirty years old, as head coach. Arians had some success during his six years, beating Pittsburgh three times and compiling two winning seasons, going 6–5 in 1984, beating East Carolina, Pittsburgh, and West Virginia, and 6–5 again in 1986. That year running back Paul Palmer (1986) was the runner-up for the Heisman Trophy and a consensus first-team All-American.

Jerry Berndt took over for Arians in 1989 and led Temple to a 7–4 season in 1990. Temple joined the Big East Conference in 1991 but was unable to compete against teams with better facilities and bigger budgets. During its fourteen years in the league, Temple won as many as three league games

TEMPLE NOTABLE
Glenn "Pop" Warner

The Hall of Fame Temple football coach from 1933 to 1938 revolutionized football with his single- and double-winged formations. He became a national celebrity, playing himself in the movie *Knute Rockne All American*, alongside Ronald Reagan (George Gipp). The Pop Warner Little Scholars, a junior football program attracting over 300,000 youths as players and cheerleaders, was named in his honor. In August 1997 the U.S. Postal Service released a thirty-two-cent stamp depicting Warner with a young football player.

in a season only once and failed to win any league games six times. Overall, the team had a 14–80 record against Big East foes. Berndt finished with an overall record of 11–33, followed by Ron Dickerson (1993 to 1997), who went 8–47, and Bobby Wallace, who won nineteen and lost seventy-one between 1998 and 2005. Temple failed to win a game in Wallace's final year.

Trustees, donors, alumni, and fans continued to hold out hope and financial assistance. To provide the kinds of football facilities and infrastructure support in place at the institutions against which the football team competed, Temple authorized funds and sought gifts of $6.8 million for the construction of an athletic practice facility dedicated exclusively to the football team. In 1999 Temple opened Edberg-Olson Hall, named for George Edberg-Olson (BS EDU 1949), professor emeritus of Spanish and a major donor. The Edberg-Olson complex covered the city blocks north and east of the campus bounded by Diamond Street, Susquehanna Avenue, Eleventh Street, and the SEPTA Regional Rail tracks. The 13,000-square-foot, two-story building included a locker room, weight room, training room, lecture hall, equipment storage, team meeting rooms, and coaches' offices. The centerpiece of the Edberg-Olson facility was a practice field with 100 yards of natural turf and 50 yards of artificial turf.

The commitment to continue to play football games in the largest available stadium before the largest possible crowds was reaffirmed in 1996 when Temple's trustees authorized the demolition of Temple Stadium. In April 2001 the thirty-two-acre site at Vernon Road and Cheltenham Avenue was sold for $4.5 million, and the next year trustees authorized expending a similar amount to construct athletic facilities on the Ambler Campus. These facilities would include baseball and softball fields, two soccer fields, and a sports administration building, which were completed in 2003.

New facilities notwithstanding, the Big East Conference dropped Temple in 2004, and for the next two seasons Temple played an independent schedule. Al Golden, Temple's twenty-fourth head football coach, started the 2006 season with raised expectations, but the team lost its first eight games before defeating Bowling Green and snapping a twenty-game losing streak, one game short of the school record. Golden's teams improved in his second and third seasons, and his overall record stood at ten wins and twenty-six losses entering the 2009 season.

Beginning in 2007 Temple's football team participated in the NCAA's Division I Football Bowl Subdivision (formerly known as Division 1-A) as a football-only affiliate of the Mid-American Conference (MAC). Temple's primary athletic conference, the Atlantic 10 Conference, did not sponsor a football league. After 114 years of competition, dating to 1894, Temple's overall football record stood at 387 wins, 506 losses, and 52 ties. Nine out of ten of the largest crowds to see Temple football were at games against Penn State, the largest being 105,950 for the 2006 game at Penn State. The largest crowd to see a Temple home game was at the 2007 Penn State game when 69,029 spectators filled Lincoln Financial Field.

Many Temple football players went on to play professional football. Fifty-eight Temple players were selected in the National Football League (NFL) draft between 1937 and 2008. Five former Owls were

Al Golden, named Temple's twenty-fourth head football coach in 2006, brought youthful vigor and an intense desire to restore former glory to a program that had lost its luster in recent years. In 2009 Golden led the Owls to nine-straight victories on the way to a 9–3 regular-season record and—for the first time in thirty years—an invitation to compete in a postseason bowl game, the EagleBank Bowl against UCLA.

on NFL rosters in the 2008 season. At least one Temple University alumnus appeared on the roster of six of the seven Super Bowl champion teams between 2001 and 2008. Temple University's Joe Klecko (CLA 1977) was the first defensive player in the NFL to be selected to the Pro Bowl at three different positions, and his son, Dan Klecko (SCT 2003), played for the Philadelphia Eagles.

Men's Basketball

Since their beginnings under Charles M. Williams in 1894, Temple's men's basketball teams have won 1,689 games (as of the end of 2008–2009 season), leaving the Owls as the sixth most successful program in the history of college basketball, trailing only Kentucky, North Carolina, Kansas, Duke, and Syracuse in total number of wins. Temple's teams have established a reputation for spirited, disciplined play and good sportsmanship. On many occasions they have risen to the top of national competition, bringing the institution valued attention and instilling pride and honor in its students and graduates.

After being idle during World War I the basketball program reestablished itself under Dr. Francis D'Eliscue (1920–1922) and Samuel L. Dienes (1923–1926), before finding substantial success with Coach James Usilton Sr., who led the team from 1926 to 1939. Playing in the Eastern Intercollegiate Basketball Conference, Usilton's Temple teams were respected for their solid fundamental play and were consistently ranked among the best in the East. The 1927–1929 teams were co-captained by Harry Litwack (BS EDU 1930), who mastered Usilton's teaching and training methods.

Temple's consistency and impressive wins over regional opponents gave the program prominence. By the 1930s the city of Philadelphia, with five outstanding teams, was a hotbed for college basketball. The final game of the 1937–1938 regular season attracted 12,000 spectators to Philadelphia's Convention Center to see Temple defeat St. Joseph's College 40–34. That year, for the first time, a postseason tournament was conducted to determine a national champion in basketball. Known as the National Invitational Tournament (NIT), it was the forerunner of the NCAA Tournament that started a year later. In the final game Temple defeated the University of Colorado 60–36 before a crowd of 15,000 in Madison Square Garden, thus claiming the first-ever national championship in the sport and completing the season with a fabulous 23–2 record.

FACT

Temple University has nine national Hall of Fame coaches, in football, basketball, soccer, baseball, lacrosse, golf, and fencing.

Usilton stepped down after the NIT win, succeeded by Ernest Messikomer, who served through 1942. With some difficulty Temple continued its basketball program during the war years. As players were drawn into the service, Temple rarely started the same group of five players in consecutive games. Don Henderson, a starter on the 1938 NIT championship team, and student manager Alan Bobrow were killed in action during World War II. Coached by Josh Cody, the 1943–1944 Temple squad managed only a 13–8 record, but two of the wins were over highly ranked opponents, including one over St. John's University at Madison Square Garden. It came as something of a surprise, then, when Temple was selected as an at-large team to compete in the NCAA postseason tournament, but no surprise when it failed to advance.

Without a decent-sized home court of their own the Temple Owls played intersectional games at Philadelphia's Convention Hall, often as part of twin bills with Villanova, St. Joseph's, or La Salle. Occasionally Temple played in high school gymnasiums. Wherever it played, Temple challenged the top teams. The 1949–1950 team chalked up victories over West Virginia and Syracuse. Costic (Ike) Borsavage (BS EDU 1951; M.Ed. 1954), who set a Temple season scoring record, and steady Johnny Ballots (BS 1951; DDS DEN 1957) led the team; both earned places on the all-city collegiate quintet. The 1950–1951 schedule included games with perennial powers North Carolina,

North Carolina State, and Manhattan, plus City College of New York, winners of the NIT and NCAA tournaments the year before. The 1950–1951 season is memorable, however, for the emergence of Bill Mlkvy (DDS DEN 1955), "The Owl without a Vowel."

Mlkvy broke a total of seventy-three college scoring records during the 1950–1951 season, amassing 731 points in twenty-five games for a 29.2 scoring average that led the nation. He scored 43 points against North Carolina. His 73 points against Wilkes College broke the collegiate single-game scoring record. On his way to 73 points Mlkvy scored 54 points in a row, the most consecutive points without a teammate scoring in a single game in NCAA history. A team player, Mlkvy averaged 18.9 rebounds (second in the nation) and 7.0 assists a game. Bill Mlkvy became Temple's first official All-American and was selected as the nation's number-one player by the Philadelphia Basketball Writers Association. "Easily the most popular guy on the campus," according to the *Temple Review*, Mlkvy was lauded for his accomplishments and also for "the modesty with which he received them."

Harry Litwack replaced Josh Cody in 1952, opening the Litwack Era in Temple basketball. Known as The Chief, Litwack was the first Temple coach to be inducted into the Naismith Memorial Basketball Hall of Fame. Under Litwack's direction Temple won another NIT championship (1969) and made two appearances (1956 and 1958) in the Final Four of the NCAA Tournament, finishing third on both occasions. Litwack led Temple to a total of six NCAA postseason tournaments. Before retiring in 1973, he compiled a record of 373 wins against 193 losses. Litwack's well-coached teams were respected for their tenacious zone defenses, unselfish style of play, unrelenting hustle, and fundamental skills. Known for teaching players how to gain the most from their innate abilities, Litwack produced many outstanding players, including All-Americans Hal Lear, Guy Rodgers, Bill "Pickles" Kennedy (1970), John Baum (BBA SBM 1969), and Bruce Drysdale (BA 1962; DDS DEN 1966).

The three most memorable seasons for the South Philadelphia–reared Litwack were those of 1956, 1958, and 1969. The 1956 team, behind Guy Rodgers's pinpoint passing and Fred Cohen's NCAA Tournament–record thirty-four rebounds against Connecticut, advanced to the NCAA Final Four, where Hal Lear won MVP honors, scoring 48 points against Southern Methodist in the consolation game.

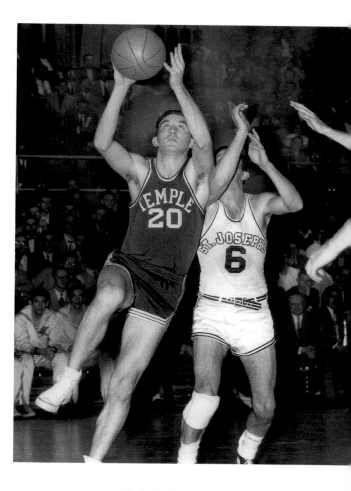

The Owl without a Vowel: Bill Mlkvy, shown driving to the basket against St. Joseph's in a 1951 contest, averaged 21.1 points per game during his Temple basketball career. Winner of many individual awards and still holder of several school scoring records, Mlkvy was Temple's first official All-American in basketball.

The 1958 squad featured Guy Rodgers, Jay Norman, Bill "Pickles" Kennedy, Tink Van Patton, and Mel Brodsky. Ranked in the top ten nationally by the major polls throughout the season, they were clearly the best in the East, as they demonstrated by winning the Eastern Collegiate Athletic Conference (ECAC) Holiday Festival in convincing style before capacity crowds in Madison Square Garden. Rodgers, a two-time All-American guard, led Temple back to the Final Four in 1958 and a third-place finish before going on to play eleven seasons in the National Basketball Association (NBA).

Sportswriters labeled Litwack's 1969 squad a "Cinderella" team after they won the NIT championship by defeating heavily favored Boston College, ending that school's nineteen-game winning streak. The Owls had stumbled through an 18–8 season, winning only two Big Five games and losing out on an NCAA bid by dropping a 68–67 Middle Atlantic Conference play-off game to archrival St.

Joseph's. Undaunted, Temple's starting five of John Baum, Eddie Mast, Joe Cromer, Bill Strunk, and Tony Brocchi prevailed against Florida, St. Peter's, and Tennessee. The championship game drew 18,311 fans and a national television audience who were entertained by a special guest appearance from Temple's own Bill Cosby. The night before, on Johnny Carson's *Tonight Show*, Cosby had predicted a Temple victory. Inspired by a locker-room visit by the "Coz" and a sensational performance by John Baum, Temple responded by routing Boston College 89–76 for its second NIT championship in eight appearances.

The Litwack years correspond with the beginning in 1954 of a regular season round-robin play-off between the Big Five teams. Many of the games were contested in the midst of total bedlam at the Palestra, the home arena for the University of Pennsylvania. For noise, intense competition, and unforgettable excitement, there was nothing comparable to a Big Five doubleheader at the Palestra. The opening of McGonigle Hall in 1969 finally provided a decent-sized 3,900-seat arena for Temple's regular-season games, although the Palestra remained a favorite place for the Big Five games. With Litwack's retirement in 1973, his assistant, Don Casey, took over the basketball helm for Temple. In nine seasons under Casey the Owls made another three NIT appearances and were a consistent threat to win the East Coast Conference championship.

Above *The men's basketball team dedicated the 3,900-seat McGonigle Hall in December 1969 with a game against St. John's University. Since 1997 the team has played home games in the 10,200-seat Liacouras Center. Temple's football team played home games in Temple Stadium from 1928 to 1974, with an occasional game at Franklin Field and, beginning in 1974, at Veterans Stadium, which was Temple's home field from 1976 to 2002. The football Owls have called Lincoln Financial Field home since 2003.*

Below *Known affectionately as The Chief, men's Hall of Fame basketball coach Harry Litwack puffed trademark cigars while leading the Owls to six NCAA appearances and twice into the Final Four.*

John Chaney joined Temple as head coach in 1982 after ten years as basketball coach at Cheyney University, where his teams won 225 games, lost only 59, and won the NCAA Division II title in 1978. A dedicated, strong-willed teacher who molded the character of his players with discipline, hard work, and common decency, Chaney grew up in South Philadelphia, starred at Ben Franklin High School, and was named Philadelphia Public League Player of the Year in 1951. Having grown up in disadvantaged circumstances, Chaney understood the predicament that many of his prospective players faced. He became determined to create what he called "access and opportunity" for young men who had neither. Playing the role of teacher, mentor, and disciplinarian, Chaney put his players through testing 5:30 A.M. practice sessions, emphasizing positive thinking, repetition of basic skills, dignity, and self-control. Famous for his matchup zone defenses, Chaney excelled at recruiting unheralded players, teaching them fundamentals, and molding them into winners. "Winning is an attitude," he often said.

Chaney's most memorable season ended with a loss to Duke in the finals of the NCAA Eastern Regional on March 26, 1988, leaving Temple with a 32–2 record and its dreams of a national championship dashed after being ranked number one in the country entering the postseason. That team featured Temple's all-time leading scorer and All-American Mark Macon (BS EDU 1991) and the phenomenal shot-blocking of Tim Perry, just two of Chaney's twenty-nine players who were drafted by the NBA. After twenty-four years as head coach, Chaney retired in 2006, leaving an extraordinary record of accomplishment. Twenty-three of Chaney's twenty-four teams played in postseason tournaments, including seventeen trips to the NCAA Tournament and five trips to the Elite Eight. His teams won six Atlantic 10 tournament championships and seven regular-season titles. Chaney was twice named the Division I Coach of the Year. He won 724 games during his career, compiling a record of 516–253 as Temple's head coach. At his retirement only three active coaches had more career victories than Chaney. In 2001 Chaney joined Harry Litwack as a member of the Naismith Memorial Basketball Hall of Fame.

In April 2006 University of Pennsylvania head coach and La Salle University alumnus Fran Dunphy was named Temple's head basketball coach. Dunphy had coached the Quakers for seventeen seasons prior to the move, making him the first person to serve as the head men's basketball coach at two Philadelphia Big Five institutions. During his tenure at Penn he won 310 games and recorded nine twenty-win seasons. Dunphy's Penn teams won three Philadelphia Big Five City Series titles, annexed ten Ivy League championships, and made nine NCAA appearances. Dunphy wasted no time in taking over the Temple reins, guiding the Owls to two straight Atlantic 10 tournament championships and their twenty-sixth and twenty-seventh NCAA Tournament appearances, thus perpetuating Temple's rich heritage of basketball excellence.

A part of Temple's connection to Philadelphia's marvelous basketball tradition can be attributed to the strength of such personalities as Dave Zinkoff (BS SBM 1932). Known as The Zink for his memorable voice and zany style as a public announcer for the Philadelphia 76ers professional basketball team, Zinkoff also served for several years in the 1950s as the tour secretary for the Harlem Globetrotters. Another connection is through the talented pen of Harvey Pollack (BS SBM 1943), who chronicled Temple's sports history and wrote knowingly and extensively on college basketball for six decades. Sonny Hill, another figure closely related to Philadelphia basketball and to the university, did not attend Temple, but his Sonny Hill League for boys aged fifteen to nineteen from all Philadelphia neighborhoods has been housed at Temple's McGonigle Hall for over four decades. In addition, several of Philadelphia's most notable and successful sportswriters began their careers writing for the *Temple News* or broadcasting over WRTI-FM at Temple, including Ray Didinger (BS SCT 1968), Herm Rogul (BS SCT 1961), Bill Conlin (BS SCT 1961), and Joe Juliano (BA SCT 1974), to name a few.

Above *Hall of Fame coach John Chaney led Temple's basketball teams into the NCAA Tournament seventeen times, reaching the elite eight on five occasions.*

Below *Coach John Chaney's teams provided many thrilling moments at the Liacouras Center, including this fast action against Rhode Island in 2000, as Kevin Lyde (#42) drives the lane, supported by teammates Lamont Barnes (#32) and Pepe Sanchez (#4).*

Baseball

The Temple baseball program ranks as the most successful college program in the city of Philadelphia. Since its beginnings in 1927, the Owls made two College World Series and fourteen NCAA postseason appearances, won twelve conference championships, and surpassed 1,300 wins. Twenty-six Temple baseball players were drafted by major-league baseball teams; sixty players enjoyed professional careers, including thirteen who made it to the major leagues.

Frank Martin coached during the first years of the program, succeeded by Walter Keating (1928–1931) and Ralph "Pep" Young, who coached for eleven years (1932–1942). The program was discontinued for two years during World War II. Pete Stevens guided the program from 1947 to 1952 before giving way to Ernie Casale (1953–1959). The future Temple athletic director guided his team to a pair of NCAA Tournament appearances in 1957 and 1959. The 1959 team compiled a 10–2 record in the Mid-Atlantic Conference, winning the conference title. Bill "Pickles" Kennedy batted .414, won All-America honors, and signed as a free agent with the Pittsburgh Pirates. Kennedy also was an All-American in basketball, drafted by the NBA's Philadelphia Warriors.

James "Skip" Wilson, a Manayunk product named the city's Most Outstanding High School Athlete of 1948, started at Temple in 1957 as a student assistant to basketball coach Harry Litwack and as an assistant to baseball coach Ernie Casale. When Casale was named athletic director in 1959, Wilson was promoted to head baseball coach and held the job until his retirement in 2005. In 1963 Wilson's team won the East Coast Conference championship, earned the program's third appearance in the NCAA Tournament, and got its first national ranking as thirteenth in the nation by *Collegiate Baseball*. Behind the pitching of Joe Kerrigan (1972), the 1972 team swept through the NCAA District II Tournament with a 3–0 record and advanced to the College World Series in Omaha. The Owls opened the College World Series with a heartbreaking 2–1 loss to Oklahoma in thirteen innings but bounced back to eliminate Iowa, 13–9. After sending Connecticut home, Temple faced off with Arizona State for the chance to play USC in the finals. Featuring a roster stacked with seven

Taking a break from an indoor practice session in Mitten Hall, two members of the 1940 baseball team, Dominic Battisto (1940) and George Nemchik (BS CHP 1941), pose daringly on the building's southeast corner. Behind them, on the horizon, lay the industrial city, and below them, to the right, is Sullivan Hall amidst the renovated row houses and former churches that constituted Temple's sidewalk campus. Nemchik, a standout in soccer, represented the United States in the 1936 Olympics and was voted into the Temple Hall of Fame.

future major leaguers, the Sun Devils edged the Owls, 1–0. The third-place national finish is the best ever in the program's history.

In 1977 Temple led the nation in hitting and finished with a 34–9 regular-season record. It ranked number eight in the nation, winning its third-straight East Coast Conference championship and qualifying for the NCAA for the fifth time in six years. Temple won the Northeast Regional with a 4–0 record but faltered at the College World Series and finished eighth overall. Six players from the 1977 team went on to careers in professional baseball.

Temple won the East Coast Conference championship in its final season in the conference in 1982 and moved into the Atlantic 10 Conference in 1983. It won conference titles in 1983 and 1984 and returned to the NCAA Tournament. Those teams were led by a trio of Temple Hall of Fame players: John Marzano (1984) (a member of the gold-medal-winning U.S. Olympic team in 1984 who played ten years in the majors), Jeff Manto (1984) (played nine seasons in the big leagues), and Bill Mendek (1984) (drafted in the ninth round by Seattle). Bobby Higginson (1992) earned All-America honors in 1991 and 1992 and went on to a twelve-year career with the Detroit Tigers.

In 2004, after seventy-eight years at Erny Field next to Temple Stadium in Mt. Airy, the baseball program was moved to new facilities at the Ambler Campus. In his forty-six years as head coach, Skip Wilson won seven East Coast Conference titles and three Atlantic 10 championships. He guided the Owls to fourteen NCAA tournaments and two trips to the College World Series. A three-time District Coach of the Year, Wilson was inducted into the Pennsylvania Sports Hall of Fame and the American Baseball Coaches Hall of Fame. When he retired after the 2005 season after 1,034 wins, he was the winningest coach in Temple history, regardless of sport. In 2006 the baseball field at the Ambler Campus was named Skip Wilson Field in his honor.

Rob Valli, who led Gloucester County (New Jersey) College to the 2005 National Junior College Athletic Association National Championship, was named Wilson's successor in the fall of 2005. One of Valli's first products, outfielder Sean Barksdale, was drafted in June 2009 by the Houston Astros.

Men's Soccer

Temple's men's soccer program has a long, distinguished history. Started in 1926 under Coach James Neely, it won instant plaudits for winning play. Dr. William "Pete" Leaness (DPM) received All-America recognition in 1929 and the next year was appointed to coach the team, leading Temple to two national championships (1951 and 1953). Five members of his teams participated in the Olympics for the United States: George Nemchik (BS CHP 1941) (Berlin, 1936), Walt Bahr (BS EDU 1949; M.Ed. 1964) and Ben McLaughlin (London, 1948), Jack Dunn (BS EDU 1955) (Helsinki, 1952), and Len Oliver (BS SBM 1955) (Tokyo, 1964). The team received NCAA Tournament invitations in 1966 and 1967.

Walt Bahr, who played on three U.S. World Cup teams and earned All-America honors as a Temple freshman in 1944, took over the team for three years, 1971 to 1973, before leaving to accept the head coaching position at Penn State. He was succeeded by John Boles, who coached the Owls until 1994, winning three more NCAA invitations in 1976, 1978, and 1985. Hugh McInaw coached from 1995 to 1999, replaced in 2000 by Dave MacWilliams, who brought an extensive background in international, professional, and youth soccer to the Temple position. Considered one of the all-time-greatest American-born soccer players, MacWilliams was a member of the 1980 U.S. Olympic team before turning professional, playing for the Tampa Bay Rowdies and Philadelphia Fury of the NASL.

Men's Gymnastics

The men's gymnastics program traces its beginnings to 1926 when Harry Nelson started the program. Max Younger took over a year later and coached until 1955, winning five EIGL (Eastern Intercollegiate Gymnastics League) championships from 1934 through 1941, adding another in 1949, along with an NCAA championship. At the 1952 Olympics Bob Stout, a Temple product, became the first gymnast ever to complete a back somersault with a full twist when he landed the move during the floor exercises. Under Carl Peterson, who coached from 1955 to 1968, Temple won two more EIGL championships. Bill Coco took charge from 1968 to 1973, replaced by Dave Thor, who compiled a 28–9 dual-meet record in three years as coach.

Fred Turoff (BS EDU 1969; M.Ed. 1991) was only twenty-nine years old when he was named Temple's head coach in 1976. He had been an assistant for six years after his undergraduate career at Temple, where he won the 1968 EIGL all-around and horizontal-bar championships. Turoff was a member of the U.S. National Team in 1969 and 1970. Five Temple University gymnasts have competed or coached in the Olympic Games. Thirteen Temple gymnasts have been NCAA national gymnastics individual champions. Alumnus Bill Roth (BBA SBM 1993) made U.S. Gymnastics Championship history in 1990 when he scored the first perfect 10.0 with his high-bar routine.

Turoff was elected to the USA Gymnastics Hall of Fame in 2009. His Temple coaching career by then had spanned three decades, during which he had guided the Owls to sixteen EIGL/ECAC titles and achieved a lifetime coaching record of 356–157 (.694). Turoff participated in the 1979 World Championships, 1991 World University Games and Pan American Games, 1992 Olympic Games, 1994 World Championships, and 1996 Pacific Alliance Championships.

Men's Crew

The men's varsity crew program began in 1966 when athletic director Ernie Casale hired Thomas Aloysius "Bear" Curran to start the team. Curran had been part of the crew that had represented the United States at the Berlin Olympic Games of 1936. Curran's crew won the Bergen Cup and Kerr Cup several times. Twice (in 1968 and 1973) the Temple heavyweight eight crew finished second in the Dad Vail Regatta. Curran retired in 1978, succeeded in 1979 by Gavin White, who coached each season except 1984–1985, when he took a sabbatical to work on a doctoral degree. Under White, the Temple men's crew enjoyed spectacular success from 1983 to 1994, winning international distinction with seven invitations to Great Britain's premier regatta, the Henley Royal Regatta on the River Thames.

Between 1983 and 2008 Temple won the Dad Vail varsity eight championship twenty-one times, as well as sixteen Bergen Cups and fifteen Kerr Cups. White coached the men's four at the 2000 Olympics in Sydney, Australia, where they finished fifth. In 2003 he was named the Schuylkill Navy Coach of the Year, and he coached the men's pair with coxswain to a gold medal at the 2003 FISA World Rowing Championships in Milan, Italy.

Men's Golf

The Temple golf program, inaugurated in 1931, was for many years guided by volunteer faculty coaches, such as history professor Arthur Cook, who managed the team during the 1940s and through 1951. One of Cook's star players was John Dyniewski (BS SBM 1951), a nationally ranked amateur and the first golfer named to Temple's Hall of Fame. Dyniewski was team captain in 1951 when Temple won the Middle Atlantic team championship and he captured the individual crown. Dyniewski won virtually every regional amateur title several times, including the Philadelphia and Pennsylvania amateur championships.

Under the guidance of Coach Gavin R. White, the men's heavyweight crew (shown here on the Schuylkill River in 2007) won the Dad Vail Regatta twenty-one times between 1983 and 2008.

Malcolm "Mac" Strow launched a more formal program in 1952 and served as golf coach until 1971, when John MacDonald (BS SBM 1965; M.Ed. EDU 1971) took over and gave shape and substance to the program, serving for twenty-nine years. Under MacDonald the team went undefeated in 1973 and went on to compile an amazing record of 139–9 in dual matches. The Owls captured their first Eastern Intercollegiate Golf Association Championship in 1975, giving them the number-one ranking in the East and an invitation to the NCAA Tournament, the first of fourteen in MacDonald's career at Temple. MacDonald's teams won seven A-10 championships. In twenty-three of his twenty-nine seasons at Temple, the Owls were represented either by the team or by individuals in the national NCAA Tournament. Eleven of MacDonald's golfers earned All-America honors. Two of his players were honored as Academic All-Americans. MacDonald was named the NCAA District II Coach of the Year twelve times. In 1987 he was inducted into the Temple University Athletic Hall of Fame. He is also a member of the Golf Coaches of America Hall of Fame. Bill Mannino succeeded MacDonald in 2001, followed by Brian Rogers in 2004 and Brian Quinn in 2007.

Cross-Country and Track

Temple has fielded men's track and cross-country teams since 1925, when Bert Barron started the programs. Max Younger coached for a couple of seasons before Ben Ogden took over the men's program in 1928, holding the position for thirty years.

Ogden's prize runner was Eulace Peacock (1937), who at the 1935 national AAU (Amateur Athletic Union) championships set the world record for the 100-meter dash at 10.2 seconds, beating Jesse Owens and Ralph Metcalf. He also won the broad jump, again defeating Owens, to become only the second man to win a double in an American track and field championship event. Looking forward to the 1936 Berlin Olympics, everyone anticipated a showdown between Peacock and

Owens to determine who the fastest man in the world was. They were scheduled to race against each other in the 1936 Penn Relays and again at the Olympic trials. However, Peacock severely injured his leg during an event at the Penn Relays and was unable to compete in the Olympic trials. Owens and Metcalf won the gold and silver medals at Berlin in the 100-meter race. Owens won a total of four gold medals in Berlin, making a mockery of Hitler's racist theories and leaving Temple loyalists regretting Peacock's absence. During his Temple career Peacock won eight Penn Relay medals, six national pentathlon titles, and two AAU championships and set world records at 100 meters outdoors and at 60 yards indoors. Peacock and Owens became friends and even business partners later in life.

Another Temple track star, Stan Wudyka (BS EDU 1935), had somewhat better luck than Peacock and qualified for the 1936 Olympics in the 10,000-meter run. During his three-year Temple career, Wudyka, who was beaten only once in NCAA competition at two miles, was disappointed with finishing nineteenth out of forty-two runners at the Olympics, but Temple was proud of his effort.

Gavin White Jr. headed the men's track program from 1958 to 1967, followed by Jack St. Clair, who held the post until 1983. Chuck Alexander, who took over the women's team in 1977, succeeded St. Clair as men's coach in 1983 and for the next sixteen years coached both the men's and women's track programs. Many fine athletes competed during these years. The 1982 women's season produced some exceptional performances. That year Edna Brown (BA CST 1983) (400 meters), Glenda Truesdale (BBA SBM 1986) (100-meter hurdles), and Sharon Mitnik (BBA SBM 1983) (shot put) earned All-America honors. Brown was the national 400-meter champion, winning the event in a national record time. Felicia Hodges (BA SCT 1988) stood out, winning the women's high jump three years in a row (1986–1988) at the Penn Relays and qualifying for the 1988 Olympic trials.

Both men's and women's cross-country were dropped in 1986, to be revived in 2005 by Stefanie Scalessa, head coach of the combined men's and women's track programs. In 2008 Eric Mobley became head coach of the combined programs.

Women's Athletics

Regrettably, there was no women's track program when Jean Shiley (BS EDU 1933) competed in the high jump for the United States in the 1932 Olympic Games in Los Angeles. The graceful five-foot-ten Shiley won the gold medal by defeating the immortal Babe Didrikson. Shiley had also competed in the 1928 Olympic Games in Amsterdam, finishing fourth in the high jump as a sixteen-year-old. She returned from Los Angeles after the 1932 Olympics, completed her Temple education, subsequently served in the navy during World War II, and married. Jean Shiley-Newhouse remained enormously proud to have represented her country, even though she was permitted nothing more than what she called "intramural stuff" as far as athletic competition was concerned during her student days at Temple.

Although one of the first universities to offer women's sports, Temple yielded to the trends of the times and abolished women's varsity sports in May 1927. The administrative ruling stated that university women were to participate only in "play dates" rather than intercollegiate competition. These play dates were argued to be better because they encouraged women to participate in sports without the need to be competitive. Most universities around the nation at this time also abolished women's varsity sports teams in favor of "physical culture" activities of a non-competitive nature so as to preserve the notion of the "fragile female." Informal and mannerly intramural games that

avoided physical contact and required only mild exertion were offered once or twice a year. And so, indeed, by the time Jean Shiley arrived on the Temple campus in 1929 there was not much other than "intramural stuff" when it came to athletic opportunities for women.

Jumping ahead to 2009, we note that Temple sponsored twelve women's varsity sports teams, compared with only ten for men. Moreover, the cumulative success of the women's programs, based on the number of national championships and individual All-Americans, is at least as strong as, if not more competitive than, that of the men's programs, even though most of the women's programs did not get fully under way until 1975. How did it come to that?

Temple first offered women's intramural sports in 1919 under the direction of C. Anita Preston and Blanche Voorhees (BA 1917). Preston directed the programs, and Voorhees coached. In 1922 Voorhees organized a women's basketball team that compiled a perfect 12–0 record against other schools and clubs. She also started short-lived programs in field hockey and swimming, but in 1927 all of the programs were scuttled. Although Voorhees returned to coach women's basketball in 1936, the success of the early years was not revived. With a general de-emphasis on both men's and women's intercollegiate sports at Temple—except for men's basketball—during the late Depression years, through World War II, and continuing into the 1950s, there was little opportunity for growth or success. Except for men's football and basketball, Temple's sports teams, including all of the women's teams, were coached or managed by part-timers or by professors who took on the chores as extra duties.

The defining moment for American women's athletics came with the issuance of Title IX of the Education Amendments of 1972, prohibiting discrimination in any educational program or activity receiving federal financial assistance. Although neither aimed at nor intended necessarily to balance gender equity in the funding of intercollegiate athletic programs, Title IX had an enormous impact on women's sports programs. In 1981 the NCAA added women's competition and championships to its jurisdiction, as well as Title IX compliance.

At Temple a seismic shift in gender balance in athletics was already under way before the NCAA insinuated itself. The turning point may be said to have occurred in 1970 with the start of the WIA (Women's Intercollegiate Athletics) program or the appointment of Dr. Barbara D. Lockhart as women's athletic director; or perhaps in 1974 with the hiring of the first full-time coaches for women's sports teams; or perhaps in 1975 when the first women athletes were inducted into Temple's Sports Hall of Fame and their portraits were hung alongside the likes of Mlkvy, Rodgers, and Litwack. Others might point to 1980 when Rollin Haffer, president of the WIA student council and captain of the badminton team, and seven women athletes filed suit against Temple in U.S. District Court. The group charged Temple with sex discrimination in its intercollegiate athletic programs said Haffer, "because something had to be done to prod the University."

Temple's undefeated 1922 women's basketball team was coached by Blanche Voorhees and C. Anita Preston. Unfortunately, Temple, like most universities, eliminated women's athletic teams in 1927. When basketball was revived in the late 1930s, competition was limited to club teams until the modern rebirth of women's intercollegiate competition in the mid-1970s.

The Haffer suit was the first legal action in the United States questioning a university athletic program's compliance with the Title IX guidelines banning sex discrimination in education. The Haffer suit pointed out that, as of 1980, Temple had thirteen men's teams (with 364 participants) and thirteen women's teams (with 249 participants) but the men's operating budget was three times as large as the women's. The suit acknowledged that Temple had steadily increased the athletic budgets for women's sports, but "it hasn't been large enough." Carole Oglesby, professor emerita of kinesiology at Temple who has written extensively on Title IX, said, "In a real sense, Temple was sued precisely because it was ahead of the game."

The Haffer case was in the courts for eight years and eventually was settled out of court when Temple agreed to put more money into women's sports. The case set a precedent by comparing the resources spent on men's and women's teams. It also laid the foundation for developing techniques for ascertaining equity in the treatment of college athletes. All of the preceding factors, then, were responsible for the spectacular expansion of Temple's women's athletics programs beginning in the mid-1970s.

Women's Basketball

Blanche Voorhees Brown guided the Lady Owls, as they were still called then, from 1937 to 1940. Over the next thirty-four years the team was coached by eleven different women, all with considerable success, including undefeated teams led by Patricia Collins Morris (1942 and 1943), Vera Egner (1944), and Virginia Middleton (1954). The modern era began in 1974, when Temple named physical education instructor Veronica "Ronnie" Maurek to the dual role of head basketball and softball coach. In 1976 Maurek led the basketball team to its first postseason appearance in the Eastern Association for Intercollegiate Athletics for Women (EAIAW) tournament.

Three years later, when Maurek chose to coach only softball, the university went outside the Physical Education Department to hire its first modern-day, full-time women's basketball coach, Andy McGovern. McGovern produced the Owls' first winning season of the modern era with a 14–10 mark in the 1979–1980 season. Prior to the 1980–1981 season, Temple named Linda MacDonald as its second full-time head coach and began the process of national recruiting and scheduling. In the 1981–1983 seasons Temple advanced to postseason appearances in the Women's National Invitational Tournament (WNIT), finishing fifth and seventh. In the 1983–1984 campaign, Marilyn Stephens (BS HPERD 1985) was named to the Kodak All-America team. In 1989 MacDonald guided the team into the NCAA Tournament and it advanced to the second round. Charlene Curtis coached from 1990 to 1995, and Kristen Foley took charge from 1995 to 2000.

The Dawn Staley era in women's basketball began in 2000. In the six years that Staley coached at Temple the women's basketball team made one WNIT appearance, won four A-10 championships, and gained five NCAA bids. Staley twice was named A-10 Coach of the Year. The 2005 team won twenty-five straight games and was ranked number fifteen in the final polls; it also made it into the second round of the NCAA Tournament. In 2006 Candice Dupree (BS CHP 2006), a three-time A-10 MVP, was selected the A-10 and Big Five Player of the Year. She became the program's first WNBA draft pick and Temple's first to earn AP All-America honors (third team). The next year Kamesha Hairston (BS THM 2008), an Honorable Mention All-American, became Temple's second player selected in the WNBA draft. Staley moved on to the University of South Carolina, replaced in May 2008 by Tonya Cardoza, former assistant coach at the University of Connecticut under Hall of Fame coach Geno Auriemma. Cardoza became the twentieth head women's basketball coach in Temple University history.

In seven seasons as head coach of Temple's women's basketball team, Dawn Staley compiled an overall record of 172–80, with six NCAA appearances and four Atlantic 10 titles. Many of those wins came while she was still actively competing in the Women's National Basketball Association. The Philadelphia-born Staley won Olympic gold three times as a member of the U.S. basketball team and was selected to carry the American flag in the opening ceremonies of the 2004 games. Tonya Cardoza took over for Staley in the 2008 season.

Lady Owls

After 1990 the Temple women's teams were no longer called Lady Owls. The word *Lady* was dropped from the name. They were known thereafter simply as the Owls.

Women's Field Hockey

Until the 1970s the Temple women's field hockey program operated on a club level through a Women's Athletic Association (WAA). Temple's teams were coached by former players. The competitions sometimes included alumnae. In 1950, for example, Temple's women competed against Bryn Mawr, Swarthmore, Beaver, East Stroudsburg, and Ursinus. An all-college team was selected to compete against teams from Boston and internationally. Grace Schuler McGoey coached the team in the early 1950s. Standouts included Alice Putnam (1947), Louise Lenco (BS EDU 1950), Agnes "Aggie" Stegmuller (BS EDU 1945; M.Ed. 1948), Marie R. Kerstetter (BS EDU 1952), and Anne Volp (BS HPERD 1943) (a five-time All-American).

Anne Volp, Joan Edenborn Stiles, and Eleanor Pepper coached the Temple field hockey team through the 1960s into the early 1970s. The modern era begins in 1974 with the arrival of Tina Sloan-Green (M.Ed. EDU 1970) from Lincoln University. She became the first full-time coach for field hockey and lacrosse. In her second and third seasons as field hockey coach she guided the team to a spot in the regional championship. Carol Sauppe Kline (BS EDU 1979; M.Ed. 1982) led Temple to its first national field hockey tournament in 1978.

In 1980 Sloan-Green turned the team over to Gwen Cheeseman-Alexander. In her eight years as head coach Cheeseman-Alexander's team made it into three NCAA tournaments (1982, 1983, and 1984) and won the Atlantic 10 championship in 1983. Coach Cheeseman-Alexander played on the 1984 Olympic field hockey team. Jane Catanzaro (BS THM 1992), a four-time All-American, won the prestigious 1990 Honda Award for outstanding achievement and excellence in intercollegiate athletics. In the four seasons from 1989 to 1992, Coach Michelle Madison's teams made four A-10 postseason tournaments, winning the championship in 1991; her teams won bids to three NCAA tournaments, twice playing into the regional final rounds. Between 1993 and 2004 Lauren Fuch's teams made the A-10 semi-final or final rounds nine out of twelve seasons, including a championship season in 1994.

By 2004 Temple's field hockey teams had finished among the NCAA's top-twenty teams no less than thirteen of the previous fifteen seasons, while producing twenty-four All-Americans. Amanda Janney took over as coach in 2004, continuing the program's success in A-10 tourney play that led the team to three consecutive postseason appearances, reaching the semi-finals each year. In 2007 Janney guided the team to its first regular-season A-10 championship.

Women's Fencing

Temple's fencing program and Dr. Nikki Franke (M.Ed. EDU 1975; Ed.D. 1988) are synonymous: Mention one and you think of the other. A Brooklyn native, Franke started the fencing program at Temple in 1972 and has guided her team to thirty consecutive NCAA Tournament appearances. In 1992, Coach Franke's squad was crowned the NCAA champion in foil competition. Overall, she has coached eleven All-Americans and has been honored four times as National Coach of the Year. Her career record is 566–143–1. She received her 500th career win in the 2005–2006 season.

Franke was a member of the 1976 and 1980 Summer Olympic teams and won a silver medal in the foil competition at the 1975 Pan American Games. In 1975 and 1980, she was the United States Fencing Association's national foil champion. She is a member of the United States Fencing Association Hall of Fame, the Temple Sports Hall of Fame, and the International Women's Sports Hall of Fame. The last, established by the Women's Sports Foundation founded by Billie Jean King in 1974, recognizes female athletes and coaches who have made history in women's sports and selects them based on achievements, breakthroughs, innovative style, and ongoing commitment to the development of women's sports.

Women's Lacrosse

Temple fielded a women's lacrosse team through the 1950s and 1960s made up of non-scholarship athletes and some alumnae who competed against local colleges. Alice Putnam, a standout in the 1940s and described as an All-American, coached Temple's team through the 1950s and organized "play days" of round-robin tournaments for other teams in the area, all on a volunteer basis.

Under the direction of the remarkable Tina Sloan-Green, who coached the team from 1975 to 1992, the Temple lacrosse program captured three national championships and won forty-three individual All-America certificates. The women's lacrosse team won NCAA national championships in 1982, 1984, and 1988. The 1988 team, led by senior All-Americans Gail L. Cummings (BS EDU 1988; M.Ed. 1991; Ed.D. 1998), Amanda "Mandee" Moore (BS EDU 1988), and Kim Lambdin-Ciarocca (BS EDU 1989; M.Ed. THM 1993), finished the regular season with a 17–0 record and ranked number one in the country. The team capped off the perfect year with a 15–7 victory over Penn State in the NCAA Division I tournament final. In addition to winning the three national championships, the lacrosse team was runner-up in 1983 and 1987 and semi-finalist in 1985, 1986, 1987, 1989, and 1990.

Mandee Moore-O'Leary, a three-time All-American and MVP of the 1988 Final Four, was also an All-American in field hockey at Temple. She was a member of the U.S. women's lacrosse World Cup team and was named to the all-century team in 1999. Moore-O'Leary is currently the head women's lacrosse coach at Yale University. The tradition of excellence continued under head coach Kim Lambdin-Ciarocca, also a member of the Owls' 1988 national championship club. Between 1992 and 2004 Ciarocca coached Temple to the NCAA Final Four in 1997, 1998, and 1999. In 1999

Dr. Nikki Franke, associate professor of health, was the first African American female fencing coach in the history of collegiate fencing and the only African American woman to coach a Division I fencing team. One of Temple's all-time winningest coaches, Franke explains: "We know we have to work for [a good season]. It's a Temple philosophy—we're working-class folks and that's just what our team is."

FACT

The women's lacrosse team at Temple University won national championships in 1982, 1984, and 1988.

and 2000 her teams were runners-up in the A-10, but champions each year from 2001 to 2004. In 2001 Ciarocca was named A-10 Coach of the Year. The winning tradition continued under Coach Jenny Ulehla (2005–2006). Bonnie Rosen took over in 2007, leading her 2008 team to the A-10 championship and a NCAA Tournament bid; Rosen was named A-10 Coach of the Year.

Women's Softball

Women's softball debuted in 1975 under Coach Ronnie Maurek, who doubled as women's basketball coach. The team won the 1978 championship of the EAIAW. After moving into the A-10 in 1983, Maurek's teams produced three first-place finishes. In 1989 Dionna Harris (BA CLA 1991) was named A-10 Player of the Year, and Maurek won the Coach of the Year award. Harris, a two-time All-Atlantic-10 Conference performer, was a starter on the 1996 gold-medal-winning U.S. Olympic softball team.

Carol Kashow took over coaching from 1991 to 1997, succeeded in 1998 by Rocci Pignoli, whose 2004 team won the A-10 Conference championship and the NCAA Tournament bid. Pignoli was named A-10 Coach of the Year. Casey Dickson became Temple's fourth coach in 2006. Adrienne Repsher (BS EDU 2007) was named A-10 Player of the Year and first-team Academic All-American in 2007. Joe DiPietro, a former La Salle coach, was named head coach in 2008. Since 2005 the softball team has played its home games at the new sports complex at the Ambler Campus.

Seeking to regain the pinnacle of success enjoyed by lacrosse in the 1980s, Temple named Bonnie Rosen as head coach in 2007. Rosen previously served as head coach at the University of Connecticut, establishing the program and leading the Huskies into the national rankings. A member of a national championship team as an undergrad at the University of Virginia and also a starter on the Team USA World Cup championship team of 1997, Rosen is a proven winner. In this photo, Berkley Summerlin (#22) advances in a 2007 game.

Women's Volleyball

Women's volleyball at Temple, launched in 1975, played its first eight seasons as an independent under a succession of coaches, beginning with Mary Kilarsky. Kay Corcoran guided the program from 1977 to 1986. S. Daniels-Oleksok, Jackie Nunez, and Ginny Alexander coached teams from 1986 to 1994. In 1993 Katie Harrigan (BS EDU 1996) was named A-10 Player of the Year, and the Owls finished as runner-up in the conference.

Bob Bertucci joined the Temple volleyball program in 1994, bringing a reputation as an architect of the game. Under Bertucci Temple teams have advanced to postseason play in every season since 1995. In fourteen seasons at Temple, Bertucci's teams earned 282 wins and captured seven A-10 regular-season titles, posting twenty or more wins nine times and earning four automatic NCAA Tournament bids. They advanced to the Sweet 16 in 2002. Bertucci won three Atlantic-10 Coach of the Year awards. Several Temple players have won A-10 Player of the Year awards, including Alma Kovaci (BS EDU 2002), Xu Yun (2002), and Yue Liu (2007). The 2004–2007 teams won three consecutive A-10 regular-season titles.

Women's Gymnastics

Evelyn Hurley was head coach for the program's inaugural three seasons, 1976 to 1979, followed by Jeff Rosenberg (1980–1985) and Ken Anderson (1986–2000). In 2003 the team set an all-time record for team score at the USA Gymnastics (USAG) national championships. Under Coach Aaron Murphy the team has continued to improve and competitively mature, placing fifth at the ECAC championships in 2007. In 2009 the team finished third in the ECAC, the best in the program's history, and Katie Canning (2009) captured first place both in the all-around and on vault and tied for second on floor, earning first-team All-America honors at the USAG championships. Kaity Watson (2009) also earned first-team All-America honors for third place on vault. Murphy was named ECAC Coach of the Year.

Other Sports

Steve Mauro took over the men's tennis team in 2004. In his first year at the helm the former Ursinus coach revitalized the Owls' tennis program, guiding the squad to a 17–8 record and a third-place finish at the Atlantic 10 tournament, the highest by a Temple team since the 2000 season. Women's tennis, which began in 1987, annexed A-10 championships in 1994 and 1995 under Drew Sorrentino, who was named A-10 Coach of the Year in 1994. The team repeated in 2003 and 2008, under Jill Breslin. In 2008 Mauro assumed women's and men's coaching duties.

Women's soccer, which started in 1991 under Eileen Richart's direction, gained its first postseason A-10 tournament bid in 1993 and improved under coaches Seamus McWilliams (1994–2003) and David Jones (2003–2009).

Athletic Administration

Temple University has had eight athletic directors throughout its athletic history, dating from Earl R. Yeomans, who oversaw the programs from their infancy in 1927. Yeomans served for twenty-five years, leading athletics through years of growth and then contraction, to be succeeded by Josh Cody in 1952. Ernie Casale took the reins in 1959, heading the program through the construction of McGonigle Hall, the expansion of the Geasey athletic complex, and the hiring of Wayne Hardin to bring Temple's football program back to prominence. Gavin White Jr., Casale's long-time assistant and an institution himself at Temple, was named athletic director in 1983. Charles Theokis and Dave O'Brien followed, along with two acting athletic directors during the 1990s—a time when Temple sought to reorganize and realign its programs, seeking the proper conference affiliations, equitable distribution of resources between men's and women's teams, and an appropriate balance of competitive levels for its many sports. In July 2002 William D. "Bill" Bradshaw, former director of athletics at DePaul University for sixteen years and an alumnus of and former athletic director at La Salle, was named to lead Temple's programs.

In 2009 former Temple athletes and friends donated funds to name the Athletic Office in honor of its second-longest-serving athletic director, Ernest C. Casale, one of the most influential athletic administrators in Philadelphia intercollegiate athletics. Casale taught mathematics at Temple in addition to his coaching and administrative duties. He served as athletic director from 1959 to 1982. The Ernest C. Casale Intercollegiate Athletics Suite acknowledges Casale's energy and dedication, as well as his personal generosity to the Temple program. "When one thinks of Temple athletics, the name Ernie Casale comes quickly to mind, so it is only fitting that our athletics suite bears his name," said Director of Athletics Bill Bradshaw in 2009.

Every organization needs an institutional memory, emotional continuity, and personal stability. All of that has been supplied for Temple's athletics program since July 1953, when Al Shrier was appointed sports information director. Shrier majored in journalism at Temple and was sports editor of the *Temple News*. He remained with the athletics department in one capacity or another for more than five decades. The peripatetic Shrier and his weathered briefcase became fixtures at Temple athletic events. Known as the dean among national college sports information directors, Shrier has received

Once described as the glue that bound together Temple athletics, Gavin White Jr. devoted more than four decades to Temple as a coach, assistant athletic director, and athletic director. His star pupil, Bill Cosby, frequently acknowledged White's steady hand and supportive role. Al Shrier, still active in 2009 as a special assistant to the athletic director, is such a recognizable figure to Temple sports fans that his likeness (complete with the ever-present brief-case) has been captured in the form of a bobble-head doll.

special tributes from the U.S. Basketball Writers Association, the National Football Foundation, and College Football Hall of Fame. Shrier has been inducted into the halls of fame for Temple University, Philadelphia Big Five, Pennsylvania Sports, and Philadelphia Jewish Sports.

Women's Sports Administration

Intramural programs and friendly "all-college" competitions between Temple women and the representatives of local colleges were conducted during the 1940s and 1950s under the auspices of a student-run WAA. The competition was apparently spirited but friendly, without scholarships and full-time coaches. In the 1950s Temple women competed in swimming, bowling, basketball, field hockey, and lacrosse against the women from Swarthmore, East Stroudsburg, Beaver, Ursinus, Rosemont, Albright, Penn, and Drexel.

Women's competition intensified in the early 1970s, and the WAA gave way to the Women's Intercollegiate Athletics (WIA) program, administered through the Department of Physical Education. In 1970 Dr. Barbara D. Lockhart became the university's first women's athletic director. She enlarged the program to twelve teams, increased the number of participants, and hired highly qualified coaches. The WIA program expanded into one of the largest and strongest in the country. When Lockhart left the post in 1974 to become assistant dean of the new College of Health, Physical Education, Recreation and Dance (HPERD), Jean Roberts (M.Ed. EDU 1975) became interim athletic director.

Dr. Kaye Hart came to Temple from the University of Tennessee in 1975 to become athletic director for women's sports. She immediately lobbied for additional equipment, facilities, and scholarships to support WIA teams. Gradually, over time, more scholarships were added. So also were more full-time coaches. In 1974 the WIA appointed two full-time coaches, Veronica "Ronnie" Maurek and Tina Sloan (later Sloan-Green). By 1977 the WIA had five full-time coaches and five part-time coaches for its twelve sports.

By the time the Haffer suit was settled in 1988 Temple had redistributed its athletic budget in proportion to the percentage of athletes who were women. Moreover, the administration and management of women's athletic programs were removed from the Physical Education Department and placed within a single consolidated athletic department. In 2005 the senior administrator for women's athletics, Kristen A. Foley, an assistant director of athletics since 2000, was promoted to associate athletic director. In her role, Foley, who also served as the department's senior women's administrator, oversees the administration of twelve varsity sports, including budget construction, scheduling contests, student-athlete crisis intervention, and evaluation and review of coaches. She also supervises the Academic Support and Compliance Units for student athletes.

Much has changed since 1927, when Temple banned women's sports competition, and since 1972 and the advent of Title IX. The last word on the subject goes to Tina Sloan-Green: "Some women, and some men, like competition," she told the *Temple Review* in 2002, "others don't. The point is to give people options and not to be judgmental about those options."

Diamond Marching Band and Spirit Squad

What is a football game without a band to perform at halftime? When Temple decided in the 1920s to field a big-time college football team and build its own stadium, a group of students decided to form a band to entertain spectators at home games and to support the team on road trips. Temple's marching band dates back to 1925, when Herbert E. McMahan (BS SBM 1926), a senior in the

FACT

Bill Hyman won the 1985 NCAA heavyweight wrestling title and was Temple's first two-time All-American.

The Pride of the Cherry and White: Temple's Diamond Marching Band, founded in 1925, owes much of its distinctive style to Arthur Chodoroff, director of university bands since 1977. The DMB performs at all football games and at other special functions.

School of Commerce, organized a forty-member all-male marching band. Professor Samuel Steiner, on behalf of the students and the Athletic Council, received approval from Laura Carnell for $800 to purchase uniforms and instruments at Sears-Roebuck and sheet music for six numbers from Presser's Music Store. According to Maureen E. Walsh (BA SCT 1986), who researched its history, the band's first uniform consisted of white trousers, with a cherry braid, white sweater, and white hat. With once-a-week rehearsals and a few marching drills from Charles Golder, a member of the Elks Band, McMahan and his cohorts formed the Temple "T" on the field for the first time in 1926.

The band's early directors introduced increasingly complex music and more intricate marching formations. Soon the band became an indispensable part of every football game. Its popularity grew in the 1930s, culminating with a performance at the first Sugar Bowl game in New Orleans in 1935. The band, like the football team, went on hiatus during the war years but vigorously rebounded in 1946 with a new director, John H. Jenny, plus new instruments and uniforms, courtesy of a special grant from President Johnson. Jenny was an assistant dean of students, and the marching band was administratively part of the Office of Student Affairs. The band grew to seventy-five members and, for the first time, added women. Elva Daniels, one of the first women to join the band and later a professor of music theory at Temple, recalled, "It was unusual for women to wear trousers back then." But, she added, "I never felt hostility."

Jenny renamed the band The Diamond Band of Temple University—The University Band Built on Acres of Diamonds. He resigned in 1953, replaced by Howard Chivian, who died in 1957. A series of directors came and went over the next few years. Meanwhile, the College of Music developed a concert band, jazz bands, and a pep band made up of Diamond Band members who played at basketball games. James W. Herbert served as director of bands from 1970 to 1976, succeeded by his assistant, Arthur D. Chodoroff (M.Mus. 1973). Dean Helen Laird brought the Diamond Band administratively under the College of Music in 1978.

Under Chodoroff's creative baton the Diamond Band performed for the 1977 and 1978 Mirage Bowls in Tokyo, Japan. It played Chodoroff's custom arrangements and adapted a more contemporary marching style, abandoning the high-stepping style used by most college bands for many years. Temple band shows became more flowing, with geometrically precise formations and persistently excellent musicianship. In 1996 Chodoroff assumed the chairmanship of the Department of Instrumental Studies, retaining his duties as director of bands but relinquishing the marching band directorship to his assistant, Bradley Townsend. Thereafter, the assistant director of bands also became director of athletic bands. In 2008 Dr. Mathew Brunner became Chodoroff's assistant and the director of athletic bands.

In recent years, as the pageantry and visual complexity of Temple's intercollegiate contests have expanded and the pace and excitement of the games themselves have accelerated, it has been due in large part to the contributions of Temple's Spirit Squad—the talented athletes and musicians who perform at Temple pep rallies, games, and special events and infuse the players and the crowds with the Temple spirit. The Spirit Squad has grown since the mid-1990s to encompass the Diamond Marching Band and Pep Band, Temple cheerleaders, and the Diamond Gems, a dedicated group of women students who perform modern, rhythmic dance routines to capture and hold the energy of the moment.

Cheerleaders have roused the Temple faithful since the mid-1890s and the beginning of Temple's athletic programs, when young men with megaphones urged the crowd to cheer on the teams. As the size of the crowds has grown at Temple games so also has the size of the cheerleading squad, reaching forty women and eight men in 2008. Cheerleading skills also changed as routines became strenuous, gymnastic performances demanding athletic strength, coordination, and stamina. Competition for the spots on the Spirit Squad, whether as a cheerleader, musician, or dancer, has intensified in recent years. Students must survive tryouts, summer training programs, and long hours of practice and rehearsals to perfect routines and to make the difficult seem easy—all to let the Temple spirit shine through.

Opposite *The* Red Owl, *a gift to Temple from Bell Atlantic, is mounted at Alumni Circle along Liacouras Walk. The university mace (inset), symbolizing the authority of Temple's president, is carried by a bearer who immediately precedes the president at each commencement procession.*

Below *The Temple alma mater, "Onward with Temple," was composed by two trumpet players in the Temple marching band, one of whom earned a Temple medical degree and the other a Temple doctorate in education.*

Temple Symbols, Traditions, and Lore

Temple's 125-year history is rich with tradition and cherry and white spirit, from Conwell's "Acres of Diamonds" speech to the Temple Owl. Some of Temple's symbols, tradition, and lore date back to the founding, but others, such as the Temple "T" (see Chapter 7), are of fairly recent vintage. Temple has always embraced change, and some of its traditional symbols and identifying emblems have changed with the times.

Consider, for example, the origins of Temple's alma mater. Temple alums returning on homecoming weekend in 1930 watched the football team defeat the University of Miami and then listened as the marching band introduced them to a new alma mater. The song, "Onward with Temple," was written by two of the marching band's trumpet players, Walter St. Clair (BS SBM 1930; MA EDU 1936; Ed.D. 1942) and Charles D. Coppes (MD MED 1932). St. Clair wrote the lyrics and Coppes supplied the melody. An arrangement for the band was written by H. Edward Pike, director of bands from 1927 to 1945 and a professor of music. "Onward with Temple" replaced an older, eminently forgettable and difficult to sing classical anthem. St. Clair, Coppes, and Pike believed their new song was more appropriate for a marching band and better suited for a football powerhouse such as Temple. Initially there was some resistance to the new song, but over time the song was accepted and its origins in the trumpet section have been ignored or all but forgotten.

The university mace, the formal symbol of authority of the president of Temple, is also a fairly recent creation. A vestige of medieval university tradition, the president's mace is presented at every commencement, carried into the area by the mace bearer, a university marshal who immediately precedes the president in the academic procession. It is now a tradition at Temple that the retiring president formally transfers the mace to the incoming president during the formal investiture ceremony. Temple's mace was created in 1964 when then-President Millard Gladfelter commissioned Tyler School of Art professor Stanley Lechtzin to design and craft the mace, which has been carried and presented at every commencement since.

The selection of the owl as Temple's mascot, as we saw in Chapter 2, was actually made by the trustees of Conwell's church. Conwell endorsed the selection, kept on his desk a stuffed owl (the gift of the Rev. Forrest Dager), and later explained that the owl was an ideal symbol for a college where ambitious young people attended classes at night to further their educations and their careers. Late-night studiers were further encouraged by Conwell's remark, "The owl of the night makes the eagle of the day." Like Temple students, the owl is perceptive and resourceful, quick and courageous, and truly a fierce fighter.

For a brief time Temple had a live owl for a mascot. In 1931 the football team received a live great horned owl, a gift from the University of Missouri football team. It was named Owliver. The care and feeding of a live owl were more than anyone at Temple—let alone anyone on the football team—was prepared for, and so the bird was donated to the Philadelphia Zoo. Owliver died in 1947. Perhaps because of the popularity of the St. Joseph's University hawk mascot, Temple decided in 1977 to introduce a human-sized mascot owl caricature and named him Victor E. Owl. The name never quite stuck, and so, just seven years later, Temple conducted another contest to name the mascot. Students voted to name him Hooter, and he has since entertained the Temple faithful at sporting events and other special occasions.

Athletes who earned starting positions or played significant roles in Temple's varsity athletic teams—such as Bill Cosby (opposite page)—were awarded a varsity "T" that they proudly displayed on letter sweaters, a practice that became déclassé sometime in the late 1960s.

FACT

Bill Cosby (BA SCT 1977) lettered in football and track while a student at Temple.

The *Red Owl* came to Temple in April 1988. The 3,000-pound sculpture of the head of an owl, hewn from flecked Italian earth-red marble, was created by Italian artist Beniamino Bufano and donated to Temple by Bell Atlantic. Located at Berks Mall and Liacouras Walk, the thirty-four-inch-high figure was perched on top of the Alumni Circle, a stone seating area and gathering place designed by Professor Brigitte Knowles of the Architecture Department.

Cherry and white, the official colors of Temple University, adorn the inside of the hoods of the academic regalia worn by Temple graduates, distinguishing them from others in academic processions. The colors are seen more often when used to identify Temple's athletic teams. Temple was the first college in the nation officially to use cherry as one of its colors. The combination of red with white is quite common, but only one other school—Rensselaer Polytechnic Institute (Troy, New York)—adopted cherry and white. The University of New Mexico uses cherry as one of its colors but combines it with silver, not white. Conscious of the fact that cherry is a color of many gradations and can range from bright red to dark red, Temple standardized the color for athletic teams, signage, and publications to Pantone Matching System (PMS) 201 on the international color chart, a color of cherry near that of a ripe and bright American black cherry.

Famous Visitors

Many celebrated persons have visited Temple to receive honorary degrees, deliver lectures, support causes, or campaign for president. A sampling of dignitaries provides some indication of Temple's importance to the outside world, beginning with four sitting presidents—Franklin Roosevelt (1936), Harry Truman (1948), Lyndon Johnson (1964), and Jimmy Carter (1980)— plus four other presidents before they were elected—Dwight Eisenhower (1950), Richard Nixon (1955), John Kennedy (1960), and Barack Obama (2008).

Ambassador At Large

Finally, if you mention Temple University to someone beyond Philadelphia, he or she likely will say, "Oh, sure, I know Bill Cosby's school." Indeed, Dr. William Henry Cosby—comedian, actor, author, television producer, activist, and Temple University trustee—is surely Temple's best-known alum. Bill Cosby returned to his native Philadelphia after four years as a hospital corpsman in the U.S. Navy, enrolled at Temple, played fullback on the football team, and was a member of the track team. Always the class clown, the Coz, as he was known, was encouraged by fellow students to take his natural humor and quick wit on stage. In 1962 Bill was a Temple sophomore doing stand-up comedy in center city clubs. In a matter of weeks he was "discovered," and after an appearance on *The Tonight Show* in the summer of 1963, the rest, as they say, is history. What followed, among other achievements, were many comedy albums; a vanguard role in the TV series *I Spy;* the educational cartoon series *Fat Albert and the Cosby Kids;* several books; and his own TV series, *The Cosby Show*, which ran from 1984 to 1992 and was one of the highest-rated sitcoms in history. Hailed as one of the 100 greatest African Americans of all time, as one of America's most influential men, and as an educator and humanitarian, Bill Cosby was a 2002 recipient of the Presidential Medal of Freedom.

Above *In April 1962 the* Temple Review *described sophomore Bill Cosby as a "multifaceted physical education major who plays fullback, high jumps, and throws the discus and javelin." In the off-season, Cosby entertained at a center city nightclub.*

Left *Two owls exchange knowing glances.*

Chapter 7
Multiversity and Globalversity, 1982–2009

By the early 1980s Temple's aspirations to become a modern, comprehensive university were largely realized. With a distinguished faculty, contemporary facilities, and a robust combination of undergraduate, graduate, and professional programs, commingled with a substantial record of advanced research and scholarship, Temple seemed imminently positioned to rise further, perhaps into the top ranks of America's universities.

Ground is broken
for a new Temple
University Hospital.

1983

Bell of Pennsylvania
Computer Center
opens.

1987

Shusterman Hall
is dedicated.

1994

TEMPLE UNIVERSITY TIMELINE

1986

The University
Honors Program
starts.

1988

Temple offers
nation's first
doctorate in African
American Studies.

1997

The Apollo of Temple
(Liacouras Center
since 2000) opens.

Temple, as always, saw new challenges and aimed higher. Rather than a *uni*versity—with emphasis on oneness of purpose—Temple gradually had become a *multi*versity, attempting to fulfill multiple missions and satisfy many different constituencies. First coined by the American historian Arthur Bestor, the term *multiversity* connotes a very large university with numerous component schools, colleges, or divisions and widely diverse functions, with multiple stakeholders and affiliated institutions. In Temple's case some constituents were overseas. And so, while Temple expanded its influence locally and nationally, it also reached farther across the seas and accepted responsibility as a globalversity, a university steadfastly devoted to international education.

Temple became the manager of several complex academic ventures and proprietor of dozens of auxiliary enterprises in health care, sports entertainment, performing arts, professional training, business and social services, public service contracts, and the like. These endeavors required the creation of new administrative contrivances, additional departments and colleges, separate campuses, and numerous research centers. Seeking to gain or hold a competitive niche, Temple emulated other multiversities, adding layers of specialization upon the academic enterprise, leading some to decry the "tyranny of specialization" that stifled cross-disciplinary cooperation and forced a reconsideration of the basic purposes of the university. Reflecting on the impact of the multiversity role, Clark Kerr, the distinguished president of the University of California, perceptively questioned the "hinge of history" on which American universities seemed to pivot.

Temple's future hinged on responding to the needs of several disparate groups or communities, including the communities of undergraduate, professional, and graduate students; faculty humanists, social scientists, and scientists; neighborhood, business, professional, and political communities; and internal communities of non-academic personnel, administrators, and auxiliary enterprises. These various aggregations, with often-conflicting and competing interests, reached out in turn to alumni, government officials, neighborhood groups, business leaders, foundation heads, and others. Put more simply, Temple University by the 1980s had become a very large, intricately complex institution with many identities.

Depending on whom you asked, there were many Temple Universities. The problem facing the leadership in the 1980s, then, was how to unbundle all of Temple's various images, unite its diverse communities, reinvigorate the university's basic mission, and restore a unified, coherent Temple. Over the course of the next two decades Temple gradually repositioned itself in the higher-education marketplace, finding a new identity as an urban residential university. By the end of the century the Temple name, place, and idea still resonated, but with new respect for its transformative powers. Outside observers marveled at Temple's tolerance of change and the extent to which Temple's historic legacy and the enduring strength of its mission united its numerous citizens within its many communities. But it was neither an easy nor an uneventful journey.

Peter J. Liacouras

On July 1, 1982, Peter James Liacouras became the seventh president in Temple's history. The son of immigrants, who were born in Messenia and Laconia, Greece, Liacouras took enormous pride in Temple's role in making the American Dream come true for its many thousands of graduates, especially first-generation college students. Liacouras's father, James Peter Liacouras, arrived in Philadelphia in September 1906 with no resources other than a strong will to succeed and a passion for hard work. He established himself as a successful small-business man and imbued his son

with a deep reverence for his heritage, as well as a strong work ethic, a profound respect for the common man, and a keen, insatiable interest in education.

Born in Philadelphia, and thus the first native Philadelphian to rise to the Temple presidency, Peter Liacouras graduated from Yeadon High School in Delaware County, earned a bachelor's degree at Drexel University, a Juris Doctor degree (in 1956) from the University of Pennsylvania, a master's degree from the Fletcher School of Law and Diplomacy (Tufts University), and a Master of Laws degree in international law from Harvard University. In addition, he was a Sterling Fellow at Yale Law School. As a scholar of international law he became a devoted defender of human rights, maintaining an unshakable commitment to human dignity and equality of opportunity. He served as an American specialist for the Department of State in India before returning to Philadelphia and to the law as a public defender, providing legal counsel for indigent persons charged with crimes.

Liacouras joined Temple's Law School in 1963, rose through the academic ranks, and was named dean in 1972. Liacouras initiated a number of new programs (see Chapter 8), expanded the size and quality of the Law School faculty, and was the driving force behind the concept of a Temple Law Center, a law school campus within the Main Campus. Many of his successful initiatives attracted wide attention, which, in turn, drew attention to the Law School and to Liacouras personally, leading in 1980 to an unsuccessful bid for the Democratic nomination for the U.S. Senate from Pennsylvania.

The six-month interregnum between presidential administrations afforded Liacouras time to assess matters before taking office. He sought advice from and listened intently to Temple students, faculty, and staff and brought in consultants, including Lennox Moak, former finance director for the City of Philadelphia, to advise him on university finances and on structuring and administering the university. Liacouras quickly reorganized the top management of the university, appointing Barbara

Peter Liacouras and President Marvin Wachman (pictured above when Liacouras was dean of the Law School) publicly differed over the depth and intensity of the financial problems facing the university at the time of Wachman's retirement.

Insisting that "change and renewal" were "constants throughout Temple's history," Liacouras outlined a bold thrust to reposition the university, challenging Temple to reach higher. Strategic initiatives included a new corporate brand (the Temple "T"), an expansive student recruitment campaign, and eventually the third wave of capital expansion in Temple's history, sandwiched around two devastating faculty strikes.

L. Brownstein, an internationally known geneticist, as provost; H. Patrick Swygert as vice president for university administration (later to be named president of Howard University); and John Rumpf as executive vice president. In short order Liacouras moved the president's office from Conwell Hall to Sullivan Hall and relocated the Diamond Club for faculty and staff to Mitten Hall, drawing both closer to the physical center of the campus. Eager to upgrade Temple's intercollegiate athletics programs, he immediately appointed a new basketball coach (John Chaney) and, after the 1982 season, a new football coach (Bruce Arians).

The lengthy transition also bred tensions, as the outgoing administration felt second-guessed by the incoming one, particularly over the state of the university's finances and faculty retrenchment. Marvin Wachman and Liacouras later publicly disagreed on the state of university finances upon Wachman's leaving. Liacouras insisted that Temple was technically "insolvent" on July 1, 1982, when he inherited a $3 million deficit in consolidated, unrestricted fund balances. In 1986 the *Philadelphia Inquirer* referred to Temple's "near bankruptcy" and the "near catastrophic" situation confronting Liacouras when he took office. Wachman, on the other hand, believed that last-minute retrenchments, along with reductions of 2,500 staff positions and other administrative reorganizations, had saved Temple perhaps as much as $30 million. Wachman insisted in his 2005 memoir that auditors' statements "showed surpluses for the university, and that Temple's financial status was absolutely solid" when he retired as president.

Wachman's explanations notwithstanding, the lingering financial crisis of the late 1970s and early 1980s was quite real. Between 1977 and 1983, total enrollments fell 17.9 percent, from 36,339 to 29,835. Liacouras was able to demonstrate slow, steady enrollment growth through the 1980s, peaking at 34,560 in 1989. However, almost all of those gains were lost during the faculty strike of 1990, which cost Temple 12.2 percent of its full-time undergraduate enrollments and 10.5 percent of its total enrollments. Recovery required many years. During the 1990s enrollments in the profes-

sional schools grew steadily, graduate enrollments declined slightly, and full-time undergraduate enrollments dropped slightly, fluctuating each year within a narrow 2 to 3 percent range. Temple's total enrollments did not again attain 1989 levels until 2003.

At the same time, commonwealth appropriations failed to keep pace with inflation, decreasing in both real and relative terms. Consider, for example, the six-year period from 1991 through 1997, during which Temple's appropriation rose by 6.6 percent ($139.6 million to $148.6 million), or 1.1 percent per year over the six years. The cumulative inflation rate for those six years was 20.6 percent, or an average yearly increase of 3.4 percent. The very modest increases in the appropriations meant Temple's relative buying power was substantially reduced. Temple was not the only Pennsylvania state-affiliated university affected. Between 1990 and 2009 Pennsylvania ranked between forty-fifth and forty-eighth out of all fifty states in per capita support of public higher education.

Over time, commonwealth funds constituted less and less of Temple's total operating budget. When the state-affiliation agreement was signed into law in 1965, Temple was assured that the commonwealth would thereafter provide the vast majority of the university's operating and capital expenses in return for lower tuition for Pennsylvania residents. However, the non-preferred status of Temple's annual appropriation bill within the General Assembly meant it was always subject to the political winds blowing through Harrisburg. The percentage of Temple's operations supported by the commonwealth appropriation steadily declined—1990 was the last year the commonwealth provided as much as half of Temple's total budget—until by fiscal year 2008–2009 the commonwealth appropriation amounted to only 23 percent of Temple's operating budget.

Turning back to 1982, the most obvious signs of financial decline were five years of deferred maintenance, freezes on hiring, moratoriums on new program development, and virtually no recapitalization of critical instructional, research, and computational equipment. Part of the problem was that the enormous capital and programmatic expansion from 1965 to 1978 had created cumulative obligations that could not be met during an era of declining enrollments and decreasing net revenues. Put another way, Temple's insistence on playing the multiversity role, trying to be all things to all people, had created more commitments than Temple had resources to meet. Compounding matters, the trustees refused to impose a larger burden on Temple's students and did not raise tuition any higher than necessary to meet bare operating expenses. How, then, was Temple expected to maintain its academic reputation and meet expanding needs?

The first, most obvious answer was to cut costs. That required tough-minded discipline, a willingness to make hard decisions, and a determined effort to steadily build financial reserves without putting the entire enterprise at risk. In his eighteen years as president, Peter Liacouras delivered eighteen balanced budgets, emphasizing administrative efficiencies and productivity. Doing more with less became the Liacouras and the Temple mantra.

To remain competitive and to satisfy diverse constituencies, Temple employed some creative approaches for leveraging available resources and developing new ones, becoming a leader in what analysts in the mid-1980s described as an "enterprising evolution" taking hold in America's universities. By necessity Temple became a more enterprising, entrepreneurial institution. Planning and managerial approaches were combined to diversify revenues, meet capital requirements, and improve the campus environment. Unable to do everything on its own, Temple sought partnerships with and assistance from an impressive array of governmental agencies, corporations, businesses, and community groups.

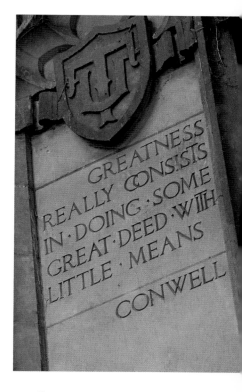

Russell Conwell's maxim engraved on the outer wall of Sullivan Hall tested Temple's leadership for 125 years, perhaps never more persistently than during the Liacouras years.

Temple Town

President Liacouras and board of trustees chairman Richard J. Fox worked closely in developing a strategy for competitively repositioning the university and for ensuring its long-term viability in North Philadelphia. Fox served for over forty years on Temple's board and was chairman from 1983 to 2000, the longest tenure of any chairman in Temple history. Besides contributing his business acumen, he was part of Temple's negotiating team during the 1969 community charrette and knowledgeable about community needs and issues.

Liacouras envisioned developing Temple's Main Campus into what he called "Temple Town." The objective was to convert Temple from a predominantly commuter institution, where fewer than 2,800 students lived on campus, to a university with a firm, vibrant residential presence and with a special identity to make all who worked and studied there proud of the association. Fox and Liacouras predicted that the effects of a more energetic campus would spill over into the neighborhood. They pledged, therefore, to maintain community services, health care, and assistance with economic revitalization, all the while building the university into a major, comprehensive research university and a center of cultural activity.

When Liacouras assumed office, the commonwealth capital program, except for funds reserved for the hospital and Dental School, had run its course. No new major capital improvements were planned for the Main Campus. Some funds remained available through the Campus Environmental Improvement Program (CEIP), launched during the Wachman years with a $6 million grant from the Pew Memorial Trust and a $1 million grant from the William Penn Foundation. The CEIP was completed in the early 1980s with renovations totaling $4.2 million on the Student Activities Center and Mitten Hall along with a complete overhaul of the Geasey Field outdoor recreation complex at Fifteenth Street, from Norris to Montgomery Avenue. Upgrades included installation of artificial turf and improved lighting on playing surfaces for field hockey, soccer, lacrosse, and football, plus a six-lane all-weather running track.

A campus environmental improvement program of the late 1970s and early 1980s added recreation and varsity athletic facilities to the Geasey complex on the east side of the campus. New facilities included an all-weather running track and a vast expanse of synthetic athletic turf for the use of physical education instruction, intramural athletics, and women's lacrosse and field hockey competitions.

Liacouras and Fox were concerned about pyramiding costs and the diffusion of influence created by staffing and maintaining multiple campuses, and so they ordered cost-benefit studies for consolidating Temple's operations at one location, including the possibility of moving the Tyler School of Art and the entire Health Sciences Center to the Broad and Montgomery campus. Tyler eventually moved to Main Campus (in 2009), but relocating the Health Sciences Center proved infeasible, because the university lacked adequate resources, space, and necessary political support.

Thus, the commitment was made to develop the Health Sciences Campus in tandem with the Main Campus and, as much as possible, physically link them along the North Broad Street corridor. Accordingly, in December 1982 trustees authorized proceeding with the long-delayed construction of a new replacement hospital at Broad and Ontario streets. Liacouras insisted on minimizing the university's long-term financial obligation and risk exposure. Funds for the new hospital came from a $115.5 million bond issue backed by the Federal Housing Administration, with $22.5 million from the commonwealth, and $7 million in private support from the Haas Family Charitable Trust, the George D. Widener Trust, plus contributions from trustees, medical staff, and members of the Hospital Board of Governors.

However, concerns remained. The Temple University Health System posed what Liacouras called an "intractable dilemma," a constant monetary drain on the university. The City of Philadelphia had closed Philadelphia General Hospital in 1975, leaving Philadelphia as the only major American city without a municipal hospital and shifting the burden onto Temple and the city's teaching hospitals. Further, the city government provided Temple no funds for treating Philadelphia's poor. At one point Temple temporarily gained additional state funding but only after resorting to a lawsuit. Even with some federal support, the costs of unreimbursed indigent care continued to mount. Liacouras feared the hospital would "become a fatal financial noose around the University." Therefore, in 1994 Temple legally separated the hospital-related activities (all but the Physicians' Practice Plan), creating a wholly owned university subsidiary, Temple University Health Systems, Inc. The arrangement freed the health system and the university to expand.

Back on the Main Campus the plan for Temple Town began with strengthening the campus spine, the pedestrian walkway known then as Park Mall (later as Liacouras Walk) running south to north from Cecil B. Moore Avenue to Diamond Street. A long-term plan called for the rehabilitation of the historically significant circa 1865 row houses along Park Mall that had served Temple since the 1880s. Many of the row houses, unused after the spurt of state construction in the 1970s, were in deteriorating condition. With grants from the Kresge Foundation and Girard Trust, the residential cornerstones of Temple Town were laid in 1984 with the conversion of two row houses at 1914 and 1916 Park Mall into ten rental townhomes and apartments available to staff, faculty, and visiting scholars. As funds became available, other row houses were renovated to provide amenities lacking at Temple prior to the 1980s, such as a convenience store, entertainment spots, and even a pub.

Once used for classrooms and dormitories, then for faculty and departmental offices, the row houses in the 1900 block of Park Mall (later Liacouras Walk) began undergoing renovations in the 1980s with intentions of creating a set of core amenities to serve visitors and a much-expanded, full-time residential student body. Two decades later, as the picture below illustrates, those intentions were grandly fulfilled.

Eager to meet a growing demand for campus living, Temple in 1984 purchased the Yorktown Apartments, a large six-story apartment building at 1200 Cecil B. Moore Avenue. The twin-tower building was renamed Temple Towers and renovated to accommodate 632 upper-class and transfer students in one-, two-, and three-bedroom furnished apartments, all with private bathrooms and fully equipped kitchens, private balconies, a fitness room, a computer lab, and a heated outdoor swimming pool. "The goal," said Liacouras in the spring of 1984, "is for the campus to become a bustling community—as active by night as it is by day—enlivened by residents, restaurants, shops and other businesses."

Arguably the most consequential initiative of the early Liacouras years was the plan for a master computing and information system assigned to Robert G. Scanlon, the former secretary of education in Governor Dick Thornburgh's cabinet who served as Liacouras's chief of staff and later vice president. Scanlon was charged with creating an integrated voice, data, and communications system to combine all of Temple's needs into one self-contained, university-wide fiber-optic telecommunications network. When completed, the $12.5 million project put Temple squarely in the forefront of higher education's technological innovators, substantially ahead of local and regional competitors. The project also produced one of the most momentous partnerships in Temple's history.

The contract for the installation of Temple's fiber-optic telecommunications system was awarded to Bell Atlanticom, a telecommunications equipment division of Bell of Pennsylvania (later known as Bell Atlantic, then Verizon). When issuing the request for proposals, Temple asked each bidder to comment on how it would assist Temple in reaching its overall development goals. In response, Raymond Smith, Bell's chief executive officer, at first considered tying Bell into Temple's Ambler Campus, perhaps by building a new corporate computer center on the campus or in a nearby industrial park. Liacouras preferred that Bell's investment be near the Main Campus in North Philadelphia.

On a warm July afternoon in 1984 Ray Smith paid a courtesy visit to Temple and was given a personal walking tour of the Main Campus by Liacouras. During their meeting Liacouras poured out

A major milestone in Temple's efforts to bring new investment and new development into North Philadelphia was reached in 1987 with the opening of the Bell of Pennsylvania corporate computer center on Temple's campus. Changes in Bell's corporate structure led eventually to Temple's acquisition and renovation of the building, adding student meeting rooms, a café, and a welcome center, plus installing more than 700 computer workstations for student use. Named the TECH (Teaching, Education, Collaboration, and Help) Center, the building opened in 2006 and quickly became the new student hub, attracting thousands of students day and night to its state-of-the-art facilities.

his hopes and aspirations for Temple and for North Philadelphia's revitalization. "Basically," Liacouras later recalled, "it was a matter of trust—and I knew that he could dream."

Whatever was said, Smith was persuaded that Bell should build its computer center at Temple and become Temple's partner in helping to revitalize North Philadelphia—if certain conditions were met and if the city and state gave full support. Eventually agreement was reached with all parties and the Bell corporate computer center was built on the Temple campus on a parking lot at the northwest corner of Montgomery Avenue and Twelfth Street. Construction of the 220,000-square-foot building cost $25 million. More than $100 million in computer equipment went into the building. An attached $2.5 million parking garage was erected for the convenience of the 173 Bell employees working in the building. Space in the building was also provided to house Temple's security force.

Bell also played a very active role in the North Philadelphia community, agreeing to hire some local residents to work in the building as well as funding job-training programs and a community development corporation. By 1990 Bell had generously invested $1 million into various North Philadelphia community programs. In addition, largely through the efforts of Charles F. Schalch (BS SBM 1955), president of Temple's Alumni Association and also a Bell executive, the Temple-Bell partnership brought Temple a $1 million gift to establish a visiting professor's chair in telecommunications and a substantial contribution to create the Camille Cosby Scholarship in Science at Temple.

Bell's decision to build in North Philadelphia, as Peter Liacouras observed at the April 1987 dedication ceremony, reversed a generation of exodus by private industry. Governor Robert P. Casey and Philadelphia Mayor W. Wilson Goode hailed the Temple-Bell joint venture as a model partnership for urban revitalization. In hopes that the details of the arrangements would be instructive to others, Bell commissioned New York University professor Larry Alan Bear to write a history of the undertaking, which he titled *The Glass House Revolution: Inner-City War for Interdependence.*

To make Temple more accessible and commuting more pleasant, Temple secured funding to upgrade its transportation portals, beginning in 1983 with significant renovations to the Cecil B. Moore/Temple University subway station on the Broad Street line and the construction of an adjoining plaza.

Expectations were that the Bell investment would spawn further development. Indeed, shortly on the heels of the Bell-Temple announcement, the Philadelphia Gas Works (PGW) decided not to leave North Philadelphia and opted instead to construct a new $29 million executive office building at Ninth and Berks streets, just two blocks from the Bell computer building. Eventually two nearby Temple buildings—the Kardon Building and the Atlantic Terminal Warehouse, two large industrial buildings abandoned during the post–World War II deindustrialization of North Philadelphia and donated to Temple—were converted by private developers into upscale apartment buildings for Temple students.

The once-desolate, blighted area on the east side of Temple's campus was further enlivened with the construction of the new $36.7 million Regional Rail station. Thanks largely to the good offices of Congressman William H. Gray—then chairman of the U.S. House Budget Committee and also minister of Bright Hope Baptist Church opposite Temple's campus at Twelfth Street and Cecil B.

Moore Avenue—federal funds were made available through a mass-transit appropriation to move the small, run-down Temple Station from Ninth Street and Cecil B. Moore Avenue closer to the center of Temple's campus at Berks and Tenth streets, adjacent to the PGW offices and one block from the Bell computer building. Temple installed a safety kiosk and arranged with SEPTA to convert Temple Station into a major stop on the Regional Rail line. When the station opened in 1993, Temple University became directly accessible to suburban residents in all of the surrounding counties and New Jersey. In 2008 Temple University station was the fourth-busiest in SEPTA's Regional Rail system, with 2,448 average total weekday boardings and 2,593 average weekday alightments.

"T" for Temple U

In 1982 Temple's blurred image was represented by many symbols and insignia, but no single compelling brand identifier. Almost everyone knew that the owl was the university mascot, but few recognized the university seal or other logos used by various units within Temple. Determined to create a unifying Temple logo, Liacouras invited students in the Tyler School of Art to create a distinctively recognizable symbol for Temple.

Students in Professor Joseph Scorscone's 1983 Tyler School of Art class welcomed the challenge. Faculty, staff, and alumni were invited to jury the best student designs. The block Temple "T" that we know today was designed by Tyler student Kristine Herrick (MFA TYL 1983). She aspired to create a logo that would be, as she put it, "bold, highly visible and somewhat collegiate." The final decision was supported by Bill Cosby and men's basketball coach John Chaney. Chaney embraced the potential of the logo from an athletic perspective, and Cosby casually promoted the logo on his television show.

The Temple "T," said Professor Scorscone, had a new, modern look "but also reflected the tradition of Temple University." Its shape suggested Greek Doric columns, connoting permanence, strength, and stability. When used on stationery, advertisements, and flags flown across the campus, the Temple "T" quickly became one of the most recognizable symbols in the Greater Philadelphia area.

Peter Liacouras also became quickly known across the region as Temple's premier cheerleader, publicly touting accomplishments and urging everyone at Temple to aim high. He also made a few bold, media-worthy promises, which were no more really than a collection of his fondest aspirations for Temple. A few of Liacouras's promises—such as reaching the "final four in '84" (the semi-finals of the NCAA national basketball championships) and a Sugar Bowl berth for the football team—remained beyond Temple's reach. Some constituents questioned his priorities when making such promises, but none questioned his dedication and devotion to Temple. Alumni were particularly proud of Temple's nationwide television image campaign featuring alumnus Bill Cosby, who reminded viewers, "I could have gone anywhere—but I chose Temple."

The makeover of Temple involved more than image and facilities. Temple's academic programs underwent substantial scrutiny by Provost Barbara Brownstein, culminating in 1986 with a ten-year academic plan, setting priorities and reserving funds to support faculty research, establish interdisciplinary research centers, and focus efforts on pursuing the coveted status of Carnegie Research I University, a goal that was attained in 1993. The academic plan fostered a reexamination of the basic, general knowledge each Temple undergraduate should possess, leading to a new undergraduate core curriculum. Additionally, the plan recommended bolstering Temple's academic reputation by expressing greater appreciation for faculty contributions. Temple subsequently established Distinguished University Professorships, Laura H. Carnell Professorships, and Great Teacher Awards, each of which carried special status, plus monetary rewards. In recognition of the lasting value of exceptional teaching, the names of each year's Great Teacher Award winners were engraved on the granite walls of Founder's Garden.

The ubiquitous Temple "T"—with us now for more than a quarter century—provides a singular identifying brand, an immediately recognizable symbol of Access to Excellence.

For all of this, the central feature of Temple planning remained the development of a vibrant residential campus, which, of course, required capital. Temple's situation was not helped when the governor frequently abated Temple's appropriation and, for a time (from 1989 to 1995), altered the commonwealth appropriation scheme by promulgating a per capita funding formula that—because of Temple's top-heavy emphasis on more costly graduate and professional education—disadvantaged Temple compared with other state-affiliated institutions. Gradually, however, through prudent investment and careful management, Temple was able to reduce short-term borrowing and to attain the requisite financial stability for the long-term borrowing necessary for improving its aging infrastructure, enhancing campus amenities, and building new dormitories and other revenue-generating projects.

The Temple Town strategy aimed to strengthen the Main Campus by bringing back many of the functions that, through the years, often were held in other parts of the city, including convocations, commencements, and major sporting events. Temple was particularly handicapped by not having a convocation center befitting a university of its size and caliber. All of Temple's annual commencements, dating back to 1932, had been held off campus, usually at the Philadelphia Civic Center. Liacouras, therefore, dedicated himself to finding the funds for the construction of a convocation center, a new classroom building, additional student housing and recreational facilities, as well as other campus amenities.

A breakthrough occurred in 1993 when Governor Robert P. Casey agreed to release capital funds to "jump-start" Pennsylvania's lagging economy, on condition that Temple match one-third of the total in private gifts. Liacouras then presented "The Commonwealth Challenge," a one-year intense development campaign to raise $30 million in exchange for a state appropriation of $61.9 million to go toward four major projects: a classroom and laboratory building, a recreation and convocation center, a student residence hall, and upgrades to eleven high-rise buildings to bring them into compliance with local building codes.

The Third Wave

The Commonwealth Challenge created the momentum to carry Temple into its third major wave of campus expansion in its 125-year history. The first wave, spanning 1922 to 1936, provided the first campus, albeit a limited, sidewalk campus. The second wave, covering the years 1956 to 1978 and funded largely by the commonwealth, enabled Temple to rise to the status of a modern comprehensive university. The third wave commenced in 1993 and reached its apex in 2009—just in time for the 125th anniversary celebrations. It established Temple as a premier urban, residential campus.

Bricks and mortar alone, of course, do not make a university. During 1995 and 1996 Liacouras guided Temple through a strategic planning process that he called the "Plan to Renew Temple's Mission." Looking back on his presidency years later, he described these two years as Temple's critical "reformative years of structural changes." Most, if not all, of Temple's major stakeholders played a role in the planning process. Liacouras's goals were to improve productivity and streamline operations, strengthen educational programs, and make Temple a top choice for undergraduates.

Experts on best practices evaluated all phases of the institution. Particular attention was devoted to marketing and promotions efforts to reposition Temple in the quickly changing higher-education marketplace. Temple's administrative procedures and the normal day-to-day office procedures were altered to create a more cordial, welcoming environment in the delivery of student services. To make Temple more marketable, undergraduate tuition rates were frozen or increased minimally. At the same time, Temple cut redundant programs, reduced its budget by 11 percent, froze salaries, and created a replenishment fund to support renewal plans.

Liacouras summarized the renewal plan in the "Report on Strategic Initiatives," approved by the board of trustees in June 1997. The plan recommended a major repositioning of Temple in response to profound changes in the higher-education marketplace and to major population shifts in the Philadelphia metropolitan area. Philadelphia County's diminishing population (down 25 percent since 1950) and the expansive growth of the Philadelphia suburbs (up 24.5 percent in the decade of the 1990s alone) mandated a new "regional strategy."

While refusing to turn its back on the city and its needs, Temple at the same time realized the inescapable need to diversify and expand its enrollment base beyond the shrinking population of Philadelphia County. The growing suburbs were producing more college-aged students and more well-prepared students than the city. The first goal of the Temple renewal plan, then, was to increase the freshman class in both size and level of academic preparation. Temple began cutting back its remedial programs, shifting much of that responsibility to the community colleges. In short order Temple struck joint admissions agreements with seven community colleges.

The second goal was to improve the total experience of Temple students by transforming the Main Campus. Temple could not flourish as an overwhelmingly commuter campus. If Temple was to grow and prosper, it had to respond to the competition from traditional liberal arts colleges and flagship state universities. Discriminating, cost-conscious consumers of higher education expected college to be a memorable life experience. More than a place to take classes, the campus had to be not only safe and attractive, but also an area for students to live, study, and grow, as well as a cultural destination filled with amenities and activities.

Temple's third major wave of capital expansion began in 1993 under the direction of Temple's executive vice president, James S. White. A retired army officer and decorated Vietnam veteran, White joined Temple in 1991 after five years of distinguished service as managing director of the City of Philadelphia. Entrusted with launching the capital expansion, White took on his first major project with the construction of a 558-bed dormitory at 2108-50 North Broad Street, formerly the site of a vacant state-owned armory. The $19 million facility featured two- and four-person living units with shared bath, large social lounges, fitness center, enclosed garden patio, and other amenities that became the new standard for Temple dormitories. White was named a trustee after his retirement in 1999, and in his honor Temple named the new dormitory the James S. White Residence Hall.

Other upgrades to residential life soon followed. In 1993 the university substantially upgraded central dining services in Johnson-Hardwick Commons, introducing a food-court style of dining with more than a dozen food and beverage stations offering the widest possible variety of meal choices for students. The $7.8 million dining facility was later dedicated in honor of Louis J. Esposito, an honorary life trustee. In 1999 a second new residence hall opened at 1940 Park Mall (now Liacouras Walk) at Norris Street on the former site of Thomas Hall, which was once a church. In June 1998 the Philadelphia Historical Commission agreed to allow demolition of Thomas Hall (formerly Thatcher Hall) to make way for the new residence hall in exchange for the university's promise to find a use for the vacant Baptist Temple. Known simply as 1940, the four-story, $17 million building provided 472 additional beds in two-bedroom suites, plus lounges, fitness room, laundries, dance studio, computer room, and other amenities.

Other projects, equally important to the growth of the campus, were not as noticeable, such as a $16 million stand-by power plant or the $19.7 million expenditure to bring Temple's buildings into compliance with Philadelphia's High-Rise Fire Code.

One of the first projects to be completed in Temple's third wave of physical expansion, the James S. White Residence Hall was fittingly dedicated in 1999 to honor the significant accomplishments of Temple's retired executive vice president.

The most noticeable of all the new buildings was The Forum at the Apollo of Temple. The multi-building recreation and convocation center covered over 270,000 gross square feet on the west side of the 1700 block of North Broad Street, from Montgomery to Cecil B. Moore avenues. Dedicated in December 1997 by Governor Tom Ridge, the $107 million complex contained six venues, including a 10,000-seat basketball arena, a theater (named in honor of lead contributor Esther Boyer, who also endowed the School of Music), athletics offices (later named in honor of Temple's long-time athletic director Ernie Casale), plus retail and support space. In February 2000 the building was rededicated and renamed the Liacouras Center in honor of Temple's seventh president. The Liacouras Center has hosted a wide array of events, including concerts, trade shows, community activities, and sporting events, such as the 2003 NCAA men's gymnastics championships and preliminary games in the 2004 and 2006 NCAA women's basketball championships.

Vivacqua Hall, next door to the Liacouras Center, underwent $1.1 million of exterior improvements to harmonize with the exterior of the Liacouras Center complex. Vivacqua Hall's ground-floor retail space was expanded, awnings and signage were added, and new paving, lighting, and tree plantings gave a new look to Temple's Broad Street portal. A six-story, 1,200-space parking garage was constructed on Fifteenth Street with a connecting bridge to the Liacouras Center.

Temple's expansion also included new facilities for student intramural athletics and leisure exercise. The centerpiece was a $73 million, 38,000-square-foot, two-level student fitness facility attached to the Liacouras Center and dedicated in 1998 as the Independence Blue Cross Recreation Center (IBC). With entrances from Fifteenth Street and Cecil B. Moore Avenue, the IBC included state-of-the-art fitness equipment, an indoor track, aerobics and martial arts centers, racquetball courts, lockers, and more. A year later Temple opened the new Student Pavilion, a $4.7 million field house

The Tuttleman Learning Center, named in honor of Stanley Tuttleman and Edna Shanis Tuttleman (BS SBM 1942), opened in 1999. At 117,000 square feet, with interior gardens, a café, and all of the accoutrements necessary to meet the learning needs of the millennial generation of students, the Tuttleman Learning Center appeared at a propitious moment in Temple's history.

dedicated to student recreation. Located adjacent to McGonigle Hall and the Geasey Field Astroturf and track complex near Fifteenth and Berks streets and just a short walk from the IBC student fitness center, the Student Pavilion was designed to accommodate a variety of recreational sports, including basketball, volleyball, indoor soccer, golf practice, and tennis. In addition, it featured six lighted outdoor tennis courts and a beach volleyball court.

The academic showpiece of the 1990s expansion was the Tuttleman Learning Center, a state-of-the-art classroom building completed in 1999 at the corner of Thirteenth Street and Montgomery Avenue. The center contained thirty multimedia classrooms, computer laboratories, three lecture halls, a library reading room, a café, and a walkway into Paley Library. The first academic building constructed on the Main Campus in twenty-one years, the Tuttleman Learning Center was made possible by grants from the Commonwealth of Pennsylvania and by the generosity of Stanley Tuttleman and his wife, Edna Shanis Tuttleman (BS SBM 1942). Edna Tuttleman told the *Temple Review* that she and her husband "perceive Temple to be the key to Philadelphia's advanced education for its citizens." She acknowledged being committed to "Temple's continued presence on North Broad Street" since she campaigned for class president in 1942 and said, "I continue to believe in it."

The Temple Town plan worked. As Main Campus facilities improved, more students opted to live on campus and total enrollments increased and diversified. An enrollment surge began in the fall 1999 semester, with a 26 percent increase in freshman enrollments, and continued through the next decade, lifting full-time undergraduate enrollments from 19,285 in 1999 to 30,034 in 2008, a 55.7 percent increase. At the same time, total Temple enrollments, including all undergraduate, graduate, and professional students at all of Temple's campuses (including Rome and TU Japan), rose from 28,932 to 37,748, or 30.5 percent.

Beginning with the fall 2000 semester, 54 percent of Temple's new students chose to live on campus compared with only 17 percent two decades earlier. The demand for student housing quickly exceeded available space. Temple also attracted larger numbers of students from beyond the

Philadelphia region. In 1996 fewer than 25 percent of Temple freshmen and transfer students were from out of state or from Pennsylvania counties beyond the five-county Philadelphia region. By 2005 that number had risen above 45 percent.

Globalversity

Temple's global reach, begun in the 1960s with a small French-language program in Paris, progressively widened in the 1980s and 1990s. As traditional national boundaries gradually blurred, increasing numbers of Temple students found it both rewarding and necessary to be more actively engaged as learners, participants, and residents of the international community. By 1997, with Temple campuses in Rome, Japan, and China, President Liacouras proudly proclaimed, "The sun never sets on Temple University."

The globalization of education was stimulated by the end of the Cold War, the once-soaring global economy, and the growing interdependence of societies, abetted by astounding advances in telecommunications. Temple's global approach to education took shape in various ways: Temple internationalized its General Education curriculum; sent students abroad to study; accepted a steadily increasing number of international students; created new international partnerships and programs; and expanded campuses abroad.

Temple's leadership role in global education stems largely from its early initiatives in establishing foreign campuses, beginning with Temple University Rome. The Rome program began as a study abroad program for Tyler School of Art students but over the years has expanded to include a semester or academic year of full-time study in one of four undergraduate components: architecture/landscape architecture, liberal arts and Italian studies, visual arts, and international business. Faculty members are selected from Temple University's Main Campus, as well as from Italy and other European countries.

Since its establishment in 1966, Temple Rome has occupied the lower floors of the nineteenth-century Villa Caproni, located on the Tiber River just north of the Piazza del Popolo and within walking distance of the Spanish Steps. The top floors are retained as the private residence of Contessa Maria Fede Caproni and her sister, Princess Letizia Caproni Giovanelli. Their father, Gianni Caproni, an aviation pioneer and manufacturer, designed Caproni airplanes on the premises. In the spring of 2009 a year-long renovation project, under the direction of Rome dean Kim Strommen, updated classrooms and study areas, created a new architecture studio, and installed a staircase linking the first and second floors to a new third-floor expansion, providing space for a new architecture studio, lounges, and classrooms and also affording room to expand. "The light-filled spaces with views of Rome," said Dean Strommen, "added even greater beauty to the facilities while maintaining the Villa Caproni's historic character."

Temple University Japan (TUJ), established in 1982, is the oldest and largest American university in Japan. Beginning with an Intensive English Language Program (later renamed Academic Preparation Program) and M.Ed. programs in the teaching of English as a second or foreign language, TUJ has since expanded into a full-fledged university with eleven undergraduate-, graduate-, and professional-degree programs, including Japanese-language instruction; courses in art, Asian studies, business administration, economics, communications, tourism and hospitality, and critical languages; plus specialized courses in architecture and business. Since 1993 Temple University's Law School has offered a Master of Laws (LLM) program, the first such program offered by an

Temple University Rome

Study in Rome can be a life-changing experience. Joe Viesti (BSW SSA 1971) recalled how in 1970 an inspiring professor of anthropology, Jacob Gruber, "pushed us to explore the museums and to make the most of the opportunity to experience the wonders of Rome firsthand." Taking Gruber's "words to heart, I did it with a camera," said Viesti, thus launching a highly successful career as a travel photographer. Joe returned in 2007 to meet with Temple Rome students, share memories, and discuss the commercial side of photography. (The photo above is of an oil painting of the Villa Caproni done in 2008 by Temple Rome faculty member Lucy Clink.)

American law school in Asia. Classes are conducted in English, and TUJ students receive the same curriculum and are conferred the same degrees as Temple's Main Campus students. This arrangement has prompted a two-way flow of students. Each year since the 1990s increasing numbers of TUJ students have opted to complete their degrees on Temple's Main Campus.

During its early years TUJ relocated several times and partnered with different Japanese business interests. However, in 1996 TUJ became a wholly owned operation of Temple University. That same year TUJ relocated to Minami-Azabu, Minato-ku in central Tokyo. TUJ's main classroom and administration building is Azabu Hall, a six-floor modern office building. A second classroom and office building, Mita Hall, is a five-minute walk away. Since 1995 TUJ also has offered graduate education programs in Osaka and since 1998 in Fukuoka.

It required several years for TUJ to gain the acceptance and full recognition of Japanese education officials, but in 2005 TUJ became the first postsecondary educational institution in Japan with overseas roots to be designated a Foreign University, Japan Campus, by Japan's Ministry of Education. By 2009 total enrollment exceeded 2,250 students. TUJ faculty numbered over 180, including Temple faculty from Philadelphia and full- and part-time faculty hired locally from among practicing professionals.

A further sign of TUJ's elevated status occurred in February 2008 when Dr. Bruce Stronach, president of Yokohama City University (Japan), was named dean of Temple University Japan. The first foreign president of a Japanese public university and a respected authority and author of several books on Japanese popular culture and politics, Stronach immediately set out to enhance TUJ's connections with Japanese institutions of higher education and to further mutual academic development. TUJ's dual mission, as set forth by Stronach, is to foster better relations between the United States and Japan and to be "a model for cross-national academic collaboration."

FACT

The Beasley School of Law at Temple University created the first and only Juris Doctor semester-abroad program in Japan.

Temple University Japan annually attracts a number of American study abroad students who learn firsthand about Japanese culture while studying in Tokyo. Here, Japanese and American students are jointly engaged in Mochi-tsuki, the traditional ceremony in which glutinous rice is soaked, cooked, and placed in a mortar (usu). Using wooden mallets (kine), the students alternate pounding the rice into a paste that is shaped into rice cakes called mochi, *a traditional food for the Japanese New Year.*

Temple's first foray into China dates back to the 1970s when President Wachman established a series of cultural exchanges. In 1980 Temple partnered with Ohio State University in establishing the first cooperative long-range educational program conducted by American universities in the People's Republic of China, operating English-language programs at two Chinese universities, Peking University and Huazhong Institute of Science and Technology. Temple administered the program through the Multilingual Education Resource Information and Training Center (MERIT) in the College of Education, directed by Professor Frank X. Sutman. During three summers, ten faculty members and doctoral students from Temple spent ten weeks in China instructing Chinese teachers in the English language.

In 1999 a permanent presence for Temple in China was established, building upon a lengthy series of meetings and negotiations led by Robert J. Reinstein. From the early 1980s until his retirement from administrative responsibilities in 2008, Reinstein doubled as Law School dean and vice president for international affairs and was the driving force behind developing and expanding Temple's international programs in China, Japan, Rome, and around the world. Reinstein worked with Temple professors Mann Chiang Niu and Joseph Schmukler—both of whom had been of assistance earlier to President Wachman in China—and their efforts culminated in January 1999 when President Liacouras and Minister Wan Xue Yuan of the State Administration of Foreign Experts Affairs signed the Agreement for Academic Cooperation between Temple and the agency responsible for state-level

Professor Emeritus Justin Vitiello conducts a class for Temple Rome students at an ancient theater in Segesta, Sicily, for a course titled "Sicily: Its Land, People, and Identity."

Left and below *In October 2008 President Ann Weaver Hart signed a renewal agreement with Ji Yunshi (right), director of China's State Administration of Foreign Experts Affairs, cementing a partnership behind Temple's Rule of Law program in China. The way was opened for the Rule of Law program in 1999, when President Liacouras and Minister Wan Xue Yuan (pictured below) signed the first Agreement for Academic Cooperation. In the first decade of the Rule of Law program, 711 Chinese legal professionals participated in at least one of the courses.*

exchange programs in China. The pact provided for scholarly exchanges and opened the way to explore further opportunities for cooperative ventures.

In September 1999 the Beasley School of Law opened a two-year Master of Laws (LLM) Rule of Law program at the China University for Political Science and Law. In 2003 the program moved to Tsinghua University in Beijing, one of China's most prestigious universities. Temple was invited to offer the courses because of its long experience in providing overseas law curriculum, and its law faculty introduced basic concepts of the rule of law to Chinese judges, lawyers, and government leaders. The first foreign degree-granting law education program in the history of the People's Republic of China and the first program approved by the Chinese Ministry of Education and the American Bar Association, it provided a historic opportunity for Temple to contribute to the development of the Chinese legal system at a propitious moment, just as China emerged from cultural isolation and its burgeoning economy drew it closer to the international community. In 2004 the U.S. Agency for International Development awarded Temple a $1.75 million grant to expand the program and to be joined by other American law schools. Over 700 Chinese legal professionals participated in the program during its first ten years.

The Fox School of Business and Management, under the leadership of Dean William C. Dunkelberg, also answered the international call. In 1994 it boldly ventured forth, creating an International Master of Business Administration (IMBA) degree program with a truly distinctive flair. The highly selective IMBA program was set up initially on two continents with a cohort of students studying together in Paris and Philadelphia. Later, students were offered the choice of beginning their program in either Paris or Mumbai and then rotating to Philadelphia and other locations around the globe.

Under Dean M. Moshe Porat, the Fox School further expanded its international reach in 1997, adding Executive MBA programs in Tokyo and at Hanyang University in the Republic of Korea. That same year Porat established the Global Enterprise Management Consulting (EMC) Practice as part of the

IMBA, providing real-time management consulting experience for all participants. Temple students in the IMBA program received management experience in diverse cultural settings, building the global business skills required to meet the demands of the changing international marketplace. The IMBA program earned the Fox School a *Financial Times* top-five ranking among U.S. business schools for international mobility and, since 2003, a *U.S. News & World Report* consistent top-twenty ranking for graduate programs in international business.

Over the years all of Temple's schools and colleges have created international exchange agreements of one kind or another, allowing its students to exchange places with students in Germany (University of Hamburg and University of Tübingen), Puerto Rico (University of Puerto Rico), and England (University of East Anglia), to name a few. Schools and colleges also established discipline-based study abroad programs, such as the College of Science and Technology (Taiwan), Liberal Arts (Latin American Studies Spring Semester in Latin America), and the Fox School of Business and Management (Lyon, Mexico City, Accra, Dublin, Paris, Tokyo, Rome, and Mumbai).

As a globalversity, Temple receives several thousand international students each year. In the fall 2007 semester, for example, Temple's student body included 2,745 students who were not U.S. citizens, representing 127 countries. The majority of Temple's international students come to study business.

By 2009 Temple's international partnerships and collaborations extended to forty countries around the globe. Temple has offered courses in Paris since 1950, in London since 1969, and in Ghana since 1993. Temple dental students have treated patients in Haiti. Temple faculty have taught environmental responsibility in Africa and provided summer programs in dozens of other countries, including England, Ireland, Greece, Israel, and Ghana, as well as Japan, China, Taiwan, and Korea. Every school and college at Temple has been involved in some form of international partnership or collaboration, with significant variation in purpose, depth of engagement, and commitment of resources.

Since Temple's founding, and owing perhaps initially to the extensive world travels of Russell Conwell, the international perspective has been an integral part of Temple's undergraduate curricula. Whether through programs called Liberal Studies, Basic Studies, Core Curriculum, or General Education, Temple demanded that students learn about societies and cultures outside of the United States. Students seeking an internationally focused major have been afforded a wide array of options, including foreign language, areas studies, international affairs, and international business. In myriad ways, then, Temple students have been encouraged to develop an international point of view and to contribute as citizens of the world.

Liberal Arts

Throughout Temple's first 100 years the faculty of the College of Liberal Arts were in the forefront of all important academic transformations. They developed and implemented most of the undergraduate academic policies and set the scholarly standards for both students and faculty; they actuated many new programs and instructional innovations; and they provided the leadership for the development of the required general undergraduate education curriculum. However, in the early 1970s the Liberal Arts faculty essentially abdicated responsibility for students' foundational curriculum. Thereafter they found their influence both diminished and diluted due largely to the proliferation of academic specializations, the rise and growth of new undergraduate schools and

Students of Temple's College of Liberal Arts and Sciences were especially blessed in the 1980s with a distinguished aggregation of celebrated authors and poets, including (top row from left to right) Toby Olson, Seaview (PEN/Faulkner Award, 1983); Joan Mellen, Kay Boyle (1994) and Hellman and Hammett (1996); Charles Fuller (1982 Pulitzer Prize for drama for A Soldier's Play and the movie A Soldier's Story); (bottom row from left to right) Sonia Sanchez, Homegirls and Handgrenades (American Book Award, 1985); Rachel Blau DuPlessis, Writing Beyond the Ending (1985) and The Pink Guitar: Writing as Feminist Practice (1990); and Susan Stewart, author of Crimes of Writing (1991) and The Forest (1995), who later won both the Christian Gauss and Truman Capote awards for literary criticism. Not pictured: David Bradley, The Chaneysville Incident (PEN/Faulkner Award, 1982), and William Van Wert, Missing in Action (O. Henry Prize and Nelsen Algren Award, 1986).

colleges, and the increasing emphasis on undergraduate study as training for a career, as opposed to learning for life.

By the late 1960s most Liberal Arts faculty regarded the Basic Studies program put in place in 1964 as overly structured, unnecessarily rigid, and basically unworkable. Moreover, it failed, on the one hand, to meet students' vocational needs and their demands for relevant educations and, on the other hand, to satisfy student and faculty opposition to rigid formality. Reflecting the sixties' spirit of tolerance and flexibility, the Liberal Arts faculty sought to make amends to neglected student needs and to liberate students to exercise greater freedom in determining their courses of study. Thus, in 1971 the Liberal Arts faculty abolished Basic Studies, leaving each school and college free to set its own requirements and allowing students to declare majors as freshmen and not wait until junior year.

The reform put students almost completely in charge of their educations; there were many choices and few specific course requirements, except those for a major, and some majors allowed students to shape their own curriculum. Liberal Arts faculty valued interdisciplinary education to the point that a student majoring in history, for example, was not necessarily required to take any history courses, as long as a faculty adviser approved the program of study. "Ironically, what was intended to liberate the student," concluded a faculty committee four years later, "may have trapped him."

Loosening degree requirements and removing the formality of a traditional liberal education left both students and faculty without relevant common ground on which to build a solid framework for advanced learning. Gradually, required courses in reading, writing, computational skills, and the understanding and development of civilization (Intellectual Heritage) were added back as requirements, but for several years there was little uniformity across the university.

Woodcut of the acclaimed Irish poet Thomas Kinsella, who joined the Temple faculty in 1970. From 1972 to 1992 Kinsella offered Temple study abroad students the opportunity to learn about "the Irish experience" in Dublin. Considered the most experimental of modern Irish poets, Kinsella authored dozens of books of poetry and criticism, including The New Oxford Book of Irish Verse (1986).

With prodding from President Liacouras's and Provost Barbara Brownstein's ten-year academic plan and with funding from a $2 million grant from the Pew Charitable Trusts, Temple in September 1988 implemented a university-wide Core Curriculum. Structured to provide a common knowledge base to facilitate communication as students move through their college careers, the Core Curriculum was required of all Temple undergraduate students, regardless of college or major. Consisting mostly of introductory courses to various disciplines in each of the undergraduate colleges, the Core Curriculum constituted thirty-three to forty semester hours of credit, depending on the student's major. It was intended to inculcate the intellectual skills and knowledge needed for academic success and, in combination with courses taken in a major field of study, produce a useful education for one's career, citizenship, and personal life. From a practical, political point of view the pact between the schools and colleges that produced the Core Curriculum signaled an end to the dominance of the Liberal Arts faculty over basic education curriculum.

Leadership of the College of Liberal Arts changed rather frequently during these years. For some, the post seemed but a stopping place on the way up the academic ladder. In July 1968 Dr. George W. Johnson, professor and chair of the English Department, was selected as dean to replace Rhoten Smith, who left Temple to take the presidency of Northern Illinois University. Among Johnson's notable accomplishments were the development of an Urban Studies program (1970), college Honors Program (1972), and a highly praised Freshman Interdisciplinary Studies (FIS) program (1975–1978) funded by a $500,000 award from the Andrew W. Mellon Foundation. FIS proved immensely popular with students and faculty alike. It brought together faculty from the sciences, humanities, and social sciences to collaborate in teaching freshmen courses centered on cross-disciplinary, problem-oriented themes. Intended to break instruction away from disciplinary strictures, FIS broadened the perspectives of both the students and the faculty. The genial, well-respected Johnson guided the college through a number of difficult issues before leaving in 1978 to become president of George Mason University.

Dr. George W. Wheeler, a physicist and former dean at Lehman College of the City University of New York, assumed the Liberal Arts deanship in February 1979. By then the college had grown to twenty-one departments, with 5,700 undergraduate students and 1,200 graduate students. In 1983 Wheeler gained the trustees' approval to change the name of the college back to the College of Liberal Arts and Sciences. The change, according to Wheeler, was necessary to reflect the large amount of teaching and research in basic sciences conducted within the college; it also restored the original name of the college, which had been shortened in 1956 to simply the College of Liberal Arts.

The number of liberal arts majors declined during the 1970s and 1980s as more and more students approached college concentrating on career goals. Many viewed the bachelor's degree as only a valuable credential for an entry-level job. To attract more students, the college expanded its Core Curriculum offerings to include non-majors, added an Asian Studies program (1979), started a Master of Liberal Arts (MLA) degree (1980) to attract graduates interested in personal enrichment, and established a cooperative degree program with Gratz College (1984), permitting students to earn degrees from Gratz and the College of Arts and Sciences simultaneously.

George Wheeler resigned in December 1983 to become provost at the University of Tennessee–Knoxville, and Dr. Carolyn T. Adams served as interim dean until Dr. Lois Cronholm took over in July 1985. Cronholm came to Temple from the University of Louisville. A biologist specializing in water quality and water resources, she sought to increase the scholarly productivity of the faculty, stiffening the standards for faculty tenure and promotion to emphasize research. When she arrived, the College of Liberal Arts and Sciences was Temple's largest college, with 420 full-time faculty members and 5,000 full-time-equivalent students. Cronholm played a guiding role in establishing a new undergraduate Core Curriculum before she left in 1991 to be provost, then interim president, at Baruch College, City College of New York.

In 1991 Adams returned as acting dean to replace Cronholm and was confirmed as permanent dean, serving seven years from 1992 to 1999. The size of the college was a lingering concern to university administrators, and so in June 1998 the board of trustees voted to reconfigure the College of Liberal Arts and Sciences, dividing it into two new colleges: the College of Liberal Arts (containing the programs in the humanities and social sciences) and the College of Science and Technology (containing the mathematics and science departments). In 2000 Dean Adams returned to her faculty position in geography and urban studies, only to be called into service as acting dean again in 2006–2007. Few faculty members have given such unsparing and loyal service to Temple University as Carolyn Adams, who also served with distinction as president of the Faculty Senate.

History professor Morris Vogel served splendidly as interim dean, filling in until the appointment of Dr. Susan Herbst in 2002. An expert on politics and communications, Herbst served previously as associate dean at Northwestern University. She minced few words regarding her ultimate objective at Temple: "Our mission," she said, "is to boost the scholarly standards [of faculty] across the college, and there's nothing complicated about it." Herbst hired forty-five new faculty, including several highly productive researchers and scholars, before moving on in May 2005 to be provost and executive vice president for academic affairs at the State University of New York at Albany.

When Dean Teresa Soufas arrived at Temple in 2006, fresh from leading a similar unit at Tulane University, the College of Liberal Arts boasted sixteen master's programs, fourteen PhD programs, twelve centers and institutes, twenty-eight undergraduate majors in sixteen departments, and ten programs (American Culture and Media Arts, American Studies, Asian Studies, Creative Writing, Environmental Studies, Jewish Studies, Latin American Studies, Master of Liberal Arts, Neuroscience, and Women's Studies). In 2009 the College of Liberal Arts added the School of Environmental Design, created out of the departments and centers of the former Ambler College. Under Dean Soufas's patient and gracious leadership, the College of Liberal Arts appeared well positioned for the future, with many of its programs already among the best in the nation and with others growing in distinction.

The *U.S. News & World Report* 2009 rankings of liberal arts programs revealed that Temple's criminal justice graduate program had vaulted from eighteenth to eleventh place nationally and first in Philadelphia. The criminal justice faculty were also ranked sixth nationally by the *Chronicle of Higher Education* Faculty Productivity Survey for their exceptional work on bail and parole conditions, crime mapping and analysis, policing research, and drug treatment evaluation. The African-American Studies Department ranked sixth in a similar survey. The English Department and History Department showed recent gains in reputational rankings as the result of new faculty hires.

The College of Liberal Arts takes particular pride in the accomplishments of its Psychology Department. Both the Clinical Training and Developmental Training programs are perennially listed among the top ten programs in the United States and, according to a nationwide ranking of psychology departments by Academic Analytics (a private firm that evaluates departments according to a faculty productivity index), the department recently ranked eighth nationally, just behind the University of California–Berkeley and ahead of Johns Hopkins and Columbia universities. Ranked annually by the

TEMPLE NOTABLE
Frank Albert Cotton

Frank Albert Cotton (BA CST 1951; ScD 1963) (1930–2007) went on from Temple to earn a doctorate at Harvard and to become, at thirty-one, the youngest person ever to reach full professor at MIT. During his lifetime he was the preeminent figure in the field of inorganic chemistry and the author of more than 1,700 scholarly papers and *Advanced Inorganic Chemistry*, the standard text on the subject. Known for his research on the chemistry of the transition metals, Cotton was the recipient of twenty-nine honorary doctorates and many awards, including the National Medal for Science, the Paracelsus Medal, the Priestley Medal, and the Wolf Prize for Chemistry. Cotton is the only American chemist ever to receive all seven of the major gold medal awards from the American Chemical Society. He was elected to the American Academy of Arts and Sciences, the American Philosophical Society, and the Royal Society, among others.

National Science Foundation (NSF) among the top ten nationally in extramural funding, the department held thirty-four extramural research grants totaling approximately $46 million, as of September 2007. In 2009 the NSF awarded Professor Nora Newcombe $15 million over three years to establish the National Spatial Intelligence and Learning Center, to be housed at Temple in collaboration with the University of Pennsylvania, University of Chicago, and Northwestern University.

Temple's psychology faculty regularly garner national recognition. Professor Laurence Steinberg, widely known for his writings on adolescent behavior, was director of the John D. and Catherine T. MacArthur Foundation Research Network on Adolescent Development and Juvenile Justice and past-president of the Division of Developmental Psychology of the American Psychological Association. Dr. Philip Kendall, recognized by the *Wall Street Journal* and the national media as a pioneer in the use of cognitive behavioral therapy in children, won a 2009 award from the Association for Behavioral and Cognitive Therapies for his "outstanding contributions." Professor Kathryn Hirsh-Pasek's book *Einstein Never Used Flashcards* won the prestigious Books for Better Life Award as the best psychology book in 2003. Professor Nora Newcombe, president of the Eastern Psychological Association, was the 2007 winner of the American Psychological Association's G. Stanley Hall Award for Distinguished Contribution to Developmental Psychology, and she became the first Temple faculty member elected to the American Academy of Arts and Sciences.

The School of Science and Technology

The division in 1998 of the College of Liberal Arts and Sciences shifted the departments of Biology, Chemistry, Computer and Information Sciences, Geology (since renamed Earth and Environmental Science), Mathematics, and Physics into the new College of Science and Technology (CST). The origins and development of Temple's science programs date back to 1894–1895 when the Temple catalog listed classes in botany, biology, chemistry, and mineralogy. Through the years the Chemistry and Physics departments, despite the lack of modern laboratory and teaching facilities, produced top-flight students, many of whom went on to graduate school and to distinction in their fields.

The lack of adequate research facilities handicapped Temple's science faculty at the Main Campus, providing them little chance of competing for and winning the large federal grants for scientific research that became available after World War II. They were grateful, therefore, when Barton Hall opened in 1960, providing Temple's first up-to-date laboratories and facilities. Four years later, Beury Hall was completed and occupied by the departments of Chemistry and Geology (Earth and Environmental Science). The Geology (Earth and Environmental Science) Department was founded in 1962 by Dr. Alice M. Weeks, a prominent uranium geologist on the staff of the United States Geological Survey. Temple's first PhD in mathematics was granted in 1970 to David Tepper, who became an associate professor of instruction in the Mathematics Department. With the addition of active faculty researchers, such as the noted chemist Daniel Swern, the basic research programs began gathering momentum in the 1970s and 1980s.

Faculty success in gaining external funding for research increased in the 1990s when Temple revised its patent, royalty, and indirect cost recovery policies and provided seed grants to incentivize faculty to secure grants and to encourage the transfer of basic technology into the marketplace. The amounts received for sponsored research funding reached $36 million for fiscal year 1991–1992. When combined with other improvements in facilities and the addition of new faculty, Temple consequently was reclassified in 1993 as a Carnegie Foundation Research I University, placing Temple

TEMPLE NOTABLE
Daniel Swern

Daniel Swern (1916–1982), holder of sixty-five patents and many American Chemical Society Awards, began work as a chemist in the U.S. Department of Agriculture in 1937, worked on the development of synthetic rubber during the war years, and finally arrived at Temple in 1963. Best known for the *Swern Oxidation*, Professor Swern helped pave the way for the ubiquitous use of plastics. His experiments with polyvinyl chlorides and water-insoluble thermoplastic resins provided the chemical key to change hard and brittle vinyl into softer and more flexible plastics. Swern's revolutionary research protocols influenced a host of Temple graduate students and chemists around the globe.

among the top 106 research universities in terms of external funding for research, breadth of program offerings, and the awarding of doctorates.

Thanks to such fine additions as Franklin Davis, winner of several top prizes in organic chemistry who joined the chemistry faculty in 1995, Temple was able to sustain Research I status. Yet Temple's basic science programs still lagged behind peer institutions in total resources and total amounts of external funding. One of the reasons for the creation in 1998 of a separate College of Science and Technology was to concentrate resources and efforts more intensely on securing additional funds for sponsored research and on improving instruction in the basic sciences.

To launch the new school, Liacouras appointed as dean Dr. Chris D. Platsoucas, then chairman of the Department of Microbiology and Immunology at the Medical School. At the time Platsoucas was directing a multimillion-dollar National Institutes of Health study of the chronic rejection of heart transplants.

Platsoucas immediately set about energizing the CST research effort, eventually creating four new research centers to foster external support for basic research. In 1999 Platsoucas established the Center for Biotechnology and the Center for Neurovirology and Cancer Biology. A year later the Center for Information Science and Technology (IST) was created to provide advanced research and education aimed at solving challenging data mining, machine learning, pattern recognition, and optimization problems for efficient knowledge discovery in large databases. The Center for Advanced Photonics Research (CAPR) began operations in 2002 focusing on interactions between the biological, chemical, optical, and physics communities with state-of-the-art laser technology. In 2002 Temple entered a partnership with Dr. Antonio Giordano and Mario Sbarro, owner of the international restaurant chain Sbarro, to fund the Sbarro Institute for Cancer Research and Molecular Medicine, under the direction of Giordano. An internationally recognized cancer and gene therapy researcher, Giordano received the 2007 Saint Valentine Prize in Terni, Italy, in recognition of his humanitarian contributions in advancing cancer research.

In January 2004 Platsoucas resigned as dean to return to his research. Dean Keya Sadeghipour of the College of Engineering served as acting dean until the appointment in January 2007 of Dr. Hai Lung Dai. A distinguished professor of chemistry and an experienced administrator at the University of Pennsylvania, Dai had secured more than $13 million to support his research. Dai expressed high hopes for the College of Science and Technology, believing it to be poised to take dramatic steps forward in advancing the quality of its research and education and thus enhancing its reputation and standing among peer institutions. Working with Provost Lisa Staiano-Coico, Dai set a specific goal to raise Temple's national Carnegie classification ranking from Research University with high activity (RU/H) to Research University with very high activity (RU/VH).

Upon Dai's arrival the College of Science and Technology added new faculty, increased external funding, and launched a new program called TUteach in collaboration with the College of Education. TUteach allows math and science majors to earn teaching certificates in education. The program was created in response to a national report, "Rising above the Gathering Storm," which found that about one-third of high school math students and two-thirds of those enrolled in physical science have teachers who did not major in the subject in college or are not certified to teach it.

On March 5, 2009, the 2,900 undergraduates, 200 graduate students, and 180 faculty members of the College of Science and Technology celebrated completion of the final phase of the Beury

TEMPLE NOTABLE
John Allen Paulos

Professor of mathematics John Allen Paulos has written eight books relating math to everyday life. His *Innumeracy: Mathematical Illiteracy and Its Consequences* spent eighteen weeks on the *New York Times* Best-seller List and was translated into six languages. His *Mathematics and Humor* and *A Mathematician Plays the Stock Market* were also best sellers. Paulos has become a nationally recognized and award-winning commentator on how mathematics and numbers are portrayed by the news media. What does he hope to give to his Temple students? "I want them to be able to bring a kind of critical intelligence to mathematical notions they come upon in the future."

Hall renovations. The five-year, $25 million makeover project included complete renovations of the infrastructure of the building, plus installation of wireless technology in classrooms and lecture halls and new, cutting-edge chemistry classrooms and research laboratories. Distinctive features include specialized instructional classrooms for physical geology and a microscope projection system in teaching laboratories. With new facilities, new leadership, and a distinct objective, the College of Science and Technology appeared to have a bright and promising future.

Engineering

The origins of the College of Engineering can be traced back to 1921 when the demand for technical education led the Philadelphia chapter of the American Society of Metals to collaborate with the Evening College of Liberal Arts and Sciences to present a course called Heat Treatment and the Metallography of Steel. Lectures were held in the Mitten Hall auditorium and workshops conducted in two Broad Street row houses. From this venture sprang the Evening Technical School in 1936, offering certificates in a wide array of technical areas, including architectural design, mechanical design, heating, ventilating and air-conditioning, blueprint reading and estimating, metallurgy, and principles of radio and television, to name a few. To accommodate working adults, many courses were held off campus in schools, hospitals, and industrial plants.

To meet the postwar educational demands of returning GIs, the Technical School began offering day programs in 1945. In 1947 the program's curriculum and admissions standards were upgraded, and its name was changed to the Technical Institute of Temple University. Two years later it merged with the Temple Community College. The institute, which was authorized to grant an associate degree in technology, was intended to provide a level of training between that of the technician and the engineer. Leadership in the early years was provided by James J. Crawford, Edward L. Fleckenstein, William A. Schrag, Theodore P. Vassallo, and William F. Melchoir. Technical Institute programs were based at the Eighteenth and Buttonwood campus but offered at locations across southeastern Pennsylvania in Chester, Reading, Harrisburg, Allentown, and Scranton. Off-campus units were

After several delays caused by intense community opposition over its location, the College of Engineering Technology building (later renamed the Engineering and Architecture building) was constructed at Twelfth and Norris streets and opened for occupancy in August 1978. The building included a separate library for engineering and architecture, plus nineteen specialized laboratories and design studios.

phased out by 1959 when the Technical Institute moved to Stauffer Hall (since demolished) at North Broad Street and Columbia Avenue (now Cecil B. Moore Avenue).

Temple's new state-related status and the 1966 Commonwealth Master Plan for Higher Education necessitated closing the Community College and eliminating most two-year programs. That opened the door for the creation of a baccalaureate degree in engineering technology and a four-year college, which was proposed initially by Edward Fleckenstein and approved by the Temple trustees in May 1969. The state-related plan called for the construction of thirteen new buildings, one of which would become the College of Engineering Technology. In August 1970 Dr. John Rumpf, former head of the Department of Civil Engineering and Mechanics at Drexel University, was appointed dean.

The new college opened that fall with 250 students selecting from programs in architectural design and construction technology, electronics engineering technology, and mechanical engineering technology. Soon added were programs in civil, electrical, mechanical, biomedical, and urban engineering technology. In 1972 an alumni association was formed and the Technical Institute was merged with the college. Dr. John Tarka headed up the Electrical Engineering Technology Department, and Professor Robert H. Creamer used a $130,000 NSF grant to develop a program in environmental technology.

To attract and build on enrollments from Philadelphia high schools, the college and the institute established the Special Technology Educational Program (STEP) for minority disadvantaged students, providing tutoring, advising, and personal counseling. In 1971 the college joined the Philadelphia Regional Introduction to Minority Education Consortium (PRIME) to encourage minorities to consider careers in engineering. And in 1974 the college received a $55,000 NSF grant to conduct a summer career program for disadvantaged minority students and later participated in a PRIME summer program for inner-city high school students. Dr. Theodore Vassallo coordinated these programs and other student services for the college.

In October 1975 ground was broken at Twelfth and Norris streets for the new College of Engineering Technology building, and the school became ready for occupancy in August 1978. Meanwhile, all of the college's associate and bachelor's degree programs gained accreditation from the Engineers Council for Professional Development (ECPD). The college lost its dean in 1976 when John Rumpf was promoted to vice president and dean of faculties at Temple. Robert Creamer served as acting dean until August 1979, when Dr. Robert M. Haythornthwaite was appointed dean. Haythornthwaite resigned two years later, and Dr. Frederick B. Higgins served as acting dean before being appointed in 1982.

Dean Higgins directed the formulation of an academic plan to establish a full-fledged engineering program. The president and trustees approved the plan in 1983, and new programs were established in civil, electrical, and mechanical engineering leading to a bachelor of science in engineering. Dr. Steven Ridenour was appointed to chair the Mechanical Engineering Department. At the same time the college was renamed the College of Engineering and Architecture to denote the shift from technology to engineering and to reflect greater visibility for the Architecture Department.

Several changes occurred in rather rapid order. In 1986 the Computer and Information Science (CIS) Department of the School of Business merged with the college, and the college was renamed the College of Engineering, Computer Science, and Architecture. That year the master's degree program in engineering science was approved. The civil, electrical, and mechanical engineering curricula were accredited in 1988 by the Accreditation Board for Engineering and Technology (ABET)

TEMPLE NOTABLE
Lynne Tarka Ewell

Lynne Tarka Ewell (BS ENG 1986) recalled "growing up" on the Temple campus watching her father, Dr. John E. Tarka, teach in his biomed lab. Professor Tarka chaired the Electrical Engineering Department and was instrumental in establishing both the electrical engineering technology and the biomedical engineering technology programs. Lynne became the first female as well as the first student accepted into the electrical engineering program at Temple's College of Engineering. In 1991, Lynne and her husband, John Ewell, founded Prism Engineering, Inc. When Dr. Tarka passed away in April 2007, Lynne and her husband and mother donated funds to establish the John E. Tarka Design and Manufacturing Laboratory within the College of Engineering.

(formerly ECPD). In 1989 Frederick Higgins stepped down as dean, and Dr. Charles Alexander was appointed acting dean. A PhD program in electrical engineering was approved that year, and all of the two-year associate degree programs were discontinued. Then, in the fall of 1992, the CIS Department was transferred to the College of Liberal Arts and Sciences and the Architecture Department was administratively combined with programs in landscape architecture and horticulture at the Ambler Campus, thus necessitating yet another name change, this time simply to the College of Engineering.

On July 1, 1995, after nearly six years with acting deans, the College of Engineering welcomed Dr. Cynthia S. Hirtzel as dean. Hirtzel resigned in June 1998. She left the university when the trustees administratively relocated the College of Engineering into the new College of Science and Technology. Dr. Keya Sadeghipour was appointed acting dean of engineering.

Engineering benefited from the general upswing in Temple enrollments that began in 1999 and from an increased demand for engineering graduates, particularly in the computer industry. In response, the college developed a computer engineering program as an option in the electrical engineering curriculum. Acting Dean Sadeghipour guided the college in the preparation of a five-year strategic plan for the growth and development of the College of Engineering. The president and trustees reacted positively, and in January 2003 the College of Engineering was removed from the College of Science and Technology and once again became an independent entity. In April, Sadeghipour was named dean.

The College of Engineering was divided into three academic departments: Civil and Environmental Engineering, Electrical and Computer Engineering, and Mechanical Engineering. Undergraduates were offered a range of professional options for majors. Graduate students could select from four master's programs and the PhD program. New areas of study were launched, including an innovative major in bioelectronics that merged electrical engineering and biological sciences to explore new approaches and technologies for the detection of environmental and physiological states.

Under Sadeghipour's leadership the College of Engineering made impressive progress in recruiting productive faculty research centers, securing external support for research, and establishing new research centers. Timely and important research on environmental engineering problems, such as the lingering effects of the Exxon Valdez oil spill, has been conducted by Professor Michel Boufadel and his students. Engineering has also strengthened its connections to local industry. For example, Professor Rominder Suri was awarded a $1.6 million grant in 2009 by the Commonwealth of Pennsylvania to establish the Center for Pennsylvania Environmental Technologies for the Pharmaceutical Industry (PETPI). The center provides technological support to the pharmaceutical industry in the Delaware Valley, making Temple a worldwide hub for research and development in dealing with the green manufacture of medicines. These and other advances leave the College of Engineering poised on the edge of a very bright future.

Architecture

Architecture was an important, though sometimes overlooked, program in the early years of the College of Engineering Technology. Evening courses in architecture were first offered in 1936, and a formal program was established in 1969. Professor John Christopher Knowles was appointed the first chairman of the Architecture Department in 1970. He built a department principally composed of highly skilled practicing architects from the Philadelphia region. Knowles put in place a four-year bachelor of science in architecture program (BS Arch) designed to develop a strong base in architectural technology and practice upon which students could develop additional areas of special competence. Graduates with the bachelor's degree in architecture were qualified for a variety of positions in architecture and related fields for which a professional degree and registration were not required.

In 1976 the department added a five-year bachelor of architecture (B.Arch) degree to meet the needs of the profession and to prepare students for professional certification and licensure. Knowles succeeded in getting the degree fully accredited by the National Architectural Accrediting Board (NAAB) in 1978. Professor William C. Fox succeeded Knowles as chair in 1979. When the architecture program came up for reaccreditation in 1980, it was only one of four accredited out of twelve applicants and only one of three in the state. In 1983 Professor George Clafen was appointed department chair, succeeded by David Glasser and then Sally Harrison.

In 1992 the architecture program was administratively moved from the College of Engineering and combined with the Landscape Architecture and Horticulture departments to form a new academic unit under the administration of the dean of the Ambler Campus. However, that arrangement was short-lived. In May 2001 the board of trustees authorized the officers to incorporate the architecture program in the Tyler School of Art, where architecture's mission and passion for educating design professionals seemed a better fit.

Believing that the mission of an architect should be to create aesthetically enriching environments built for the needs of human beings, to revitalize the urban fabric, and to serve as stewards of the global environment, the department created the Tyler Architecture Institute summer program in 2008 to introduce the field of architecture to high school students. Through design problems, lectures, and site visits, students come to understand that architecture is a creative search based on both imagination and precedents. Like full-time students in the program, the summer institute students learn that architecture is a reflective process and that self-criticism and motivation are their greatest resources.

Reflecting the department's global values and reach, Lindsay Bremner, an expert on urban planning in post-apartheid South Africa and the former chair of architecture at the University of the Witwatersrand in Johannesburg, was appointed to chair the Architecture Department in 2005. That year the department opened a program at Temple University Japan. Indeed, study abroad has been a feature of the program for many years, as several hundred architecture students have availed themselves of the opportunity to study at Temple Rome. The program's core values have long emphasized its location in Philadelphia and the importance of engaging students in the forces of global restructuring and the critical issues of the urban condition.

The College of Education

No school or college at Temple University or in the Philadelphia region has a longer, deeper, or more direct involvement in the urban environment than the College of Education. Since its founding in 1919 the college has cultivated a special relationship with the School District of Philadelphia, collaborating to address the pressing needs of Philadelphia students and their families. Throughout its history the College of Education has provided the school district and the Philadelphia region with more teachers than any other college. Temple's diversity of people and perspectives has historically strengthened and enriched the college and influenced all aspects of its academic life. More recently, the College of Education has become a national center for excellence in both teaching and research with an international presence.

FACT

Temple University operates the largest school of education in the metropolitan area and among the largest in the state and country.

Laura Carnell laid the foundation blocks for Temple's College of Education. She first emphasized teacher training in 1894 with courses on kindergarten theory, and in 1902 she established a department of pedagogy. From this evolved a normal program (an outdated name for a program instructing teachers in how to teach) and then a Teachers College, which functioned as early as 1916 but was not formally established until 1919 with the appointment of George E. Walk as the first dean. The name of the college was changed to the College of Education in 1960.

Walk organized undergraduate programs in commercial education, health or physical education, kindergarten-primary education, home economics, nursery school education, nursing education, and religious education. For most of its early years Temple's Teachers College emphasized undergraduate instruction in pedagogy and the preparation and retraining of elementary and secondary public school teachers.

Dean Walk served twenty-nine years, retiring in 1948. He organized a strong, adaptable teacher education curriculum to meet the needs of first-generation teachers, plus he offered evening, summer, and graduate programs to serve the professional needs of the teachers and administrators of the Philadelphia school system. He introduced graduate education in 1923 and the Doctor of Education degree. With the closing of the Philadelphia Normal School in 1938, Temple became the primary training site for Philadelphia schoolteachers, and the relationship has grown stronger in the years since. With Walk's guidance the college became the largest school in the university, with more than 2,800 total enrollments, counting day, evening, and off-campus programs.

Walk was succeeded as dean by J. Conrad Seegers, who joined the faculty in 1927 and had served as dean of men, director of the Oak Lane Laboratory School, and associate dean.

Responding to heightened public concerns over the quality of public education, Dean Seegers envisioned a new, broader mission for the college, insisting that it be not simply a teacher-training institution but that it also be concerned with developing teachers' "social sensitivity." Moreover, the college, according to Seegers, was obligated "to develop an understanding of children and adolescents."

Seegers resigned in 1953 to assume the presidency of Muhlenberg College, his alma mater. Dr. Joseph Butterweck served as acting dean until the arrival in 1955 of D. Willard Zahn, former associate superintendent of the Philadelphia schools. Zahn's tenure corresponded with the peak of a national teachers' shortage, the impact of the *Brown v. Board of Education* decision (1954) desegregating America's schools, and the public outcry over the poor state of American education revealed by the Soviet Union's launch of Sputnik in 1957. To recruit new teachers, Zahn used a Ford Foundation grant to create an Intern Teaching Program for liberal arts graduates leading to a master's degree while they were teaching as interns. The program attracted over 400 persons to enter the teaching field who would not have otherwise. To reform teacher education, the college introduced the General Education Program for Teachers, a master's degree curriculum designed to broaden the intellectual horizons of teachers trained too narrowly in pedagogy at the bachelor's level. In 1960 Zahn gained approval to change the name of the college to the College of Education. Before retiring in 1963 Zahn was permitted to begin planning for a new building, Ritter Hall, which opened in October 1965.

Dr. Paul W. Eberman, former associate dean of the School of Education at the University of Wisconsin, was appointed dean in 1963. He brought five years of experience teaching in New York public elementary schools, a doctorate from the University of Chicago, and a substantial publication record. Eberman and the College of Education faced a new set of issues in the 1960s as the federal government became more actively involved in setting educational policies and in mandating changes in the nation's schools. Congress passed a series of acts as part of Great Society and War on Poverty legislation intended to improve schooling in poor neighborhoods; to make a larger place in public schools for children with mental, physical, and emotional disabilities; and to prepare students for more effective service in minority schools and communities.

Temple's College of Education vigorously responded by creating departments of Special Education and Urban Education, establishing bilingual education programs, launching programs for teaching English to speakers of other languages, and participating in the Teacher Corps, Get Set, and Head Start programs. A dizzying array of special programs and acronyms evolved. For example, the Junior Honors Mathematics Internship Program (JHMIP) sent liberal arts students to tutor inner-city youths. The Philadelphia school district and Temple University School Improvement and Teacher Education Program (SITE) were aimed at improving the quality of education in North Philadelphia. In recognition of these and other efforts to improve the Philadelphia school system the College of Education received the 1972 Distinguished Achievement Award from the American Association of Colleges for Teacher Education.

Eberman resigned as dean in 1973, replaced by Benjamin Rosner, who died suddenly ten months later. Professor Roy Kress served briefly as acting dean before Dr. Jay Scribner was appointed in 1975. Scribner and his colleagues responded to a new public attitude in which the emphasis shifted to basic skills, standardized curriculum, minimum competency tests, and statewide requirements for high school graduation. Under Scribner the college also significantly expanded its international programs, offering an M.Ed. program in Nigeria, forming partnerships with universities in China and

TEMPLE NOTABLE
Ruth Wright Hayre

Pioneering educator Ruth Wright Hayre (Hon. DHL, 1989) (1910–1998) was the first full-time African American teacher in the Philadelphia public school system, the first African American senior high school principal, as well as the first female president of the Philadelphia Board of Education (elected in 1990). She also served for eleven years on Temple's board of trustees (1969–1980). An inspiring, forceful advocate for programs in support of urban teenagers and eager to deal with the high dropout rate among high school students, Dr. Hayre in 1988 promised all 116 sixth-grade pupils in two North Philadelphia schools a free college education if they graduated from high school. She titled her program "Tell Them We Are Rising" and chose Temple's College of Education to manage and coordinate the program's trust fund. In 1994 a special ceremony attended by the governor was held to honor the first thirty-six of seventy African American students to benefit from Dr. Hayre's generosity.

Puerto Rico, and designing remedial education programs for U.S. servicemen and servicewomen through TEAM, or Temple European Army Mission (see Chapter 5).

During the 1980s and 1990s, under the direction of Deans Richard M. Englert and Trevor Sewell, the college continued to respond imaginatively and energetically to society's broader concerns over the state of American public education and to anticipate the social, economic, and technological changes affecting society and thus the way children learn and teachers teach. Taking just two examples, in 1988 the college received a $357,000 grant to model a program to retrain teachers to effectively utilize computers in the classroom. And in 1995, when the Philadelphia Navy Yard closed, Temple's Secondary Teacher Education and Placement Project placed a dozen out-of-work engineers in high school classrooms to teach math and science.

In 2003 Dr. C. Kent McGuire was appointed dean. As a former assistant secretary of the U.S. Depart-ment of Education and an experienced program officer with the Pew Charitable Trusts and Eli Lilly Endowment, McGuire brought a wealth of talent and connections to the position. In short order the college announced a series of new program initiatives. For example, in 2005 Temple and PNC Bank announced their support of a professorship to advance research focusing on early childhood educa-tion and literacy. In 2007 a grant of $2.4 million was awarded to launch TUteach—a science and math teacher preparation program in collaboration with the College of Science and Technology—and in 2008 the Governor's School for Urban Teaching was established as a five-week summer training program to show high school students the challenges and rewards of teaching in an urban environment.

McGuire inherited a college with seventy faculty members and over 1,800 undergraduate and 650 graduate students. Offering an extensive array of programs within three divisions, the college prepares students for teaching and for careers as school administrators, counselors, school psy-chologists, researchers, policy makers, and professors of education. In recent years the College of Education has advanced its research and public service agenda largely through the coordinated efforts of a notable group of research centers and partnership arrangements.

The College of Education boasts an impressive and productive assemblage of research and service centers, among them the Career & Technical Education (CTE) center; the Center for Frontier Sciences (CFS); the Institute on Disabilities (IOD); and the Center for Research in Human Development and Education (CRHDE).

In 2002 the School District of Philadelphia asked Temple to lead and support a group of four public schools in the neighborhoods surrounding its Main Campus in North Philadelphia. Out of this came Temple University's Office of Partnership Schools. The partnership assembled intellectual capital from across the university to support the schools in a comprehensive reform process that the four schools began implementing in fall of 2003. The Urban Education Collaborative (UEC), formed in 2005 with support from the William Penn Foundation, was designed to correct a lack of coordination between local school improvement efforts and professional evaluations by institu-tions of higher learning.

Throughout its history the College of Education has contributed an astonishing number of teachers and educators dedicated to fulfilling the potential of America's youth. Building on the successes of alumni such as Happy Fernandez, Constance Clayton, Linda Darling-Hammond, and the thousands of teachers who have passed through the portals of Ritter Hall, the College of Education looks forward to a rich and productive future.

Faculty

As the administrative and financial arrangements of Temple's schools and colleges were stabilizing in the 1980s and 1990s, professors' roles and their relationships to the university were changing. Professorial activism had transformed the governance structure of Temple during the 1960s and early 1970s, and those reforms carried through into the 1980s and beyond. Traditionally active in university affairs, Temple's dedicated faculty were instrumental in creating and shaping the curriculum, setting the academic mission, vetting and monitoring colleagues' scholarly performances, serving as gatekeepers into their professions through doctoral training programs, assessing their colleagues' fitness for tenure and promotion, reviewing and approving new and existing academic programs, and advising the administration and trustees on matters of general import to the university. But something had changed.

After 1973 faculty members in the unionized schools and colleges still expected to exercise influence over the university's strategic direction and the management of its administrative affairs. But how to do it? The union agreement required that management prerogatives be defined and separated from those of the bargaining unit. Because of the necessarily adversarial relationship dictated by a union-management agreement, the channels of communication between faculty and administration had become less open and more formalized. Moreover, the rise of the faculty union led to the relative decline of the Faculty Senate as both a policy body and broad representative faculty forum. Although goodwill prevailed in most quarters, two faculty strikes left some faculty members permanently poised to dissent, desirous of a stronger management role, yet reluctant to abandon the relative security of a collective bargaining agreement and fearful of the alternative.

Gradually, full-time and tenured faculty members relinquished their formerly predominant roles in advising and teaching undergraduates. In the modern multiversity those roles became increasingly the function of a professional staff retained specifically for that purpose. Moreover, undergraduate instruction, particularly at the introductory level, was left mostly to part-time instructors and graduate assistants, as the majority of the senior faculty devoted themselves to graduate education and research that offered the greatest personal and professional rewards.

Some of Temple's faculty may not have liked it, but the sheer size of the modern multiversity necessitated a business approach to the enterprise. Charles Beury first brought business procedures into the university during the 1930s. Robert Johnson's background was in business. As Temple grew larger and more complex and as its consolidated university and hospital budget approached and passed $1 billion, Temple's trustees, cognizant of their fiduciary responsibilities, demanded that the administration adopt sound financial practices and required it to make sometimes difficult decisions to ensure the continued solvency of the enterprise. Faculty at Temple often questioned administrative decisions and occasionally demanded a greater role in the setting of priorities and allocation of resources.

Faced with declining net revenues and increasing costs, Liacouras had no choice in the early 1980s but to impose strict budgetary discipline, reduce or eliminate discretionary spending, curtail or judiciously limit the development of new programs, and institute faculty and staff hiring freezes. While those actions benefited the university's bottom line and were welcomed by trustees and legislators, they had a chilling effect on faculty morale, particularly since faculty expectations had been grandly elevated from the mid-1960s to the mid-1970s, the years of nearly unrestricted growth. Liacouras reported annually to the legislature on the increased faculty productivity, on decreases in the number of full-time faculty, and on increases in the average number of students taught by faculty. The faculty retrenchments of 1979 and 1982, the tightening of faculty account-ability and productivity, plus the relative stagnation of program growth as compared with prior years, exacerbated by the inability to renew and refresh academic departments through new faculty appointments, all contributed to persistent faculty uneasiness, punctuated by two devas-tating strikes in 1986 and 1990.

Faculty expectations and university financial exigencies explosively collided in the fall of 1986 when the American Association of University Professors (AAUP) faculty union walked out. A bitter strike ended with an agreement, but faculty-administration tensions remained unresolved, as were faculty frustrations with the AAUP. The national AAUP offices, openly ambivalent toward collective bargain-ing, provided little direct support during the 1986 Temple faculty strike.

Seeking to retain local autonomy but desirous of connecting to organizations with greater politi-cal clout, Temple's faculty union, under the leadership of English professor Philip Yanella and then business professor Arthur Hochner, considered several alternatives before voting in the spring of 1987 for a joint affiliation with AAUP and the American Federation of Teachers (AFT), changing the organization's name to the AAUP/AFT. However, the burden of paying dues to two organizations, plus the advantages of AFT's considerable experience with collective bargaining and its connections within the state through AFT Pennsylvania, led the faculty, effective May 1, 1990, to drop the AAUP affiliation. By an overwhelming vote, the Temple faculty (minus the law, medicine, and dental faculty) approved full affiliation with the AFT, plus a name change to the Temple Association of University Professionals (TAUP), to include librarians and academic professionals.

The TAUP strike from September to October 1990 decimated undergraduate enrollments, costing Temple over 3,500 students who withdrew or simply did not return to classes when the strike ended and forcing the university to cut $12.9 million from the budget. After the strike the governor further com-pounded Temple's problems, twice abating appropriations at mid-point in the fiscal years of 1990–1991 and 1991–1992, taking away $11.5 million in appropriated funds. Temple's enrollments and budgets eventually rebounded in the late 1990s, but the tensions between the TAUP faculty and the administra-tion resonated into the next decade and into two subsequent presidential administrations.

The Liacouras Era

When Peter Liacouras stepped down from the Temple presidency on June 30, 2000, he had served longer (eighteen years) than any president except Conwell (forty-one years). In recognition of his achievements, the Board of Trustees of Temple University named Liacouras University Professor of Law and Chancellor of Temple University. Additionally, the university's massive six-building Apollo complex was renamed the Liacouras Center in his honor as was the European-style piazza along the spine of the Main Campus (Liacouras Walk).

By the time Liacouras retired, Temple's annual consolidated (hospital and university) operating budget was $1.3 billion, with more than 10,000 employees, 210,000 alumni, 29,946 students from 110 nations, and substantial support from the private sector. During his presidency, the College of Podiatry and the School of Tourism and Hospitality were added (see Chapter 8) and Temple became a Carnegie Research I University. Liacouras accelerated the opening of the professions, graduate programs, and administration to minorities and increased Temple's historic diversity, particularly among African Americans within the institution. In May 2003, Liacouras was elected a member of the Academy of Athens, the successor to Plato's Academy and the highest honorary scientific association in Greece. Liacouras's book, *Toward Universal Access to Higher Education — The American Experience*, was published by the Academy of Athens in 2004.

To his lasting credit, Peter Liacouras strategically repositioned Temple, creating the impetus and direction for a new surge of enrollments that came after he stepped down as president. By the time his dream of Temple Town had become a reality, it was accepted, perhaps even taken for granted, as though it were a natural, organic transition. In reality, however, Liacouras bent history and changed the flow of events with transforming ideas and dreams. Those aspirations were culminated in the first decade of the new century.

As enrollments increased and commonwealth appropriations steadied in the mid-1990s, the university's financial situation improved markedly, permitting investments in new programs and faculty and the long-delayed revitalization of university infrastructure, including greater attention to the landscaping and campus streetscape. Temple upgraded lighting, public access ways, and the general physical appearance of the campus, as many more prospective students and their parents visited the campus with heightened expectations of what a college campus should offer and how it should look.

Chapter 8
From Sidewalk Campus to Urban Village

The first nine years of the new millennium represented a period of intense, very positive change for Temple University. For the amount of concentrated, pervading change that occurred across the university and in the external perceptions of Temple, there was no other era in Temple's history to compare, save perhaps for the period from 1965 to 1970, when the huge building and programmatic endeavors were a direct result of state affiliation.

TEMPLE UNIVERSITY TIMELINE

David Adamany is elected Temple's eighth president.
2000

Entertainment and Community Education Center opens.
2004

New General Education curriculum is inaugurated.
2008

2001
Retail stores and the Conwell Inn open on Liacouras Walk.

2006
TECH Center opens. Dental School is renamed in honor of Maurice H. Kornberg.

2009
Tyler School of Art relocates to the Main Campus. Alter Hall is dedicated. New Medical School building opens.

Page 220 *Temple's Main Campus in 2008, a bright, shining presence in North Philadelphia.*

The difference, however, is that the changes from 2000 to 2009 took place not because of a massive infusion of commonwealth aid—although state capital support surely helped—but, rather, largely because of Temple's own strategic initiatives to attract more highly qualified students and to increase enrollments; to revitalize the Main Campus and environs; to adjust its learning and teaching strategies to meet new demands and circumstances; and to attract major, transformative gifts—all of which vastly improved Temple University as a place and as a quality institution of higher learning.

Many challenges awaited Temple. More high school students than ever opted to go to college, but competition for those students was greatly intensified by the proliferation of aggressive, for-profit proprietary institutions of higher education, by the high costs of technological infrastructure essential to higher education, and by the heightened consumer expectations related to the commodification of higher education. Moreover, rapid technological transformations and significant shifts in America's socioeconomic structure demanded nimble adjustments in both the substance and delivery of general education. Temple had to adapt to new ways of delivering information and new ways of learning. In the post-information millennial age, technological access to information and knowledge of the complex, interdependent global society required new skills to manage in the workplace or in professional life. Temple had to be prepared to impart those skills.

Temple foresaw these changes and responded accordingly, positioning itself advantageously in the intensely competitive market, succeeding in increasing full-time enrollments, creating a new General Education curriculum, enhancing the technological infrastructure, responding with new programs of study and new learning approaches, expanding and improving professional education, rebuilding its faculty with hundreds of new hires, completing an ambitious program of physical improvements, stimulating economic partnerships to benefit both Temple and the community, enhancing Temple's presence as a cultural anchor in North Philadelphia, and providing the living spaces and amenities to convert Temple from a predominantly commuter institution to a residential campus.

Seemingly in a twinkling, Temple changed from a sidewalk campus to a bustling urban academic village. Its location in North Philadelphia, for many years a drawback, gradually became an asset. The city and Temple were resurgent—their aspirations parallel. The strategic groundwork for change was laid during the eighteen-year presidency of Peter Liacouras. Within nine years of Liacouras's departure from office, Temple had two presidents, including its first female president. But, as we shall see, the pace of change accelerated markedly behind vigorous, inspired leadership, leaving Temple University stronger and more confident than at any time in its history.

David Adamany

Temple University's eighth president, David Adamany, much like his immediate predecessor, was an active agent for change. Guided by an inner-directed confidence in what the future ought to bring, Adamany kept a keen eye directed toward the broader course of events, yet, to lessen entropic tendencies toward mediocrity, he also steeped himself in the details of the university's bureaucracy. A proficient multitasker and an astute manager of complex issues, Adamany was determined to build on the firm foundation laid by Peter Liacouras and to press the university to reach higher.

Like Wachman and Liacouras, Adamany was the son of immigrants. His father arrived in the United States from Lebanon and his mother, too, via Canada. They settled in Green Bay, Wisconsin, where Adamany's father operated a restaurant. In high school David Adamany demonstrated exceptional academic promise and leadership prowess, winning election as class president and gaining admission to Harvard. Aspiring to a law career, Adamany graduated from Harvard College in 1958 with an AB in government and then earned a JD degree from Harvard Law in 1961. Active in campus politics at Harvard, he returned to Wisconsin after receiving his law degree and immediately became engaged in state politics, serving briefly on the attorney general's staff, campaigning for the successful gubernatorial candidate, John W. Reynolds Jr., and moving then into the governor's office, where, though only twenty-three years old, he served as pardon counsel to the governor. Three years later he was appointed to the Public Service Commission, regulating Wisconsin's public utilities, and then served a stint as chief assistant to the lieutenant governor.

Meanwhile, Adamany completed all of the course work and requirements for MS (1963) and PhD degrees (1967) in political science at the University of Wisconsin, where he taught part-time and, as he told the *Temple Review* in 2001, "fell in love with the teaching profession." Adamany took an academic appointment at Wesleyan University, a private liberal arts school in Middletown, Connecticut, first as a professor, then as dean. In 1970 he returned to Wisconsin to help Patrick J. Lucey win the governorship. Adamany held several positions in state government, including secretary of the Department of Revenue and chairman of the State Elections Board. Between 1972 and 1974 he held appointment as professor of political science at the University of Wisconsin–Madison.

President David Adamany pauses in May 2006, during his final commencement procession, to share a moment with delighted graduates.

David Adamany's career in higher-education administration began in 1977 when he was appointed vice president for academic affairs at California State University at Long Beach. In 1980 he moved on to accept the same position for the five-campus system at the University of Maryland. Two years later he was elected to the presidency of Wayne State University. Adamany reversed enrollment declines, raised academic standards and research productivity, and restored financial stability to the troubled Detroit institution, encountering both success and controversy before retiring in 1997. Two years later the governor of Michigan and the mayor of Detroit asked Adamany to serve one year as interim chief executive of the Detroit school district, where he helped rebuild the foundering system and restore its finances.

The author or editor of four books on government, including a prescient discourse on election finance reform, plus more than fifty articles, reviews, and essays, Adamany planned to return to teaching and research at Wayne State in 2000 when Temple's presidential search committee sought him out and recommended his election to succeed Peter Liacouras. Taking office in August 2000, Adamany spent several weeks listening to Temple's students, faculty, and staff, evaluating Temple's resources, and analyzing the challenges and opportunities confronting the university. Afterward, he delivered a lengthy "Self-Study and Agenda," setting a series of specific goals for Temple.

David Adamany addresses the Temple community upon his acceptance of the Temple presidency on May 17, 2000, acknowledging the contributions of and promising to build on the legacy of Peter Liacouras (foreground).

By the time he stepped down as president in June 2006, Adamany had succeeded either in achieving or in positioning Temple to accomplish most of the critical elements he outlined in his self-study. Undergraduate applications increased by 40 percent and overall enrollments by 17 percent; average SAT scores for incoming undergraduate students were sixty-two points higher in 2005 than in 2000 (and seventy points above the national average); the Core Curriculum was replaced with a new General Education program; enrollments in University Honors increased by 40 percent; by January 2006 Temple had added 151 new tenured or tenure-track faculty members to address enrollment expansion and faculty retirements; Temple's libraries were technologically upgraded; a massive $400 million program of physical construction and building renewal was under way; selected centers of national excellence were upgraded through the appointment of new faculty and added resources; externally funded research awards increased by 28 percent; the critical stages of Temple's first university-wide capital campaign since the 1970s were completed; relationships with the community were strengthened through partnerships that yielded more than $180 million of private investment in the Temple neighborhood; and student financial aid was increased by $80 million.

Adamany worked closely with board chairman Howard Gittis to restrain tuition and increase financial aid, thus maintaining Temple's historic commitment to provide educational opportunities for able young men and women of all backgrounds. At the same time he increased alumni giving and secured several major gifts. By the end of his five-year term in office David Adamany had nearly doubled Temple's net assets, increased unrestricted cash and investments, and raised the university's bond ratings, laying a solid foundation for Temple's continued success.

The basic soundness of Adamany's leadership and the overall fitness of the university were confirmed in November 2005, when the Middle States Commission on Higher Education reaffirmed Temple's accreditation, finding the university in compliance on all sixteen accrediting standards and noting that Temple "continues to add to its list of accomplishments." The leader of the review team concluded, "It appears that Temple is seeking to fulfill its potential to rank among the finest public universities in the nation."

In his final address to the university community, Adamany graciously acknowledged that by 2006 President Liacouras's vision of a "residential community of scholars" in North Philadelphia "has come to pass, even well beyond his hopes and dreams." Much of Adamany's presidency was dedicated to ensuring the success of that vision, building new dormitories, renovating and expanding the Student Activities Center, completing construction of the new TECH Center, relocating the Tyler School of Art from Elkins Park to the Main Campus, planning a major addition to the Fox School of Business and Management, launching construction of a new Medical School building, planning renovations to the Baptist Temple, and completing the new Entertainment and Community Education Center as part of a broader community partnering to develop the area around the Main Campus.

Two major factors energized and propelled Temple toward reifying the Liacouras Temple Town vision: first, the changing needs and expectations of students as higher-education consumers, which were part of the broader commodification of higher education, and, second, the amazing changes that occurred in Philadelphia, beginning in the 1990s and steadily transforming the city over the course of two decades, bringing long-awaited private and public investments and an invigorating sociocultural renaissance that was especially appealing to young adults. To use a word favored by President Ann Weaver Hart, Philadelphia and Temple were "hot."

Sharp competition among universities and steadily increasing tuition rates in the 1980s and 1990s gradually changed the relationship between students and universities, transforming students into discriminating consumers and requiring universities to institute management reforms, improve student services, and provide facilities and amenities to meet enlarged expectations of what a college experience must entail. One unintended consequence of this trend was the commodification of higher education, or the perception of university services as commercial activities to be valued largely in terms of their price and customer satisfaction. Many university activities normally untainted by commerce—including the acquisition of the final product, the degree—were viewed by consumers as a commodity. Almost all universities, Temple included, responded accordingly.

Converting a public, non-profit service into a commodity necessitates branding to delineate distinguishing features and to differentiate it from competitors, leading some consumers to buy on name recognition alone. Ironically, in the higher-education market, less discriminating consumers often associate quality with price alone: The more expensive a college education, the better it must be, or so some consumers would reason. The costly and prestigious Ivy League universities bore the ultimate in higher-education brands. This led some colleges and universities to increase tuition substantially to create a perception of quality, justified or not, associated with their name and brand—a ploy that Temple steadfastly and proudly refused to exercise.

Instead, Temple judiciously responded to students' (and parents') expectations by improving student services, providing amenities and conveniences, and treating students like consumers by providing online applications and registration systems, electronic grading, and other streamlined business services. Presidents Liacouras, Adamany, and Hart insisted that all university offices practice simple and cordial business procedures when serving students and the public. They understood also the need to enhance campus amenities to give students places to gather and to be entertained. The commodification of higher education required the campus to be more than a place to study; it also had to be a lively cultural, recreational, and entertainment destination.

Certainly a substantial part of the explanation for Temple's enrollment surge lies in its excellent academic reputation and in the vast improvements to the campus. But Philadelphia, too, had changed. It became safer, more accessible, and more welcoming. Prospective students increasingly cited Temple's urban location as one of the reasons for enrolling. In 2006 more than 60 percent of Temple's newly admitted students acknowledged "location in a large city" was a "very positive factor" influencing their decision to attend Temple. In 1997 only 40 percent of new students had agreed. What had changed?

Philadelphia's population had declined from 2.1 million to 1.5 million people between 1950 and 2000, but the decline slowed after 2000 as Philadelphia became a more desirable place in which to live and work. Indeed, analysts projected Philadelphia to show a population increase after 2010. Various explanations are offered for what drew people back to the city—tax abatements, a new convention center, historically undervalued housing, a restaurant renaissance, new sports stadiums, waterfront improvements, and continuing redevelopment of the old city—but few of those issues matter to college freshmen. Surveys of student applicants indicate they were attracted to Temple by a combination of factors, not the least being the breadth and depth of its excellent academic offerings, but also by Philadelphia's lively entertainment, sports, and cultural attractions, plus general improvements in personal security, amenities, and the relative ease of access into the city and to Temple by subway and regional rail.

Beginning in 1999 Temple steadily became a more popular choice for suburban students within the Philadelphia Metropolitan Statistical Area (PMSA), that area covering the four Pennsylvania counties around Philadelphia, reaching into South Jersey, and extending south to Wilmington, Delaware. Philadelphia is the fifth-largest metropolitan area in the United States. In 2006 more than 5.8 million people resided within the metropolitan area. The Philadelphia MSA was also the fourth-largest media market in the United States. To compete successfully within this sizable market, Temple knew it must begin with the revitalization and enhancement of Main Campus facilities and amenities.

Main Campus Revitalization

Revitalizing Temple's Main Campus and its surrounding area could not be completed in a decade or two, but substantial progress began in the Liacouras years and was significantly advanced by the administrations of David Adamany and Ann Weaver Hart. When considered individually, the changes may not seem that significant, but their cumulative impact effectively remade the Main Campus and its image.

The success of Temple's revitalization effort is best measured by the large increase in Main Campus and full-time undergraduate enrollments and by the number of students living on or near the campus. Another positive sign is the increase in the number of Main Campus visitors. One objective of the 2008 strategic academic compass was the creation of Destination Temple, or the remaking of the campus into a lively, welcoming place teeming with cultural and entertainment attractions. In 2008 more than 32,500 prospective students and their families, friends, and counselors visited the Main Campus, almost doubling the number who visited just three years earlier.

Expectations are that the number of Main Campus visitors will increase once The Temple (aka Baptist Temple—see Chapter 1) is converted into a major performing arts center on the northern Avenue of the Arts, expected to open in 2010. Two foundation projects of the Destination Temple plan were completed in 2009 with the relocation of the Tyler School of Art into its new Main Campus building and the opening of Alter Hall, the new home of the Fox School of Business and Management. These endeavors capped off a significant amount of renewal under way since 1999, including Liacouras

Walk renovations, new residence halls, an expansion of the Student Activities Center, and substantial private investment in the immediate area of the Main Campus.

Tyler School of Art

Since 1935 the Tyler School of Art has offered students the opportunity to pursue study of the arts within small learning communities while providing the advantages afforded by a large, comprehensive research institution (see Chapter 3 for Tyler's early history). A recognized leader, Tyler offers programs that have long been considered among the finest in the nation. The school was ranked fourteenth in the nation by *U.S. News & World Report* in 2008, leaping seven spots since art school rankings were last issued in 2003. Tyler's programs in ceramics and photography (ranked nineteenth and eighteenth, respectively, in the nation in 2008) entered the national top-twenty for the first time, joining the school's long-standing top-ranked MFA programs in painting and drawing (seventh), sculpture (eighth), and printmaking (seventeenth).

The Tyler School of Art relocated to the Main Campus in January 2009 in a striking new building adjacent to the Boyer College of Music and Dance and the School of Communications and Theater, thus creating an imposing arts enclave on the northern edge of campus. Architect Carlos Jimenez's bold exteriors and roomy, functional interior designs dramatically repositioned Tyler, both in relation to Temple's other schools and colleges and within the Philadelphia arts community.

For all of its success, Tyler's relative academic isolation and the costs of duplicative services and facilities at the Elkins Park campus over the years became academically and administratively problematic. Temple's administration first considered relocating the art school in the mid-1980s, when President Liacouras conducted a series of studies and tasked various committees with exploring the costs and academic ramifications of moving it to the Main Campus. When the decision to move was finally made in 1998, few applauded. Dean Rochelle "Rocky" Toner's leadership helped calm skeptics, who feared that the distinctive character of the school was being sacrificed for expediency. However, the university promised the Tyler students and faculty new studio, classroom, and production facilities in a building of their own.

Spectacularly equipped and brilliantly lit art studios greeted Tyler School of Art students in January 2009, offering new inspirational venues for fostering creativity.

Funding for the new $75 million arts facility came primarily from a $61.5 million commonwealth capital appropriation, and the remainder was provided by gifts and Temple allocations. Designed by award-winning architect Carlos Jimenez, the 234,000-square-foot, three-story structure that opened in January 2009 provides 40 percent more usable studio space than available in Elkins Park, four times the amount of gallery space, and the largest green space on Temple's Main Campus. The building adjoins the Boyer College of Music and Dance and is adjacent to the School of Communications and Theater, forming a vibrant and exciting arts compound within the Main Campus that will expand Tyler's interdisciplinary outreach to other departments and schools. Being on the Main Campus allows arts and artists to be a more visible and active part of university life, plus it offers Tyler's talented students and distinguished faculty greater access to Temple colleagues in other disciplines, to Temple's technological resources, and to the Philadelphia arts community.

Tyler's students found a creative way to remind Philadelphia's other art schools that they now had company. On the morning of March 18, 2009, students and faculties of Philadelphia's four other art schools found life-sized Trojan horses on their premises, with notes declaring an "art war" and announcing: "We the students of Tyler School of Art have been rerouted and relocated. However, our waters are as steady and strong as they have ever been." The symbolic gifts meant no harm; they were merely ways of marking Tyler's arrival and opening a dialogue with the other schools. As Tyler junior Alyssa Brubaker explained, "It's all positive."

Another positive development occurred in December 2008, when Jack Wolgin, Philadelphia real estate developer, philanthropist, and prominent art patron, presented the Tyler School of Art with a pledge of $3.7 million to endow the world's largest annual art prize. Wolgin's gift, the largest received by Tyler since its inception, created the Wolgin International Prize in the Fine Arts. An annual $150,000 prize will be awarded to artists who create work that transcends traditional boundaries and exemplifies the highest level of excellence in painting, sculpture, printmaking, photography, ceramics, metals, glass, or fibers. The winning artworks will be exhibited at Tyler's gallery.

FACT

Tyler School of Art at Temple University administers the Wolgin International Prize in the Fine Arts, the largest prize of its kind in the world.

The relocation of the entire art school from Elkins Park to Philadelphia was a complicated and difficult undertaking that fell largely on the capable shoulders of Tyler's acting dean, Theresa Dolan. Once settled, however, Tyler's students and faculty adjusted well to their new surroundings. The new studios teem with activity and excitement. Dedicated students work day and night, sharing ideas and inspiration. The close proximity of Tyler's programs to Temple's other artistic programs and to the heart of the university enterprise enhances the educational experience for Tyler's gifted students, each one poised to make a significant contribution to an increasingly interdisciplinary and multimedia artistic culture in the twenty-first century.

Liacouras Walk

For decades, Temple's Main Campus lacked adequate amenities—the retail shops, convenience stores, social spaces, and visitors' accommodations—to attract and hold visitors and students. Many such features were added following renovations to the historically certified nineteenth-century row houses along the 1900 block of Liacouras Walk. In September 2001 Temple completed $1.7 million in exterior improvements, installing new paving, an elevated walkway, plantings, and lighting. Private developers then rehabilitated the interiors for use as retail spaces. When finished, Liacouras Walk resembled a European-style piazza that included a 7-Eleven, PNC Bank, cellular store, eatery, dry cleaner, and unisex hair salon—topped off by a twenty-two-room boutique hotel, the Conwell Inn.

Five years later, at the other end of Liacouras Walk in the 1800 block, Temple completed a $18.6 million restoration and adaptive reuse project, converting the row houses to recapture approximately 75,000 gross square feet of space that had been unusable for many years. From the 1930s into the late 1960s the row houses had been used as a women's dormitory, known as Williams Hall, but they were too costly to maintain and the entire block fell into disrepair. The restoration plan, reviewed by the Philadelphia Historical Commission, permitted retention of the historic features on the south and east facades (now facing Alter Hall). The renovated spaces accommodate Student Health Services, the Academic Resource Center, and the College of Liberal Arts advising center, modern meeting rooms, and administrative offices.

Above *The Conwell Inn, which opened in September 2001, is situated in the middle of the campus along the 1900 block of Liacouras Walk, with an entrance on Polett Walk (formerly Berks Mall) opposite Sullivan Hall. The privately owned, three-story, twenty-two-room inn, created out of renovated historic row houses, provides upscale boutique hotel rooms for visitors to the Main Campus.*

Left *In 2006 Temple totally remodeled the historic row houses in the 1800 block of Liacouras Walk (formerly the site of a women's dormitory known as Williams Hall) to accommodate student health services, undergraduate advising facilities, administrative offices, and executive conference space.*

The Student Activities Center, first opened in 1971, underwent a remarkable exterior renovation (pictured below) and a dramatic two-phase expansion between 2001 and 2005. It was renamed the Howard Gittis Student Center in 2006 in honor of the longtime member and former chairman of Temple's board of trustees (inset below). The redesign was the work of Martin Kimmel (B.Arch. TYL 1989) of the firm Kimmel and Bogrette.

With more students living on campus and enrollments on the rise, the available student activities spaces became crowded and overtaxed. The Student Activities Center (SAC) on the southeast corner of Thirteenth Street and Montgomery Avenue underwent a major overhaul and an addition that provided over 86,000 square feet of new construction to the four-story structure built in 1971. Phase I renovations were completed in 2001, adding a 700-seat food court, an entry atrium, and a striking building facade, featuring the Temple "T" in bold modern relief. Phase II renovations, completed in November 2005, added a four-story annex that included lounges, cinema, game room, non-alcoholic student entertainment center, student organization offices, meeting rooms, and administrative offices. In October 2006 Temple's board of trustees renamed the renovated building the Howard Gittis Student Center in honor of the former board chairman and generous benefactor.

The 700-seat food court in the renovated SAC served students who lived in a splendid new residence hall opened in the fall of 2001 at 1300 Cecil B. Moore Avenue. Known simply as 1300 for its address, the five-story building constructed by the university on the former site of the Cooney Apartments housed 1,000 students in standard dormitory rooms, plus 142 apartment units and 188 suites. The building also included common areas, study lounges, a convenience store, fitness center, laundries, and other amenities.

North Philadelphia Renewal

When Temple moved forward in 1995 with major plans for the restoration of its Main Campus facilities, the university leadership carefully assayed the impact of every move on the community around Temple. Because such care was taken beforehand, Temple's neighbors, in contrast to their reactions in the late 1960s, proved helpful and supportive, allowing Temple to move ahead with its plans and also play a central role in revitalizing North Philadelphia. A broadly inclusive Temple-Community Task Force, chaired by executive vice president James White, included the distinguished North Philadelphian Floyd W. Alston, founding president of the Beech Corporation, later Beech Interplex, a real estate and community development corporation. Over the next decade Alston and Temple worked together with business, government, and non-profit entities to restore the Cecil B. Moore neighborhood, which had experienced a period of economic decline.

Temple offered the community immediate and long-term technical and financial assistance totaling more than $10 million toward the renaissance of the area on Cecil B. Moore Avenue between Broad and Sixteenth streets. Temple became the prime tenant in the Beech Corporation's redevelopment of a landmark four-story building at Fifteenth Street and Cecil B. Moore Avenue. Known as the Entertainment and Community Education Center, the building serves, among other things, as a community education center and as home to radio station WRTI.

Between 2001 and 2008 the university worked with private contractors to stimulate the development of over 1.5 million square feet of new residential and commercial space, representing a private investment of approximately $200 million in the surrounding community, with plans for more to come. Six large-scale student housing projects, immediately adjacent to or within a few blocks of the Main Campus, added residential space for 3,166 students. The university-owned Kardon Building at Berks and Tenth streets was renovated in 2002 by Philadelphia Management Corporation, a private real estate development company, converting the eight-story former box company building into rental apartments for 500 students, with two floors of parking and two floors for university use. The same corporation also renovated the adjacent Atlantic Terminal warehouse building in 2003, adding rental apartment units for 140 students. In 2004 University Village opened at 1701 North Tenth Street at Cecil B. Moore Avenue, with apartments for another 750 students.

On the other side of the campus, Elmira Jeffries, a four-story complex at the corner of Jefferson and Fifteenth streets, opened in 2003, offering furnished apartments to 156 upperclassmen and transfer students. Oxford Village, a Beech Interplex project on North Fifteenth Street, was completed in 2004, adding beds for 420 students. The Edge, located on the southeast corner of Fifteenth and Oxford streets, opened the next year with accommodations for 1,200 students.

The development of these six apartment complexes was absolutely essential to accommodate swelling student demands. Unable to guarantee on-campus housing beyond a student's sophomore year, Temple welcomed the new residential developments. As Temple-sponsored housing options, these sites were assigned professional staff members during the academic year to organize activities and provide residence life services. Knowing that safety is always a concern in an urban setting, Temple also hired more safety officers, increased the range of its security patrols, and added off-campus security kiosks and Owl Watch patrols throughout the campus. Additionally, Temple replaced conventional streetlights with bright stadium-style lighting and extended lighting into nearby neighborhoods.

Temple kept its promise to the community, breaking ground in November 2002 for the 61,000-square-foot, $16 million Entertainment and Community Education Center (ECEC) at 1509 Cecil B. Moore Avenue. At its opening in 2004 the ECEC provided retail space on the ground floor, classrooms and offices for Temple's Pan-African Studies Community Education Program on the second floor, and a new home for WRTI-FM, plus a performance studio available to cultural organizations for making commercial-quality recordings to benefit Philadelphia's cultural community. A major resource for community residents, the ECEC offers access to job listings, computers, and educational and meeting space. Temple's Partnership Schools program, a collaborative effort linking the university, the School District of Philadelphia, and six neighborhood schools, is also housed in the ECEC.

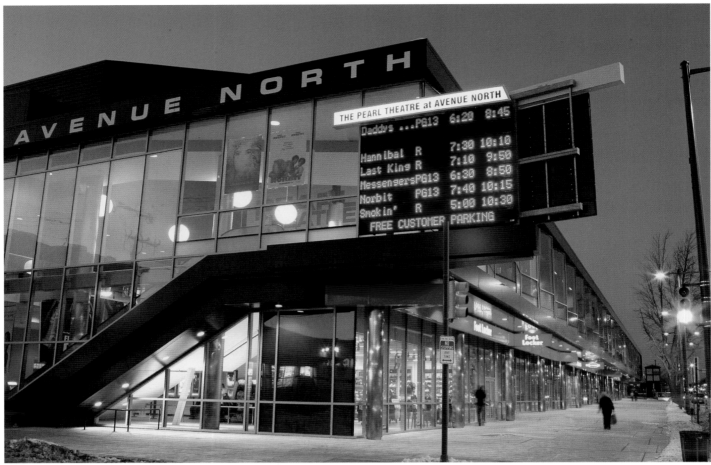

Above *Avenue North, a huge $183 million retail-entertainment complex, opened in 2006. Extending on the west side of Broad Street from Oxford Street to Cecil B. Moore Avenue, it became the first non-Temple commercial and retail development in North Philadelphia in several decades. The brainchild of Temple graduate Bart Blatstein (BA CLA 1976), Avenue North contains restaurants, apartments, and retail stores, plus the Pearl Theater, the first movie theater to open in North Philadelphia in more than three decades.*

Center *University Village, another Temple–private partnership venture, opened in 2004, housing 750 students.*

Right *Private investment in the development of nearby student apartment complexes accelerated after 2001, when the university opened a 1,000-bed complex at 1300 Cecil B. Moore Avenue. New construction at 1500 North Fifteenth Street added even more student accommodations.*

A major step forward in the North Philadelphia renewal occurred in 2006 with the opening of Avenue North, a $183 million retail and apartment complex located on North Broad Street between Cecil B. Moore Avenue and Oxford Street. The first non-Temple commercial and retail development in North Philadelphia in several decades, Avenue North was the brainchild of Temple graduate Bart Blatstein (BA CLA 1976), president of Tower Investments. Blatstein's Avenue North contains seven movie theaters plus restaurants, retail stores, and apartments. Said Blatstein in 2006, "It's the biggest and most visible symbol of the development now going on all over North Philadelphia—something you didn't see a decade ago."

The Edge at Avenue North, 1601 North Fifteenth Street, offers fully equipped studio and two-, three-, and four-bedroom apartment living spaces for 1,200 Temple students. Additional living spaces were needed to accommodate the burgeoning undergraduate enrollment, which expanded by more than 28 percent between 1998 and 2003 alone.

All of this did not take place without raising some community concerns. Residents were apprehensive about rising property taxes, competition for parking spots, and student parties. "There are still fears of the big institution taking over," said City Councilman Darrell L. Clarke. "I'm not going to tell you there's no concern," he continued, "but it's minimal. The student housing has created an environment that's going to bring in retail development that's needed by the community." State Senator Shirley M. Kitchen told the *Temple Times*, "I can say that Temple has been a good neighbor, because we have avenues of communication on all things." Asked what is changed, she replied that Temple "has afforded us a seat at the table. That has kept down tension."

The quickened pace of development around Temple's campus attracted additional investors. Governor Edward G. Rendell announced in 2006 that the state would invest $5 million in renovating Progress Plaza on Broad Street between Oxford and Jefferson streets. And in June 2009 Philadelphia's City Council approved a $250 million community development plan for the 5.5-acre site of the former John Wanamaker Middle School at Twelfth Street and Cecil B. Moore Avenue. These joint ventures and community partnerships evoke the Conwellian legacy of community service and bode well for the future of Temple and its surrounding communities.

How Did Those Vendors' Trucks Get There?

Visitors to the streets of the Main Campus are often struck by the presence of trucks and kiosks of food vendors offering a wide variety of American and international foods. Those enterprising operations have become a recognized and accepted part of the Temple culture. Yet, one wonders: How did they get there?

Food vendors first appeared in numbers in the early 1960s. In the beginning they arrived each day and parked their carts and trucks along Thirteenth Street just west of Paley Library. Gradually they began to stay overnight. University officials were concerned about the potential health and safety risks posed by the vendors and tried to limit their activities. Two early vendors who resisted university requests with organized vendor protests were the brothers Milton and John Street. University resistance crumpled in March 1966, when Temple students unexpectedly found themselves eating in temporary dining areas in College Hall and in the basement of Conwell Hall after the luncheonettes

Temple University earned national recognition for its ongoing dedication to providing students, faculty, and staff with consistent access to state-of-the-art technology.

FACT

Temple University is one of the top twenty-five most technologically "connected" campuses in the United States according to *The Princeton Review.*

personalized communications codes. Subjected to mandatory testing from their earliest years in school, they demonstrate rising proficiency in math, science, and standardized tests. Millennial students think it is cool to be smart. They tend to use trial and error as the key learning strategy, derived from Nintendo logic or the popularity of electronic games. When it came to the classroom environment, Temple's professors learned that it was essential to engage with technology and to generate course content dynamically, but to teach with content and to ensure the portability and usefulness of information.

The arrival of these students required Temple to adjust the way it delivered its educational services, to find new ways to engage students, and to redefine what it considered essential to the college learning experience. Three specific adjustments merit mention: the upgrading of Temple's technological capacity across the university but especially in the library and in the building of a new TECH Center; the establishment of a new General Education curriculum; and the expansion of the University Honors Program.

Temple University thoroughly embraced the Information Revolution and its new learning technologies and innovative methods of classroom organization and course delivery. Temple began early, repositioning itself in the 1980s to respond to new Information Age educational technologies, by installing a fiber-optic telecommunications network, creating a wired campus, and upgrading its computer capacity for instructional, research, and administrative purposes. Plans for all new and existing classroom buildings included Smart Classrooms, providing instructors and students with fingertip connectivity to the latest in computer, audiovisual, Internet, and state-of-the-art teaching and learning technologies. Faculty members participated directly in planning the new learning technologies for the Tuttleman Learning Center, new Tyler School of Art building, and Alter Hall, ensuring that Temple's classroom facilities remained on the cutting edge of academic technology.

New learning technologies are perfectly embodied in Temple's TECH (Teaching, Education, Collaboration, and Help) Center. In response to Millennial student needs, Temple constructed a 76,000-square-foot facility—the largest of its kind in the nation when it opened in January 2006—to provide state-of-the-art technology catering to new learning modalities. Located on the first two floors of the former Bell building on the northeast corner of Twelfth Street and Montgomery Avenue, the TECH Center was designed with a variety of work spaces to enable students to work collaboratively or individually. The facility includes 700 generalized and specialized computer workstations; a twenty-four-hour help desk with members trained to support specialized software; thirteen break-out rooms; specialized labs for video editing, graphic design, and music composition; an Instructional Support Center and a Teaching and Learning Center to assist faculty; a cyber lounge; and even a Starbucks café to fuel dedicated scholars. Open 24/7 during the school year, the TECH Center has become the social hub of the campus, a place for students to meet, study, collaborate, and relax.

Temple's Paley Library has changed greatly since its 1966 dedication. The card catalog has long since been replaced by computer workstations. The mandatory silences of years ago—enforced by shushing librarians—has given way to the steady hum of students gathered in small groups collaborating on projects. Clicking computer keyboards are heard as often as the sounds of turning pages. Yet, for all of this constant activity, some people believe that libraries may no longer be needed in the age of the Internet. In fact, they are needed more than ever.

Temple University Libraries form an extensive network of services and resources that support the educational and research needs of the university's students and faculty. The libraries directly support the schools and colleges on the Main Campus, Temple University Ambler/Fort Washington, the Harrisburg Center, and the Temple University Center City Campus. The Health Sciences Center Libraries serve the Schools of Dentistry, Medicine, and Pharmacy, the College of Health Professions and Social Work and the Temple University Hospital. The Law Library supports the faculty and students of the School of Law on the Main Campus. The university also provides library services for students attending Temple University Japan and Temple University Rome.

Temple students enjoy the advantages of a bright, open interior walkway and the modern technologies of classrooms and facilities in the Tuttleman Learning Center.

Temple's library system employs the latest technology in providing access to more than three million volumes, 27,000 journal subscriptions, and more than 350 electronic research databases. Special collections include the Urban Archives, the University Archives, the Rare Books and Manuscripts Collection, Contemporary Culture Collection, Science Fiction and Fantasy collections, and the Charles L. Blockson Afro-American Collection. Many of the books, monographs, and archival material of greatest importance to researchers remain only in hard copy and must be carefully accessioned and cataloged. In recent years, for example, Paley Library has become a mecca for scholars and students of Philadelphia history. Temple's Urban Archives attract students, professors, and visiting scholars to explore the photojournalism collections, newspaper morgues, and records of hundreds of impor-

tant Philadelphia institutions. Since its establishment in 1967, the Urban Archives has amassed more than ten million items, including the defunct *Philadelphia Evening Bulletin* morgue files and 20,000 videotapes of news footage from CBS 3 (KYW-TV). In 2009 the Urban Archives added the holdings of the Philadelphia Jewish Archives Center, the major collector and preserver of historical records of the Philadelphia Jewish community dating to the nineteenth century.

To manage Temple's large and growing electronic and hard-copy collections, Larry Alford, formerly of the University of North Carolina, was appointed in 2005 as vice provost and dean of Temple's seventeen libraries. Alford immediately tackled the problem of severe overcrowding in the library by overseeing the preparation of an off-site depository. He also improved student and faculty access to the libraries' rapidly expanding collection of electronic resources. Paley Library has undergone a significant internal renewal since 2005, and more changes are in store for the years ahead. But Temple will soon need a new, larger library to continue to serve as the guidepost to knowledge for Temple scholars.

University Honors

Throughout its long history Temple University has attracted and nurtured some of the finest minds in America, those rare few, truly exceptional students who were among the best and the brightest of their generations. Exceptional students often found a faculty mentor or a cohort of similarly gifted students with whom they could open and explore new venues of knowledge or deepen their artistic or creative gifts. As Temple grew and matured, the number of outstanding students increased. Professor Joseph Butterweck's X-Group experiment, lasting from 1932 to 1938 (see Chapter 3), was Temple's first effort at isolating talented students and giving them greater latitude in course selection and freedom to develop selected interests. The idea was revived in the 1960s within the College of Liberal Arts and Sciences and the School of Business Administration when faculty began to offer exceptionally talented students extra attention by grouping them in special, more challenging and demanding Honors courses.

By the mid-1960s a formal Honors Program had taken shape within the College of Liberal Arts and Sciences. The program sought superior students motivated to explore new ideas and interested in discovering as well as solving problems. The Honors courses stimulated students' creativity, strengthened their analytical skills, extended their vision beyond their limited backgrounds, and deepened their understanding of themselves and their capabilities. As more and more superior students elected Temple, the demand for Honors courses and individualized attention increased. Several Temple schools and colleges set up Honors programs, but standards and requirements varied widely.

In 1986 French professor James Mall, director of the College of Liberal Arts and Sciences Honors Program, thought it time for a full and complete discussion. That year a Faculty Senate committee chaired by Mall recommended that Temple establish a University Honors Program, using the College of Liberal Arts and Sciences program as a model. The proposal was approved in March 1987, and the new university-wide program was phased in during the 1987–1988 academic year, beginning with 287 students under the leadership of its first director, Ronald Hathaway. Temple found itself in the forefront of a national development. Many universities followed suit in the 1990s and established honors programs.

Following Dr. Hathaway's untimely death in 1991, a series of directors guided the program until 1995, when Professors Dieter Forster (Physics) and Ruth Ost (Religion) became co-directors. To classes of twenty or fewer Honors students, select, full-time faculty members taught challenging, specially designated courses. By 1995 the program admitted about 175 carefully screened students annually. Originally housed in the Ritter Hall Annex, the University Honors Program moved

What is so special about University Honors?

Let Joe Ament (2011), an Honors student and English major, explain: "The Honors Program offers all of the benefits of a large university while combining it with the personal connections characteristic of a small school. Most notably, Honors students make up a diverse group, ethnically, geographically, and personality-wise, that share a zeal for learning. While everyone in Honors loves to have fun, they also respect academics, making the college experience both enjoyable and satisfying."

in 1999 to the Tuttleman Learning Center, to be ensconced in new, larger quarters dedicated exclusively to Honors. That year President Liacouras directed that the Honors Program capacity be doubled. By 2009 the University Honors Program was admitting 400 students annually and serving a total of 1,550.

Since 1996, admission to the program has been determined on the basis of high school grades, SAT scores, letters of recommendation, and personal interviews. Many of the Honors courses are in the liberal arts and the sciences, but each of the undergraduate schools and colleges offers some Honors courses. Honors students may opt for an eight-course program, leading to the Honors Certificate, or a four-year focus, culminating with a thesis or comparable accomplishment and designation as Honors Scholars. Under Ruth Ost's direction since 2004, Honors students have won many prestigious individual awards, including several Fulbright, Marshall, and Truman scholarships and Morris K. Udall fellowships.

General Education

Temple's new learning strategies were not confined to the brightest and most technologically savvy students. In 2004 Temple decided to jettison its Core Curriculum requirements for all undergraduates, substituting a new General Education curriculum that emphasized problem-solving skills and intellectual connections. New courses were designed specifically to satisfy requirements within one of the eleven areas of the General Education curriculum that included Analytical Reading and Writing, Mosaic (a two-semester Great Ideas course), Arts, Human Behavior, World Society, U.S. Society, Race and Diversity, Science or Technology, and Quantitative Literacy. The program, so ably guided by business professor Terry Halbert, went into effect beginning with the fall 2008 semester.

In the 1980s, when the Core Curriculum was constructed, the Temple faculty debate centered principally on content, about what belonged in the common body of knowledge to which every Temple student should be exposed. Much has changed since then. Technology has vastly accelerated the rate at which information is created and accessed. What there is to know is increasingly complex and beyond any person's capacity to learn or contain it all. The makers of the General Education requirements believed students needed to learn how to make sense of the blizzard of information confronting them daily and to know how information is linked, or how seemingly disparate pieces of information are interrelated.

General Education courses were designed to allow students to make connections across disciplinary boundaries. Each course in the General Education curriculum is built upon a foundation of three desirable goals: to help students develop thinking, learning, and communication skills; to develop skills in identifying, accessing, and evaluating sources of information; and to promote curiosity and lifelong learning. Courses were set up to ensure the portability and usefulness of knowledge. Students learn that the resolution of complicated issues increasingly requires the ability to see a problem from many angles and to synthesize divergent perspectives. Ultimately, the General Education program assists students in knowing themselves, their place in the world, and the limit and reach of their skills.

Professional Schools

As Temple University entered its 125th year, its professional school enrollments ranked fifth largest among America's 199 Carnegie High and Very High Research Universities. Temple has trained more

(1989–2008), the number and quality of student applications grew, the incoming class average for LSAT scores rose to the 85th percentile, and job placement rates annually exceeded 90 percent.

For many of the years during which Reinstein led the Law School he was also the university's vice president responsible for leading the expansion and maturation of Temple's international programs. Temple's globalversity reputation evolved in large part as a result of Reinstein's role in developing several successful Law School initiatives, including international law study programs in Japan; the Master's in Transnational Law in Tokyo, Rome, Athens, and Tel Aviv; and the Master of Laws Program for Chinese students in Beijing—China's first foreign degree-granting law program (see Chapter 7). In recognition of these achievements, Reinstein received the 2002 National Friendship Award from the Chinese Government. In congratulating Dean Reinstein on the award, Secretary of State Colin L. Powell said, "The State Department is pleased that it has been able to support Temple's efforts to establish its program. The rule of law in China is important for American economic and political interests."

Reinstein also proved an adept fund-raiser. The springboard for a major campaign was the year-long celebration that marked the Law School's 100th year in 1995. William H. Rehnquist, chief justice of the United States, received an honorary degree and spoke at the Centennial Convocation on April 2, 1996. The Centennial Campaign raised more than $10 million for the Law School.

One of the lead gifts in the campaign came from Murray H. Shusterman (BA CLA 1933; LLB LAW 1936), whose $1 million gift went toward the careful restoration and renovation of Park Hall (see Chapter 4), a then-unused English Gothic-style building along Liacouras Walk just south of Sullivan Hall, and its conversion into a multi-purpose educational and meeting facility to serve the Law School and the university. In September 1997 the completely renovated building was dedicated as Shusterman Hall, named in honor of the distinguished senior partner at Fox, Rothschild, O'Brien & Frankel.

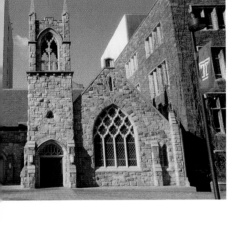

A generous gift to the School of Law Centennial Campaign by Murray H. Shusterman (BA CLA 1933; LLB LAW 1936) and his wife, Judith, permitted renovations to Park Hall, converting the former church into a meeting center with the latest technological advancements. The renovated building was rededicated in 1997 as Shusterman Hall (pictured above following renovations). Mr. Shusterman (second from right) is pictured with (from left) Dean Robert Reinstein, Arthur Raynes, and Howard Gittis at the Centennial Campaign kickoff dinner on October 27, 1994.

Shusterman's generosity dated back to 1981, when he established the Murray H. Shusterman Fellowship to support the exchange of Temple and Israeli law students, faculty, and scholars.

In March 1998 the Law School received another major gift. Leonard Barrack (LLB LAW 1968) and his wife, Lynne Barrack, donated $2.5 million for student financial aid, faculty research, and the establishment of the Barrack Public Interest Fellowship Program to assist law graduates in repaying student loans while they work on public interest jobs. Leonard Barrack, a Temple trustee and senior partner and founder of Barrack Rodos and Bacine in Philadelphia, also chaired Temple's capital campaign, appropriately titled "Access to Excellence." In recognition of the Barracks' gift, Temple's trustees renamed College Hall (see also Chapter 1) Morris and Sylvia Barrack Hall, in memory of Leonard Barrack's parents, who were immigrants to the United States. The restored College Hall received major historic preservation awards in 2002 and 2003.

A destiny-altering donation arrived at the Law School in 1999 when James E. Beasley (LLB LAW 1956), a prominent litigator of national importance, contributed $20 million, the largest gift in Temple's history and one of the largest ever made to any American law school. A World War II veteran, who collected, restored, and piloted World War II–vintage fighter aircraft, Beasley was considered one of America's outstanding trial lawyers. In grateful recognition of the long-standing support that Beasley gave Temple University and its Law School, the university board of trustees changed the official name of Temple Law School to the James E. Beasley School of Law of Temple University and renamed Watts Walk as Beasley Walk.

James Beasley's gift sparked other sizable contributions, the largest of which came in January 2000 when the Beasley School of Law received a $9 million unrestricted bequest from the estate of noted Philadelphia attorney Leonard Rubin (BA CLA 1943; LLB LAW 1949). He graduated from Olney High School in 1939, earned his Temple pre-law degree in 1943, enlisted in the army, and was a decorated veteran when he entered law school in 1946. A general-practice lawyer, Rubin lived frugally, was a selfless philanthropist, and was described as a "man of simple needs" and as a diligent student of the law. His higher purpose, according to those who knew him, was to "make a high-quality legal education available to students of modest means."

JoAnne A. Epps was appointed the tenth dean of the Law School in July 2008. Prior to joining the Temple law faculty in 1985, Epps was assistant U.S. attorney for the Eastern District of Pennsylvania (1980–1985) and, before that, deputy city attorney for the City of Los Angeles (1976–1980). Epps inherited a law school ranked sixty-fifth overall by *U.S. News & World Report*, but preeminent reputations were noted for its programs in legal writing (seventh), trial advocacy (second), and part-time instruction (seventh). With a solid reputation, firm and devoted alumni support, creative and energetic faculty, and resourceful leadership, the Beasley School of Law is ideally positioned to build on its illustrious history and to reach even greater heights in the years ahead.

The Health Sciences Center

Four of Temple's professional schools—Medicine, Pharmacy, Dentistry, and Podiatry—are directly associated with the Health Sciences Center, Temple University Hospital, and the Temple University Health System. Their parallel, sometimes overlapping missions and histories developed concurrently and in close proximity. Once the commitment was made in 1982 to develop Temple's Health Sciences Center in tandem with the Main Campus (see Chapter 7), momentum gathered for a great many changes. By the first decade of the new century William Parkinson's dream of a great medical center to rival those of Columbia and Johns Hopkins was not yet achieved, but Temple had pro-

Loyal alumnus and Temple trustee Leonard Barrack (LLB LAW 1968) and his wife, Lynne Barrack, donated $2.5 million to Temple University's Beasley School of Law to establish the Barrack Public Interest Fellowship Program. "We give to Temple," says Barrack, "because we believe in Temple, we have confidence in its leadership, and we see very clearly the difference philanthropy makes in the lives of its faculty and students."

gressed into the first ranks in professional education and medical research, while extending its peerless contributions in community health service.

Temple University Health System

The new, nine-level Temple University Hospital that opened in 1986 provided 606 patient beds and an expanded emergency department, one of the busiest in the city. An ancillary building and outpatient building were added, and the former hospital tower (Parkinson Pavilion) was renovated for outpatient clinical services, physicians' offices, and support facilities.

Until the late 1980s the leadership of Temple's health care system was divided between the Health Sciences Center (Dr. Frank Sweeney, vice president), the hospital (Michael Jhin), and Medical School (Dr. Sol Sherry). Gradually, leadership was entrusted to Dr. Leon Malmud, professor of diagnostic imaging and renowned nuclear physician, who served as vice president for the Health Sciences Center from 1988 to 2000, dean of medicine from 1997 to 2001, and CEO of the health system from 1994 to 2000. Under Malmud, Temple Hospital employed a strategy of mergers and affiliations to help create an improved payer mix, put the hospital on a firmer financial footing, and stay current with the fast-developing technological demands of modern health care.

In 1994 Temple University's trustees formed the Temple University Health System (TUHS) to create a separate organization to manage its hospital and growing health care services and reduce the university's financial exposure (see Chapter 7). Through strategic mergers and affiliations the TUHS soon expanded into one of the region's major providers. In January 1995 Northeastern Hospital became part of TUHS, followed in 1996 by Jeanes Hospital and in 1997 by Episcopal Hospital. Temple also created affiliation agreements with the Neumann Medical Center and the Fox Chase Cancer Center. To reach further into the community, TUHS created Temple Physicians, Inc., a network of community-based physician practices.

Above *A new Temple University Hospital opened in 1986. In 2009 the 746-bed teaching hospital included seventeen operating rooms, four cardiac catheterization labs, 176 critical care unit beds, and a Level 1 Trauma Center. In fiscal year 2007–2008 there were 123,191 outpatient visits, 65,291 emergency department visits, and 2,726 births registered.*

Opposite *An expansive period in the 1990s led to several mergers with other hospitals, plus the construction of a seventy-bed Temple Children's Medical Center and the relocation of the Shriners Hospitals for Children to Temple. The two facilities (pictured at right) opened in 1998. (Temple Children's Medical Center closed in 2008, and the space was converted for other clinical uses.)*

Plans were quickly put forward and approved for the construction of Temple Children's Medical Center on North Broad Street between Venango and Tioga streets. Ground was broken in October 1994 for the $39 million, seventy-bed facility. Meanwhile, the Shriners Hospitals for Children, then located on Roosevelt Boulevard and the site of much collaboration with Temple physicians, decided to move to the Temple Health Sciences Center. A new $50 million Shriners Hospitals went up alongside Temple Children's Medical Center.

Confident of the future and constantly in need of updated facilities, Temple Hospital, between 1996 and 1998, added an ambulatory care building, a cardiac care addition, a cancer center, and two parking garages. The hospital expanded to provide an array of inpatient and outpatient services to its surrounding community and highly specialized tertiary services to the entire Philadelphia region. Well known for its expertise in cardiology, pulmonary medicine, sports medicine, and gastroenterology, Temple University Hospital has been ranked consistently as one of the nation's top hospitals for respiratory disorders by *U.S. News & World Report* in its *America's Best Hospitals* guide.

In 2000 Leon Malmud stepped down as CEO of the Temple University Health System. He was succeeded by Joseph W. "Chip" Marshall III, chairman of the TUHS board and a Temple trustee and alumnus (BA CLA 1975; JD LAW 1979). A Temple Owl through and through, Marshall has family associations with Temple that extend back six decades. One of the founding members of the Health System Board of Directors that created the hospital system, Marshall quickly oversaw a number of improvements. In January 2006 a new $75 million Ambulatory Care Center at Temple Hospital was completed, adding more than 125,000 square feet of clinical space, with expanded capabilities for radiation oncology and medical oncology. In addition, a new Digestive Diseases Center opened, and the Emergency Department was expanded. Marshall also guided the renovation of the former Budd Company site on West Hunting Park Avenue into a splendid new corporate headquarters.

The challenges confronting urban health systems throughout the country and the Temple University Health System in particular continued to mount as the economic meltdown commencing in 2006 lengthened and deepened. In 2007 the Temple Children's Medical Center, facing a declining patient census and worsening deficits, agreed to send its pediatric physicians and faculty to practice and teach at St. Christopher's Hospital for Children. The building that housed the Children's Medical Center was redeployed for other health care delivery services.

In December 2008 Marshall was replaced by Edmond F. Notebaert. A few months earlier President Hart had appointed Notebaert as senior executive vice president of health sciences. Notebaert was the former CEO of the University of Maryland Medical System and former president and CEO of the Children's Hospital of Philadelphia. Further cost cutting in 2009 raised the ire of some members of the community served by Northeastern Hospital, which faced severe cutbacks in service. But, as *Philadelphia Inquirer* editors observed, "The health of Philadelphia is in part tied to the health of these [Temple Health System] facilities. Each one must receive appropriate treatment."

As changes in national health care policies loom on the horizon, Temple remains ever mindful of its historic legacy to serve the health care needs of Philadelphians. The Temple University Health System also has an enormous impact on the region's financial health, employing more than 10,000 people and contributing more than $1.9 billion to the Greater Philadelphia economy each year. Since 2008, Temple University Health System's expenditures have supported nearly 19,400 jobs in Greater Philadelphia each year. For all of this, however, one must also remember that the Temple University Hospital, in support of the educational mission of Temple University, serves as the chief clinical training site for the Temple University School of Medicine.

School of Medicine

Since its opening in 1901, Temple University's School of Medicine has been guided by a commitment to educate superior physicians, enhance research and knowledge, and improve health care in the North Philadelphia community and beyond.

An acceptance and encouragement of diversity, as President Ann Weaver Hart proudly noted at the 2006 groundbreaking for the new Medical Education and Research Building, have been hallmarks of Temple medicine since its beginnings, dating to the graduation in 1906 of Sara Allen and Mary E. Shepard, the school's first women graduates. Temple conferred their degrees seven years before the University of Pennsylvania admitted female medical students and fifty-five years before Thomas Jefferson Medical College admitted women. In 1908, Agnes Berry Montier became the first African American woman to graduate with a Temple MD. She practiced general medicine in Philadelphia

Medical School Notable Facts

- Professor Herbert Stauffer designed the first television stereoscopic fluoroscope (1966).

- Temple established the nation's first state-sponsored HMO in two North Philadelphia neighborhoods, providing approximately 12,000 families with access to complete medical and dental care (1973).

- Donald Taylor Jr., a professor of rehabilitation medicine and biomedical engineering, led the development of the first artificial arm that was fully mobile and operated on command from the brain (1973).

- Temple opened the world's first university-based sports medicine center (1974).

- Dr. Jacob Kolff led a Temple team that accomplished the world's fifth implantation of an artificial heart (1982).

- The first combined heart and kidney transplant in the region was performed at Temple (1989).

until her death in 1961. According to the 2006 edition of *Diversity in the Physician Workforce*, Temple University ranked fifth in the nation in the total number of African Americans who graduated from medical schools between 1950 and 2004.

Temple medicine has encouraged diversity in other ways. Take, for example, David William Hartman (MD MED 1976), who has been blind since the age of eight. "As a visually impaired senior at Gettysburg College," Hartman recalled in 2009, "I had the audacity to apply to Temple University School of Medicine to pursue a medical career, though no student who was blind had been admitted to a medical school in the twentieth century. Thanks to Dean Prince Brigham, I was admitted in 1972 as the 151st student—an experiment some called Brigham's folly!" Hartman's efforts to overcome prejudice and to graduate from medical school were re-created in the two-hour television movie *Journey from Darkness*. He also co-authored a book about his experiences, *White Coat, White Cane*. In 2009 Hartman was practicing psychiatry in Salem, Virginia.

The School of Medicine has always sought students of the highest academic caliber, with a demonstrated capacity for volunteerism, altruism, and a genuine desire to help those in need. Temple medical students are trained to provide outstanding medical care to a culturally diverse population and to be exceptionally well prepared for further training and lifelong career development. Temple's medical faculty members have remained abreast of the latest pedagogical and technological advances in learning modalities. For example, to facilitate the learning of clinical and procedural medicine and promote patient safety, Temple established the Institute for Clinical Simulation and Patient Safety (ICSPS), with a Simulation Center that uses inanimate, programmable simulators to imitate physiologic and clinical conditions and a Skills Center that uses Standardized Patients, that is, actors trained to portray a patient scenario for purposes of training medical students in examining skills. The education of Temple's medical students centers on a solid foundation in the basic sciences integrated with clinical medicine and extensive hands-on clinical training.

Toward those ends, the Medical School has enjoyed a close educational and working relationship with the Temple University Health System and its hospitals: currently Temple, Episcopal, and Jeanes. It also created major teaching affiliates across the commonwealth, reaching as far west as Pittsburgh and Johnstown, north to Bethlehem and Allentown, and across the Philadelphia region to Abington and Fox Chase, permitting Temple students to become experienced in caring for individuals with simple to highly complex illnesses in a variety of settings.

In September 2002 Temple University's Medical School turned an important page in its remarkable history with the appointment of a new dean. A Philadelphia native and Temple alumnus, John M. Daly, MD, FACS (MD MED 1973), returned to his alma mater after compiling a truly distinguished professional record. Previously, he had chaired the Department of Surgery at the Weill Medical College of Cornell University in New York and been chief of surgical oncology at the Hospital of the University of Pennsylvania. Under Daly's dynamic and farsighted leadership, Temple's School of Medicine progressed and expanded on many fronts.

In the span of seven years Daly recruited nearly 300 outstanding new faculty members and 100 faculty scientists from leading institutions around the nation to rejuvenate educational programs and to rebuild the Medical School's research capacity. Included in those numbers were eleven new department chairs and the leadership for three new research centers in obesity, neurovirology, and minority health, to complement existing centers in cardiovascular disease, substance abuse, cancer,

TEMPLE NOTABLE
Sol Sherry, MD

A pioneer in the field of thrombosis, Dr. Sherry (1916–1993) served as chair of medicine at Temple from 1968 to 1984. He founded the Thrombosis Research Center that bears his name and was dean of the School of Medicine from 1984 to 1986. He revolutionized the treatment of acute myocardial infarction through the first therapeutic use of streptokinase and through his pathbreaking work in thrombolytic therapy. Named a university distinguished professor, Sherry trained many of today's leaders in the field of thrombosis and hemostasis. He founded the Council on Thrombosis of the American Heart Association and the International Society of Thrombosis and Haemostasis.

molecular biology, thrombosis, and pulmonary disease. External funding for research increased more than 40 percent, studies of new drugs and devices doubled, and the number of clinical research trials increased significantly.

Led by groundbreaking research in lung disease, obesity, drug addiction, and cancer, the School of Medicine in 2009, for the first time in its history, received a national research ranking. It placed fifty-sixth out of 146 medical schools nationwide, second in Philadelphia, and third in Pennsylvania. A major contributor to advancing the Medical School's research agenda was the establishment in August 2008 of the Keystone Institute for Translational Medicine (KITM). Directed by Drs. Richard Coico and Henry Parkman, the KITM is a joint endeavor with the Fox Chase Cancer Center of Philadelphia and the Geisinger Health System of Danville, Pennsylvania. Headquartered at the School of Medicine, the KITM became the nexus between collaborative translational science research, clinical and translational education and training, and community outreach aimed at improving health outcomes. KITM research focuses on reducing the prevalence of at-risk lifestyles and the incidence and severity of diseases associated with them.

Dean Daly and his colleagues take greatest delight in the new Medical Education and Research Building that opened in the fall of 2009. Located on the west side of North Broad Street between

The new Medical Education and Research Building (pictured below) was officially dedicated on October 30, 2009, in ceremonies led by President Ann Weaver Hart, assisted by Philadelphia mayor Michael Nutter and other dignitaries.

Venango and Tioga streets, the eleven-story, 480,000-square-foot Medical Research and Education Building is outfitted with the latest technologies for learning and discovery. Designed for current and emerging trends in medical education, such as virtual learning, clinical simulations, smart classrooms, interdisciplinary collaborations, and small-group endeavors, the building facilitated the addition of more students and faculty, plus a significant expansion in medical research, since seven floors are dedicated to laboratory research.

Funding for the new $160.4 million building was provided by a $50 million grant from the Commonwealth of Pennsylvania, $50 million from a Temple University bond issue, and $50 million from the Medical School, with additional assistance from the Kresge Foundation and faculty gifts. During planning stages for the building, the university explored the impact of the construction on the surrounding area and worked with community and church groups to address their concerns. As a consequence, Ballinger, Inc., architects created a design that lets servicing for the building take place below street level. Trucks can load or unload supplies and equipment without blocking traffic. A third-floor bridge, crossing Tioga Street, connects the new building with current teaching and research facilities. The building includes an attractive café, a spacious and comfortable lobby, and ample study and meeting space. Educational features include a clinical skills and robotic simulation center, where students practice doctoring and surgical skills with mannequins, simulators, and actor patients. A combined 50,000-square-foot library for the Health Sciences Center brings together resources for medicine, dentistry, pharmacy, podiatry, and related health professions as well as multimedia and wireless technology. In addition, an all-glass collaborative learning and research tower offers dramatic views of the center city skyline.

The more than 450 full-time and 1,160 volunteer faculty members take great satisfaction in the excellence of the Medical School's teaching, service, and research programs. They also give back. Asked by Dean Daly to raise $1 million toward construction of the new medical building, the medical faculty responded by raising $2 million. They are also a distinguished group. More than fifty Temple Medical School faculty members are listed in the 2007–2008 edition of the *Best Doctors in America*. And more than a dozen routinely appear on *Philadelphia* magazine's annual Top Doctors list.

Fully accredited by the American Medical Association Liaison Committee on Medical Education, the School of Medicine admitted 180 medical students in 2009 (a number that has been fixed since 1976 but is expected to increase after 2010 when the new building is fully operational). Competition for those few positions has intensified since 2000. Temple University's dynamic growth has contributed to the Medical School's increasing share of the national pool of medical school applicants. For example, the Medical School received 9,886 applications for the class of 2011, a 17.5 percent increase over the previous year. Temple's entering students boast better grade point averages and MCAT scores than preceding classes and in aggregate rank above the national average.

More than 10,000 living alumni of Temple University's School of Medicine are engaged in academia, clinical practice, business, industry, and public service around the globe. Over 4,300 Temple medicine alumni live and work in Pennsylvania; there is a Temple doctor practicing in every county in the state. Over 2,200 Philadelphia-area physicians, constituting 22 percent of all practicing physicians in the Philadelphia region, are graduates of Temple's School of Medicine.

Looking to the future, the final word belongs to Dean John Daly, who called the opening of the new medical building—the largest building project in the university's history—"the first step for Temple University School of Medicine in realizing a bold new vision." The building, as he explained, "visibly demonstrates a steadfast commitment to the surrounding neighborhood and to the City of Philadelphia." These investments, he reminds us, "enable Temple to be faithful to its missions for many years to come."

School of Pharmacy

Much has changed in the medicinal and pharmaceutical worlds since the first pharmacy classes were offered at Temple in 1901. Students in the early days were trained primarily in the apothecary skills of compounding herbs and powders to make pills and potions. Even through the 1960s it was not unusual for pharmacists still to be compounding medications to fill physicians' prescriptions. With the development in the mid-twentieth century of synthetic, manufactured drugs, the training of pharmacists shifted largely to professional preparation for their responsibilities concerning the lawful dispensing of drugs.

Even greater transformations occurred in the latter half of the last century. Flurries of breakthrough advances came in pharmaceutical sciences, medicinal chemistry, and the development of new drugs and increasingly sophisticated drug delivery systems and dosage forms. Whole new disciplines were created, such as biopharmaceutics and pharmacokinetics, to establish suitable dosing regimens. To respond to these rapid and profound transformations, the Pharmacy School accordingly adjusted its curriculum and various programs of professional preparation.

Led by Deans Alfred N. Martin (1968–1972), Paul Zanewiak (1972–1974), Joseph D. McEvilla (1974–1985), and Adelaide Van Titus (1985–1990), the Pharmacy School steadily upgraded its curriculum to meet the changing demands of the times and also pioneered a number of important advances. To respond to the significant changes occurring in the regulatory processes overseeing drug safety, efficacy, and quality control, the school in 1968 established an MS degree in Quality Assurance/ Regulatory Affairs (QA/RA), aimed principally at meeting the needs of professionals in the pharmaceutical industry. And in 1972 the School of Pharmacy established the first undergraduate program in radiopharmacy in the United States.

Pharmacy's needs for modern classrooms and updated research and instructional laboratories were met in 1974 when the Pharmacy School moved out of the Dental School building one block north into a new $8 million, six-story building at 3307 North Broad Street, on the northeast corner of Broad Street and Rising Sun Avenue. Constructed by the commonwealth, with funding assistance from Temple and a $2.3 million federal grant, the new building was shared with the College of Allied Health Professions. Still, it was large enough to accommodate the growing student demand for pharmacy courses and to provide needed pharmacological research space, contributing in 1980 to discoveries generated by a team of researchers led by pharmacology professor Ronald Gautieri that for the first time linked cocaine use with birth defects.

Beginning in 1990, under the creative leadership of Dean Peter Doukas, the pharmacy program made important new strides. It acquired additional external support for research and reached out to industry leaders, such as Merck & Co. and Wyeth, and to the U.S. Food and Drug Administration (FDA) for assistance in developing new research protocols and instructional techniques to stay ahead of major developments in the field. When several leading pharmaceutical companies became located in Philadelphia's northern suburbs, the Pharmacy School responded by moving its MS program in QA/RA in 1999 to the Fort Washington Campus. There it offered flexible scheduling and innovative methods for delivering classroom materials, attracting several hundred professionals from the pharmaceutical and related industries each semester.

FACT

The School of Pharmacy at Temple University established one of the first undergraduate programs in radiopharmacy in the United States in 1973.

In 1998, the school changed its core pharmacy curriculum to comply with the mandate from the American Council on Pharmaceutical Education (ACPE) to require a total of six years of study to earn the doctor of pharmacy (PharmD) degree, which became the new entry-level standard for the profession. Students entering the Temple pharmacy program thereafter were required to complete two years of pre-professional education followed by four years of rigorous professional study.

To provide pharmacists with the medication-related expertise they are expected to contribute to patient care, the modern doctor of pharmacy curriculum includes hundreds of hours of instruction in pharmaceutics and pharmacokinetics, plus study in anatomy, physiology, pathophysiology, infectious diseases, immunology, and biochemistry; pharmacology, medicinal chemistry, therapeutics, biostatistics, and literature evaluation; pharmacoeconomics, law, drug information, and patient counseling. These studies culminate in patient-oriented clerkship rotations in a variety of settings. With this preparation Temple pharmacy graduates are ready for positions in a wide range of corporate environments, care organizations, the pharmaceutical industry, and governmental agencies.

The Pharmacy School prides itself on a number of instructional innovations, research centers, and successful collaborations with the pharmaceutical industry. For example, in 2000 the school collaborated with the nonprofit Institute for Safe Medication Practices (ISMP) and the FDA to develop the nation's first program in medication safety as an elective within Temple's PharmD program. In 2006 the Pharmacy School opened a facility for Current Good Manufacturing Practices (CGMP), only one of six based at universities nationwide. The School of Pharmacy's status as a major contributor to pharmaceutical research was enhanced further in September 2008 when Dr. Magid Abou-Gharbia joined the faculty as director of the Moulder Center for Drug Discovery Research (MCDDR). Abou-Gharbia brought twenty-six years of experience working in the area of drug discovery and development, most recently as senior vice president and head of chemical and screening sciences at Wyeth. His research bridges the gap between pre-clinical and clinical research in support of translational medicine.

Many more changes lie ahead for the Pharmacy School. The mapping of the human genome allows for the development of countless new drugs that will enable health care practitioners to individualize therapies. In preparation for these developments, the Pharmacy School in 2007 opened the Jayne Lebow Haines Center for Pharmacogenomics and Drug Safety, named for the 1954 Pharmacy alumna and designed to enhance the safety and efficacy of genetically based drug therapy. Temple's School of Pharmacy has adjusted successfully to more than a century of change and is well positioned to continue its enviable record of innovative responses to meet society's needs for advanced pharmaceutical research and educational excellence.

Maurice H. Kornberg School of Dentistry

In 1947 Temple's School of Dentistry welcomed the move to its new home in the former Packard Building at North Broad and Allegheny streets (see Chapter 4). For the next three decades it continued to focus on the preparation of dentists for service as general practitioners, first under Dean Charles Howell and then Dale F. Roeck, who succeeded Howell as dean in 1976. The larger facility allowed a greater emphasis on community health and clinical services to its North Philadelphia neighbors. However, with the passage of time, technological advancements, and new demands on the dentistry profession, Dean Roeck and American Dental Association (ADA) accreditors expressed grave concerns over the inadequacy of the clinical training facilities.

Leon O. (Lonnie) Moulder Jr., president and CEO of MGI Pharma, and his wife, Sharon, both 1980 graduates of Temple University School of Pharmacy, generously provided funding to launch the Moulder Center for Drug Discovery Research. "The pharmacy education I received and the people I met at Temple made a real difference in my life," said Lonnie, when he and Sharon decided the time was right to help their alma mater. The mission of the Moulder Center is to advance discoveries by testing hypotheses to increase understanding of the physiological and pathophysiological processes relevant to drug discovery, with the ultimate goal of bridging the gap between pre-clinical and clinical research in support of translational medicine. The Moulder Center also provides students, faculty, and future researchers with excellent training and a solid understanding of modern drug discovery and development.

The much-needed and much-awaited Dental School clinical annex (shown here circa 2000) was completed in 1990, securing full ADA accreditation and advancing the school's long-standing efforts to provide clinical services to the community.

Renovating the old structure (originally built in 1925) would address only a portion of the Dental School problems and likely not appease ADA accreditors, who warned the school that its accreditation was at risk if new facilities were not forthcoming. Roeck succeeded in gaining the Wachman administration's support for a new clinical teaching building, and the commonwealth agreed to set aside funds to pay for construction. Roeck also won university support to add new faculty and to change the name of the degree awarded to dental graduates from Doctor of Dental Surgery (DDS) to Doctor of Dental Medicine (DMD), beginning in 1984.

Dr. Martin F. Tansy, professor and chairman of the Physiology Department, was appointed as Temple's twelfth dental school dean in 1986. He immediately urged moving ahead with Roeck's proposals to construct a new clinical facility. However, with the introduction of fluoride in the 1970s, fewer dentists were required and several dental schools, including Georgetown and Emory, closed in the 1980s. Moreover, during the ten-year academic planning process, Temple's provost, Dr. Barbara Brownstein, raised serious doubts concerning the high costs of dental education and the meager research productivity of Temple's dental faculty, questioning whether the school ought to continue. To answer those concerns, President Liacouras assembled a blue-ribbon committee of dental educators to assess the school's future.

Dean Tansy advised the blue-ribbon committee of the critical importance of the Temple Dental School to the citizens of Philadelphia and southeastern Pennsylvania. He also provided new direction for the school, eventually establishing an implantology clinic, teaching cosmetic dentistry, and expanding dental research. With the committee's favorable endorsement, construction proceeded on the $36 million clinical facility, funded by the Commonwealth of Pennsylvania and private gifts. The new facility, constructed as an annex to the existing building, opened in 1990 with over 100 individual dental operatories and advanced clinical and pre-clinical training facilities.

Subsequent external reviewers and accreditors praised the state-of-the-art quality of Temple's dental education programs and gave the clinics their highest commendations. Every seven years, each of the nation's fifty-six dental schools is visited by the American Dental Association's Commission on Dental Accreditation (ADA-CODA) to review the school's accomplishments and suggest ways it could improve. The most recent ADA-CODA accreditation review occurred in 2004, and the Kornberg School of Dentistry received a perfect score, along with an unprecedented thirteen commendations for particular areas of excellence.

One of the Kornberg School of Dentistry's excellent features is its pre-clinical training laboratory. Before dental students work with real patients, they spend two years practicing with plastic teeth and jaw and head mannequins to perfect basic dental skills in the pre-clinical laboratory. In 2006 the School of Dentistry fittingly dedicated the Dr. John and Joan H. Ballots Preclinical Laboratory in recognition of the Ballotses' generous scholarship support of Temple dental students. Few Temple loyalists have matched the pride and spirit of Joan Ballots (BS EDU 1953). A university trustee, faithful follower of Temple athletics, and generous donor to the basketball program, she has demonstrated unflagging support of Temple over several decades. Her late husband, John Ballots (DDS DEN 1957), was a standout basketball player for Temple, as well as a Dental School graduate with a highly successful family practice.

The long, distinguished history from which the Kornberg School of Dentistry evolved has been on display since 2003 in the Edwin and Trudy Weaver Historical Dental Museum at Temple University, which houses some of the finest museum-quality dental antiquities in the United States. The museum features the school's unique collection of dental artifacts and presents the history of dentistry in America. Displays include a richly varied collection of photographs, instruments, and the personal possessions of former students, faculty, and alumni. Here one can trace the beginnings of dentistry in America through three generations of dentists— from Josiah Flagg and his Revolutionary War–era practice to his grandson, J. Foster Flagg, who in 1863 was a founder and member of the faculty of the Philadelphia Dental College. The college, which was the second oldest dental school in the country, merged with Temple in 1907. Temple's Dental School history is evoked by museum depictions of dental educational techniques and photographs of student laboratories, clinics, and operatories, highlighting the contributions of Temple alumni and faculty to the advancement of dental education and to the growth of the dental profession.

In December 2006 Leonard and Madlyn Abramson and the Abramson Family Foundation committed $10 million to Temple University in support of student scholarships. In recognition of their gift, the trustees named the Dental School the Maurice H. Kornberg School of Dentistry after Madlyn's father, a member of the class of 1921. Proud of its distinguished past and mindful of its noble obligation to educate dentists for general practice, the Maurice H. Kornberg School of Dentistry and its 500 students and 130 faculty members provided more than 300,000 patient procedures in 2009, attesting to the school's unshakable commitment to community health. Additionally, seven research laboratories and collaborative research projects currently focus on HIV/AIDS, oral cancer, and the impact of various factors on oral health care.

Martin Tansy retired in 2008, and Amid I. Ismail was selected to lead the Kornberg School of Dentistry. Coming to Temple from the University of Michigan, where he was professor of health services research and cariology in the School of Dentistry and professor of epidemiology and director of the program in dental public health in the School of Public Health, Dr. Ismail brought substantial expertise and a passionate advocacy for the delivery and improvement of dental health care for

TEMPLE NOTABLE
Maurice H. Kornberg

The son of Jewish immigrants from Eastern Europe, Maurice Kornberg (DDS DEN 1921) was the first in his family to attend college, working his way through. Dr. Kornberg practiced family dentistry in center city and South Philadelphia. In his memory, Dr. Kornberg's daughter, Madlyn Abramson, and her husband, Leonard, made a $10 million gift to Temple in 2006. "Our gift is in honor of my father," said Madlyn Abramson. "It was a great accomplishment for him to get through school. We really wanted our support to go to scholarships for students in need."

the underserved in urban areas. Under his leadership the Maurice H. Kornberg School of Dentistry remains committed to excellence in dental education and to fulfilling its mission of serving the community's dental health needs.

School of Podiatric Medicine

Temple University's School of Podiatric Medicine is one of only eight in the United States offering accredited training in the branch of medicine concentrating on the diagnosis, treatment, and prevention of problems and diseases of the foot, ankle, and lower extremities. Graduates of the school are awarded a Doctor of Podiatric Medicine (DPM) degree. Practitioners, once known as chiropodists, are now called podiatrists. Temple opened the School of Chiropody in 1915 but closed it in 1960 because of low enrollments (see Chapter 2). In 1963 several members of the faculty obtained a charter from the Commonwealth of Pennsylvania to open a new, independent podiatry school, which they called the Pennsylvania College of Podiatric Medicine (PCPM). Initially, PCPM functioned in rented facilities, before moving in 1965 to Eighth and Pine streets and then in 1973 to a building at Eighth and Race streets customized to accommodate podiatry.

In July 1998 President Liacouras invited PCPM to merge with Temple University and become Temple's fourth professional school, elevating Temple's professional enrollments to the fifth largest in the country. Following a national search, Liacouras appointed Dr. John A. Mattiacci, one of the nation's leading podiatrists, as dean of Temple's School of Podiatric Medicine. Mattiacci brought to the post nearly three decades of experience as a practicing podiatrist and surgeon. He had served as director of surgical residency at the Neumann Medical Center and Northeastern Hospital, as well as president of the Physicians' Guild. Mattiacci smoothly guided the transition of PCPM into the Temple family of professional schools.

Temple's podiatry campus includes student classrooms and laboratories at Eighth and Race streets, plus a seven-story student residence complex at 801 Cherry Street, providing apartments for 126

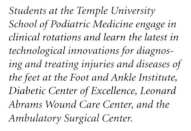

Students at the Temple University School of Podiatric Medicine engage in clinical rotations and learn the latest in technological innovations for diagnosing and treating injuries and diseases of the feet at the Foot and Ankle Institute, Diabetic Center of Excellence, Leonard Abrams Wound Care Center, and the Ambulatory Surgical Center.

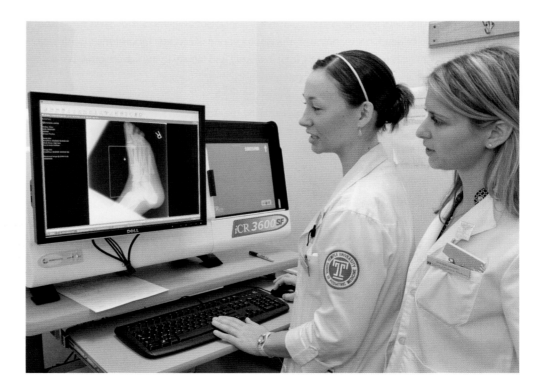

professional and graduate students. The main podiatry building includes a Shoe Museum with approximately 1,000 pairs of shoes, 250 of which are on display on the sixth floor. Many of the items are part of the Dr. H. Augustus Wilson Shoe Collection on extended loan to the Temple University School of Podiatric Medicine from the Mütter Museum of the Philadelphia College of Physicians. Dr. Wilson (1853–1919), a noted Philadelphia orthopedist, collected footwear from over thirty nations. The Shoe Museum, which contains the shoes of first ladies Nancy Reagan, Mamie Eisenhower, Betty Ford, and Lady Bird Johnson, was created during the nation's bicentennial in 1976 as an added attraction for visitors to the Liberty Bell and Independence Park, just two blocks from the podiatry campus.

The School of Podiatric Medicine operates a medical clinic known as the Foot and Ankle Institute, located in the 800 block of Cherry Street. The largest facility of its kind in the Philadelphia area and one of the most comprehensive centers for podiatric treatment in the world, the Foot and Ankle Institute's specialists diagnose and treat problems of the lower extremities. Treatments are directed by members of the podiatry faculty, who are aided by third- and fourth-year students. Every April the School of Podiatric Medicine holds a rite-of-passage ceremony honoring second-year podiatry students, who are given their white coats to mark the beginning of their clinical work in the school's Foot and Ankle Institute in the fall. Clinical experiences are also available through the Diabetic Center of Excellence located at Temple University's Health Sciences Campus; it focuses on diabetes treatment, wound care, and amputation prevention. The Ambulatory Surgical Center (ASC) at the Foot and Ankle Institute offers common surgical procedures on an outpatient basis. The Leonard S. Abrams Center for Advanced Wound Healing (LAC) treats wounds of the lower extremity that may arise from diabetes or vascular, neuropathic, or traumatic causes.

Temple's podiatry students can elect a variety of specialties, such as orthopedics, surgery, sports medicine, pediatrics, diabetic foot care, and geriatrics. The course of study toward the DPM has

FACT

The School of Podiatric Medicine at Temple University is the only such school in the United States that is part of a large research university, and the only one with a connection to a major university health system.

been fully accredited by the Council of Podiatric Medical Education (CPME). Dual degree programs are available through Temple's School of Medicine, the Fox School of Business and Management, and the College of Health Professions. In addition, the school offers post-professional certificate programs in specialties such as pedorthics (the art of orthotics manufacture).

Research conducted in the Gait Study Center has significantly advanced knowledge of the care and treatment of diabetes. For example, Dr. Jinsup Song, director of the Gait Study Center and assistant professor of podiatric medicine and orthopedics, recently used a four-year $650,000 grant from the National Institutes of Health to test the effectiveness of a personalized, visual diabetic foot education strategy developed by using clinical information collected at the Gait Study Center. Whether through research, clinical treatments, or the education of new cohorts of doctors of podiatric medicine, Temple University plays a major regional and national role in advancing the care and treatment of problems of the lower extremities.

Health Professions

Through the years, extending back to the 1890s, Temple has taken a leadership role in the education and training of personnel in the health professions allied with and supportive of physicians. Of those professions, nursing was the earliest and most critical.

Nursing

Temple's nursing program began in 1893 as the Training School for Nurses within Samaritan Hospital, the twenty-bed hospital at Broad and Ontario streets founded by Russell Conwell in 1892. Nursing then was seen mostly as a necessary hospital service rather than as a profession. The goal of the program, first directed by Emma Mathias-Darnley, was "to train young women of good moral standing and common school education to nurse the sick." The first class of four students completed a two-year course of study in 1895. They were personally congratulated by Conwell, who performed the pinning ceremony. Conwell liked the nurses' two-color uniforms of cherry and white, which, according to one source, he then chose as Temple's official colors.

In 1899, when Daisy O'Hara was appointed director of nursing, she added a third year to the basic requirements. When Temple merged with the Philadelphia Dental College in 1907, the nursing program added an affiliation with the Garretson Hospital. The Nurses' Alumni Association formed in 1909. The teaching department separated from the hospital in 1917, the same year that Edna L. Moore (RN 1905) was appointed as the first full-time nursing instructor. Four years later the Samaritan Hospital School of Nursing merged with the Garretson Hospital School of Nursing, and in 1929 they became the Temple University Hospital School of Nursing (TUHSN). Over time the Nursing School created affiliation agreements with nearly a dozen hospitals, including St. Christopher's, Abington, Episcopal, Northeastern, and Frankford hospitals. In 1932, when the Medical School moved to Broad and Ontario streets, it assumed responsibility for the School of Nursing and offered classes in the new Medical School building.

The Home Economics Department in Temple's Teachers College (College of Education) introduced a course in nursing education in 1925, making Temple the first university in the commonwealth to offer a university course in nursing. However, a full degree program did not develop until 1938, when the Teachers College offered a bachelor of science degree in nursing. Intended for registered nurses (RNs), the program granted advanced standing for completion of the three-year nursing diploma at the Medical School and hospital. With the opening in 1969 of a Department of Nursing in the College of Allied Health Professions (CAHP), both the College of Education nursing program and the Temple University Hospital School of Nursing were formally dissolved. The last twenty-six of the more than 3,000 graduates of the Temple Hospital School of Nursing received their nursing diplomas in 1971, and the last of the College of Education degrees were awarded in 1972.

The nursing program in CAHP grew rapidly after the first students were admitted in 1969. Earlier in the decade the growth of nursing as a profession and the demand for qualified nurses had prompted Temple to construct Jones Hall, a ten-story women's dormitory on Ontario Street at Park Avenue. Named for Edith Bolling Jones and opened in September 1962, Jones Hall accommodated 453 women students in nursing, medical technology, and other schools and colleges at the Health Sciences Center.

As nursing matured as a profession, the CAHP nursing program placed greater attention on graduate education, offering a master of science degree in nursing beginning in 1991, and later adding a number of specializations and nurse-practitioner tracks. Continually concerned with meeting community health care needs, the Department of Nursing in 1996 opened the Temple Health Connection, a neighborhood nursing center that operated out of Norris Homes, a public housing development next to Temple's Main Campus.

College of Health Professions and Social Work

In 1966 Temple brought together a group of health-related disciplines to form the College of Allied Health Professions, to be known after 2003 as the College of Health Professions and after 2009 as the College of Health Professions and Social Work (see Chapter 5). When first formed, the college was intended, according to then-president Millard Gladfelter, to upgrade "the training of technicians to take over more of the physicians' tasks." With the expansion of the health care industry and the enlarged demand for nurses and other highly qualified technical personnel, the college became one of the fastest growing of Temple's colleges, adding several new programs and attracting many new students.

Early in its history the college absorbed the medical technology program and added programs in occupational therapy, physical therapy, and medical records library science (health records administration). In 1998 the college added the Communication Sciences Department (formerly Speech and Hearing), which shifted over from the School of Communications and Theater. Therapeutic recreation and health education (renamed Public Health) were moved into the college in 2003 upon the dissolution of the College of Health, Physical Education, Recreation, and Dance (HPERD). In July 2005 the Department of Kinesiology (formerly known as Physical Education) was moved from the College of Education into the College of Health Professions. Then, in May 2009, the School of Social Administration merged with the college, and the name was changed to the College of Health Professions and Social Work.

The first dean of CAHP was Aaron L. Andrews. A recognized leader in the field, Andrews helped found the American Society of Allied Health Professions and was influential within the organization for many years. Administrative offices were located initially in a row house at 3424 Carlisle Street. In 1974 the College of Allied Health Professions moved into a new building at Broad Street and Rising Sun Avenue, which they shared with Pharmacy.

When CAHP opened in 1966 it had but one program: medical technology. The program was moved into the new college from the Medical School, where it had begun back in 1933 as the School for Laboratory Technicians. Bachelor's degrees in medical technology were first offered in 1939. The

TEMPLE NOTABLE
Glenda Price

Glenda Price (BS CHP 1961; M.Ed. EDU 1969; PhD EDU 1979)—one of at least sixteen Temple alumni who have become college presidents— received her initial degree in medical technology, accepted a position as a cytotechnologist at Temple Hospital, and taught at Temple for ten years, working her way up to professor of clinical laboratory science. She served as assistant dean of the College of Allied Health from 1979 to 1986, before leaving Temple to become dean of the School of Allied Health Professions at the University of Connecticut. From there she went on to become provost of Spelman College in Atlanta and then president of Marymount College in Detroit, retiring in 2006. Dr. Price served as president of the American Society for Clinical Laboratory Sciences and received many professional awards during her long and distinguished career.

Pathbreaking Research

The College of Health Professions was the first to establish a virtual reality laboratory for the diagnosis of balance disorders. Dr. Emily Keshner, chair of the Department of Physical Therapy, uses virtual reality technology to demonstrate how the central nervous system recalculates movements based on its surroundings. Retroreflective markers are placed on patients wearing 3-D glasses and body harnesses to measure and record their movements as they view images intentionally created to throw them off-balance.

program trained students in laboratory skills to aid doctors and nurses in tracking the nature and causes of disease. The first CAHP graduates in May 1967 were twenty-nine students who received bachelor's degrees in medical technology. The program changed its name to Clinical Laboratory Sciences in the 1980s, but the program closed in 1990.

Dean Andrews established baccalaureate programs in occupational therapy and physical therapy and began admitting students in September 1967. As the demand for occupational therapists increased nationally and as professional requirements stiffened, the master's degree became the profession's desired entry-level degree. Temple responded by approving an MS program in 1985, followed by a Master's of Occupational Therapy (MOT) and a Doctor of Occupational Therapy (DOT). Eventually, the BS degree was phased out, graduating the last class in January 2002. Similarly, the Department of Physical Therapy, chaired in 1967 by Hyman L. Dervitz, took a farsighted approach, preparing for the eventual escalation of professional standards associated with enlarged clinical responsibilities of physical therapists. The college moved to an MS degree, then a Master of Physical Therapy (MPT), a PhD, and, finally, in 2000 a Doctor of Physical Therapy (DPT) as the entry-level degree in the profession.

A program in medical records library science was established in 1969, later changing its name to Health Records Administration and then to Health Information Management to be consistent with the designation of the national professional association. An integral part of patient care, health records administration soon developed stringent professional training standards. As health care became more complex, hospitals shifted responsibility to medical librarians and medical historians, who verified insurance claims and provided information to physicians and medical researchers.

The Communication Sciences Department, known previously by various names, began in 1950 as the Speech and Hearing: Rhetoric Department within the College of Liberal Arts and Sciences, migrated to the School of Communications and Theater in 1984, and then in 1998 moved, in part, to the College of Health Professions. The department offers five degrees in speech-language-hearing, linguistics, and communication sciences and houses the Speech-Language-Hearing Clinic. Another frequent traveler is the Department of Public Health. It began in 1966 as a program in the College of Education, moved to the College of Health, Physical Education, Recreation, and Dance (HPERD), and was briefly a part of the School of Social Administration, before joining the College of Health Professions in 2003. The program offers a bachelor's degree, plus the PhD and five master's degree tracks in various public health specializations. The College of Health Professions added programs in therapeutic recreation in 2003 and kinesiology in 2005.

The growth of the College of Health Professions and Social Work, as the above discussion attests, has been nothing short of phenomenal. Besides the proliferation of programs, the college has witnessed a spectacular increase in research productivity and external funding. Since the arrival from the Medical University of South Carolina of Dean Ronald T. Brown, a leading pediatric psychologist, the college has quickly moved up the ranks of health professions colleges receiving funding from the National Institutes of Health—from sixteenth place in 2004 to eighth in 2006. Four of the college's graduate programs ranked among the top fifty of their type, according to *U.S. News & World Report*. In just over forty years the College of Health Professions and Social Work has demonstrated a remarkable capacity to adapt to the complex demands of the health care and social service delivery systems and to anticipate new developments, all of which bodes well for the future of the college and for Temple University.

Fox School of Business and Management

Temple's School of Business (see Chapter 2) can trace its informal beginnings back to the earliest days of Temple College and its formal roots to 1902, when Dr. Milton Stauffer first headed a Department of Commercial Education, and to 1918, when the School of Commerce was created. In 1943 the school was renamed the School of Business and Public Administration and then in 1963 the School of Business Administration. Another change occurred in 1987, when trustees approved changing the name to the School of Business and Management. Finally, in 1999, the school was renamed the Richard J. Fox School of Business and Management, in honor of Richard J. Fox, a member of Temple's board of trustees for more than forty years, chairman of the board for eighteen years, and a prominent member of Philadelphia's business and philanthropic communities.

Under the steady hand of Dean Harry A. Cochran, the Fox School first earned full accreditation in 1934 by the American Association of Collegiate Schools of Business (AACSB), now called the Association to Advance Collegiate Schools of Business (AACSB International). The Fox School has maintained its accredited status ever since. Credit goes to Cochran for placing the school on such a firm foundation. He assembled a solid faculty contingent, taken largely from graduates of America's most prestigious institutions. He also personally shaped the undergraduate and graduate curricula, securing approvals for a master of science in 1939 and the master of business administration (MBA) in 1943. Both were predominantly part-time evening programs, with many of the students and adjunct professors drawn from the city's downtown businesses. A daytime MBA program was first offered in 1951.

Cochran served as dean for twenty-six years, retiring in 1960. By then the school had grown to nearly 1,300 day students and 2,500 evening students, including over 650 MBA students. Cochran's close ties with the Philadelphia business community ensured a steady flow of students and professors and provided access for Temple graduates seeking employment. During the Cochran years the basic learning schemes of the school were laid. The most valued approach to learning at Temple's School of Business was through the study of tangible everyday life experiences and problems drawn from real life.

Many companies went to Cochran with requests for the school to analyze and offer recommendations for the solution of practical business problems. When the demand grew particularly large after World War II, Cochran created the Bureau of Economic and Business Research. The bureau produced research reports, studies, and economic bulletins, many of which found their way into *The Economics and Business Bulletin*, founded in 1949. In 1972 the name was changed to the *Journal of Economics and Business*. The Fox School later added several more academic journals and by 2009 was home to seven national academic and professional journals, among them the *Benefits Quarterly* (1991), the *Journal of International Management* (1997), the *Journal of Product Innovation Management* (2004), and the *Journal of Risk Finance* (2004).

Cochran was succeeded by Charles E. Gilliland Jr., who served for five years, during which he assisted in the creation of programs in Third World countries and encouraged students to contribute to public service. His most notable contribution was developing the programming for the construction of Speakman Hall (see Chapter 5), making sure that when it opened in 1966 the building anticipated future needs. Gilliland and Acting Dean W. Roy Buckwalter, who filled in for two years after Gilliland stepped down in 1965, organized a fund-raising campaign that drew more than 9,000 alumni and other donations to the Speakman Hall building fund.

TEMPLE NOTABLE
Richard J. Fox

Richard J. Fox, Temple University trustee and past board chairman (1982–2000), founded Fox Companies, one of southeastern Pennsylvania's major building, development, and real estate management firms. For his immeasurable contributions to Temple, Fox was awarded an honorary Doctor of Humane Letters (1993) and the Alumni Association's Diamond Award (1996), its highest award for a non-alumnus. Fox and his brother, Robert A. Fox, were joint recipients of the Musser Award for Excellence in Leadership (2007), given annually to honor outstanding achievement and service by a distinguished member of the business community.

Following an extensive international search, Dr. Seymour Wolfbein accepted the deanship in 1967, fresh from serving as deputy assistant secretary of labor for Presidents Kennedy and Johnson. A renowned expert in manpower policy, Wolfbein established a Manpower Research Institute, which he directed. The number of full-time tenure-track faculty in the school increased almost fourfold during Wolfbein's deanship, as the school added new departments in computer information science, statistics, health care administration, and insurance and risk. Wolfbein strengthened the Economics Department, building on the master of arts (first offered in 1964) and the PhD (1966). Eager to boost the research capacity of the school, Wolfbein also established institutes for social insurance and social economics, urban studies, economic organizations, and international development. During his tenure the MBA program was accredited by the AACSB, and new graduate programs in operations research, health care administration, and information sciences were offered. Other new programs created during these years offered a bachelor of business administration (BBA), an MBA in health administration, a PhD in statistics (1971), and a PhD in business administration (1973).

Dr. Edward M. Mazze was appointed dean in 1979, coming to Temple after serving as dean of business at Seton Hall University. Mazze was responsible for a long list of innovations, including the establishment in 1984 of an undergraduate Honors Program (directed by Professor Terry Halbert), a bachelor of business administration in international business administration (1984), and the Executive MBA program (1985). Also added during the Mazze years were a master of science in taxation, two joint-degree programs in health care/financial management and occupational safety and health/MBA in management, a PhD program in computer science, and a Small Business Advisory Council.

Professor John C. "Jack" Ritchie Jr. filled in as acting dean for two years until the arrival of Dr. William C. Dunkelberg in 1987. Dunkelberg drew a great deal of attention to the school as a result of his frequent appearances in the national media as the chief economist of the National Federation of Independent Business. He focused on the local, North Philadelphia businesses, assisting them through the Small Business Development Center (SBDC) and the Center for the Advancement and Study of Entrepreneurship (CASE). Dunkelberg also made several major advancements in international education. In 1994 he launched the International MBA (IMBA) program with partners in France (later in Tokyo, Mumbai, and Shanghai) and an Executive MBA (EMBA) program at Temple University Japan (see Chapter 7).

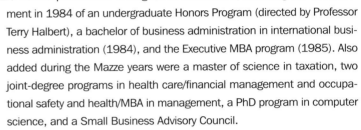

The ultra-modern Alter Hall (pictured above) opened in January 2009. Named for Dennis Alter (BS EDU 1966) and his wife, Gisela, Alter Hall is an eight-story, 217,000-gross-square-foot building that includes a three-story atrium (pictured opposite), a 277-seat auditorium, separate breakout rooms for MBA students, two computer teaching laboratories, student lockers, sixty offices, room for nine research institutes, and an alumni lounge, among other features.

Dunkelberg returned to teaching in 1995, and his associate dean, Dr. Jonathan Scott, filled in until a national search elevated Dr. M. Moshe Porat from the chairmanship of the Risk Management, Insurance, and Actuarial Science Department to the dean's office. Influenced by three megatrends—the global economy, exploding information technology, and the worldwide spread of entrepreneurship—Dean Porat launched several initiatives to keep the Fox School even with or ahead of megatrend developments. Responding to technology trends, the Fox School in 1998 became the first school at Temple to establish its own Office of Information Technology, intended to make the school a leader in incorporating information technology into teaching and learning. The school created a partnership with International Business Machines (IBM) to make Temple an IBM ThinkPad University, allowing mobile computer users to share information. In 1999 the Fox School established an Honors Laptop Community, awarding laptops to incoming Honors Program freshmen to use during their first two

years at the Fox School. Further, the formation in 2000 of the Management Information Systems Department had as its purpose the production of graduates with technological savvy.

Responding to globalization, Porat increased the Fox School's involvement in international education in several ways. The International MBA was expanded with the creation of a partnership with the Welingkar Institute of Management, Development and Research in Mumbai; a full-year undergraduate international business program was established in Rome; and a bachelor of business administration was offered in Tokyo. In addition, the Center for International Business and Research (CIBER) was established in 2002 to serve as a regional and national resource to help improve understanding of international trade, commerce, and economics among businesspeople, students, and teachers at all levels. Partnerships formed by Dean Porat with top-flight schools in France, Israel, India, Colombia, and China have brought many truly excellent foreign students to study at Temple in the Fox School.

To better serve the Fox School students, the Center for Student Professional Development was set up in 1997 to provide career services for undergraduates, and the Graduate Career Management Center was established in 2002 to help Fox School graduate students learn about their career options. In hopes of preparing Fox graduates to be responsible and ethical practitioners, the school in 2002 began offering Business, Ethics and Society, an undergraduate ethics program. External developments persuaded the faculty in 2005 to make the course mandatory, making the Fox School one of the few schools in the United States to require undergraduates to take an ethics course.

Capitalizing on the surge of interest in entrepreneurship, in 1997 the Fox School began offering an undergraduate program in entrepreneurship to integrate the knowledge and experiences gained in other disciplines. In 1999 the Fox School created the Innovation and Entrepreneurship Institute (IEI) to promote the entrepreneurial spirit across the university. Additionally, the Fox School participated in a collaborative effort in 2000 to create the League for Entrepreneurial Women to serve as an advocacy initiative addressing the challenges and interests of entrepreneurial women at Temple and in the Greater Philadelphia region. The Fox Women's Leadership Initiative, established in 2005, was a networking group for MBA students, connecting them to the Women's Leadership Network at Rohm & Haas and other area corporations.

All of these efforts paid handsome dividends for the Fox School of Business and Management. In recent years the number of applicants to Fox School programs has increased dramatically. The quality of the applicants is also appreciatively greater. On average, applicants to the school's advanced graduate programs score in the 95th percentile on the GMAT. In 2008 the Fox School broke into the top-fifty rankings for the first time, placing forty-seventh among all U.S. business schools as ranked by the Social Science Research network. The *Financial Times* ranked the school's MBA program among the top ten in the United States for "value for money." The Executive MBA is ranked seventeenth overall and is in the top ten for the number of female students and for career progress. In 2008 the *Chronicle of Higher Education* placed the finance faculty and management information sciences faculty in the top ten for research productivity. *U.S. News & World Report* ranked the Fox School's undergraduate international business program and its risk management and insurance program in the top ten in the United States.

In January 2009 the Fox School moved into a new $80 million, eight-story modernistic facility at Montgomery Avenue and Thirteenth Street on the former site of Curtis Hall and directly connected to Speakman Hall. The new building was named Alter Hall in honor of Dennis Alter, CEO of Advanta

Faculty in the Fox School of Business and Management were absolutely delighted with the Alter Hall classroom and teaching facilities when the building opened for classes in the spring 2009 semester. Pictured above is Dwight Carey, an instructor in the Department of General and Strategic Management, teaching a class in entrepreneurship.

Corporation, and his wife, Gisela, who provided the lead gift of $15 million—the largest in the school's history—to launch the capital campaign for the building. Alter Hall provides space enough to bring together in a single building academic departments, classes, centers, and institutes that were formerly spread among nine buildings. The building is equipped with the most advanced technology available, including dual projection screens, robotic cameras, ambient microphones, WiFi, and digital annotation.

Everything considered, the 45,000 living alumni of and the current 5,700 students in the Fox School of Business and Management rightfully take pride in their past, point with satisfaction to their collective accomplishments, and face the future with confidence in the continuing capacity of their school to meet and anticipate society's most important needs.

School of Tourism and Hospitality Management

In 1998 President Liacouras appointed a task force, headed by trustee Edward Rosen, to investigate how Temple University ought to respond to the Philadelphia area's burgeoning hospitality industry. Acting on the task force recommendations, the trustees established the School of Tourism and Hospitality Management (STHM) on July 1, 1998. Recognizing the importance of the travel and tourism industry and the need to educate and train persons for positions in those fields, the task force recommended that the new school be formed out of units within the recently dissolved College of Health, Physical Education, Recreation, and Dance (HPERD), namely the Sport Management and Leisure Studies Department.

Trustees designated the School of Tourism and Hospitality Management to be administratively affiliated with the Fox School of Business and Management, and Dean Moshe Porat was appointed to serve as the dean for both schools. Dr. Elizabeth Barber, the driving force behind the creation of the school, was appointed as the school's first director and later the school's first associate dean. The school started with only six faculty members, three staff members, and 200 students in Sport Management and Leisure Studies but quickly grew to include fourteen faculty members, eight staff members, and over 600 students enrolled in five degree programs: bachelor of science programs in Tourism and Hospitality Management and Sport and Recreation Management, a Master of Tourism and Hospitality Management (MTHM), an M.Ed. in Sport and Recreation Administration, and a PhD in Business Administration (offered in the Fox School of Business and Management) with a concentration in Sport and Tourism.

Notable achievements in the school's brief history include co-sponsorship, with the Fox School and the School of Communications and Theater, of an annual Women's Entrepreneurship Conference that started in 2000. And in 2003 the school established an Executive in Residence Program that has included Ted Turner, chairman of Turner Enterprises, and Jonathan Tisch, chairman of the Loews Corporation. In 2004 the school established the 2+2 Program with Temple University Japan (TUJ), a program designed for TUJ students in Tourism and Hospitality Management to study two years at TUJ in Tokyo and two years on the Main Campus in Philadelphia. Dr. Michael Jackson brought much positive attention to the school with his successful program in Sport and Recreation Administration. Dr. Dan Fesenmaier, regarded as the leading producer of tourism research in the world, was appointed to the faculty in 2004, bringing the school to prominence early in its history with innovations such as the National Laboratory for Tourism and eCommerce. After only ten years, the School of Tourism and Hospitality Management is the most comprehensive and largest of its kind in the Greater Philadelphia region.

Branch Campuses

After 125 years Temple is still very much Philadelphia's university, but over the years it also has become a metropolitan university, serving the needs of the greater Delaware Valley, with its destiny tied to the entire Philadelphia region. Russell Conwell insisted that the "Temple Idea" was transportable and that Temple University ought to serve educational needs wherever they may be found. Toward that end, over the last fifty years Temple established four regional campuses—Ambler, Center City, Fort Washington, and Harrisburg—each serving slightly different populations with a fairly wide array of programs.

Responsibility for coordinating and overseeing the branch campuses falls to the dean of the University College, a position created in 2004 and held, along with other responsibilities, by Dr. Richard Englert. The primary foci for University College are to coordinate effective instruction and services to students across the regional campuses, build capacity and support the special strengths of each of these locations in response to regional needs, and at the same time create new initiatives to expand Temple's outreach.

Ambler Campus

Temple University acquired the Ambler Campus in 1958 through a merger with the Pennsylvania School of Horticulture for Women (PSHW), which began on the site in 1911. Jane Bowne Haines, founder of the school, purchased a seventy-one-acre tract known as the McAlonan Farm and situated along Meetinghouse Road near Ambler Borough. A Bryn Mawr College graduate and a Quaker, Haines believed that the training of young women in horticulture and gardening provided them a worthy outlet for their energy and talents, which were denied a place in the workforce during the early years of the twentieth century, and also an opportunity to accomplish good for society by espousing the virtues of conservation and wise use of natural resources.

As an institution founded, funded, and operated by women, the Pennsylvania School of Horticulture for Women represented an important building block in the history of both American women and American gardening and horticulture. The National Women's Farm and Garden Association, a major

Right *Students in the Pennsylvania School of Horticulture for Women, which merged with Temple in 1958, work on garden designs for Professor James Bush-Brown's landscape design course circa 1947.*

Opposite *Temple Ambler Arboretum's historic formal gardens (top left) were inspired by schemes presented by Beatrix Jones Farrand, the first American woman licensed as a landscape architect, and developed by James Bush-Brown. The Ernesta Ballard Healing Garden (top right), named in honor of the first chair of the Ambler Board of Visitors, was installed by students and faculty of the Landscape Architecture and Horticulture Department and dedicated in 2009. The green roof atop the Sports Administration building at Ambler (bottom), made possible by a grant from PECO, manifests the spirit of environmental sustainability that is the hallmark of the Temple Ambler Campus.*

advocacy group for sustainable environmental gardening practices and for horticulture as a career path, was founded on the PSHW site in 1914.

Elizabeth Leighton Lee became director in 1915 and served until 1924, succeeded by Louise Carter Bush-Brown, who remained until 1952, providing the vision and energy to realize Jane Bowne Haines's original dream. Louise Carter Bush-Brown and her husband, James Bush-Brown, who taught at the school, published the number-one-selling general garden book, *America's Garden Book* (1939), which seven decades later remains the classic guide to American gardening. Ambler's formal gardens were created from designs by James Bush-Brown and Beatrix Jones Farrand, the first woman licensed as a landscape architect in the United States.

Several buildings were added, including greenhouses and a potting shed (1938), a dormitory (1929) for fifty students, and a library (1951). In 1940 a nearby property was purchased, bringing the PSHW property to approximately 151 acres. The PSHW declined after Louise Carter Bush-Brown's retirement, and in 1955 the PSHW proposed an affiliation with Temple University. By then the PSHW had sixty students and an endowment of $50,000, pledged as security for current loans. Temple's trustees refused the offer. In 1957 the PSHW changed its name to Ambler Junior College. The next year the offer to Temple was on the table again. By then PSHW enrollments had dropped to thirty-nine women, but the property was appreciating and expected to double in value in ten years.

In 1958 Temple University assumed the assets and liabilities of the PSHW and merged to become the Ambler Junior College of Temple University. Temple later bought thirty-six additional acres adjacent to the campus, bringing the total campus acreage to 187. Temple immediately used a part of the PSHW endowment, combined with Temple funds, to build a new multi-purpose building at Ambler, with five classrooms and a library, lunchroom, and recreation room. Opened in 1960 the building was called Bright Hall, named in honor of the mother of Jane Linn Erwin Bright, a PSHW graduate and a major contributor to the building's fund. Many of the PSHW students and instructors became prominent in the fields of gardening and horticulture. That tradition carried on after the PSHW affiliated with Temple. Two prime examples are Ernesta Ballard (AS SED 1954), president of the Pennsylvania Horticultural Society (PHS) from 1963 to 1981, and her successor, Jane Guest Pepper (AS SED 1974), who has headed the PHS since 1981. Among their other good works, Ballard and Pepper oversaw the expansion of the Philadelphia Flower Show into the world's largest and most prestigious event of its kind.

Temple did not purchase the Ambler land with the thought of one day relocating Main Campus operations there. Quite the contrary, by 1958 Temple had decided to remain in North Philadelphia. Ambler's allure was found in population studies indicating a steadily increasing movement of people into Bucks and Montgomery counties and, thus, educational needs to be met.

In 1961 the name was changed to the Ambler Campus of Temple University. Temple initially offered only an associate's degree, retaining the PSHW teachers and staff and continuing courses in horticulture, landscape design, and horse husbandry, but opening them to men as well. Several PSHW students remained and received Temple degrees. Horse husbandry was terminated in 1965, and all livestock were removed from the campus. In March 1963 Dr. Eugene Udell became dean, and he arranged to offer advanced courses in liberal arts and business. Udell's greater challenge came in the summer of 1963, when the former PSHW dormitory was destroyed by fire. A temporary dormitory, Cottage Hall, was quickly erected, and trustees authorized building a new dining hall and dormitories for 300 residents that were completed and opened in 1965.

FACT

Temple University's Ambler Campus is designated as an arboretum and features gardens that have won national awards in recent years.

Small classes, a rural setting, and individual instruction were all part of Ambler's charm. By 1965 enrollments reached 500. Presidents Gladfelter, Anderson, and Wachman were particularly enthusiastic about Ambler's prospects, seeing its location as a substantial opportunity for generating new revenues and for offsetting the unpredictable cycles of Main Campus enrollments. Ambler was in full bloom from 1967 to 1980, when the Music Festival thrived and several four-year programs were added. The campus underwent a substantial expansion during the eleven years of Dr. Sidney Halpern's deanship from 1971 to 1982. A pre-fabricated general-purpose building served as a library and computer center, and five temporary modular units helped meet a classroom shortage. During these years, when suburbanites found travel into Philadelphia an unwelcome prospect, as many as 6,500 students registered for at least one course each semester on the Ambler Campus or in rented classrooms at Upper Dublin High School.

Ambler found its champion in trustee F. Eugene "Fitz" Dixon Jr., who arranged funding through the will of George D. Widener for the construction of George D. Widener Hall, a 15,000-square-foot multi-purpose classroom building that opened in 1978. A two-story science facility and classroom building was dedicated in 1982, named for F. Eugene Dixon, who provided a substantial portion of the funds for its construction. The future of Ambler was debated often during the Anderson and Wachman years, with some supporting a semi-autonomous campus with faculty of its own and others insisting it should be a branch campus, with the Main Campus departments and colleges determining program offerings. The latter notion prevailed.

In 1987 the two remaining programs of the PSHW—landscape architecture and horticulture—were converted to four-year programs within a new department reporting to the dean of Ambler. The Department of Landscape Architecture and Horticulture retained and amplified the trailblazing contributions of the Pennsylvania School of Horticulture for Women, taking care to preserve and expand the formal gardens, requiring courses on the significance of landscape traditions, conserving PSHW's facilities, and commemorating the school's importance with an official historic marker placed on the campus in 2002 by the Pennsylvania Historic and Museum Commission. In 2002 the Department of Landscape Architecture and Horticulture was combined with Temple's Center for Sustainable Communities, established in 2000, and a new Department of Community and Regional

An aerial view of the academic facilities of the Temple University Ambler Campus (circa 2000) reveals the verdant beauty of Temple's "Green Campus." In 2009 Temple Ambler and Fort Washington enrolled over 3,800 students for courses in liberal arts, business, education, pharmaceutics, health professions, communications, and social work. The Ambler Campus is home to the School of Environmental Design.

Planning to form Ambler College, Temple's seventeenth school or college. In 2009 Ambler College was renamed the School of Environmental Design and administratively placed under the College of Liberal Arts.

Meanwhile, Ambler Campus underwent a number of improvements, beginning in 2000, when the Temple Ambler Campus was officially designated an arboretum, meeting the requirements of the American Association of Botanical Gardens and Arboreta. A new greenhouse followed in 2001. Substantial improvements were made to the formal gardens with the addition in 2008 of the Philip and Barbara Albright Winter Garden and with the installation in 2009 of the Ernesta Ballard Healing Garden. The gardens were named to honor Ernesta Ballard's and Phil Albright's volunteer leadership of the Ambler Board of Visitors and their generosity to the university.

In 2004 the university expended $4.5 million to relocate its NCAA Division I sports teams in baseball, softball, and men's and women's soccer to Ambler and to construct a new sports administration building. For Ambler students and faculty, the most important change came in the fall of 2006 with the opening of the 72,000-square-foot Learning Center, featuring advanced teaching technologies and modern equipment throughout.

With the establishment of the Center for Sustainable Communities and Department of Community and Regional Planning, combined with the existing programs in landscape architecture and horticulture, the Ambler Campus became the centerpiece of Temple's "Green" agenda in environmental stewardship. In 2003 Temple Ambler held its first EarthFest event, an outdoor educational celebration of Earth Day for students of all ages. By 2009 the event had grown substantially, attracting ninety-five exhibitors and over 12,000 actively engaged schoolchildren learning firsthand about the importance of conserving resources and sustaining the environment.

In addition to serving as Temple's "Green Campus," Temple University Ambler provides a range of programs in the liberal arts, business, education, and pre-professional training to meet the needs of residents in Montgomery and Bucks counties and particularly to offer a convenient, accessible location for returning adult students.

EarthFest, Temple Ambler's annual educational carnival in celebration of Earth Day, has attracted a total of more than 50,000 students to the campus since EarthFest was inaugurated in 2003. Students are eager to see and participate in educational exhibits, activities, and demonstrations intended to invest in them a respect for the environment and an obligation to sustain the earth's resources for future generations.

Fort Washington

Temple University's Fort Washington Campus, located in two buildings on Commerce Drive within the Fort Washington Industrial Park, opened in August 1997 as the Temple University Center for Advanced Technology (TUCAT) to promote liaison with area corporations and businesses. TUCAT proved short-lived, but a focus on graduate and professional education endured. Designed to serve adult professional graduate students and the educational needs of area businesses, Temple's Fort Washington services and facilities provide a corporate atmosphere in a convenient, professional setting.

Fort Washington's location, virtually at the hub of the region's impressive assemblage of major pharmaceutical companies, was suited for the School of Pharmacy's MS programs in Quality Assurance/Regulatory Affairs (QA/RA), which opened in 1999 and flourished thereafter. The campus also serves the Fox School of Business and Management Professional MBA program and the College of Education M.Ed. program in educational administration. In addition, Fort Washington serves as a satellite of Temple University Ambler, offering a lively set of non-credit and certificate programs and an active Lifelong Learning Society for senior learners. Fort Washington features easy automobile access from the Pennsylvania Turnpike, free parking next to the buildings, and a cordial, welcoming atmosphere for older students interested in personal enrichment or career advancement.

Temple University Center City

In January 1973 the Westinghouse Corporation made Temple a gift of a building at 1619 Walnut Street in center city Philadelphia. Not just any building, the KYW Building constructed in 1937 was the first ever built specifically for the new medium of television. The former Westinghouse Broadcasting Studio, it later housed the CBS affiliate KYW, and its studios were used in the 1950s and 1960s to telecast nationally syndicated shows, including the highly popular Mike Douglas and Ernie Kovacs shows. The radio, television, and film program in the School of Communications and Theater was already using the facility for classes when other departments began offering classes in the fall of 1973.

The new site was called Temple University Center City (TUCC). Enrollment growth was phenomenal, necessitating the lease of additional space in the twenty-five-story building across the street at 1616 Walnut Street. Fourteen of Temple's schools and colleges offered courses at TUCC. The Law School; the colleges of Liberal Arts, Communications and Theater, Education, and Music; and the Fox School of Business became significant presences at TUCC. In addition, several credit and non-credit institutes took root, including real estate, data processing, and court reporting. TUCC also became a major cultural center in downtown Philadelphia, with theater productions, art exhibits, poetry readings, and classic films at the Cinematheque Theater. In 1985 the Tyler School of Art Gallery opened on the ground floor of 1619 Walnut Street in space designed by the famed architect Robert Venturi. However, with renewed interest in the Main Campus, beginning in 1999, course offerings and enrollments at TUCC dwindled.

In need of more modern space and greater technological capabilities, Temple sold the building at 1619 Walnut Street and did not renew the lease at 1616 Walnut Street. Instead, Temple leased six floors at 1515 Market Street, authorizing $14 million for a three-phase renovation for classrooms, computer laboratories, a bookstore, and cultural performance spaces. William E. Parshall, the new director of Temple University Center City, directed the renovations and the relocation of the campus, which was ready for students in the fall of 2001.

Temple University Center City is the adult education destination in center city. Surrounded by the home offices of major national corporations and just across the street from City Hall, TUCC is near the city's cultural and entertainment resources. TUCC also serves as a social, cultural, and continuing education center for retired center city residents, several hundred of whom regularly attend programs sponsored by the Temple Association of Retired Professionals (TARP). TUCC's goal is to serve the credit and non-credit education needs of area corporations and their employees and to provide enrichment opportunities for Philadelphia-area residents.

Temple University Harrisburg

Temple has been a presence in central Pennsylvania at various locations for more than forty years, beginning as a cooperative venture with other colleges and universities in offering classes at the Harrisburg Center, the site of a former military academy. Temple shared classrooms and administrative space with Pennsylvania State University, the University of Pennsylvania, and Elizabethtown and Lebanon Valley colleges. In the 1980s the institutions decided to go their separate ways.

After operating for several years at downtown sites near the state capital, Temple moved in 1998 to 234 Strawberry Square, a retail business complex located in the heart of downtown Harrisburg, close to Pennsylvania's capitol and nearby state associations and businesses. Temple leased additional space in 2000 for a library, computer center, and more classrooms for graduate professional degree programs in education, social work, and community and regional planning, plus a graduate certificate in play therapy. Temple University Harrisburg caters to the busy adult, providing a convenient evening and weekend course schedule. A telecommunications suite permits students to enroll in selected classes taught at Temple's other campuses. Harrisburg also serves as a base for other Temple programs offered at extension sites in Lancaster, Huntingdon, Pottsville, and Dallastown.

Diversity University

Known and respected for the breadth of its tolerance, Temple had a transforming influence on other institutions because of its democratic spirit and its history of offering higher-education opportunities, regardless of race, gender, religious background, or station in life. Temple led the way in fostering multiple perspectives and taking enormous pride in the diverse nature of its student body, faculty, and staff. By the time the university was chartered in 1888, several women had enrolled in classes, and four women walked with the first graduating class in 1892. The School of Medicine was the first coeducational medical college in Pennsylvania that awarded the MD degree to women and to African Americans.

Throughout its history Temple purposely cultivated an aura of diversity. Even during the growth years from 1999 to 2009, when Temple reached out to the suburbs, it steadfastly sustained diversity as a goal and became even more diverse, in terms of both gender and racial ethnicity. The 2006 edition of *The Best 361 Colleges*, the annual guide from *The Princeton Review,* ranked Temple number two on its list of most diverse student populations. In the guide's main entry on Temple, one student was quoted as saying, "We call it Diversity University." Other students called Temple a "huge melting pot" in which "everyone's differences become their connection to other people."

None of this occurred by chance. All was done intentionally, dating to Temple's founding years and carefully expanded upon from generation to generation. Temple has always welcomed talented students of every background. Temple's School of Medicine has achieved some particularly notable results in affirmative action, recently ranking third in the nation in enrolling first-year-medical minority

Opposite *In 2001 Temple University Center City moved to a new location at 1515 Market Street, conveniently located across from Philadelphia's City Hall.*

What do Temple's students say about the value of diversity?

Here is what Steve Smith (2010), an Honors student in psychology and political science, had to say: "I am from a small town, and I always wanted something with a little more excitement, and a little more diversity, than what my hometown offered. I figured Temple was the place for me, and I was right. There are people from all walks of life, races, religions, and backgrounds, with all kinds of different thoughts, opinions, and attitudes. I am in the heart of the melting pot, and I am pretty excited about it."

"On all sides the fences fall which formerly hemmed a woman's life into such a narrow sphere, and universal social and business equality is the aim of all classes. If any woman wishes an honorable station let her try to obtain it. The sea will divide."

Russell H. Conwell

students. Only two predominantly black institutions (Howard and Meharry) enrolled more minorities. Temple has taken pride in its accessibility to all who were qualified and motivated, without restrictions. In the fall of 2008 nearly one-third of Temple's entering freshmen students reported their ethnicity as African American, Hispanic, Asian, or Native American. The fastest-growing minority groups among entering students since 2000 are Asians and Hispanics. However, an increasing number of Temple students (around 10 percent) list "other" when asked about their ethnicity, suggesting a diminishing concern among young people for such identifiers.

In 1971 President Anderson established the Office of Affirmative Action, charged with ensuring university compliance with government directives and assisting in the recruitment of minority employees. At first ineffective, the office expanded its reach over the years, and Temple established more energetic procedures to recruit minority and women faculty members with increasing success in recent years. In the fall 2002 semester, minorities constituted 15.7 percent of the total faculty of all ranks. By the fall of 2008, the number had grown to 21.5 percent, or 392 in 1,826 members of the university's full-time instructional staff.

Gender Equity

Temple began as a college for "working men," but Russell Conwell, an advocate of the rights of women to obtain "an honorable station," quickly modified the charter to include "working women" and their children. For the first 100 years, more men than women attended Temple, but in the fall 1988 semester the sea divided, and each year thereafter women students outnumbered men. By the fall 2008 semester 19,516 women attended Temple—more than double Villanova University's total enrollment that fall—constituting 54.4 percent of Temple's total enrollment. Since the late 1980s women have received a majority of the degrees conferred annually. Women received 49.1 percent of the bachelor's degrees conferred in 1987, rising to 56 percent in 1997 and to 57.9 percent in 2007. Women also now receive the majority of Temple's master's and doctoral degrees and are gaining each year in the number of first professional degrees. Only 38.9 percent of Temple's first professional degrees were awarded to women in 1987, but by 2007 the number had grown to 49.4 percent.

The women's rights movement of the late 1960s and early 1970s had its counterpart advocates at Temple, led by a spirited and dedicated group of faculty and staff who organized the Temple Women's Rights Coalition (TWRC). Drawing on 250 persons, counting males and females among its members, the TWRC in 1971 proposed to establish a special commission to bring to light any discriminatory practices based on sex at Temple and to ensure compliance with new federal directives. Faced with mounting pressure, President Anderson basically co-opted the TWRC idea and that year appointed his own committee, named the Presidential Advisory Committee on Employment Practices Related to Women at Temple (PACOW). After nearly two years of study and deliberation, PACOW reported the existence of gender inequities in both rank and academic salary and the conspicuous under-representation of females at the higher ranks of the university. PACOW's recommendations prompted a stronger commitment to affirmative action by the university's officers, improved data collection to identify inequities, and greater attention to recruitment, promotion, and job-posting procedures.

Over the last thirty years the proportions of women holding full-time, tenured, and tenure-track faculty positions at Temple have steadily increased. In 1977 women constituted only 22.7 percent of the full-time faculty. By 1987 the proportion increased to 24.6 percent and then to 30.8 percent in 1997. In the fall of 2008, women made up 34.8 percent (636 in 1,826) of the full-time instructional staff.

One of the outgrowths of the women's movement of the 1970s was the establishment of a women's studies program in the College of Liberal Arts and Sciences. Thanks to the leadership and advocacy of Professors Rachel Blau DuPlessis, Sonia Sanchez, Julia Ericksen, Sally Mitchell, Denise O'Brien, and Louise Kidder, a women's studies program won approval by the board of trustees in October 1978. It began as a certificate program and then by 1980 became a full major leading to a BA degree. Recently expanded and renamed, it is now called Women's Studies and Lesbian, Gay, Bisexual, and Transgender Studies, offering courses that analyze gender, sexuality, and sexual orientation as they are understood by various disciplines and in cross-cultural perspectives.

Diversity Initiatives

The intentional nature of Temple's strategic approach for ensuring diversity and its impact on other institutions were perhaps no better illustrated than by the Liacouras administration's approach to building a new Temple University Hospital in 1983. An affirmative action plan—known as the Temple Plan and later widely emulated by other institutions, including the City of Philadelphia when constructing a new Convention Center—was created to ensure fair opportunity in contracts for women and minority firms, employment for minorities living in Philadelphia and near the hospital, and acceptable participation rates by women and minority workers in the skilled trades. The plan set an initial target of a 33 percent minority participation rate. When completed, 38 percent of the nearly 1 million work hours and 35 percent of the dollar value of all construction contracts went to female and minority workers. The Temple Plan demonstrated the power of an institution to effect profound social change.

Temple is fortunate to house the Charles L. Blockson Afro-American Collection, one of the nation's leading university-based resource centers for the study of the history and culture of people of African descent. Charles Blockson, noted author and bibliophile, chose to place his collection at Temple University in 1984 because of the university's diverse student body and its location in the heart of the African American community in North Philadelphia. The Blockson Collection consists of rare first-edition texts, slave narratives, art, three-dimensional artifacts, books, manuscript collections, pamphlets, broadsides, photographs, and rare ephemera, numbering over 500,000 significant items in African American history. Blockson served as curator of his collection, which was provided a highly visible home in Sullivan Hall, directly beneath the president's office. Blockson authored many books, including *The Underground Railroad* and *Liberty Bell Era*. In 2005 he stepped down as curator, succeeded by Diane Turner, who earned her PhD in history from Temple.

Another noteworthy initiative in the celebration of America's diversity by Temple University was the creation in 1990 of the Myer and Rosaline Feinstein Center for American Jewish History. Founded in cooperation with the Philadelphia Chapter of the American Jewish Committee, the Feinstein Center was dedicated to promoting the study of the Jewish experience in America and to encouraging and nurturing a new generation of scholars to devote their talents and energies to researching and teaching American Jewish history. Dr. Murray Friedman, noted author of works on Jewish history and a member of the U.S. Civil Rights Commission, served as founding director until his death in 2005.

Community Service Projects

Temple from its beginning has embraced and sustained a culture of community service, an ethos that places service to others above self. Students, faculty, and staff volunteer more than 35,000 hours of service annually in Philadelphia and beyond. They contribute their services year-round, taking part in community cleanups, medical programs, income tax preparation, legal assistance,

TEMPLE NOTABLE
Charles L. Blockson

Born in Norristown, Pennsylvania, Charles Leroy Blockson excelled in football and track, earning him a scholarship to Penn State University. After college he served in the army and opened a janitorial service. An inveterate reader, collector, and student of African American history, Blockson became an adviser for human relations and cultural affairs at the Norristown Area High School, taught African American history, helped found the Afro-American Historical and Cultural Museum in Philadelphia in 1976, and launched a project to erect sixty-four historical markers commemorating the contribution of African Americans to Philadelphia. As one of the foremost experts on the Underground Railroad, he is a prolific researcher and author, whose writings include the seminal *Black Genealogy* (1976), a series of profound African American narratives in *The Underground Railroad* (1987), and an illustrated map of the railroad for *National Geographic*. Wherever he travels Blockson exudes the Temple spirit of diversity, equality, and accessibility.

business consulting, and much more. In its immediate neighborhoods, the university has established training programs and hosted job fairs to support local residents and has begun a home ownership program to help Main Campus and Health Sciences employees put down roots in the community where they work.

A 2008 survey of Temple's community service activities identified 325 community service programs university-wide and hundreds of individuals contributing personal services in the community. The university provides a broad range of community programs, including hiring and housing initiatives, educational support, health services, arts and cultural activities, and volunteer efforts to assist individuals and community groups.

Each of Temple's schools and colleges has contributed to the culture of service. The School of Social Work was founded on the principle of public service, and its Center for Social Policy & Community Development (CSPCD) has been actively serving the community for more than forty years. Similarly, the African-American Studies Department and Pan-African Studies Community Education Program (PASCEP) in the College of Liberal Arts sprang from Temple's dual commitment to diversity and community service (see Chapter 5).

In the fall of 2009 approximately 250 volunteers, including many Temple students, performed 100 Hours of Power, a service marathon to revitalize the playground and recreation center located at Twelfth Street and Susquehanna Avenue near Temple's Main Campus. The volunteer effort was part of a year-long commitment called MLK 365, organized by Temple's University Community Collaborative of Philadelphia (UCCP) and directed by political science professor Barbara Ferman. UCCP was formed in 1997 to leverage the university's human capital resources to assist neighborhood-based organizations in their community-building efforts. UCCP also sponsors Temple Youth VOICES, a mentorship program involving college students assisting young people in urban communities to develop the critical skills necessary to navigate their environments more effectively.

Another among many examples of academically oriented community service is the College of Engineering program called Philadelphia FIRST (For Inspiration and Recognition of Service and Technology), which has promoted involvement in science and technology among high school students since 1989. In the program, Temple engineering students team with counterparts from an area high school to build robots that vie with entries from other schools. Temple's Tyler School of Art sponsors Art in the Community and Artworks in Different Places, demonstrating the role artists can play in the life of an urban community. Artists work in cooperation with local social service, educational, and cultural groups, involving the communities in workshops, exhibitions, and performance. Temple's architecture program formed the Urban Workshop in 2002 to engage the community in exploring complex design problems that emerge in restructuring neighborhoods.

Extending back to the 1890s, Temple has delivered community health care services in many forms. Besides offering the wide range of clinical medical services provided directly through Temple's schools of dentistry, medicine, pharmacy, and podiatry (see above), Temple has served the community through its research centers. One example is the Center for Obesity Research and Education (CORE). A particular focus of CORE is a greater understanding of the causes, treatment, and prevention of obesity among minorities of lower socioeconomic status, among whom obesity is more prevalent. Further, Temple's medical researchers found that people in North Philadelphia suffer from preventable and treatable health conditions at a disproportionately high rate. In response, the Center for Minority Health and Health Disparities (CMHHD) has developed more effective diagnostic,

Equal Opportunity

In 1993 Temple University was the first university to receive the U.S. Department of Labor's E.V.E. Award (Exemplary Voluntary Efforts) in recognition of Temple's innovative programs advancing equal opportunities for employees, including minorities, women, and individuals with disabilities.

treatment, and prevention strategies for this underserved population by working with community-based health programs and serving as a partner and resource for disease prevention and health promotion.

At one point Temple was directly involved in the education and training of the developmentally disabled, known as the mentally retarded back in 1974, when the Pennsylvania Department of Welfare constructed the Woodhaven Center, an entirely new facility for multiple-handicapped, mentally retarded individuals. Temple was contracted to operate the site. Woodhaven was intended as an alternative to "warehousing" retarded people, sometimes for their entire lives, in state asylums or mental institutions. The center was located on a seventy-two-acre tract on Southampton Road near Woodhaven Road in Northeast Philadelphia. The 300 residents were housed in small, cottage-type facilities, where they received attention from a staff of 600 Temple employees. To operate Woodhaven, Temple drew on the talents and skills of faculty in fourteen departments from six schools and colleges. Even the College of Music was involved: Professor Ken Bruscia, who joined the Temple faculty in 1974, helped establish the clinical music therapy program at Woodhaven.

Dr. Valaida Smith Walker served as the first commissioner of mental retardation for Southeast Pennsylvania and the first director of the Woodhaven Center, one of nine state-funded institutions for people with developmental disabilities in Pennsylvania. Walker later served as chair of special education, associate dean of the College of Education, and vice provost for administration. Temple's Institute on Developmental Disabilities, established in 1974 and housed in the College of Education, coordinated the direct provision of services and training at Woodhaven. Since the abandonment of the concept and the closure of Woodhaven in the 1980s, the institute has mirrored the changes in the field of developmental disabilities, evolving from a specialized-service model to a model of self-determination and individualized supports in the community, concentrating on research and advocacy. The institute today is one of the sixty-seven University Centers for Excellence in Developmental Disabilities Education, Research and Service funded by the Administration on Developmental Disabilities, U.S. Department of Health and Human Services.

Several Temple research centers have combined research in public policy with the hands-on delivery of services to the urban community. A brief sampling includes the Temple University Institute on Aging, which has served as the focal point for Temple activities in the field of aging, promoting interdisciplinary education, research, and outreach since 1978. The Center for Intergenerational Learning has created opportunities for youth and elders to contribute to their communities to promote productive aging since 1979. Young people provide respite services to frail elderly and their families, conduct oral history interviews with nursing home residents, and teach English to older immigrants and refugees. Older adults serve as literacy tutors, mentors, parent outreach workers, oral historians, after-school volunteers, and child care aides.

The Temple University Center for Research in Human Development and Education (CRHDE), established in 1986 by the late Dr. Margaret Wang, brings together resources in the College of Education and the School District of Philadelphia to research the problems of children, youth, and families challenged by the circumstances of economic and educational disadvantage. Temple University's Institute for Public Affairs, based in the College of Liberal Arts, conducts, supports, and disseminates interdisciplinary research to inform and improve public policy, focusing particularly on Philadelphia, the greater metropolitan area, and the Commonwealth of Pennsylvania. Temple's Institute for Survey Research (ISR), founded in 1967, is one of only three university-based survey-research facilities in the United States capable of conducting large-scale, in-person surveys representative of the entire

U.S. household population. Accordingly, ISR has made numerous contributions to policy planning at local, state, and national levels.

Many Temple students today are actively engaged in community and social service. Instead of going to Florida during spring break in 2009, several students opted to work for Habitat for Humanity. In past years students have responded to natural disasters such as Hurricane Katrina or volunteered assistance to community service organizations. Temple encourages students to engage in community service from their first day on campus. Each fall before the beginning of classes freshmen volunteer one day for FreshServe, a community cleanup program to help clear streets, sidewalks, and public spaces of trash and debris. In recognition of these exemplary service efforts, Temple was named in 2009 to the President's Higher Education Community Service Honor Roll by the U.S. Corporation for National and Community Service.

Alumni Association

The General Alumni Association (GAA) of Temple University—the umbrella organization for the alumni associations in Temple's schools and colleges that is now called the Temple University Alumni Association—was launched with some fanfare by President Beury in June 1926 (see Chapter 2). However, few university resources were allocated to the effort, which relied almost entirely upon alumni volunteers, the most important being Raymond L. Burkley (BS EDU 1928). As an undergraduate at Temple, Burkley was involved in many campus activities, serving as president of Student Council, managing the band, chairing various organizations, and participating on the swimming team. He also served as an unpaid, part-time director of alumni affairs, continuing in that role after graduation while holding a teaching position at Girard College. In November 1931 Burkley's volunteer contributions were formalized when he was elected executive alumni secretary, a part-time position that became full-time two years later.

In 1996 the Raymond L. Burkley Alumni Center moved from center city to Mitten Hall. Shown below at the ribbon-cutting ceremony are (left to right) Mary Connell, vice president of the Alumni Association; Judge Theodore Davis, Alumni Association president; Executive Vice President James White; and John MacDonald, executive director of the Alumni Association.

Under Burkley's tireless, dedicated direction the Alumni Association took form, establishing the annual Founder's Dinner and Homecoming celebrations, creating distinguished alumni awards, setting up regional clubs, and endowing many scholarships and book funds. A beloved figure, affectionately known as Dean of Alumni, Burkley retired as executive director on January 31, 1966, after thirty-five years of full-time service to Temple and the alumni. Regrettably, he passed away just a few months later. In many respects Burkley devoted his entire adult life to Temple and to its alumni. The 1927 *Templar* described Mr. Burkley as "a true Temple man, and his Alma Mater is proud of her son who has given so unstintingly of his time, efforts, and even health itself, that she might be exalted."

Burkley was succeeded by John H. MacDonald (BS SBM 1961; M.Ed. EDU 1966). As an undergrad, MacDonald thoroughly enjoyed his years at Temple and was much involved in campus activities. He joined the staffs of the *Temple News* and WRTI and was active in a fraternity. Temple remained in his blood. After graduation he took a job as administrative assistant to Vice President Earl Yeomans and went on to earn his master's degree from Temple. He was appointed as Burkley's assistant and then as his successor in 1966. From 1966 to 2004 the friendly, outgoing MacDonald was the personification of Temple alumni affairs, organizing forty Founder's Dinners, making each a showcase affair, all the while winning the support of thousands of alumni and broadening Temple's reach.

Deborah W. Fowlkes joined Temple in 2005, coming to Temple from Duke University and inheriting the weighty task of carrying on the Burkley-MacDonald legacy. In 2006 the GAA underwent an administrative makeover, revamping its bylaws and changing its name to the Temple University Alumni Association. The Founder's Dinner was expanded to an Alumni Weekend, an extended celebration each spring when the campus and its amenities are showcased to all Temple alumni and friends. By 2009 the total number of living alumni surpassed 260,000 worldwide, many of whom were eager to learn more about the substantial changes at Temple and to reconnect with their alma mater.

Through the years alumni have been active contributors to university governance through informal advising, service on search committees, and participation on ad hoc committees at various levels of university administration. Temple's board of trustees, beginning in the 1960s, routinely elected immediate past-presidents of the Alumni Association to one term as a university trustee. In 2003 the trustees decided as a matter of policy to elect the sitting alumni president to a full term on the board. To involve alumni more closely in university affairs and to draw upon their wise counsel and good services, Temple in 2001 established a board of visitors for each of its schools and colleges and for academic entities, such as Paley Library and Temple University Press. Alumni fill the majority of seats on the boards of visitors. With the same objectives in mind, President Hart has made extensive use of a president's advisory committee as a means of broadening Temple's leadership and maximizing the human resources of Temple's alumni and friends.

Inspired by Fowlkes, the Alumni Association extended its outreach, expanding its Senior Scholars program to allow older alumni to audit Temple classes, offering educational foreign travel packages, and establishing Shared Interest Groups—such as the Temple University Black Alumni Alliance (TUBAA), Temple University Young Alumni (TUYA), and Temple LGBT (Lesbian, Gay, Bisexual, and Transgender) Alumni—and Affinity Reunions, for groups such as the *Temple News*, University Honors Program, Temple Rome, and Diamond Marching Band. In recent years Temple has also conducted a series of highly successful events known as Temple on the Road, featuring faculty lectures and a university update from President Ann Weaver Hart. President Hart has greeted Temple alumni in scores of venues across the country and around the world, including Rome, Tokyo, and Beijing, proving again that Temple Owls are everywhere.

The Spirit of Temple

The Spirit of Temple is found in the noble sacrifices of those dedicated, caring persons who served for the greater benefit of all. Many unsung heroes and heroines, following the model of Laura Carnell, quietly labored to keep Temple running. Many, like Laura Carnell, were Temple graduates who remained at the university and literally dedicated their lives to Temple. There are too many unsung Temple heroes and heroines to list and properly recognize in this small space, but two—Marie B. Cooney and Theodore (Ted) Quedenfeld—epitomize the spirit of Temple.

9/11

Everyone alive on September 11, 2001, vividly recalls the day. People remember where they were and who they were with. For Temple students, September 11 was the equivalent of the bombing

The Spirit of Temple: Sacrifice, Dedication, Loyalty

Marie B. Cooney (BS EDU 1941) epitomized the spirit of Temple. She served Temple unstintingly for forty years in a number of capacities and was assistant vice president for budget and administration in the provost's office at the time of her death in 1986. A conference room in Conwell Hall named in her honor commemorates her selfless, devoted service.

Theodore (Ted) Quedenfeld (BS EDU 1960; M.Ed. EDU 1962) earned varsity letters in three sports, served as Temple's top athletic trainer, and in 1974 played a key role in establishing the Temple Sports Medicine Center, the first university-based sports medicine center in the United States. Quedenfeld trained over 300 certified athletic trainers, substantially advancing professional standards for the field. He was also known for his ebullient personality and wonderful sense of humor. At the time of his premature passing in 2001, Ted's total association with Temple, counting his student days, extended over nearly fifty years of his life.

of Pearl Harbor and the assassination of JFK for previous generations, marking a turning point in their lives. Joseph Dittmar (BS SCT 1978) miraculously escaped from the 105th floor of Two World Trade Center, but no Temple alumni are known to have lost their lives in the 9/11 terrorist attacks. Lew Serviss (BS SCT 1976) was among the many Temple alumni responding to the crisis. Serviss, who was then the *New York Times* metro chief copy editor, worked around the clock to keep the newspaper rolling off the presses and keep New York and the rest of the world informed of what happened only a few minutes from his workplace.

On the campus President David Adamany reminded all in the Temple community that "Respect for all people is at the very core of Temple's purpose and history. At this difficult time, let us act with special care to reaffirm Temple's values." Students reacted with a mixture of solemnity and consternation, quietly availing themselves of impromptu teach-ins and symposia organized by the faculty. An all-day discussion on September 13 helped students begin to understand the context of 9/11 and to put it into perspective, acknowledging that none of their lives would be the same thereafter.

Alumni Remembrances

Recent graduates will always remember 9/11. All of Temple's alumni have special remembrances of their associations with Temple. Here are a few.

Temple opened its arms to many who were the first in their families to attend college. Eli Hoffman (BS SBM 1959), whose father emigrated from Russia to the United States, grew up in Newark, New Jersey. The first in his family to seek a college education, Hoffman was determined to be an accountant. He enrolled at Temple in February 1956, because, as he said, "Temple was one of the few universities that admitted freshmen in mid-year. . . . I applied, I was accepted, and that's where I went." Vince Manze (BS SCT 2001) is proud of his "blue-collar upbringing" and his first-generation Italian American parents, describing himself as "a Conshohocken boy" who was "born and raised first of all in Norristown and then we moved to the richer suburbs of Conshohocken, where I lived my whole life."

Before the Student Activities Center was built, many first-generation commuter students gathered between classes in Mitten Hall. Alums from the 1950s and 1960s remembered that groups informally staked out sections of the Great Court. African American students, for example, tended to cluster in the western alcove. "We had a South Philly contingent," John Tolomeo (BBA SBM 1977) recalled. "And we resided at the center oak table at Mitten Hall. You had to have an invitation to put your books or even just 'hang' with the South Philly guys." But Tolomeo fondly remembered "making many international friends" who were invited to hang with the South Philly guys.

Alumni recollections frequently include comments on Temple's diversity and tolerance, recognizing the importance of Temple's role in broadening America's social contours. For example, basketball great Harold C. ("Hal") Lear Jr. (BS SBM 1956) recalled the difficulty that he and other African American teammates faced when traveling into the South to compete against the top teams in the region. "We [the basketball team] would travel south by train. It was a lot of fun because we would take these overnighters and we would be . . . hanging out having fun and sleeping in these rooms with berths." However, in "the days before Martin Luther King," as Lear put it, the team often faced hostile segregated crowds in games against some southern universities. "The fans would be dressed up in confederate clothes, screaming and hollering [and] Blacks weren't allowed in to see the game."

The value of studying and living alongside persons of diverse cultures, ethnicity, and beliefs was nicely summarized by Kathleen Desmond (MSW SSA 1989): "Professors challenged me beyond my own frame of reference and forced me to consider other possibilities. My classes forced me to confront my own biases, prejudices and misconceptions about populations and communities. I came to a place where I had a better understanding of difference. That was Temple's thrust for all of us, to expose us to different experiences and expand our point of view."

Countless romances and marriages have been spawned on the Temple campus. Laura Brooks Golanoski (BS CHP 1985) recalled, "My husband and I met and fell in love while we were students at Temple in 1984." Brooks Golanoski, a nursing student living in Jones Hall at the Health Sciences Center, met her husband, Lee Golanoski (B.Arch. TYL 1989), when he was assigned a room at the medical campus because of Main Campus overcrowding. "We are thankful for this glitch, which allowed us to meet," she said.

More than a few former students returned to Temple for their weddings. David Murphy (BS SCT 1985), meteorologist for Philadelphia's 6ABC, and historian Barbara Horvath (BA CLA 1987) decided to "come back to Temple," where they met, for their 1987 wedding in Mitten Hall and a Diamond Club reception. Similarly, Rachel Oliver Gionta (BS SCT 2005; MS EDU 2008) and her husband, Matthew Gionta (BS THM 2004), fondly recalled their courtship when Temple students, and so they also elected a Mitten Hall wedding and reception, complete with a Temple "T" groom's cake decorated with cherry and white icing.

The most cherished memories of other alumni are those reflecting their individual journeys of personal discovery and professional development. Christine Mello (BS MUS 2006) spoke for many: "Temple was the place where I learned who I truly was as a professional and as a person. I truly grew into myself during my years at the university, and I received the tools to fully realize my goals and dreams and make it completely possible. Temple is an amazing place!" Thomas Madden (BS SCT 1962), a reporter for the *Philadelphia Inquirer* and eventually the owner of his own public relations firm, said, "I'll always be grateful for the liftoff I got from Temple into journalism." Reflecting on his superb professors in the Boyer College of Music and Dance, Kirk Muspratt (B.Mus. MUS 1978), a successful musician and conductor, said, "Temple taught me everything I know about music. I hear music professor Alexander Fiorillo in my ear when I'm conducting, even after years of other experiences." Or take the example of Ursula Gerhart (BA CLA 1948), who said, "Temple had a great English and philosophy department in its liberal arts studies. That, as well as the neighborhood, inspired me to become a social worker, and later a social work professor."

Temple alumni speak eloquently of the importance of their Temple educations in preparing them for life. Loretta Duckworth (BA CLA 1962; MA CLA 1965; MA TYL 1992), former Alumni Association president and a Temple trustee, stated, "I'm a true believer in the liberal arts. That kind of education is priceless. If you know how to think and how to be rational, you can do anything you want to do. I find that I can hold my own and that I'm an educated person. Temple did that for me." The final words belong to Dr. Sandra Harmon-Weiss (BA CLA 1971; MD MED 1974): "Temple influenced my life profoundly. It enabled me to choose among promising career paths and gave me excellent role models and mentors. At Temple, I became engaged in a lifelong search for learning, open to innovation and new challenges."

Chapter 9
Access to Excellence

Temple started with the man, the speech, and the "Temple Idea." Russell Conwell's amorphous dream was built on his aspirations of meeting every social need he could, whether it was the community's spiritual and health care needs or its comprehensive educational needs. A builder and a dreamer, Conwell took risks, for he was truly an entrepreneur, a captain of erudition.

TEMPLE UNIVERSITY TIMELINE

2006
Ann Weaver Hart is named Temple's ninth president.

2007
Access to Excellence campaign is launched.

2009
President Hart introduces her *Temple 20/20* development plan.

Page 280 *The half-rose window of Russell Conwell's Temple (aka the Baptist Temple) reopened in 2010 as a performing arts center.*

TEMPLE NOTABLE
Shirley M. Tilghman

Shirley M. Tilghman earned her Ph.D. from Temple in 1975. She took office as Princeton University's nineteenth president in June 2001, becoming the first woman to hold the position and the second female president in the Ivy League. A molecular biologist who served on Princeton's faculty for fifteen years before being elected president, Tilghman is renowned for her pioneering research in mammalian developmental genetics. During post-doctoral studies at the National Institutes of Health, she made a number of groundbreaking discoveries while participating in the cloning of the first mammalian gene. In keeping with the Temple spirit and tradition of supporting diversity and access, Tilghman is also known for her national leadership on behalf of women in science and for promoting efforts to make the early careers of young scientists as meaningful and productive as possible.

Conwell's desire to provide free education, open to all—"Do whatever you must," he told Laura Carnell—to meet and accommodate the demand for education, was soon compromised by the realities of the marketplace and a lack of resources. He guided Temple through growing pains that sometimes left him overwhelmed by higher education's costs and complexities. Failing to land a large-scale philanthropic donor—though he tried mightily—Conwell and his successors nonetheless became honor-bound by the persistence of his demand that the burden of paying for education should fall as lightly as possible on students.

The consequence, of course, was the creation of a durable gap between Temple's ambitions and its abilities to meet them. When other universities raised their tuition and fees, Temple clung to the idea of taxing itself first, lowering costs, and achieving greater operational economies rather than encumbering students. Hopefully, alumni beneficiaries of Temple's resolute support of this simple maxim may now appreciate the faculty and staff sacrifices made on their behalf throughout Temple's history.

Conwell's complex bequest is best expressed by his frequent assertions that greatness consists of serving the community in which one lives and accomplishing noble deeds with limited means. When reality intruded and his splendid experiment seemed destined to fail, Conwell fortuitously turned in desperation to the governor of Pennsylvania. Over time the commonwealth assumed a share of Conwell's self-imposed responsibilities for higher education, medical education, and health care for residents of North Philadelphia. By Conwell's death in 1925, Temple University had established a physical framework, a sidewalk campus of Broad Street row houses, with College and Conwell halls in place and a third building that became Carnell Hall. Programs in medicine, dentistry, law, liberal arts, business, and education were also firmly established. Conwell had placed Temple on a sound footing.

The relationship between Temple and the commonwealth, established by Conwell in 1911, ebbed and flowed through the years, yet it made all the difference to Temple's success, providing assistance with operating expenses and keeping the university solvent. But Temple operated on the edge, carefully balancing costs against available resources, keeping tuition affordable, but remaining unable for most of its existence to build reserves or endowments.

The Depression years tested Temple, but it emerged stronger, without retrenchment or layoffs, with an enhanced academic reputation and increased enrollments, an improved physical plant, and its mission intact. By then Temple could claim only a sidewalk, row house campus, but it was a campus all the same—one that sparkled with activity and enthused students. In addition, Temple was a recognizable and proud entity, with a solid identification and far-flung reputation. It possessed distinguished academic programs and renowned faculty scholars, proud alumni, and all the accoutrements of the collegiate ideal, including sororities and fraternities as well as a mascot, songs, and marching band to cheer a winning football program and a national championship basketball team. When the world was again struck by war, Temple contributed substantially to the American effort and emerged in a world of brighter opportunity, yet one filled with enormous challenges.

Temple's middle passage from 1945 to 1965 was a transition era, a time for recharting its voyage. To respond to the postwar challenges, Temple greeted thousands of returning GIs, managing to acquire and fill every available classroom. An even greater challenge, however, was being caught in the midst of one of the twentieth century's most important periods of change, the transformation of America and Philadelphia from an industrial to a postindustrial society and to a service economy.

North Philadelphia changed overnight as white flight to the suburbs and urban blight reduced the neighborhoods around Temple and tinged the university's reputation.

Temple thought briefly and seriously of reducing its presence in North Philadelphia and building a new liberal arts and undergraduate campus in the suburbs. Realizing that location was destiny, however, Temple renewed its commitment to serve the community, to improve and revitalize the neighborhoods, and to continue to serve its neighbors, at least to the extent that the university's resources permitted. With the support of the city and the commonwealth, Temple emerged into a period of rapid growth and physical expansion, as each year new enrollment milestones were surpassed and new buildings appeared at the Main, Health Sciences, and Ambler campuses.

After its middle passage Temple accepted its limited abilities to meet every educational need and focused on its importance as an institution of higher education, emphasizing undergraduate, graduate, and professional degree programs. Temple closed the High School and Community College and, in return for state affiliation and support, carved a niche as one of the growing "multiversities" in American higher education. In many ways Temple was ideally positioned for its new multiversity role; it had, after all, been providing a wide range of services and meeting many diverse needs for most of its existence.

Where the university was less prepared, however, was in responding to the postwar growth of federal support for scientific research. While the Medical School and Temple Hospital had kept pace with innovations in medical and biological research, the Main Campus science programs lacked the physical facilities, laboratories, and support systems necessary to be competitive in the grantsmanship world that pivoted around federal support of scientific research. Only belatedly did Temple find the resources to build faculty, facilities, and services capable of competing. Temple has been playing catch-up ever since in a game dominated from the outset and still today by a select group of elite institutions.

Temple's growth did not come easily or without tension. Neighbors initially saw no benefit in Temple's expansion and shared only indirectly in its success. They saw only steady encroachment on their properties and their spirits. The charrette agreement between Temple and the surrounding community limited the university's ambitions for further expansion but reawakened its sense of social obligation. Temple can point with pride to its record of community public service and its promotion of social change, combining an unprecedented dedication of resources to serving its communities with a determination to train graduates to better the societies in which they live and work.

Nor was Temple immune from the disruptions in America spreading across civil society and localized in universities and cities in the 1960s. The new, expanded version of Temple University struck many as too large, too impersonal, and too remote from their personal ideals. At Temple and other large universities during the era, the bureaucratic scale and corporate style of the omnibus, multiversity tended to alienate and repel. Students, faculty, and neighbors took up the cudgels of spirited advocacy, as many believed the sheer size and scale of the modern university neglected its social obligations and was by definition anathema to the cherished values of individualism and personal quest. Still, Temple emerged wiser and tempered by the disruptions, a more open institution with greater transparency in its governance and policy apparatus and a renewed commitment to serve the community and its wider needs.

"As educators, we must confront the simple fact: Globalization changes everything. If we do not internationalize our teaching, our research, and our community outreach, we will be increasingly left behind in a dynamic and changing world."

Ann Weaver Hart, President

Temple's strength rests historically on the exceptional quality, breadth of experience, and extraordinary dedication of its highly valued faculty members, such as Dr. Robert Yantorno, professor of electrical and computer engineering (above). Temple faculty and staff regard the university as a good place to work. A 2008 survey by the Chronicle of Higher Education recognized Temple as among the most desirable academic workplaces nationally, bestowing a "best in class" ranking.

No sooner had Temple settled into its new state-affiliated role than it was confronted seemingly with one financial crisis after another. The enrollment spurt brought by the baby-boom generation ended in the early 1970s and enrollments steadily declined, just as double-digit inflation and absurd escalations of energy costs drove up university expenses. During these same years the city withdrew from its responsibility for public health care, leaving Temple Hospital and Medical School to assume even larger burdens. Declining enrollments, coupled with political intransigence within the Commonwealth General Assembly and extraordinarily high interest rates for short-term borrowing, at one point left the university on the verge of insolvency and its leadership in a prolonged state of crisis, their credibility frequently challenged.

The 2008 edition of The Princeton Review's *annual college guidebook,* The Best 366 Colleges, *ranked Temple's undergraduate student body the most diverse in the nation.*

Weathering program retrenchment, two faculty strikes, and a gradual reduction in the relative share of commonwealth support, Temple fought back, as always, and emerged in the 1990s stronger, more financially stable, and more exuberant than ever. With concerted single-mindedness, Temple defied trends and admonitions that it must get smaller faster. Temple also defied the city leaders' emphasis on an East-West development scheme, insisting instead on the rightness and propriety of revitalizing North Philadelphia. To anchor that revitalization, Temple launched plans for a residential campus—"Temple Town," as Peter Liacouras fondly labeled it—and slowly, inexorably the sidewalk campus—peopled largely by commuting students, faculty, and staff—morphed into an urban village, a residential urban university of a scope and magnitude hardly imagined a few decades prior.

Over the last three decades Temple has essentially reinvented itself, becoming a multiversity with a global reach, anchored in a residential campus proudly a part of North Philadelphia. It was done with steadfast and imaginative leadership, with the continued dedication of its faculty and staff, including the infusion of hundreds of new faculty, with a mighty onslaught each year of anxious and determined freshmen, and with the unflinching support of alumni and the assistance of many generous friends.

Temple University has existed through twenty-four of the forty-four U.S. presidential administrations and nine presidents of its own, two world wars, several regional wars, two major industrial depressions, and a dozen recessions. Temple faced insolvency more than once and occasionally found itself skirting dissolution and despair. Too often we are apt to assume that because an institution like Temple is large and has existed for a long time that its continued existence is inevitable.

What we learn from its history is that Temple's growth, development, and continued existence were by no means certain. Temple University has survived and thrived because it faced hardship and misfortunes in a realistic, determined manner; because its mission is rooted in the very essence of the American Dream, which can never be denied; and because it has maintained a youthful vigor, a transcendent respect for its heritage, and an eagerness to meet new challenges and to adjust and adapt to changing conditions.

The Recent Past

On July 1, 2006, Ann Weaver Hart assumed the Temple presidency. Hart came to Temple from the University of New Hampshire, where she had served as president for four years. Prior to that, she was provost and vice president for academic affairs at Claremont (California) Graduate University. A native of Utah, she also held positions as professor of educational leadership, dean of the Graduate School, and special assistant to the president at the University of Utah. The first woman to head Temple, Hart enthusiastically endorsed the Temple mission. "My life was transformed by having access to a first-rate education at a great urban public university," Hart has said. "Temple has that very same transformative power, and I embrace it."

President Hart immediately set forth an agenda to strengthen Temple's leadership in research, innovation, and entrepreneurship; to take a leadership role in developing innovative ways to practice and demonstrate environmental citizenship; to advance the ambitious capital improvements under way; to create a culture of philanthropy to ensure a secure financial future; and to expand Temple's international study program and reinforce the university's role in the global community. In just a few short years she has made substantial progress toward fulfilling that agenda.

A passionate advocate of international education, President Hart launched several dramatic initiatives early in her presidency. To encourage students to study abroad so they may expand their horizons and compete in the international marketplace, she and her husband, Randy, personally established a scholarship program to pay student fees for passport applications. In October 2007, during a two-week Asian tour, Hart renewed Temple's agreement with the Chinese government partnering with Temple's innovative Rule of Law programs and also signed an agreement in Taipei inaugurating a groundbreaking dual-degree program with six Taiwanese universities.

One of President Hart's first acts was to appoint a Sustainability Task Force to survey Temple's current programs in environmental sustainability and energy conservation. Soon after receiving the group's report, she created the Office of Sustainability to keep the campus active in and informed on matters of environmental responsibility. As part of Earth Day 2008 observances, Hart signed the American College and University Presidents Climate Commitment, pledging to undertake short-term actions while working to develop a long-range plan to achieve carbon neutrality and improve the planet's climate.

To strengthen Temple's community attachments, the university created Community Outreach and Hiring, a joint program with local businesses to assist nearby residents in applying for positions at Temple and with other North Philadelphia employers. And in October 2007 President Hart unveiled the Employee Home Ownership Program in partnership with the City of Philadelphia's Neighborhood Transformation Initiative. Temple offered financial help for

Ann Weaver Hart, Temple's ninth president (shown holding the university mace at her March 2007 inauguration), made an immediate impact, expanding Temple's global reach, building consensus around an Academic Strategic Compass, and winning trustee approval for Temple 20/20, an exciting vision for Temple's future. Hart's Temple 20/20 plan focuses on the flagship Main Campus and its Broad Street corridor, creating a twenty-first-century library, increasing research facilities, adding more on-campus housing, providing additional green space, and expanding recreation facilities, all without going beyond the current campus footprint or disrupting the surrounding neighborhoods.

Provost Lisa Staiano-Coico (above) earned a bachelor of science degree from Brooklyn College of the City University of New York in 1976 and a doctorate in microbiology and immunology from the Cornell University Graduate School of Medical Sciences (now Weill Cornell Medical College) in 1981. She held appointments at Cornell University as professor of microbiology in surgery and professor of microbiology in dermatology. On announcing Staiano-Coico's appointment President Hart hailed her energy and commitment "to the power and reach of urban universities," both of which were abundantly evident in her leadership and development of Temple's Academic Strategic Compass.

its employees who purchase a home in the communities surrounding the Main Campus and Health Sciences Center in North Philadelphia. "Temple University is tied to its neighborhoods, offering many gateways through which community and university resources pass," said Hart in announcing the program. "Our goal is continued growth and investment in our city, from Main Campus south to City Hall, and north to the Health Sciences Center," she said.

A further indication of Temple's commitment to the city occurred in March 2008 when President Hart, in partnership with the School District of Philadelphia, announced a new scholarship program. Every year four talented and motivated Philadelphia high school students with demonstrated financial need will each receive full tuition through the Temple University Philadelphia School District Scholarship.

To lead Temple's academic affairs as provost, President Hart selected Lisa Staiano-Coico, formerly dean of Cornell University's College of Human Ecology. The appointment marked the first time a Philadelphia university had women simultaneously in the positions of president and provost. Under Provost Staiano-Coico's leadership the university continued to recruit highly qualified faculty to replace retiring teachers and to staff new programs. The faculty rejuvenation effort commenced in 2004 added 290 new senior-level faculty members by the fall of 2008.

The Present

A few straightforward numbers illustrate Temple's compelling story. From its humble origins in Russell Conwell's study, Temple had risen in 2009 to be ranked as the twenty-sixth-largest university and the fifth-largest provider of professional education in the United States. Its seventeen schools and colleges offered more than 300 academic degree programs to more than 37,000 students studying at nine Temple University campuses worldwide. Enrollments between 1998 and 2008 increased by nearly 10,000 students, and each freshman class in recent years has set records for its size and for the quality of its academic preparation.

In recent decades the number of Temple degrees awarded has steadily increased from 4,993 degrees in 1997 to an all-time high of 7,694 in 2008. An important reputational measure of a modern university, the number of graduate and first professional degrees awarded also increased. Temple's 2008 commencement conferred 1,276 master's, 414 doctoral, and 818 first professional degrees (Law, Medicine, Dentistry, Podiatry, and Pharmacy). In 2009 one in every eight Greater Philadelphia college graduates held a Temple University degree. More than 260,000 Temple University alumni were living in all fifty states and 145 countries. Temple could count more than 140,000 Pennsylvanians as alumni.

Temple's importance can also be measured by its contributions to the local economy. The university is the third-largest private employer in Philadelphia, with annual spending in 2009 that accounted for 30,000 jobs and generated an estimated $2.7 billion for the Delaware Valley; this amount includes annual operating spending of $850 million that creates or supports 6,439 jobs, $1.09 billion in employee spending that maintains an additional 5,299 jobs, and $631 million in student and visitor spending resulting in another 5,212 jobs. Temple in recent years annually laid out $95.5 million in construction spending, creating 868 jobs. Temple's Main Campus revitalization program spurred more than $200 million in private residential and commercial development in North Philadelphia. Temple graduates also contribute to the economy, with an overall estimated economic impact of $8.7 billion supporting over 42,000 jobs.

The Future

Temple's basic mission, said President Hart in her inaugural address, "is to generate new knowledge, new ideas; to stimulate public service; to bring to bear creativity and life-altering research to build a better world; and to change lives." In the pursuit of that mission, she stressed, Temple University must continue to "provide access to an intellectual and creative space where academically talented, highly motivated and prepared students can achieve excellence, regardless of their status or station in life."

Russell Conwell would surely have welcomed and endorsed those remarks, for they directly acknowledge and update his own views, which he summarized in the Temple Idea. Over the years the description of Temple's mission has been shortened to a simple mantra: "Access to Excellence." As President Hart takes pains to explain, Temple's mission is about "access *and* excellence, not "access *or* excellence." Fulfilling the Conwell mission and providing access to excellence cannot be done without careful planning and sufficient resources.

At President Hart's direction, the university launched a comprehensive tripartite plan to ensure Temple's future. Provost Staiano-Coico led a strategic planning process involving a wide array of the university's thought leaders to examine academic programs and recommend a series of initiatives to carry Temple through the next decade. The result of more than a year of intense study, analysis, collaboration, and brainstorming by the faculty and administrative leadership, the *Strategic Compass*, reports Staiano-Coico, "identifies points that will enable us to continue as a force of growing vitality and impact, enhancing the quality of life for current and future generations."

The four points on the Strategic Compass are to enhance opportunities for student success; to advance research excellence through investigation, innovation, and entrepreneurship; to build on Temple's record of diversity and to further Temple's engagement with the city and the region; and to increase Temple's global commitment. At the center of the compass is the campus—Destination Temple: A Lifetime Connection—a vibrant, welcoming campus with permeable boundaries, educational and performance venues, and recreational, residential, and social spaces to which students, alumni, and friends will return again and again. Part of this plan includes a continued commitment to build the Avenue of the Arts northward to make Temple a regional and national center of excellence for the arts, culture, and entertainment.

The provost's Strategic Compass was integrated into the university's master financial plan, prepared under the leadership of Anthony E. Wagner, vice president and chief financial officer, and fitted into a new, comprehensive Main Campus master development plan, called *Temple 20/20*. With the opening in 2009 of four state-of-the-art facilities devoted to business, medicine, art, and music, and with the demands for additional facilities and amenities to accommodate Temple's enrollment growth, facilitate scientific research, and meet the ever-growing demands for technological support for teaching and research, it is necessary to plan carefully for Temple's future.

Regrettably, many today who could benefit most from a college education often find it least accessible, largely because of the rising costs of higher education. Thanks to visionaries like Russell Conwell, twentieth-century Americans benefited from a general widening of access to and the gradual democratization of higher education as it ceased to remain the prerogative of a wealthy elite. But increases in the price of attaining a college degree threaten to reverse this trend the farther we move into the twenty-first century.

"We want every student athlete and Temple fan to be enriched by lifelong friendships, comforted by shared memories of joys and challenges, of competitions lost or won, and inspired to make a lifelong connection to Temple and its global community."

Fran Dunphy,
Men's Basketball Coach

Therefore, to sustain its historic mission, Temple must shape its own destiny. Relying so extensively on the commonwealth is no longer a viable alternative. The commonwealth has many obligations and costly responsibilities. Too often in Temple's history the commonwealth has found it necessary to withhold or withdraw promised support, leaving Temple to resort to borrowing and indebtedness.

History points us away from a future of large state appropriations and directs us, instead, toward solutions of our own devising. The era of vast government support for higher education has passed; direct subsidies and government subventions have dwindled and, given the changed economic situation of recent years, are likely to decline until they either constitute a very small part of Temple's operating revenues or disappear completely. Temple must find alternative revenue sources and cultivate a spirit of giving and philanthropy. As President Hart explained, "We must create a different and lasting balance in our sources of revenue."

Toward that end, in October 2007 Temple University launched the public phase of its first comprehensive fund-raising campaign before more than 1,000 supporters gathered at the National Constitution Center. Called Access to Excellence: The 125th Anniversary Campaign for Temple, the initiative set an original goal of raising $350 million by December 31, 2009. That goal was surpassed, and by late December over $370 million had been raised.

"Temple stands at a remarkable point in its history," President Hart observed in 2007. "Never before have we moved forward with such momentum; never before have so many opportunities for progress stood so close within our reach." She urged all who care about Temple to change the way they think and act regarding the practice of philanthropy. To sustain the Temple Idea and to achieve Temple's goals, President Hart stresses the need to create "a different and lasting balance in our sources of revenue and focus new energy on funding for scholarships, for buildings, for faculty and research, and for an endowment that sustains the extraordinary achievement of which Temple is capable."

Many challenges lie ahead, but Temple University faces the future confident in the rightness of the Temple mission, proud of what has been accomplished so far, and assured that its timeless message will prevail. Temple's faith in the future rests comfortably on the shoulders of its current and future students. As the embodiment of all of Temple's hopes, we continue to learn from them, because Temple students today—just as those who have gone before—are aspiring, audacious, and accomplished.

From this survey of the history of Temple University we learned that the Temple spirit remains within our students throughout life. A large part of the Temple Story, then, is the collective character of Temple, as reflected in its faculty and staff and infused within its students and alumni. It is a gritty, no-nonsense approach to life's larger struggles, a realistic you-can-do-it-if-you-try attitude that eschews self-pity or a sense of entitlement. Whatever comes about in life, Temple people know they must earn it. All we truly value requires hard work and sacrifice. In short, we know the truth of our motto—*Perseverantia vincit*—"Perseverance conquers"!

Temple student Scott Blanding (above left) tutors a student from Belize during a service immersion trip in March 2007. Blanding and other students also worked on infrastructure improvements at La Democracia Village School in Belize. Their service is just one example of Temple's passionate commitment to the Conwellian ideal of volunteer service to others.

PERSEVERANCE CONQUERS

Chronology

1882 Russell H. Conwell moves to Philadelphia to pastor the Grace Baptist Church.

1884 Conwell begins tutoring a group of seven young workingmen.

1888 Temple College receives a Charter of Incorporation. All classes are offered in the evening. Temple opens a high school for adults seventeen years of age and older.

1891 The Temple (aka the Baptist Temple) opens with seating capacity for 4,600, making it the largest Protestant church in the United States at the time. Temple College Charter is amended to include women. The Day Department opens (unofficial founding of the College of Liberal Arts).

1892 Temple College confers first degrees (bachelor of oratory). Conwell opens Samaritan Hospital for the North Philadelphia community.

1893 Laura Carnell joins Conwell's staff and gradually becomes his chief assistant.

1894 College Hall opens, housing college offices, classrooms, a library, and a gymnasium. Men's varsity football and basketball teams are organized. Business Department offers shorthand, typing, bookkeeping, and penmanship.

1895 The Philadelphia Law School of Temple College is established. Department of Music is formed.

1897 School for Nurses is established at Samaritan Hospital. Theology School is founded.

1901 Law School graduates sixteen students (all previously admitted to the bar). School of Medicine opens, becoming Pennsylvania's first coeducational and first evening medical school. Pharmacy School is founded. Temple's first student yearbook, *The Record,* is produced.

1905 Temple acquires the Philadelphia Dental College (founded in 1863) and Garretson Hospital (opened in 1878) at Eighteenth and Buttonwood streets. College of Liberal Arts is established.

1906 Sara Allen and Mary E. Shepard receive MD degrees from Temple School of Medicine.

1907 Temple College is reincorporated as Temple University.

1910 Samaritan and Garretson hospitals merge into Temple University.

1911 Jane Bowne Haines founds the Pennsylvania School of Horticulture for Women in Ambler. Temple University receives first biennial state appropriation ($110,000).

1913 Bachelor of science degree in Education is authorized.

1915 School of Chiropody opens—only the second school of chiropody in the United States.

1918 School of Commerce (later renamed the Fox School of Business and Management) is established.

1919 Teachers College (later renamed the College of Education) is formally established.

1922 Cornerstone is laid for Conwell Hall (dedicated in 1924). Women's varsity basketball and men's baseball teams are started.

1925 Laura Carnell is named associate president. Russell H. Conwell dies on December 6 at age eighty-two.

1926 Charles Ezra Beury is named Temple's second president. Temple's General Alumni Association is organized. Men's varsity soccer program is started.

1927 Temple and other universities ban intercollegiate competition for women. Department of Journalism opens in the School of Commerce. First issue of *The Temple Law Quarterly* is published. Temple Stadium, seating 34,200 for football, opens at Cheltenham Avenue and Vernon Road.

1928 Physical Rehabilitation Department—the nation's first—opens at the School of Medicine. School of Medicine affiliates with the Jewish Hospital of Philadelphia, now the Albert Einstein Medical Center.

1929 Samaritan Hospital becomes Temple University Hospital. Carnell Hall is dedicated. Temple's trademark iron gates are erected at the Eighteenth and Buttonwood campus.

1930 Chevalier Jackson, MD, developer of the bronchoscope, opens the Jackson Clinic at the School of Medicine.

1931 Paul E. "Pop" Randall founds the Department of Theater. Mitten Hall is dedicated. Oak Lane Country Day School merges with Temple University.

1932 The Medical School moves into a new building at 3401 North Broad Street.

1933 Glenn S. "Pop" Warner is hired to coach Temple football. Law School day program becomes accredited.

1935 Stella Elkins Tyler donates her Elkins Park estate to Temple to house an art school. Temple University football team is invited to the inaugural Sugar Bowl, New Year's Day in New Orleans.

1936 President Franklin Delano Roosevelt dedicates Sullivan Hall (Temple's first freestanding library building).

1937 The *Temple University News* is established. Evening Technical School is established (forerunner of the College of Engineering).

1938 Men's basketball team becomes national champion after winning first-ever National Invitational Basketball Tournament.

1939 Temple physicians O. Spurgeon English and Edward Weiss open the first clinic for psychosomatic medicine. Louise Carter and James Bush-Brown co-author *America's Garden Book,* the number-one-selling general garden book in the country.

1941 Robert Livingston Johnson is elected Temple's third president.

1943 Master of business administration (MBA) is first offered. School of Music is discontinued (Department of Music Education is retained).

1945 Postwar extension sites open at Olney High School, Cedarbrook Center, and Brookline Country Club (Havertown).

1946 Turngemeinde Hall is acquired and renamed South Hall to house physical education, art studios, and a community swimming pool.

1947 Dr. Harry Shay opens Fels Institute at the Medical School. Dentistry and Pharmacy schools move to 3223 North Broad Street. Chemistry Department offers Temple's first PhD program.

1948 Temple Community College opens at Eighteenth and Spring Garden streets in facilities vacated by Dentistry and Pharmacy the year before. WRTI begins broadcasting.

1949 W. Edward Chamberlain designs the first biplane stereoscopic x-ray machine. Temple Law School organizes Moot Court competitions.

1951 Men's soccer team wins its first intercollegiate national championship. President Harry S Truman dedicates the Chapel of the Four Chaplains.

1953 School of Dentistry opens public dental clinic. Law School moves to Main Campus and into Reber Hall (dedicated in 1954 by Chief Justice Earl Warren). Law School opens Legal Aid Clinic. Philosophy professor Barrows Dunham is dismissed.

1956 Curtis Hall, Temple's first modern air-conditioned classroom building, is dedicated. It contains fifty classrooms. (The building is demolished in 2006 to make way for Alter Hall.) Peabody Hall opens.

1957 Temple Law School publishes *The American Journal of Legal History.*

1958 Ambler Junior College, formerly the Pennsylvania School of Horticulture for Women, merges with Temple University.

1959 Millard E. Gladfelter is named Temple's fourth president. Chiropody School closes. (It reopens in 1963 as Pennsylvania College of Podiatric Medicine at St. Luke's and Children's Medical Center, to merge with Temple in 1998.) Theology School closes. (Religion Department in College of Liberal Arts opens in 1961.)

1960 John F. Kennedy campaigns at Temple. Graduate School is established. Physics chair J. Lloyd Bohn designs and builds the Micrometeorite Impact Counter for the U.S. Explorer 1 space satellite.

1961 Barton Hall (Physics) is completed. Johnson Hall dormitory opens.

1962 College of Music is reestablished. The Rev. Martin Luther King Jr. speaks at Temple.

1963 Temple students win the GE College Bowl championship.

1964 Beury Hall (Chemistry) is dedicated. Basic Studies program is adopted.

1965 Ritter Hall is dedicated as home of the College of Education. Temple University is designated a state-related institution. Speakman Hall (School of Business Administration) is dedicated.

1966 Temple University Rome is established. Paley Library opens. College of Allied Health Professions is founded. Pearson Hall (Physical Education) opens.

1967 Paul R. Anderson is elected Temple's fifth president. Presser Hall (College of Music) opens. School of Communications and Theater is organized. Annenberg Hall (School of Communications and Theater) is dedicated.

1968 Ambler Music Festival is started. Temple Community College, Temple Technical Institute, and Temple High School close, per agreement with the state to focus on baccalaureate, graduate, and professional education. Tomlinson Theater hosts first performances.

1969 College of Engineering is established. African-American Studies Department is started. McGonigle Hall (sports arena) is dedicated. Biology–Life Sciences Building opens. The School of Social Administration is established. Men's basketball team wins NIT title.

1971 Student Activities Center is completed. Sol Sherry Thrombosis Research Center is established. Nation's first program in postdoctoral studies in communications is offered.

1972 Temple revives women's intercollegiate athletic competition, hiring a women's athletic director and full-time coaches. Fire destroys the Klein Law School Library (formerly Keneseth Israel Synagogue).

1973 Marvin Wachman is selected Temple's sixth president. Social Sciences (Gladfelter Hall) and Humanities (Anderson Hall) open. Temple University Center City opens at 1619 Walnut Street. Klein Law Center opens.

1974 World's first university-based sports medicine center is started at Temple. Temple quarterback Steve Joachim receives the Maxwell Award.

1975 Weiss Hall (Psychology) is dedicated. Women's varsity softball and volleyball teams are inaugurated.

1976 College of Engineering Technology is founded (renamed the College of Engineering and Architecture in 1984 and the College of Engineering in 1993).

1977 WRTI establishes the nation's first radio service for the hearing impaired.

1978 Widener Hall opens at Ambler Campus. Mathematics and Computer Sciences building (later renamed Wachman Hall) opens. College of Engineering Technology building opens for classes.

1979 Deng Xiaoping (first vice premier of the People's Republic of China) is awarded an honorary degree. Asian Studies program is introduced. Temple football team defeats California in the Garden State Bowl.

1980 President Jimmy Carter conducts a town hall meeting in McGonigle Hall. Ambler Music Festival closes.

1981 Fellowship Exchange of Israeli and Temple Law Students is established.

1982 Peter J. Liacouras is selected Temple's seventh president. Temple University Japan (TUJ) opens, becoming the first campus of an American university in Japan. Women's lacrosse team wins the first of three national championships (repeated in 1984 and 1988).

1983 Students in a Tyler School of Art graphic arts studio create the Temple "T." Renovated Cecil B. Moore/Temple University subway station and plaza open. Construction begins on the new 504-bed Temple University Hospital.

1984 Charles L. Blockson Afro-American Collection is established at Temple.

1985 College of Music is renamed the Esther Boyer College of Music in honor of Esther Boyer Griswold. Executive MBA (EMBA) is offered.

1986 University Honors Program is established. The New School of Music merges with the Boyer College of Music.

1987 Bell of Pennsylvania constructs its Philadelphia Computer Center on Temple's Main Campus.

1988 Core Curriculum is introduced. Temple launches a doctoral program in African-American Studies, the first in the nation. Men's basketball team ranks number one in the nation.

1992 Temple's fencing team wins the NCAA championship.

1994 Reber Hall is renovated as a chamber music recital hall and renamed Rock Hall in honor of Shirley and Milton Rock. International MBA (IMBA) is first offered in Paris.

1997 Park Hall is renovated as a multi-purpose building and renamed Shusterman Hall in honor of Murray Shusterman. Fort Washington Graduate and Professional Education Center opens. WRTI adds classical music to daytime programming, jazz in the evening. Apollo of Temple opens (renamed the Liacouras Center in 2000).

1998 School of Tourism and Hospitality Management is established. Temple merges with Pennsylvania College of Podiatric Medicine, creating the Temple College of Podiatric Medicine. Independence Blue Cross Student Recreation Center opens. Law School launches the Rule of Law program in the People's Republic of China. College of Arts and Sciences divides into two schools: the College of Liberal Arts (Humanities and Social Sciences) and the College of Science and Technology (Mathematics and Sciences).

1999 School of Business Administration and Management is renamed the Richard J. Fox School of Business and Management. Law School is renamed the James E. Beasley School of Law of Temple University. "1940" residence hall (1940 Liacouras Walk) opens. Tuttleman Learning Center is dedicated in honor of Stanley and Edna Shanis Tuttleman. James S. White Residence Hall is dedicated.

2000 David Adamany is elected Temple's eighth president. Center for Sustainable Communities is established at Ambler (School of Environmental Design). Edberg-Olson Hall (football practice facility) opens.

2001 "1300" residence hall (1300 Cecil B. Moore Avenue) is readied for students.

2002 Center for Advanced Photonics (College of Science and Technology) is established. College Hall is rededicated as Morris and Sylvia Barrack Hall in recognition of a gift to the Law School from Leonard and Lynne Barrack. The building is named in honor of Mr. Barrack's parents.

2003 Ambler Campus hosts first "Earthfest" (Earth Day Celebration). Plans are launched for adaptive reuse of The Temple (aka the Baptist Temple) for the performing arts.

2004 Home fields for baseball, softball, and men's and women's soccer teams move to Ambler Campus. Temple University Opera Theater wins first National Opera Award. National Laboratory of Tourism and eCommerce is established.

2005 Fox Women's Leadership Initiative is established. Temple University Japan is designated as the first Foreign University Japan Campus by the Japanese Ministry of Education.

2006 Ann Weaver Hart is elected Temple's ninth president. Learning Center is dedicated at Ambler Campus. School of Dentistry is renamed the Maurice H. Kornberg School of Dentistry in honor of the 1921 graduate, father of Madlyn Abramson, and in recognition of a gift from Leonard and Madlyn Abramson and the Abramson Foundation. Student Activities Center is renamed the Howard Gittis Student Center to honor the late chairman of the board of trustees. Ambler baseball field is renamed Skip Wilson Field. TECH Center opens in the former Bell of Pennsylvania Computer Center.

2007 Boyer College establishes the George and Joy Abbott Center for Musical Theater.

2008 Temple Symphony Orchestra debuts at Carnegie Hall. Tyler School of Art relocates from Elkins Park to a new building at the Main Campus.

2009 New School of Medicine Education and Research building is dedicated. Alter Hall (Fox School of Business and Management) opens, named in honor of Dennis and Gisela Alter. Berks Mall is renamed Polett Walk in honor of former board chairman Daniel Polett. Temple football team is invited to play in the EagleBank Bowl in Washington, D.C. President Hart announces *Temple 20/20*, a bold development plan for the Main Campus in North Philadelphia. Temple celebrates 125 years of service to Philadelphia, the nation, and the world.

Acknowledgments and Notes on Resources

Author's Note about Writing a History of Temple

This history of Temple University is intended primarily to strengthen the emotional and intellectual ties that bind the Temple family. Being a part of this marvelously successful experiment in higher education enlarges our sense of who we are and where we fit in the grander scheme, allowing us to share something larger and more important than ourselves.

Surprisingly, for all of its attachment to its historically significant mission, Temple University, until this volume, lacked a formal written history. No institution of this size and impact should be without a sense of itself and its past. Moreover, until recently, Temple had shown relatively little appreciation for recording and maintaining its history or for expending resources to capture and sustain its past in an organized manner. Temple offers a graduate program in archival management but lacks a historical records retention policy. Hopefully, this study will bring greater attention to Temple's history, to finding the will and resources for compiling oral histories, to involving itself in the ongoing study of university history, and to addressing the issues of digital records retention, all focused on enhancing access to the university's past. Temple's history may not provide direct analogies to the present, but it is useful for learning how not to make the same mistake twice.

University historians, like political historians studying the nation's past, often find it necessary and convenient to focus on presidential administrations as catalysts for change and as a means for summarizing an institution's history according to what is accomplished or not during a president's term. We know, of course, that many of the most important transformative changes in higher education occurred irrespective of who filled a university presidency or when. Still, the changing of the guard often affords universities an opportunity to take stock, summarizing and evaluating what changed and what did not. This history of Temple attempts to avoid the presidential synthesis or the notion that the only important events in a university's history, like those in a nation's history, were those fostered or promulgated by presidential order, but in many instances undeniable credit for effecting change rightly belonged with the university leadership.

In truth, Temple has many histories, many grand narratives flowing at once. All of the units within Temple have distinguished records of accomplishment, each competing for recognition and space within this volume. It is the nature of the modern multiversity and globalversity. Hopefully, this book will encourage the many important parts of Temple University to examine their pasts and compile their own interesting and compelling histories. All of the details and subtleties of the players, events, and issues influencing the many units within Temple University over 125 years could not be captured or analyzed in this single volume. The author apologizes for omissions, accepts responsibility for errors, and invites readers' corrections.

Resources

The author concedes an enormous debt to those who attempted in the past to create histories of Temple but for one reason or another were not published. The groundwork for this study was laid in the 1950s by history professor Arthur Cook, who began to collect resources, create an oral history archive, and draft a history of Temple. Professor Cook's unfinished work was taken up first by journalism professor J. Douglas Perry in "Incredible University" (unpublished ms, Paley Library, 1970) and then by George Ingram Jr., former director of the Temple News Bureau and associate vice president for University Relations, whose "Temple University History, Part II: Anderson and Wachman Years: Epilogue: Liacouras" (unpublished ms, Paley Library, 1985) picked up where Perry left off. The author has also drawn upon milestone summary histories published over the years, including Marianne Lynch, "A Discourse on the Origin and Progress of Temple University on the Occasion of Its 75th Year," Temple Review (1959); Al Carlisle, "We Build Upon a Firm Foundation," Temple Review (January 1960); Miriam Crawford, "Walk 100 Years in One-Hundred Feet" (Temple Publications Office, funded by the Centennial History Committee, 1984); and Betsy Winter Hall, "125 Years: Celebrating Access to Excellence," Temple Review (2009).

Sincere appreciation goes to the past and present curators of the Conwellana-Templana Collection and the University Archives in Paley Library, including Marianne Lynch, Miriam Crawford, Thomas Whitehead, and Carol Ann Harris. Thanks also to Philip T. D'Andrea of the Paley staff for assistance with historic photographs and to Brenda Galloway-Wright, John Petit, and Margaret Jerrido of the Temple University Urban Archives. Special thanks to Larry Alford, dean and vice provost of libraries, for kindly making these talented people available to assist on this project.

Some of Temple's schools and colleges have compiled histories and chronological narratives that were useful in the compilation of this study. J. Douglas Perry authored several highly informative articles for the Temple Review containing portions of the histories of the Medical School and hospital. Also very helpful was Janet Tighe, "Defying All Predictions: A History of the Temple University School of Medicine, 1901–1980" (unpublished ms, Medical School Library, 1988). Professor Emeritus Theodore (Ted) P. Vasallo's "Chronology [1921–2003] of Technology, Engineering & Architecture at Temple University" (College of Engineering, 2003) was also very helpful. For the histories of other schools and colleges the author acknowledges Joseph S. Butterweck, "The Story of Teacher Education [1893–1963] at Temple University" (College of Education Library); William W. Cutler III, "Recognizing Our Past: The Paradox of Public Education," Temple Review (1990); "The First 100 Years [Law School]," Temple Review (Fall 1995); and "Fox Retrospectives: Celebrating 90 Years of Excellence at the Fox School of Business" (2009).

Special appreciation is extended to the authors and editors of the *Temple Review.* This study borrows liberally from and usually without direct attribution to the hundreds of articles published in the *Temple Review* over the course of Temple's history. Very often those articles involved tenacious historical research, making them valuable secondary historical resources. Without those many *Temple Review* articles this history simply could not have been compiled. The author especially thanks the former and current *Temple Review* editors, including Bonnie Squires, Ruth W. Schultz, Betsy Winter Hall, and Maria Raha.

Special thanks to the following *Temple Review* authors: Lewis Beale (BA CLA 1969; MA 1970), Ralph Bernstein (BS EDU 1943), Bob Bloss (BS SBM 1977), Robert Brothers (for his "Temple Trivia"), Alice Leroy Cochrane, Fred Cohen, Stephanie Cohen (BA CLA 1959; AS SED 1990), John Di Carlo (BS SCT 1998, 2006), Melissa DePino Cooper, David Driver, James Duffy, Kim Fischer, Prudence Fleming (BS EDU 1929), Greg Fornia, Phyllis T. Garland, Alix Gerz, Harriet K. Goodheart, Scott Hockenberry, Hillel J. Hoffman, Lucille Hoshabjian, the late Ralph Howard, Morton Hunt, George Ingram Jr., William G. Kelley (BS 1965; MJ SCT 1974), Henry L. Klein, Fred Maher (BA SCT 1985; MA SCT 2001), Thomas F. Maxey, Joseph McLaughlin, William Mooney, Virginia K. Nalencz, Harvey Pollack (BS SBM 1943), Maria Raha, Ilene Raymond Rush, Michael Richman (M.Ed. THM 1993), Marian Robinson (BA CLA 1961), Al Shrier (BS SBM 1953), Karen Shuey, Ron Silvergold, Samuel L. Singer, Ann Marie Strigari (BA CLA 1973; MA CLA1976), Philip Terranova, Maureen Walsh, and Richard N. Westcott.

Several Temple faculty authored important pieces for the *Temple Review*, and the author particularly acknowledges David Bradley, Burton Caine, Eunice E. Clarke, William W. Cutler III, Lawrence Ealy (BA CLA 1934), George Edberg-Olson (BS EDU 1949), Sandra Featherman, C. Tsehloane Keto, Jay Lamont, Herbert W. Simons, and Morris Vogel.

This study also draws frequently from articles and photographs published initially in the *Temple University News* and the *Temple Times,* and we gratefully acknowledge and thank the past and current editors and authors, whose reportorial skills provided basic background information and in some instances the colorful details necessary for understanding and appreciating the context of key events.

For assistance from Temple's schools, colleges, and departments in compiling their histories, the author thanks his colleagues on the Council of Deans and various individuals, including Crisbel Baez, Jim Duffy, Sylvia Studenmund, Sandra Thompson, Stephanie Cohen, Jenny Rose Carey (Ambler Campus and School of Environmental Design); John Daly, Albert Finestone, Janet Tighe (Medicine); Joseph "Chip" Marshall (Temple University Health System); William M. Hammell, Micah Kleit, Janet Francendese, Alex Holzman (Temple University Press); Joseph Butterweck, Joseph DuCette, Jay Scribner, Kent McGuire (Education); Peter Doukas (Pharmacy);

Keya Sadgehipour, Theodore (Ted) Vasallo (Engineering); Robert Reinstein, Joanne Epps, Debbie Feldman (Law); John Mattiacci, David Burt (Podiatry); Hai Lung Dai, Ralph Jenkins, Joel Bryan (Science and Technology); Moshe Porat, Diana Breslin Knudsen, Jennifer M. Fitzgerald (Fox School of Business and Management); Ruth Ost, Dieter Forster (Honors); Ira Shapiro (Health, Physical Education, Recreation, and Dance); Betsy Barber, Ira Shapiro (School of Tourism and Hospitality Management); Theresa Dolan, Jo-Anna Moore (Tyler School of Art); Robert Stroker, Linda Fiore, Arthur D. Chodoroff, Janet Yamron (Boyer College of Music and Dance); Concetta Stewart, Betsy Anderson (School of Communications and Theater); Teresa Soufas, Carolyn Adams (College of Liberal Arts); Linda Mauro (School of Social Administration); Ronald Brown, Jane M. Kurz, Ricky L. Swalm, Ashley Lomery, Mary Sinnott, Donna Weiss, Roberta Newton (College of Health Professions and Social Work); Kim Strommen (Temple Rome); Bruce Stronach (Temple Japan); Rachel Blau DuPlessis (Women's Studies); Theresa Powell, Amy Hecht (Student Affairs); Bill Bradshaw, Al Shrier, Larry Dougherty, Fran Dunphy (Athletics); Richard Hetherington (Data Management/Payroll); Jodi Laufgraben, Martyn Miller, Stephanie Gillan, Tim Walsh, Bill Wilkinson (Provost's office); Janet Carruth (Secretary's office); and Mellissa Coopersmith (President's office).

Note on Historical Sources

This volume draws extensively upon the archives in the Conwellana-Templana Collection and the Urban Archives within Temple University's Paley Library. The Conwellana-Templana Collection provided a wealth of materials for the history of Temple from its beginnings through the mid-1970s. Information for the later periods, however, has not been as systematically collected, archived, or accessioned as for the earlier period; that is due to no fault of the university archivists but rather to the advent and widespread use of computers and the lack of a mandatory, university-wide policy of records retention and archival management.

This study relied greatly on the Conwellana-Templana Collection, which includes the papers and correspondence of Russell Conwell, board of trustees minutes, plus selected university memoranda, policy statements, and press releases. Also of tremendous value were the internal publications of the *Temple News, Temple Times,* and *Temple Review*; Temple's catalogs, advertisements, and printed alumni documents of schools, colleges, and departments; and Web sites, brochures, and printed publications of Temple's various administrative offices, schools, colleges, departments, and centers. Of great help were the personal interviews recorded by Professor Betsy Leebron Tutleman for the celebration of Temple's 125th anniversary. Finally, there were the author's personal interviews with members of the Temple family and his personal recollections of events over a forty-year association with Temple University.

There are many books and articles on the life and works of Russell Conwell, including Joseph Carter, "Acres of Diamonds Man" (unpublished ms,

Paley Library, 1981); William C. Higgins, *Scaling the Eagle's Nest: The Life of Russell H. Conwell* (Springfield, Massachusetts: James D. Gill, 1889); Jane Conwell Tuttle, *Life with Grandfather Conwell and His "Acres of Diamonds"* (Northampton, Massachusetts: Gazette Printing Company, 1900, rev. 1940); Agnes Rush Burr, *Russell H. Conwell: The Man and the Work* (Philadelphia: John C. Winston, 1905); Robert J. Burdette, *The Modern Temple and Templars: A Sketch of the Life and Works of Russell H. Conwell* (Boston: Silver, Burdett and Company, 1894); Albert Hatcher Smith, *The Life of Russell H. Conwell: Preacher, Lecturer, Philanthropist* (Boston: Silver, Burdett and Company, 1899); Clyde K. Nelson, "The Social Philosophy of Russell H. Conwell" (PhD dissertation, University of Pennsylvania, 1968); Russell F. Weigley, "Foreword," in Russell H. Conwell, *Acres of Diamonds* (Philadelphia: Temple University Press, 2002). Conwell himself offered his recollections of the history of Temple University in hundreds of lectures and sermons. He also gave us written summaries of his recollections regarding the founding and growth of Temple. See in particular "The Temple College" in *The City of Philadelphia as It Appears in 1894* (Philadelphia: George S. Harris & Sons, 1894) and *Angel's Lily and History of Temple University* (Philadelphia: The Judson Press, 1920).

Other sources directly relating to or containing parts of Temple's history include Larry Alan Bear, *The Glass House Revolution: Inner-City War for Interdependence* (Seattle: University of Washington Press, 1990); Millard E. Gladfelter, "Recollections One and Recollections Two" (unpublished typescript, 1978, in the Millard E. Gladfelter Presidential Papers, Temple University Archives); James W. Hilty, "Introduction," in Barrows Dunham, *The Tradition of Tenderness in American Culture* (Philadelphia: Tyler Offset Workshop, 1982); Marvin Wachman, *Education of a University President* (Philadelphia: Temple University Press, 2005), with "Introduction" by James W. Hilty; Peter J. Liacouras, *Toward Universal Access to Higher Education—The American Experience* (Athens, Greece: The Academy of Athens, 2004); Peter Liacouras and Barbara Brownstein, "Ten-Year Academic Plan" (Temple University Academic Strategic Plan, 1986); Lisa Staiano-Coico, "Strategic Compass" (Temple University Academic Strategic Plan, 2008).

A partial list of resources consulted on the history of higher education includes Philip G. Altbach, "Students: Interests, Culture, and Activism," in *Higher Learning in America, 1980–2000*, edited by Arthur Levine (Baltimore: Johns Hopkins University Press, 1993); Philip G. Altbach, Robert O. Berdahl, and Patricia J. Gumport, *Higher Education in American Society* (New York: Prometheus Books, 1994); W. Bruce Leslie, *Gentlemen and Scholars: College and Community in the "Age of the University," 1865–1917* (University Park: Pennsylvania State University Press, 1992); Laurence R. Veysey, *The Emergence of the American Research University* (Chicago: University of Chicago Press, 1965); William Bruneau, "Large and Complicated Universities: Toronto and Melbourne," in *History of Universities*, edited by Mordechai Feingold (Oxford, England: Oxford University Press, 2005); Christopher Jencks and David Riesman, *The Academic Revolution* (New York: Doubleday, 1969); Clark Kerr, *The Uses of the University* (Cambridge, Massachusetts: Harvard University Press, 1963); Frederick Rudolph, *The American College and University: A History* (Athens: University of Georgia Press, 1962); Richard Angelo, "The Students at the University of Pennsylvania and the Temple College of Philadelphia, 1873–1906," *History of Education Quarterly* (1999); John R. Thelin, "Institutional History in Our Own Time: Higher Education's Shift from Managerial Revolution to Enterprising Evolution," *International Journal of Educational Advancement* (June 2000), pp. 9–23. Of particular value was John R. Thelin, *A History of American Higher Education* (Baltimore: Johns Hopkins University Press, 2004), which updates Veysey and Rudolph and synthesizes much of the recent literature on higher education.

Also of importance are Lee Benson, Ira Harkavy, and John Plunkett, *Dewey's Dream: Universities and Democracies in an Age of Educational Reform* (Philadelphia: Temple University Press, 2007); William G. Bowen and Harold T. Shapiro, *Universities and Their Leadership* (Princeton, New Jersey: Princeton University Press, 1998); Donald Kennedy, *Academic Duty* (Cambridge, Massachusetts: Harvard University Press, 1997); George Keller, *Academic Strategy: The Management Revolution in American Higher Education* (Baltimore: Johns Hopkins University Press, 1983); and Paul Starr, *The Social Transformation of American Medicine* (New York: Basic Books, 1984).

For student generations, see the several works of Howe and Strauss, including Neil Howe and William Strauss, *Millennials Rising: The Next Great Generation* (New York: Vintage, 2000), and Neil Howe and William Strauss, *Generations: The History of America's Future, 1584 to 2069* (New York: Harper Perennial, 1992), as well as Michael D. Coomes and Robert DeBard, *Serving the Millennial Generation* (New York: John Wiley & Sons, 2004); *Higher Education in Transition: The Challenges of the New Millennium*, edited by Joseph Losco and Brian L. Fife (Westport, Connecticut: Bergin & Garvey, 2000).

To understand Temple, one must learn about Philadelphia. The following is a partial list of sources that proved useful in that regard: *Philadelphia: A 300-Year History*, edited by Russell F. Weigley (New York: W. W. Norton & Company, 1982); Barbara Ferman, "Leveraging Social Capital: The University as Educator and Broker," in *Social Capital in the City: Community and Civic Life in Philadelphia*, edited by Richardson Dilworth (Philadelphia: Temple University Press, 2006); John K. Brown, *The Baldwin Locomotive Works, 1831–1915* (Baltimore: Johns Hopkins University Press, 1995); Thomas R. Heinrich, *Ships for the Seven Seas: Philadelphia Shipbuilding in the Age of Industrial Capitalism* (Baltimore: Johns Hopkins University Press, 1997); Philip Scranton, *Endless Novelty: Specialty Production and American Industrialization, 1865–1925* (Princeton: Princeton University Press, 1997); Sam Bass Warner Jr., *The Private City: Philadelphia in Three Periods of Its Growth* (Philadelphia: University of Pennsylvania Press, 1968); Philip Scranton and Walter Licht, *Work Sights: Industrial Philadelphia, 1890–1950* (Philadelphia:

Temple University Press, 1986); Bruce Kuklick, *To Every Thing a Season: Shibe Park and Urban Philadelphia, 1909–1976* (Princeton: Princeton University Press, 1993); Gary B. Nash, *First City: Philadelphia and the Forging of Historical Memory* (Philadelphia: University of Pennsylvania Press, 2002); Frederic M. Miller, Morris J. Vogel, and Allen F. Davis, *Still Philadelphia: A Photographic History, 1890–1940* (Philadelphia: Temple University Press, 1983); Philip S. Benjamin, *The Philadelphia Quakers in the Industrial Age, 1865–1920* (Philadelphia: Temple University Press, 1976); *The Peoples of Philadelphia: A History of Ethnic Groups and Lower-Class Life, 1790–1940,* edited by Allen F. Davis and Mark Haller (Philadelphia: University of Pennsylvania Press, 1973, 1998); Carolyn Adams, David Bartelt, David Elesh, Ira Goldstein, Nancy Kleniewski, and William Yancey, *Philadelphia Neighborhoods: Division and Conflict in a Postindustrial City* (Philadelphia: Temple University Press, 1993); Carolyn Adams, David Bartelt, and David Elesh, *Restructuring the Philadelphia Region: Metropolitan Divisions and Inequality* (Philadelphia: Temple University Press, 2008).

Author's Personal Acknowledgments and Thanks

I wish to extend my sincere appreciation to President Ann Weaver Hart, Provost Lisa Staiano-Coico, and Deputy Provost Richard Englert for their personal support and gracious encouragement throughout the development of this project; to former vice president for development Stuart Sullivan for finding the resources and providing assistance to launch the project; to Chancellor David Adamany, who provided the early impetus for determining the feasibility of such a book; and to Chancellor Peter J. Liacouras for useful insights, helpful suggestions, and personal encouragement.

My particular thanks go to the faculty and staff at the Ambler Campus for their personal support and for their willingness to shoulder additional burdens during those times when the book drew much of my attention and energy. Special thanks to Crisbel Baez, Sarada Jailal, Saul Katzman, Linda Lowe, and Lolly Tai. This is my third project with Temple University Press and my admiration and thanks go out to all who made this project a reality, particularly Charles Ault, Micah Kleit, and Alex Holzman. Thanks also to Nanette Bendyna (BA SCT 1981) for her superb copyediting and Jane Barry for her expert proofreading. Phil Unetic is responsible for the creative and resourceful layouts that bring the Temple story to life.

Matthew Hanson was at my side throughout this project, providing invaluable research support, constructing chronologies, and working with representatives of units across the university to locate important documents and photographs. His remarkable energy, dedication, and devotion can never be fully repaid, but they are gratefully acknowledged and appreciated.

This book is dedicated to the Temple family. All who are a part of Temple value our associations with the university and treasure the memories and fond attachments to its people and ideals. In forty years at Temple I have made many dear and lasting friends, too many to list, but in my heart I thank them all.

Finally, this book is dedicated to my family—all of whom have become attached to Temple or fallen within its orbit: to my daughter, Carolyn Rene Hilty Marland, her husband, Robert Marland, and their daughters, Rachel and Lyndsey Marland (CHP 2011); to my son, Robert Daniel Hilty, PhD (BS ENG 1989), his wife, Carol Ann Welsh Hilty (BA CLA 1990), and their children, Eleanor, Samuel, and Martha; and to my daughter, Maura Kathleen Hilty (TYL 2012). My greatest and most profound debt is to my wife, Kathleen Griffin-Hilty. Without her unstinting patience and without her steadfast support and wise counsel, this book could not have been written and my life would be far less complete.

James W. Hilty
Fall 2009

Illustration Sources

The author and publisher wish to thank the following individuals and institutions for their help in providing illustrations for this volume.

Temple University

Ambler Campus Public Relations (James Duffy, Coordinator)

Alumni Communications (Betsy Winter Hall, Director, Development Support Services, Alumni Communications)

Athletics (Larry Dougherty, Associate Director of Athletics; Karen Auerbach, Assistant Director, Sports Media Relations)

Beasley School of Law (John Smagula, Director, Foreign LLM Program)

Boyer College of Music and Dance (Linda Fiore, Director)

College of Health Professions (Emily Keshner, Chair, Department of Physical Therapy; Frances Ward, Chair, Nursing)

Creative Services, Photography Department (Elizabeth Manning, Coordinator of Photography; Ryan Brandenberg, Photographer; Joseph V. Labolito, Senior Photographer)

Honors Program (Amanda Neuber, Associate Director)

International Programs (Sara Sequin, Assistant Director, Japan Education Operations)

Office of the Provost (Betsy Leebron Tutelman, Senior Vice Provost and Dean of Students)

School of Communications and Theater (Ashley Lomery, Director of Development and Alumni Relations)

School of Podiatric Medicine (Jeanne M. Lockner, Art Media and Website Manager)

Temple University Libraries

Ambler Campus Library (Sandra M. Thompson, Head, Suburban Campus Libraries)

Ginsburg Health Sciences Library (Mary Ellen Post, Reference Librarian)

Special Collections—Conwellana Templana Collection (Thomas M. Whitehead, Head; Carol Ann Harris, Bibliographic Assistant)

Urban Archives (Brenda Galloway-Wright, Associate Archivist and Interim Head; John Pettit, Assistant Archivist, Curator of Photographs)

Tyler School of Art (Jo-Anna J. Moore, Chair, Art and Art Education Department)

University Communications (Ray Betzner, Assistant Vice President for Communications)

Individuals

Lucy Clink

William H. Cosby Jr. (Bill Cosby)

Linda Darling-Hammond

Anita Guerra

Melody Holmes

Joan Mellen

Mrs. Theodore Quedenfeld

Kevin Sprouls, Kevin Sprouls Illustrations, Sweetwater, New Jersey

John F. Street

Institutions

Marygrove College, Detroit, Michigan (Karen Wood, Director of Communications and Marketing)

Moore College of Art & Design, Philadelphia (Amanda Mott, Director of Communications, and Gary Horn, Photographer)

The Philadelphia Education Fund (Jenifer Trachtman, Director of Development and Marketing)

Philadelphia Museum of Art

Princeton University, Office of the President

Project H.O.M.E., Philadelphia

WHYY, Philadelphia affiliate of the Public Broadcasting System

Publications

Burr, Agnes Rush. *Russell H. Conwell and His Work.* Philadelphia: John C. Winston Company, 1926.

Keel, Thomas H. *Forgotten Philadelphia: Lost Architecture of the Quaker City.* Philadelphia: Temple University Press, 2007.

O Globo (Rio de Janeiro, Brazil).

Index

Illustrations are indicated by *italicized* page numbers.

A

Abbott, George, 145, 146, *151*

Abbott, Joy Valderrama, 145, *151*

Abou-Gharbia, Magid, 251

Abramson, Leonard, 253, *253*

Abramson, Madlyn, 253, *253*

Academy of Music, 116

 "Access to Excellence," 2, 195, 287

Access to Excellence Campaign, 224, 242, 243, 281, 288

"Acres of Diamonds," 6–8, 11, 15, 78, 107, 145, 179, 180

Adamany, David, 16, 221, 222–226, *223, 224*, 278

Adams, Carolyn T., 75, 206, 207

Adkins, Edwin P., 105

Alberti, Sarah, 147

Albert M. Greenfield Conference Center, 113

Albright, Phil, 268

Alexander, Charles, 212

Alexander, Chuck, 170

Alexander, Ginny, 176

Alford, Larry, 238

Alger, Horatio, 8

Ali, Muhammad, *104*

Alice Tully Library, 145

Allegheny House, 68

Allen, Sara, 27, 246

Allied Health/Pharmacy Building, 82

Al's Lunch Wagon, 234

Alston, Floyd W., 231

Alter, Dennis, *260*, 262

Alter, Gisela, *260*, 263

Alter Hall, 85, *85*, 97, 221, 226, 229, 236, *260, 261*, 262, *262*, 263

Alumni Circle, 182

Alumni House, 43

Amar, Henri, 137

Ambler Arboretum, 264, *265*

Ambler Campus. *See* Temple University Ambler

Ambler College. *See* Temple University Ambler

Ambler Junior College. *See* Temple University Ambler

Ambler Learning Center, 268

Ambler Music Festival, *144*

Ambler Sports Administration Building, 264, *265*

Ambulatory Care Center, 246

Ambulatory Surgical Center, 254, 255

Ament, Joe, *238*

Ancillary Services and Out-Patient Building, 83, *83*

Anderson, Ken, 176

Anderson, Paul R., 90, 99, 108, *108*, 111, 115, 116, 119–131 passim, *122, 130*, 160, 267, 272

Anderson, Thomas, 134

Anderson Hall, 115, 234

Andrews, Aaron L., 257, 258

Annenberg, Leonore, 109, *109*

Annenberg, Walter, 109, *109*, 112

Annenberg Hall, *109*, 112, 146, *149*, 150, 151, 152, 154

Apollo of Temple, The. *See* Liacouras Center

Architecture. *See* College of Engineering and Architecture

Arians, Bruce, 160, 188

Art School. *See* Tyler School of Art

Arts and Quality of Life Research Center, 145

Ashburn, Richie, *74*

Atkinson, Sterling, 76

Atlantic Terminal Warehouse, 193, 231

Auriemma, Geno, 173

Avenue North, 232, *232, 233*

Avenue of the Arts, 16, *198*, 226

Axinn, Sidney, 97

Azabu Hall, 201

B

Babcock, W. Wayne, *26*, 27

Baez, Joan, 143

Bahr, Walt, 167

Baldino, Frank, Jr., 234

Baldwin Locomotive Works, 8–9, 34

Ballard, Ernesta, 264, *265, 266, 268

Ballots, Joan, 253

Ballots, John, 162, 253

Baptist Temple, *37*, 44, 54, 70, *101, 119*, 127, 146, 197, 225, 226. *See also* Temple, The

Baptist Union of Philadelphia, 12

Barba, William, 123

Barber, Elizabeth, 263

Barclay Hotel, 67

Barksdale, Sean, 167

Barnes, Lamont, *165*

Barrack, Leonard, 19, 243, *243*

Barrack, Lynne, 19, 243, *243*

Barrack Hall, *19*, 106, 243. *See also* College Hall; Morris and Sylvia Barrack Hall

Barron, Bert, 169

Bartlett, David M., 106

Barton, Samuel Goodwin, 86

Barton Hall, 86, *88*, 89, 112, 208

Bass, Herbert J., *116*

Battisto, Dominic, *166*

Baum, John, 163, 164

Bear, Larry Alan, 193

Beardall, John R., *68*

Beasley, James E., 240, *241*, 243

Beasley School of Law, 87, 201, 203, 240–243, *243*, 286. *See also* Klein Law Library; Philadelphia Law School of Temple University; School of Law

Beasley Walk, 4, 243

Bellevue Stratford Hotel, 130

Bell of Pennsylvania Computer Center, 185, *192*, 193, 194

Bell Tower, *98*, 107, *110, 138*

Benjamin, George, Jr., 70

Benn, William, 70

Berks Mall, *101*, 182, 234. *See also* Polett Walk

Berks Walkway, 115

Berndt, Jerry, 160, 161

Bertucci, Bob, 176

Bestor, Arthur, 186

Beury, Charles Ezra, 23, 29, 31, 32, *42*, 43, 45, 48–51 passim, *49, 51*, 53, 59–67 passim, 75, 86, 148, *156*, 157, 158, 217, 276

Beury Beach, *107*, 108

Beury Hall, 86, 108, 112, 208, 209–210

Beury Stadium. *See* Temple Stadium

Biava, Luis, *143*, 146

Biology–Life Sciences Building, 112

Birdsong, Henry E., 148

Black Panthers, 124, 125

Blai, Boris, *4*, 6, 44, 55, *55*, 56, 57, 69, *70*, 89

Blanding, Scott, *288*

Blatstein, Bart, 232, *232*

Blockson, Charles Leroy, 273, *273. See also* Charles L. Blockson Afro-American Collection

Bobrow, Alan, 162

Bohn, J. Lloyd, 68, *86*

Bok, Curtis, 85

Boles, John, 167

Bolton, Thaddeus L., 62

Borneman, Henry S., 33

Borsavage, Costic "Ike," 162

Boufadel, Michel, 212

Bovaird, Kathryn F., 15

Bowman, John, 53

Boyer, Benjamin Franklin, 34, 240

Boyer Griswold, Esther, 145, *145,* 198

Boyer College of Music and Dance, 56, 142–148, *149, 227*, 228, 279. *See also* College of Music; Esther Boyer Theater

Boyle, Kay, *205*

Bradley, David, *205*, 234

Bradley, Ed, 153

Bradshaw, William D. "Bill," 177

Brakin, Joseph, 82

Bremner, Lindsay, 213

Breslin, Jill, 177

Brigham, Prince, 247

Bright, Jane Linn Erwin, 266

Bright Hall, 266

Bright Hope Baptist Church, 193

Broad Street, 2, 15, 19, *35, 41*, 43, 50, *53, 58*, 62, 65, 74, 75, 77, 81, 82, 86, 87, 88, *93*, 95, 101, 111, 115, *120, 135*, 143, 145, 190, *193*, 198, 210, *232*, 233, 234, 250, 257, *282, 285. See also* North Broad Street

Brocchi, Tony, 164

Brodhead, Richard, 145, 146

Brodsky, Mel, 163

Brookline Square Country Club, 74, 75, *76*

Brooks, Richard, *95*

Broomell, I. Norman, 32

Brown, Edna, 170

Brown, Elaine, 93, 146

Brown, Joe, *112*, 113

Brown, Ronald T., 258

Brownstein, Barbara L., 187–188, 195, 206, 252

Brubaker, Alyssa, 228

Brubeck, Dave, 144

Brunner, Mathew, 180

Bruscia, Ken, 275

Bucher, Robert M., 83

Bucknell, William, 13–14, 20

Buckwalter, W. Roy, 259

Budd, Edward G., 59

Bufano, Beniamino, 182

Bunche, Ralph, 128

Bunting, John R., *90*, 133

Burk, Alfred E., 127

Burkley, Raymond L., 43, 276, *276, 277*

Burk Mansion, 127

Burnett, Emory W., 63

Burney, Leroy E., 83, *83*, 132, 133

Bush-Brown, James, *264, 265*, 266

Bush-Brown, Louise Carter, 266

Business School. *See* Fox School of Business and Management

Butterweck, Joseph S., 57, 58, 59, 215, 238

Buttonwood campus. *See* Eighteenth and Buttonwood campus

C

Caldwell, William T., 90

Camp, Walter, 157

Camp Hilltop, *95*

Canning, Katie, 177

Caproni, Gianni, 200

Caproni, Maria Fede, 200

Capus, Steve, 153

Cardoza, Tonya, 173, *173*

Carey, Dwight, *262*

Carnegie, Andrew, 7

Carnell, Laura, 18, 23, 35, 37, 38, 41–45 passim, *43, 44*, 59, 60, 128, 158, 179, 195, 214, 277, 282

Carnell Hall, *35*, 45, 49, 50, 65, *85*, 111, 115, 282

Carter, Jimmy, 99, *113*, 183

Carter, Joseph C., 4

Casale, Ernie, 160, 166, 168, 177, 198

Casey, Don, 164

Casey, Robert P., 193, 195

Catanzaro, Jane, 174

Cecil B. Moore/Temple University Subway Station, 62, 86, *193*

Cedarbrook Center, 74, 75, *76*, 104

Cedarbrook Country Club, 75, 76

Center City Campus. *See* Temple University Center City (TUCC)

Center for Advanced Photonics Research, 209

Center for Biotechnology, 209

Center for Community Studies, 123

Center for Frontier Sciences, 216

Center for Gifted Young Musicians, 144

Center for Information Science and Technology, 209

Center for Intergenerational Learning, 275

Center for International Business and Research, 262

Center for Minority Health and Health Disparities, 274

Center for Neurovirology and Cancer Biology, 209

Center for Obesity Research and Education, 274

Center for Research in Human Development and Education, 216, 275

Center for Social Policy and Community Development, 127, 274

Center for Sustainable Communities and Department of Community and Regional Planning, 267–268

Center for the Advancement and Study of Entrepreneurship, 260

Center for the Study of Federalism, 105

Chamberlain, W. Edward, 80

Chaney, John, *140*, 164, *165*, 188, 194

Chang, Sarah, 144

Chapel of the Four Chaplains, 15, *15*

Chapman, Francis, 33, 34

Charles Klein Law Center, 87, 115, 240, 241

Charles Klein Law Library, *33*, 34, 237, 240. *See also* Klein Law School Library

Charles L. Blockson Afro-American Collection, *52*, 237, 273, *273*

Chase, Agnes Barr, 80

Chase, Theodore L., 80

Cheeseman-Alexander, Gwen, 174

Chestnut Hill, 76, 113

Children's Hospital of Philadelphia, 246

China, Temple programs in, 135, *136,* 200, 202–203, *203,* 204, 215, 242, 262

Chirchman, Mrs. Richard W., *82*

Chiropody Class 1934, *65*

Chivian, Howard, 179

Chodoroff, Arthur D., 179, *179*, 180

Christian Church, 15

Christian Science Church. *See* Park Hall; Shusterman Hall; Stauffer Hall

Cinematheque Theater, 269

Clafen, George, 213

Clarke, Darrell L., 233

Clarke, Eunice, 58

Clayton, Constance E., 216, *216*

Cliburn, Van, 143

Clink, Lucy, *200*

Clinton, Bill, *57*

Clinton, Hillary, *57*

Cochran, Harry A., 37, 149, 259

Coco, Bill, 168

Cody, Josh, 160, 162, 163, 177

Cohen, Fred, 163

Coico, Richard, 248

College Hall, *18*, 19, *19*, 21, 26, 27, 33, 34, 41–45 passim, 50–53 passim, *52*, 106, 109, 151, 155, 156, 233, 243, 282

College of Allied Health Professions, 250, 256–258, *257, 257. See also* College of Health Professions and Social Work

College of Communications, 86

College of Education, *19, 43*, 111, 125, 127, 136, 137, 147, 209, 213–216, *214, 215*, 256, 257, 258, 269, 275. *See also* School of Education; Teachers College

College of Engineering, 99, 209, 210–212, 274

College of Engineering, Computer Science, and Architecture, 211

College of Engineering and Architecture, 211

College of Engineering Technology, 105, 211, 212–213. *See also* Temple Technical Institute

College of Health, Physical Education, Recreation and Dance, 147, 148, 178, 257–258, 263. *See also* School of Tourism and Hospitality Management

College of Health Professions and Social Work, 128, 237, 256, 257, 258, *258. See also* College of Allied Health Professions; Health Sciences Center

College of Liberal Arts, 90–91, 95, 105, 115, 126, 139, 148, 149, 204–208, 229, 268, 269, 274, 275. *See also* College of Liberal Arts and Sciences

College of Liberal Arts and Sciences, 23, 39, 41, 45, 60, *205*, 208, 212, 238, 258, 273. *See also* College of Liberal Arts

College of Music, 86, 111, 142, 144, *145*, 154, 269, 275. *See also* Boyer College of Music and Dance

College of Podiatry, 218

College of Science and Technology, 204, 207, 208–210, 216. *See also* Center for Frontier Sciences; Center for Information Science and Technology; College of Liberal Arts and Sciences

College of Theater, 86

Collins, Judy, 143

Columbia Station. *See* Cecil B. Moore/Temple University Subway Station

Commerce Drive, 269

Community Mental Health Center, 122, 123, *125*

Computer Activity Building, 115

Conant, Dave, 154

Conlin, Bill, 165

Connell, Mary, *276*

Contemporary Culture Collection, 237

Conwell, Russell Herman, 1–21, *5, 6, 7, 10*, 23–45 passim, *25, 27, 29, 35, 45*, 51, *51*, 53, *53*, 54, 59, 84, 87, 90, 95, 106, 130, 145, 155, 180, 182, *189*, 204, 218, 256, 264, 272, *280*, 281, 282, 286, 287

Conwell, Sarah F., 4, *6*, 18, 38, 44, 45, 87

Conwell Dance Theater, 147

Conwell Hall, 21, *22*, 34, *35, 36*, 44, 45, 49, 50, 53, 62, *62, 74, 85*, 97, 108, 109, 111, *116*, 147, 154, 156, 188, 233, *277*, 282

Conwell Inn, 221, 229, *229*

Conwell School of Theology, 41

Conwell's Temple. *See* Temple, The

Cook, Arthur, 168

Cooke, Alistair, 16

Cooney, Marie B., 277, *277*

Cooney, Russell Conwell, 113

Cooney Apartments, 113, 230

Copland, Aaron, 144

Coppes, Charles D., 180

Corcoran, Kay, 176

Cornelius, Jeffrey, 142, 145

Corson, Frederick P., 77

Cosby, Bill, 97, *104*, 154, 164, *177*, 182, *182*, 183, *183*, 194, 195

Cosby, William Henry. *See* Cosby, Bill

Costello, Josephine K., *82*

Cottage Hall, 266

Cotton, Frank Albert, *207*

Crawford, James J., 210

Creamer, Robert H., 211

Cromer, Joe, 164

Cronholm, Lois, 206, 207

Cummings, Gail L., 175

Cunningham, Ed, 153

Curran, Thomas Aloysius "Bear," 168

Curtis, Charlene, 173

Curtis, Cyrus H. K., 53, 85

Curtis Hall, 73, 85, *85*, 86, *97*, 108, 262

Curtis Tower of Learning, 53

Cutler, Jon, 120

D

D. William Zahn Instructional Media Center, 111

Dager, Forrest E., 40, *40*, 182

Dai, Hai Lung. *See* Hai Lung Dai

Daly, John M., 247, 248, 249

Daniels, Elva, 179

Daniels-Oleksok, S., 176

Darling-Hammond, Linda, 216, *216*

Darwin, Pat, 97

Dash, Samuel, 123

Davies, Charles M., 11, 12

Davis, Franklin, 209

Davis, Theodore, *276*

Del Aguila, Kevin, 152

D'Eliscue, Francis, 157, 162

Deng Xiaoping, 135, *136*

Dental/Pharmacy Building, 82, *82*, 250

Dental School, 32, 108, 190, 252. *See also* Maurice H. Kornberg School of Dentistry; Philadelphia Dental College

Dental School Clinical Annex, *252*

Dervitz, Hyman L., 258

Desmond, Kathleen, 279

Dewey, John, 54, 57

Diabetic Center of Excellence, 255

Diamond Band of Temple University, 179, *179*

Diamond Club, 113, 279

Diamond Gems, 180

Diamond Marching Band, 277

Diamond Marching Band and Pep Band, 180

Dickerson, Ron, 161

Dickson, Casey, 176

Didinger, Ray, 165

Dienes, Samuel L., 162

Digestive Diseases Center, 246

DiPietro, Joe, 176

Disston, Henry, 9, 10

Dittmar, Joseph, 278

Divinity School. *See* School of Theology

Dixon, D. Brenda, 147

Dixon, F. Eugene "Fitz," Jr., 113, *113*, 133, 267

Dixon House. *See* Eleanor Widener Dixon House

Dobrin, Peter, 145

Dolan, Theresa, 228

Donovan, William J., *15*

Dotson, John L., Jr., 150

Doukas, Peter, 250

Downes, Robin Atkin, 152

Dr. John and Joan H. Ballots Preclinical Laboratory, 253

Drexel, Anthony J., 20

Drysdale, Bruce, 163

Duckworth, Loretta, 279

Dunham, Barrows, 94, *94*, 95

Dunham, James Henry, 39, 60, 90, 94

Dunkelberg, William C., 203, 260

Dunn, Jack, 167

Dunphy, Fran, 165, 287

DuPlessis, Rachel Blau, *205*, 273

Dupree, Candice, 173

Durant, Thomas, 80, 81

DuVall, Everett, 127

Dyniewski, John, 168

E

Ealy, Lawrence O., 156

Earhart, Amelia, *61*

Earle, George H., 48, 67

Earnest, Ernest P., 93

Eberman, Paul W., 215

Ecole de Beaux Arts, 56

Edberg-Olson, George, 161

Edberg-Olson Hall, 161

Edge, The, 231, *233*

Edwin and Trudy Weaver Historical Dental Museum, 253

Egner, Vera, 173

Eighteenth and Buttonwood campus, 27–32 passim, *28*, *29*, *31*, *37*, 49, 62, 73, 81, 82, *101*, 104, 210

Eisenhower, Dwight, 16, 183

Eisenhower, Mamie, 255

Eleanor Widener Dixon House, 113, *113*

Elesh, David, 75

Elkins, William L., 10, 55

Elkins, William M., 75

Elkins Park, 55, 56, 225, 228

Elmira Jeffries (building), 231

Engineering and Architecture Building, 115, *210*

Englert, Richard M., 216, 264

English, Maurice, 105, 106

English, O. Spurgeon, 47, 80

Entertainment and Community Education Center, 154, 231, *231*

Episcopal Hospital, 244, 247

Epps, JoAnne A., 243

Ericksen, Julia, 273

Ernesta Ballard Healing Garden, *265*, 268

Erny, Charles G., 59, 75, *156*, 157, 158

Erny Field, 167

Esposito, Louis J., 197

Esther Boyer College of Music and Department of Dance. *See* Boyer College of Music and Dance; College of Music

Esther Boyer Theater, *145*

Evening Technical School, 210

Ewell, John, *211*

Ewell, Lynne Tarka, *211*

F

Faculty Club. *See* Diamond Club

Fagan, Jay, 128

Farrand, Beatrix Jones, *265*, 266

Fell, Norman, 154

Ferdun, Edrie, 147

Ferman, Barbara, 274

Fernandez, Happy Craven, 216, *216*

Fesenmaier, Dan, 263

Fiorillo, Alexander, 279

First Methodist Episcopal Church, 40

Fitzgerald, Ella, 143

Flagg, J. Foster, 253

Flagg, Josiah, 253

Fleckenstein, Edward L., 210, 211

Flexner, Abraham, 30, 32

Flour fight, *64*

Foley, Kristen A., 178

Fonda, Jane, *104*

Food vendor trucks, 233–234, *234*

Foot and Ankle Institute, 255

Ford, Betty, 255

Ford, Charles A., 60, 104

Forster, Dieter, 238

Fort Dix, 69

Fort Washington Campus. *See* Temple University Fort Washington

Forum, 19

Founder's Garden, 44, *45*, 195

Fowlkes, Deborah W., 277

Fox, Richard J., 124, 190, 259, *259*

Fox, Robert A., *259*

Fox, William C., 213

Fox Chase Cancer Center, 244

Fox School of Business and Management, 23, 34, 35, 85, 86, 149, 203, 204, 211, 225, 226, 256, 259–263, *262*, 269. *See also* School of Commerce

Franke, Nikki, 175, *175*

Franklin Field, *66*, *157*, 158, *164*

Friedman, Murray, 273

Fritz, W. Wallace, 26, 27

Fuch, Lauren, 174

Fuller, Charles, *205*

G

Gable, Fred B., 82

Gait Study Center, 256

Gamble, John, 147

Garretson-Greatheart Hospital, *29*

Garretson Hospital, 23, 28, 29, 31, 256

Garretson Hospital for Oral Surgery, 27

Garrett, Allen, 145

Gates, Thomas S., 48

Gautieri, Ronald, 250

Geasey, Robert V., 78

Geasey Athletic Complex, 177

Geasey Field, 78, 190, *190*, 199

General Alumni Association, 23, 31 (Medical School), 43, 193, 211, 212, 256 (School of Nursing), 276–277, *276*, 279

George, Jason, 152

George and Joy Abbott Center for Musical Theater, 146

George D. Widener Hall, 267

George E. Walk Auditorium, 111

Georgian Terrace, *55*

Gerhart, Ursula, 279

Gholson, Eva, 147, 148

Gies, William J., 32

Gilliland, Charles E., Jr., 259

Gimbel's Department Store, 34

Gionta, Matthew, 279

Gionta, Rachel Oliver, 279

Giordano, Antonio, 209

Giovanelli, Letizia Caproni, 200

Gipp, George, *160*

Gittis, Howard, 224, *230*, *242*

Gladfelter, Millard E., 54, 59, 73, 76, 81, *82*, 83, 84, 90, 92, 102, 103, *103*, 104, 108, 109, *109*, 115, *118*, 120, 122, 123, *130*, 134, 142, 182, 257, 267

Gladfelter Hall, 6, 115

Glasser, David, 213

Golanoski, Laura Brooks, 279

Golanoski, Lee, 279

Golden, Al, 161, *161*

Golder, Charles, 179

Goldstein, Leonard, 97, *97*

Goode, W. Wilson, 193

Goodman, Benny, 144

Gordon, A. J., 41

Gordon, John, 40

Gordon-Conwell Theological Seminary, 41

Gottschild, Hellmut, 147

Grabfelder, Rick, 97

Grace Baptist Church, 6, 9, 12, 13, 14, 15, 16, 18, *40*

Grace Baptist Temple. *See* Temple, The

Graham, Billy, 16, 41

Grant, Ulysses S., 4

Gratz College, 54

Gray, William H., 193

Great Court of Mitten Hall, 50, *50*

Greatheart Hospital, 25, *29*

Greenberg, Robert, 152

Greenfield, Albert M., 51, 59, 113, *121*

Griswold, Earle, 145, *145*, 198

Griswold, Esther Boyer, 145, *145*

Gruber, Jacob, *200*

H

H. Evert Kendig Memorial Museum, 82, *82*

Hadden, Britton, 67

Hafed, Ali, 6

Haffer, Rollin, 172

Hai Lung Dai, 209

Haines, Jane Browne, 264, 266

Hairston, Kamesha, 173

Halbert, Terry, 239, 260

Hall, Daryl, 142

Hall, G. Stanley, 20

Halpern, Sidney, 267

Hamelin, Marc-Andre, 146

Hamilton, Andrew, 21

Hamilton, Hughbert, 105

Hamilton, Ida, 25

Hamlin, Arthur T., 107

Hammond, Frank C., 30, 31, 32

Hardin, Wayne, 160, 177

Hardt Building, 87

Hardwick, Aaron W., 88

Hardwick, Ida Seal, 88

Hardwick Hall, 10, 88, 97

Harland, Alan, 146

Harmon-Weiss, Sandra, 279

Harnwell, Gaylord P., 102

Harper, William Rainey, 20

Harrigan, Katie, 176

Harris, Dionna, 176

Harrisburg Campus. *See* Temple University Harrisburg

Harrison, Sally, 213

Harrison, William H., 216

Hart, Ann Weaver, *203*, 225, 226, *246*, *248*, 277, 281–288 passim, *285*, *286*

Hart, Kaye, 178

Hart, Randy, 285

Harting, Hugh E., 54

Hartman, David William, 247

Harwood, Kenneth, 150, 152, 154

Hathaway, Ronald, 238

Haverford College, 21

Hayden, Jennie P., 4

Hayre, Ruth Wright, *215*

Haythornthwaite, Robert M., 211

Health Sciences Center, *37*, *81*, 83, *83*, 108, 123, *125*, 133, 190, 234, 237, 243, *244*, *245*, 249, 255, 257, 267, 279, 283, 286

Hedley, Robert, 151

Heller, Napoleon, 62

Henderson, Don, 162

Henry, George, 80

Henry Disston & Son Saw Works, 9

Herbert, James W., 179

Herbst, Susan, 207

Herrick, Kristine, 194

Hershovitz, Jerry, 97

Hervey, John G., 33

Hess, Nancy, 144, *144*, *146*

Higgins, Frederick B., 211, 212

Higginson, Bobby, 167

Higher Education Center, 105

Hill, Sonny, 165

Hires, Charles E., 18

Hirsh-Pasek, Kathryn, 208

Hirtzel, Cynthia S., 212

Hochner, Arthur, 218

Hodge, Derrick, 146

Hodgens, Helen Williams, 41

Hodges, Felicia, 170

Hodgkinson, Harold L., 131

Hoffman, Eli, 278

Hogner, Nils, *15*

Hohl, Daryl. *See* Hall, Daryl

Holmes, Edward W., 27

Holzman, Alex, 106

Honors Program, 58–59, 238–239, *238*

Hope-Jones, Robert, 15

Horvath, Barbara, 279

Hostettler, Gordon, 149

Howard Gittis Student Center, 230, *230*. *See also* Student Activities Center (SAC)

Howell, Charles L., 82, 251

Huganir, George H., 92

Hunting Park, 76, 157, *157*

Hurley, Evelyn, 176

Hyman, Annie D., 126

Hyman, Bill, 178

I

Icard, Larry D., 128

Independence Blue Cross Recreation Center, 198

Independence Hall, *117*

Independence Park, 255

Independence Square, 33

Ingram, George, 108

Institute for Clinical Simulation and Patient Safety, 247

Institute for Survey Research, 105, 275

Institute on Developmental Disabilities, 275

Institute on Disabilities, 216

Instruction Materials Center, *214*

Ismail, Amid I., 253

J

J. Conrad Seegers Student Lounge, 111

Jackson, Chevalier, 80

Jackson, Chevalier Lawrence, 80

Jackson, Jesse, 128

Jackson, Michael, 263

Jacobson, Susan, 150

Jacobson, Thomas, 152

James, Henry, 108

James E. Beasley School of Law. *See* Beasley School of Law

James S. White Residence Hall, 197, *197*

Janney, Amanda, *174*, 175

Japan, Temple programs in. *See* Temple University Japan (TUJ)

Jarmoluk, Mike, 70

Jayne Lebow Haines Center for Pharmacogenomics and Drug Safety, 251

Jeanes Hospital, 244, 247

Jeffries, Clifford, 123

Jencks, Christopher, 89

Jenny, John H., 179

Jhin, Michael, 244

Jimenez, Carlos, *227*

Ji Yunshi, *203*

Joachim, Steve, 160

Johnny Ring Garden, 6, 89

Johnson, George W., 206

Johnson, Lady Bird, 255

Johnson, Lyndon B., 100, *121*, 183, 260

Johnson, Peggy, 67

Johnson, Robert Livingston, 40, 47, 66–71 passim, *68*, 75–78 passim, *77*, 83, 84, 85, 88, 91, *91*, 92, 94, 102, 105, 108, *111*, 160, 179, 217

Johnson Hall, 10, 88, 97, *109*

Johnson-Hardwick Commons, 197

Johnson-Hardwick Hall, 10. *See also* Hardwick Hall; Johnson Hall

John Wanamaker Middle School, 233

Jones, David, 177

Jones, Edith Bolling, 83, 257

Jones, Shirley, *95*

Jones Hall, 83, 257, 279

Jordan, David Starr, 20

Joseph, Ulrick "Rico," *212*

Joyce, John St. George, 59

Juliano, Joe, 165

K

Kardon Building, 193, 231

Kashow, Carol, 176

Kassi, Bob, 154

Katz, Stephen M., 150

Kawal, Albert, 160

Keating, Walter, 166

Keener, Becca, *174*

Keener, Kaylee, *174*

Keller, Helen, 16, *58*

Kendall, Philip, 208

Kendig, H. Evert, 28, 82, *82*

Keneseth Israel Synagogue, *33*, 34, 40, 87. *See also* Klein Law School Library

Kennedy, Bill "Pickles," 163, 166

Kennedy, John Fitzgerald, 73, 97, *97*, 100, 183, 260

Kensington, 10

Kensington Neighborhood House, *20*

Kerr, Clark, 131, 132, 186

Kerr, Mrs. S. Logan, *82*

Kerrigan, Joe, 166

Kerstetter, Marie R., *174*

Keshner, Emily, *258*

Keystone Institute for Translational Medicine, 248

Kidder, Louise, 273

Kilarsky, Mary, 176

Kimmel, Martin, *230*

King, Billie Jean, 175

King, Martin Luther, Jr., 16, 118, *119*, 128, 278

Kinsella, Thomas, *205*

Kitch, Carolyn, 150

Kitchen, Shirley M., 233

Klecko, Dan, 162

Klecko, Joe, 162

Klein, Charles, 34, 59, 67, *103*, *118*, 240

Klein, Lew, 153

Klein Law School Library, 87, *114*, 115, 241. *See also* Charles Klein Law Library; Keneseth Israel Synagogue

Kline, Carol Sauppe, 174

Kline, Lawrence C., *118*

Kline, Reba, *118*

Knowles, Brigitte, 182

Knowles, John Christopher, 212, 213

Knox, Simmie, *57*

Kolff, Jacob, 246

Kolmer, John A., 80

Kolotouros, Jason, 152

Kornberg, Maurice H., *253*

Kornberg School of Dentistry. *See* Maurice H. Kornberg School of Dentistry

Kotin, Paul, 133

Koufax, Sandy, *104*

Kovaci, Alma, 176

Krauskopf, Joseph, 40

Kress, Roy, 215

Kris's Coffee Truck, 234

L

La Democracia Village School, *288*

Laird, Helen, 145, 179

Lambader, Frank, 18, 155

Lambdin-Ciarocca, Kim, 175, 176

Lancaster, Burt, *95*

Lashner, Marilyn, 153

Laurel Hill Cemetery, 44

Law School of Temple College. *See* School of Law

Lawrence, David, 86, 102

Leaf, Hilda, 64

Leaness, William "Pete," 167

Lear, Harold "Hal," 156, 163, 278

Leason, Lyman S., 39–40

Lechtzin, Stanley, 182

Le Clair, Charles G., 56, 134

Lee, Elizabeth Leighton, 266

Legal Aid Clinic, 126

Lenco, Louise, 174

Leonard, Curtis, 121, 128

Leonard S. Abrams Center for Advanced Wound Healing, 255

Levine, Barry, 153

Levy, J. Leonard, 40

Lexington, Massachusetts, 6

Liacouras, James Peter, 186

Liacouras, Peter James, 99, 133, 139, 154, 186–189, *187*, *188*, *189*, 190–196 passim, 202, *203*, 206, 209, 217–228 passim, *224*, 234, 238, 241, 252, 254, 263, 273, 284

Liacouras Center, 141, *145*, *164*, *165*, 185, 198, *198*, 218

Liacouras Walk, 10, *11*, 18, 63, 182, 191, *191*, 197, 218, 226–227, 229, *229*, 234, 242

Liberal Arts College. *See* College of Liberal Arts

Lillie, Walter Ivan, 80

Lincoln Financial Field, 161, *164*

Lindorff, Joyce, 146

Lingle, James M., 18

Lisken, Sydney, 82

Littlefield, John, 152

Litwack, Harry, 162, 163, 164, *164*, 166, 172

Liu, Yue. *See* Yue Liu

Llewellyn, Robert, 137

Lockhart, Barbara D., 172, 178

Logan, James D., 128, 129

Lonsdale, Thomas P., 13, 16, 18

Low, Seth, 20

Luce, Henry R., 67

Lucey, Patrick J., 223

Lyde, Kevin, *165*

M

MacDonald, John, 169, 276, *276*

MacDonald, Linda, 173

Macon, Mark, 164

MacWilliams, Dave, 167

Macy, Anne Sullivan. *See* Sullivan, Anne

Madden, Thomas, 279

Madison, Michelle, 174

Main, The, 31

Makris, George, 160

Mall, James, 238

Malloy, Maureen, 154

Malmud, Leon, 244, 246

Mann Chiang Niu, 135, 202

Mannino, Bill, 169

Manpower Research Institute, 260

Manto, Jeff, 167

Manze, Vince, 278

Mao Tse-tung, 135

Marsalis, Wynton, 147

Marshall, Joseph W. "Chip," III, 246

Marshall, Joseph W., Jr., 241

Marshall, Thurgood, 128

Martin, Alfred N., 250

Martin, Frank, 166

Marzano, John, 167

Massachusetts, 3, *3*, 6

Mast, Eddie, 164

Mathias-Darnley, Emma, 256

Matthews, Chris, 153

Mattiacci, John A., 254

Maurek, Veronica "Ronnie," 173, 176, 178

Maurice H. Kornberg School of Dentistry, 27, 32, 251–254, 286. *See also* Dental School; Philadelphia Dental College

Mauro, Linda, 128

Mauro, Steve, 177

Mazze, Edward M., 260

McBride, Christian, 144

McCarthy, Joseph R., 94

McConnon, Joan Dawson, 127

McCurdy, Will, 44

McEvilla, Joseph D., 250

McGoey, Grace Schuler, 174

McGonigle, Arthur T., 112

McGonigle Arena, 143, 147

McGonigle Hall, 99, 112, 124, *124*, 126, 164, *164*, 165, 177, 199

McGovern, Andy, 173

McGovern, George, 16

McGrath, Earl J., 105

McGuire, C. Kent, 216

McInaw, Hugh, 167

McKevitt, John G., 108

McKinley, Albert E., 39

McLaughlin, Ben, 167

McMahan, Herbert E., 178, 179

McPherson, James, 4

McWilliams, Seamus, 177

Mead, Margaret, 16

Medical Education and Research Building, *83*, 84, 246, 248, *248*, 249

Medical School. *See* School of Medicine

Mehta, Zubin, 146

Melchoir, William F., 210

Mellen, Joan, *205*

Mello, Christine, 279

Mencken, H. L., 44

Mendek, Bill, 167

Merton, Robert King, *53*, *204*

Messikomer, Ernest, 162

Metcalf, Ralph, 169, 170

Metzger, Charles E., 54, 68

Middleton, Virginia, 173

Midvale Steel Works, 9, 34

Miller, Henry J. "Heinie," 158

Miller, Leigha Swayze, *20*

Minehart, John R., 28

Mita Hall, 201

Mitchell, Sally, 273

Mitnik, Sharon, 170

Mitten, Thomas E., 50, *50*

Mitten Hall, *2*, 4, 6, *37*, 43, 47–53 passim, *50*, *51*, *52*, 65, 67, *67*, 69, 87–97 passim, *92*, *101*, 109, 113, 127, 143, 147, 151, *166*, 188, 190, 210, *276*, 278, 279

Mlkvy, Bill, 77, 163, *163*, 172

Moak, Lennox, 187

Mobley, Eric, 170

Montier, Agnes Berry, 27, 246

Montoya, Carlos, 143

Monument Cemetery, 44, 87

Moore, Edna L., 256

Moore, Jack, 154

Moore-O'Leary, Amanda "Mandee," 175

Morris, Patricia Collins, 173

Morris and Sylvia Barrack Hall, 243. *See also* Barrack Hall

Morrison, Roy, 160

Moss-Coane, Marjorie "Marty," *155*

Motten, Clement G., 80

Moulder, Leon O. "Lonnie," Jr., *251*

Moulder, Sharon, *251*

Moulder Center for Drug Discovery Research, 251, *251*

Multimedia Urban Reporting Lab, 150

Municipal Auditorium, 15

Murase, Kenneth, 69

Murphy, Aaron, 176, 177

Murphy, David, 279

Murrow, Edward R., 16

Music School, 33, 40. *See also* Boyer College of Music and Dance; College of Music

Muspratt, Kirk, 279

Muti, Riccardo, 146

Myer and Rosaline Feinstein Center for American Jewish History, 273

N

Naismith, James, 155

Nash, Gary, 10

National Spatial Intelligence and Learning Center, 208

Nayyar, Kunal, 152

Neely, James, 167

Nelson, Harry, 168

Nemchik, George, *166*, 167

Neumann Medical Center, 244, 254

Newcombe, Nora, 208

Newhouse, Jean Shiley, 70

New School Institute of Music, 145

Newton, Huey P., 124

Newton Seminary, 6

Nicetown, 9

Nichols, Henry, 136

Niebuhr, Herman, Jr., 111, 123

1940 Residence Hall, 86, 197

Niu, Mann Chiang, *See* Mann Chiang Niu

Nixon, Richard M., *91*, 135, 183

Noel, Curt, 97, *97*

Nolen, James A., 59, 81

Nolen, James A., Jr., 89

Norman, Jay, 163

Norris Homes, 257

North Broad Street, 10, 16, 18, 25, *25*, 28, *33*, 44, 47, 76, 82, 87, 112, 113, 115, 127, 190, 197, 198, 199, 211, 232, 234, 244, 248, 250, 251. *See also* Broad Street

Northeastern Hospital, 244, 246, 254

Northern Liberties, 10

North Philadelphia Station, 62

North Tower, 130

Norvell, Ralph, 129, 240, 241

Notebaert, Edmond F., 246

Nunez, Jackie, 176

Nutter, Michael, *248*

O

Oak Lane, 54

Oak Lane Country Day School, 47, 54, 68

Oak Lane Laboratory School, 214

Oates, John, 142

Obama, Barack, 183, *216*

O'Brien, Dave, 177

O'Brien, Denise, 273

Ockenga, Harold J., 41

Ogden, Ben, 169

Oglesby, Carole, 173

O'Hara, Daisy, 256

O'Lenik, Dolores, 97, *97*

Oliver, Len, 167

Olney High School, 74

Olson, Toby, *205*

Orkis, Lambert, 146

Ormandy, Eugene, 146

Orwell, George, *74*

Ost, Ruth, 238, 239

Ovsiew, Leon, 102, 137

Owens, Jesse, 169, 170

Owl Stadium. *See* Temple Stadium

Oxendine, Joseph, 147

Oxford Village, 231

P

Packard Building, 28, 81, 251

Packel, Israel, 241

Page, Robert, 146

Palestra, 164

Paley, Samuel, 106

Paley, William S., 106

Paley Library, *52*, 99, 106, *106*, 107, *107*, *111*, *135*, *148*, 199, 233, 234, 237, 238, 277. *See also* Temple University Libraries

Palmer, Paul, 160

Panaro, Hugh, 146

Pan-Hellenic House, 64, 95

Park Avenue Methodist Church, 86

Park Hall, 86, 242, *242*. *See also* Shusterman Hall; Stauffer Hall

Parkinson, William N., 31, 32, *32*, 66, 78, 80, 81, 82, 83, 91, 133, 243

Parkinson Pavilion, 83, *83*, 244

Park Mall, 89. *See also* Liacouras Walk

Parkman, Henry, 248

Parshall, William E., 269

Pasternak, Jill, 154

Paulos, John Allen, *209*

Peabody, Gertrude D., 50, 63, 64, 88, *95*

Peabody Hall, 6, 87, 97

Peacock, Eulace, 169, 170

Pearl Theater, *232*

Pearson, Albert "Reds," 112

Pearson, Lester B., *118*

Pearson Hall, 112, 126

Pearson-McGonigle Complex, *112*

Penn Center Academy. *See* Temple High School

Pennsylvania College of Podiatric Medicine, 254. *See also* School of Podiatric Medicine; School of Podiatry

Pennsylvania Company, 67

Pennsylvania Railroad North Broad Street Station, *9*

Pennsylvania School of Horticulture for Women, 264, *264*, 265–267. *See also* Temple University Ambler

Pennsylvania State Office Building, 89

Pepper, Eleanor, 174

Pepper, Jane Guest, 266

Perkins, Bob, 154

Perry, J. Douglas, 3, 19, 31, *40*, 149, 150

Perry, Tim, 164

Peterson, Carl, 168

Pete's Tavern, *87*

Pew, J. Howard, 41

Pharmacy School. *See* School of Pharmacy

Philadelphia City Hall, *270*, 286

Philadelphia Civic Center, 195

Philadelphia Dance Collection, *148*

Philadelphia Dental College, 253, 256

Philadelphia Gas Works, 193, 194

Philadelphia Law School of Temple University, 33

Philadelphia Normal School, 48, 214

Philadelphia Rapid Transit Company, 50, *50*

Philadelphia School of Music, 40

Philadelphia School of Music of Temple College, 39

Philip and Barbara Albright Winter Garden, 268

Pignoli, Rocci, 176

Pike, H. Edward, 180

Pinchot, Gifford, 48

Platsoucas, Chris D., 209

Polett Walk, *229*. *See also* Berks Mall

Poling, Daniel K., 15

Pollack, Harvey, 165

Porat, M. Moshe, 203, 260, 262, 263

Powell, Colin L., 242

Powell, Shirley, 153

Powell, Walter, 138

President's Hall, 56

Presser, Theodore, 111

Presser Hall, *109*, 111, 112, *135*, 143, 146

Preston, C. Anita, 171, *172*

Price, Glenda, *257*

Progress Plaza, *122*, 233

Public Ledger Building, 33

Putnam, Alice, 174, 175

Q

Quedenfeld, Theodore (Ted), 277, *277*

Quinn, Brian, 169

R

Raines, John C., 118

Randall, Paul E. "Pop," 112, 148, 149, 150, 151, *151*

Randall Laboratory Theater, 112, 151

Randall Morgan Estate, 76

Rare Books and Manuscripts Collection, 237

Raynes, Arthur, *242*

Reading Station, *194*

Reagan, Nancy, 255

Reagan, Ronald, *160*

Reber, J. Howard, 34

Reber Hall, *33*, 34, 86, 145, 240. *See also* Rock Hall

Red Owl, *181*, 182

Reeb, James J., *117*

Reese, Merrill, 154

Reference Reading Room in Sullivan Memorial Library, *52*

Regional Rail Station, 193. *See also* Cecil B. Moore/Temple University Subway Station

Rehnquist, William H., 242

Reimel, Theodore, *90*

Reinstein, Robert J., 202, 241, *241*, 242, *242*

Rendell, Edward G., 233, *235*

Repsher, Adrienne, 176

Reynolds, John W., Jr., 223

Rhoads, John M., 59, 74, 128

Rich, Thaddeus, 40

Richan, Willard, 127

Richards, Dorothy Lerner, 97

Richart, Eileen, 177

Ridenour, Steven, 211

Ridge, Tom, 198

Riesman, David, 89

Ring, Johnny, 3–4, *4*, 6, 89

Ritchie, John C. "Jack," Jr., 260

Rittenhouse Building, 29

Rittenhouse Square, 10

Ritter, Rolland, 111, *214*

Ritter Hall, 111, *214*, 215, 216

Ritter Hall Annex, 111, *214*, 238

Rizzo, Frank, 116, 132

Roberts, A. Addison, 133

Roberts, Jean, 178

Roberts, John B., 149, 150, 153–154

Robinson, Ann McKernan, *147*

Robinson, Armand I., *147*

Rock, Milton, *33*, 145

Rock, Shirley, *33*, 145

Rockefeller, John D., 20

Rock Hall, *33*, 87, 145. *See also* Reber Hall

Rockne, Knute, 158, *160*

Rodgers, Guy, 156, 163, 172

Rodin, Auguste, 56

Roeck, Dale F., 251, 252

Rogers, Brian, 169

Rogul, Herm, 165

Rome (Italy), Temple programs in. *See* Temple University Rome

Roosevelt, Eleanor, *61*, 93

Roosevelt, Franklin Delano, 16, *46*, 47, 51–53, *51*, *52*, 69, 183

Rosen, Bonnie, 176, *176*

Rosen, Edward, 263

Rosenberg, Jeff, 176

Rosenthal, Mark, *152*

Rosenthal, Seymour J., 28, 127

Rosner, Benjamin, 215

Ross, David, 97, *97*

Rossky, William, 84

Roth, Bill, 168

Rubin, Leonard, 243

Rumpf, John, 139, 188, 211

Ruth, Mandi, *174*

S

S.S. *Temple Victory*, *71*

Sabatini, Raphael, *118*

SAC. *See* Student Activities Center

Sadeghipour, Keya, 209, 212

Saget, Bob, 153, 234

Samaritan Hospital, 23, 25, *25*, 26, *26*, 29, 31, 32, *40*, 47, *83*, 256. *See also* Temple University Hospital

Samoff, Zelda, 127

Samuel, Bernard, 76

Sanborn, Sarah F. *See* Conwell, Sarah F.

Sanchez, Pepe, *165*

Sanchez, Sonia, *205*, 273

Sandburg, Carl, *61*, *92*

Sawallisch, Wolfgang, 146

Sax, Reuben. *See* Brooks, Richard

Sbarro, Mario, 209

Sbarro Institute for Cancer Research and Molecular Medicine, 209

Scalessa, Stefanie, 170

Scanlon, Robert G., 192

Schalch, Charles F. (Chuck), 77, 193

Schmieder, Eduard, 146

Schmukler, Joseph, 202

School for Laboratory Technicians, 257

School of Art. *See* Tyler School of Art

School of Business, 23, 35, 211, 259

School of Business Administration, 111, 125, 238, 259. *See also* Fox School of Business and Management

School of Business and Management, 259

School of Business and Public Administration, 149, 259

School of Chiropody, 27, *28*, 28–29, *29*, 254. *See also* School of Podiatric Medicine; School of Podiatry

School of Commerce, 60, 61, 65, 86, 148, 179, 259. *See also* Fox School of Business and Management

School of Communications and Theater, 112, 146, 148, *149*, 150, *150*, 152, 153, 154, *227*, 228, 257, 258, 263, 269. *See also* College of Communications

School of Dentistry, 27, 28, *28*, 29, *29*, 73, 81, *81*, 83, 137, 237, 243, 251, 253. *See also* Maurice H. Kornberg School of Dentistry

School of Domestic Sciences and Art, 35

School of Education, 19, 35. *See also* College of Education; Teachers College

School of Environmental Design, 207, *267*. *See also* Temple University Ambler

School of Industry for Women, 35

School of Law, 1, *19*, 33–34, *33*, 73, 81, *90*, 129, 134, 137, 145, 200, 240, 241, *241*, 242, *242*, 243, 269. *See also* Beasley School of Law

School of Liberal Arts and Sciences, 35. *See also* College of Liberal Arts

School of Medicine, 1, 25–27, 30, 31, 32, 35, 41, 47, 61, 66, 68, 78–83, *78*, 81, *83*, 122, 123, 133, 134, 137, 209, 221, 225, 243, 244, 246–250, 256, 271, 283, 284, 286

School of Music, 35, 40, 142

School of Nursing, 35, 256. *See also* College of Health Professions and Social Work

School of Oratory, 35

School of Pharmacy, 27–28, *28*, *29*, 73, 81, *81*, 82, 83, 108, 237, 243, *251*, 259–261, 269, 286

School of Podiatric Medicine, 27, 28, 81, 254–256, *255*, 286. *See also* School of Chiropody; School of Podiatry

School of Podiatry, 29, 243

School of Science and Technology. *See* College of Science and Technology

School of Social Administration, 99, 111, 127–128, *214*, 257, 258. *See also* College of Health Professions and Social Work

School of Social Work, 274

School of Theology, 35, 40. *See also* Conwell School of Theology; Theology School

School of Tourism and Hospitality Management, 218, 263

Schrag, William A., 210

Schultz-Herda, Eva, 97

Schwartzkopf, Elizabeth, 143

Science Fiction and Fantasy Collection, 237

Scorscone, Joseph, 194

Scott, Jonathan, 260

Scranton, William W., 102, 103, *103*, 111

Scribner, Jay, 136, 215

Scullion, Mary, *127*

Seegers, J. Conrad, 50, 63, 64, 214, 215

Seltzer Building. *See* Vivacqua Hall

Seviss, Lew, 278

Sevy, Roger, 133

Sewell, Trevor, 216

Shafer, Raymond, 123, 125

Shanis, Edna, *61*

Shapp, Milton J., 129, 133

Sharp, William F., 136

Shaw, Artie, *67*

Shay, Harry, 80

Shea, James M., 116

Sheen, Fulton J., *61*

Shepard, Mary E., 27, 246

Sherry, Sol, 244, *247*

Shikler, Aaron, *56*

Shiley-Newhouse, Jean, 170, 171, *171*

Shimkin, Michael, 80

Shoe Museum, 255

Shrier, Al, 177, *177*, 178

Shriners Hospital for Children, *244*, *245*

Shumway, Walter B., 40

Shusterman, Judith, *242*

Shusterman, Murray H., 86, 242, *242*, 243

Shusterman Hall, 86, 185, 242, *242*. *See also* Park Hall; Stauffer Hall

Sills, Beverly, 144

Simons, Herbert W., 117, 118

Simpson, George E., *204*

Simpson, Marietta, 146

Singletary, Bill, 160

Singley, Carl E., 241

Skip Wilson Field, 167

Skoglund, Mrs. S. Palmer, *82*

Slavin, Simon, 127

Sloan, Tina. *See* Sloan-Green, Tina

Sloane, Roberta, 151

Sloan-Green, Tina, 174, 175, 178

Small Business Development Center, 260

Smith, Raymond, 192, 193

Smith, Rhoten, 91, 206

Smith, Robert, 152

Smith, Steve, 271

Smith, Suzanne, 153

Snively, I. Newton, 27

Snyder, Morris, *68*

Solow, Jeffrey, 146

Sol Sherry Thrombosis Research Center, 115, *247*

Sorenson, Corey, 152

Sorrentino, Drew, 177

Soto, Merian, 148

Soufas, Teresa, 207

South Hall, 86, *87*, 97, 126, 143

South Tower, 130

South Worthington, Massachusetts, *3*

Speakman, Frank M., 111, *111*

Speakman Hall, 106, 111, *111*, 259, 262

Speech-Language-Hearing Clinic, 258

Spiegel, Ernest A., 80

Spring Garden Station, 62

Sproul, William C., 31

Sprouls, Kevin, *134*

Sprowls, Joseph B., 82

St. Christopher's Hospital for Children, 246

St. Clair, Jack, 170

St. Clair, Walter, 180

Stafford, Terrell, 147

Stagg, Amos Alonzo, 157

Staiano-Coico, Lisa, 209, 286, *286*, 287

Staley, Dawn, 173, *173*

Stauffer, Herbert, 246

Stauffer, Milton F., 37, 86, 87, 259

Stauffer Hall, 54, 86, 105, 134, 211. *See also* Park Hall; Shusterman Hall

Stegmuller, Agnes "Aggie," 174

Steinberg, Laurence, 208

Steiner, Samuel, 179

Stella Elkins Tyler School of Fine Arts. *See* Tyler School of Art

Stephens, Marilyn, 173

Stern, J. David, 51

Stern, Yair, 153

Stetson, John B., 9, 18

Stetson Hat Company, *8*

Stevens, Pete, 160, 166

Stevenson, John A., 59

Steward, Orlando T., 12

Stewart, Concetta, 152

Stewart, Susan, *205*

Stiles, Joan Edenborn, 174

Stokowski, Leopold, 40, 54

Stone, David L., 142, 143, 145, 146

Stout, Bob, 168

Strand, A. L., *71*

Strategic Compass, 286, 287

Strawberry Square, 128, 271

Street, John F., 233, *235*

Street, Milton, 233

Stroker, Robert T., 145

Strommen, Kim, 200

Stronach, Bruce, 201

Strow, Malcolm "Mac," 169

Strunk, Bill, 164

Student Activities Center (SAC), 113, 155, 190, 225, 227, 230, *230*, 234, 278. *See also* Howard Gittis Student Center

Student Handbook, *48*

Student Pavilion, 198, 199

Subin, Richard, 97

Subway exit, *63*

Sugarloaf, 113

Sugarman, Jack, 70

Sullivan, Anne, 16, *58*

Sullivan, Leon, *122*, 125

Sullivan, Mark, 51

Sullivan Hall, 45, *46*, 47, 49, 51, *51*, *52*, 86, 106, 109, *166*, 188, *189*, *229*, 242, 273

Sullivan Memorial Library, 51, *52*

Sullivan, Thomas D., 51, *52*

Summerlin, Berkley, *176*

Suri, Rominder, 212

Surrency, Edwin C., 240, 241

Sutman, Frank X., 202

Sweeney, Frank, 244

Swern, Daniel, 208, *208*

Swidler, Leonard, 105

Swygert, H. Patrick, 154, 188

T

Tacony, 10

Taft, R. B., 80

Talbott, Betty, *68*

Tansy, Martin F., 252, 253

Tarka, John E., 211, *211*

Tasca, Henry, 134

Tate, James H. J., *118*

Taylor, Donald, Jr., 246

Teachers College, 20, 37, *38,* 40, 43, 45, 48, 54, 57, 60, 61, 142, 148, 256. *See also* College of Education

TECH (Teaching, Education, Collaboration, and Help) Center, 155, *192,* 221, 225, 236, 237

Temple, The, 13–16, *13*, 18, 19, *28*, 51, *58,* 221, 226, *280*, 281

Temple alma mater, *180*

Temple brochure, *59*

Temple Children's Medical Center. *See* Temple University Children's Medical Center

Temple College, 11–12, 33, 35, 39, 40, 54, 86, 214

Temple College Academies, *17,* 19, 34, 54

Temple Community College, 73, 104–105, 210, 211, 283

Temple Free Press, 116

Temple Health Connection, 257

Temple High School. *See* Temple University High School

Temple Hospital. *See* Temple University Hospital

Temple Law School, 243. *See also* Beasley School of Law

Temple of Learning, 53, *53*

Temple News. See Temple University News

Temple Opera Theater, 142

Temple Owl (mascot), 40, *40,* 180, *181,* 182, 194

Temple Spirit Squad, 180

Temple Sports Medicine Center, *277*

Temple Stadium, *76,* 104, 141, *156, 157,* 158, 161, *164,* 167

Temple Station. *See* Cecil B. Moore/Temple University Subway Station; Regional Rail Station

Temple "T," 179, 180, 188, 194, *195,* 230, *230,* 279

Temple Technical Institute, 87, 104, 105, 211. *See also* College of Engineering Technology

Temple Times, 116, 233

Temple Towers, 192

Temple Town, *11,* 191–199, 219, 225, 284

Temple 20/20, 287

Temple University Ambler, 58, 113, 141, 143 *144,* 155, 161, 167, 176, 192, 212, 213, 264–268, *264, 265, 267, 268,* 269, 283

Temple University Center City (TUCC), 264, 269, *270,* 271

Temple University Center for Advanced Technology, 269

Temple University Children's Medical Center, *145,* 244, *245,* 246

Temple University Fort Washington, 237, 264, *267,* 269

Temple University Harrisburg, 237, 264, 271

Temple University Health Sciences Center. *See* Health Sciences Center

Temple University Health System, 244–246

Temple University High School, 54, 84, 87, 104, 283

Temple University Hospital, *31,* 32, 47, 68, 69, *78,* 81–84, *83,* 122, 132, *145,* 185, 190, 237, 243, 244, *244,* 246, 247, *257,* 273, 284. *See also* Medical Education and Research Building; Samaritan Hospital

Temple University Hospital School of Nursing. *See* College of Health Professions and Social Work

Temple University Institute on Aging, 275

Temple University Japan (TUJ), 99, 136, *184,* 200–201, *201,* 213, 260, 263

Temple University Jazz Band, 147

Temple University Libraries, 4, 19, 27, 32, *33,* 34, 40, 51, *51, 52, 70,* 87, 92, *98,* 99, 104, 106–107, *106, 107,* 111, *114,* 115, 134, *135,* 145, *148, 149,* 152, 154, 199, 210, 233, 234, 236–238, 240, 241, 249, 266, 267, 271, 277, 285. *See also* Alice Tully Library; Charles L. Blockson Afro-American Collection; Klein Law School Library; Paley Library; Sullivan Memorial Library

Temple University Music Festival and Institute, 143–144

Temple University News, 61, 65, 113, 116, 165, 177

Temple University Press, 104, 105–106, *105,* 113, 277

Temple University Rome, 99, *134,* 145, 199, 200, *200, 202,* 213, 237, 277

Temple University Rule of Law program in China, 202–203. *See also* China, Temple programs in

Temple University seal, *x, 24, 37, 101,* 194, *289*

Temple University Station. *See* Cecil B. Moore/Temple University Subway Station; Regional Rail Station

Temple University Symphony Orchestra, 146

Tepper, David, 208

Terry, Clark, 147

Thatcher, William D., 86

Thatcher Hall, 86. *See also* Thomas Hall

Thelin, John R., 158

Theokis, Charles, 177

Theology School, 86

1300 (building), 113, 230, *232*

Thomas, J. S. Ladd, 40–41

Thomas, Morgan H., 86

Thomas Hall, 86, 143, 154, 197

Thomas Jefferson Medical College, 246

Thompson, Frank A., 29

Thompson, Polly, *58*

Thor, Dave, 168

Thornburgh, Dick, 192

Thorpe, Jim, 158

Tilghman, Shirley M., *282*

Timmins, Raye, *61, 82*

Timmons, Gerald D., 81

Tioga Baptist Church, 84

Tisch, Jonathan, 263

Tolomeo, John, 278

Tomlinson, Rebecca, 112

Tomlinson, William W., 78, 112

Tomlinson Theater, *109*, 112, 147, 150, 151, *152*

Toner, Rochelle "Rocky," 228

Torg, Joseph, 84

Tower, Josh, 152

Townsend, Bradley, 180

Training School for Nurses, 256

Trayes, Ed, 150

Truesdale, Glenda, 170

Truman, Harry, 15, *15, 74,* 183

TUCC. *See* Temple University Center City

TUJ. *See* Temple University Japan

Turner, Diane, 273

Turner, Ted, 263

Turngemeinde Hall. *See* South Hall

Turoff, Fred, 168

Tuttle, Jane Conwell, 15

Tuttleman, Edna Shanis, 199, *199*

Tuttleman, Stanley, 199, *199*

Tuttleman Learning Center, *87*, 199, *199*, 234, 236, *237*, 239

Tyler, George F., 47, 55, *55*

Tyler, Stella Elkins, 47, 55, *55*, 56

Tyler School of Art, 4, 6, 47, 55–56, 69, *70*, 89, *118,* 134, 141, 146, *149,* 182, 190, 194, 200, 213, 221, 225, 226, 227–228, *227, 228,* 236, 269, 274. *See also* School of Domestic Sciences and Art

U

Udell, Eugene, 58, 266

Ulehla, Jenny, 176

Union League, 77

Unit No. 1. *See* Conwell Hall

Unit No. 2, 45. *See also* Carnell Hall

University Archives, 237

University Services Building, 113

University Village, 231, *232*

Upper Dublin High School, 267

Urban Archives, 237–238

Usiton, James, Sr., 62

V

Vachon, Ann, 147

Valderrama, Joy. *See* Abbott, Joy Valderrama

Valli, Rob, 167

Van Patton, Tink, 163

Van Titus, Adelaide, 250

Van Wert, William, *205*

Vargus, Ione D., 128, 134

Vassallo, Theodore P., 210, 211

Venturi, Robert, 269

Vermeil, Dick, 153

Veterans Guidance Center, 126

Veterans Stadium, *164*

Viesti, Joe, *200*

Villa Caproni, 134, 200, *200. See also* Temple University Rome

Vitiello, Joseph, *202*

Vivacqua, John J., 113

Vivacqua Hall, 113, 198

Vogel, Morris, 207

Volp, Anne, 174

Voorhees Brown, Blanche, 171, *172*, 173

W

Wachman, Marvin, 95, 99, *113,* 115, 128–136, *129, 136,* 138, *138,* 139, 188, *188,* 190, 202, 222, 252, 267

Wachman Hall, 115

Wagner, Anthony E., 287

Walk, George E., 38, *43,* 214, *214*

Walker, Valaida Smith, 275

Wallace, Bobby, 161

Wallace, Robert Burns, 62

Walsh, Maureen E., 179

Wanamaker, John, 20, 44

Wang, Margaret, 275

Wan Xue Yuan, 203, *203*

Warner, Glenn Scobey "Pop," 158, 160, *160*

Warren, Earl, 34

Warrick, Joby S., 150

Washington, Linn, 150

Watson, Bernard C., 134

Watson, Kaity, 177

Watts Walk. *See* Beasley Walk

Webster, David H., 138

Webster, Herbert, 67

Weeks, Alice M., 208

Weigley, Russell F., *206*

Weinhouse, Sidney, 80

Weiss, Abram, 115

Weiss, Edward, 47, 80

Weiss, Helen, 115

Weiss Hall, 115

Welsh, Kariamu, *147,* 148

West Oak Lane, 23

Wheeler, George W., *206*

WHIP (radio station), 155

White, Andrew, 20

White, Gavin, Jr., 170, 177, *177*

White, Gavin R., 168, *169*

White, James S., 197, 231, 276

White House, *57*

WHYY (Public Broadcasting System affiliate), 112, 152, 155

Wiatt, Hattie May, 13, *13,* 63

Wiatt Hall, 63

Widener, George D., 267

Widener, P.A.B., 10, 25

Widener Estate, 75

Wiebe, Robert, 25

Wildowson, J. Howard, *68*

William H. Harrison School, *216*

Williams, Charles M., 21, 155, 156, 162

Williams, Clarence J., III, 150, *150*

Williams Hall, 63, 229, *229*

Willkie, Wendell, 67

Willoughby, Ralph R., 29

Wilson, H. Augustus, 255

Wilson, James "Skip," 166, 167

Wilson, Woodrow, 41

Wilson Building, 33

Winston, Herbert, 127

Wolfbein, Seymour, 260

Wolgin, Jack, 228

Woodhaven Center, 275

WRFT (radio station), 155

Wright, Charles A., 53, 65

WRTI (radio station), 153–155, *153,* 165, 231, *231,* 276

WRTI (Radio Teaching Institute), 141, 153–155

Wudyka, Stan, 170

Wyndmoor Property, 76, 77

Wyndmoor Station, 76

X

Xiaoping, Deng. *See* Deng Xiaoping

Xu Yun, 176

Y

Yale University, 3

Yancey, William, 75

Yanella, Philip, 218

Yantorno, Robert, *283*

Yellow Cab Company, 50, *50*

Yeomans, Earl R., *156,* 157, 177, 276

Yetter, Doris M., 67

Yorktown Apartments. *See* Temple Towers

Young, Johnny, *75*

Young, Ralph "Pep," 166

Younger, Max, 168, 169

Yuan, Wan Xue. *See* Wan Xue Yuan

Yue Liu, 176

Yun, Xu. *See* Xu Yun

Yunshi, Ji. *See* Ji Yunshi

Z

Zahn, D. Willard, 215

Zanewiak, Paul, 250

Zimmerman, Floyd J., 40

Zimring, Fred, 95

Zinkoff, Dave, 165

James W. Hilty, professor of history and dean of Temple's Ambler Campus, has written extensively about American politics, including *Robert Kennedy: Brother Protector* (Temple). He has provided political commentaries for various publications, including the *Philadelphia Inquirer,* and served as historical consultant to news media, including C-SPAN, NBC News, NPR, and others. A Temple faculty member since 1970, Hilty also wrote the introduction to Marvin Wachman's *The Education of a University President* (Temple).

Matthew M. Hanson, a visiting instructor at Saint Joseph's University, has taught United States history for over three decades and held administrative positions at Penn State and Villanova universities. For the last twenty years he has instructed Temple students in United States, European, and Third World history at three different campuses, coming to know Temple quite well. Hanson and his family reside in North Wales, Pennsylvania.

Additional illustration research was provided by **Betsy Winter Hall** and **Carol Ann Harris.** The book was designed and typeset by **Phillip Unetic,** using Helvetica Neue LT and Minion typefaces. Illustrations were prepared for printing by **Jay's Publishers Services. Nanette Bendyna-Schuman** copyedited the text and checked the proofs. Proof was read by **Jane Barry,** and **Robert Swanson Associates** prepared the index. **Charles Ault** directed production and supervised printing. The book was printed at **L.E.G.O./Eurografica** in Vicenza, Italy.